lengthy, interesting paper on *Table Blessings Set to Music*. There is an essay by John Ward: *Parody Technique in 16th-Century Instrumental Music*, and an elegantly written study of Masini's *Deer Hunt*, by Alexander Main.

Dragan Plamenac ingeniously tracks down the identity of tunes incorporated into four 15th-century Duodlibets; Karl Geiringer traces the 300-year history of a song by Ahle, down to its use by Alban Berg.

The late Jaap Kunst, wishing to contribute but too ill to prepare new material, culled for the volume his valuable *Fragments from Diaries Written During a Lecture Tour in the New World*.

ABOUT THE EDITORS

GUSTAVE REESE is Professor of Music in the Graduate School of Arts and Sciences of New York University and has been a Visiting Professor at Harvard University, the University of California at Los Angeles, and elsewhere. He was a close associate of Curt Sachs, to whose memory this work is dedicated. Professor Reese is internationally recognized as an authority on Medieval and Renaissance music and has produced outstanding publications on these subjects, notably *Music in the Middle Ages* and *Music in the Renaissance*.

ROSE BRANDEL, ethnomusicologist and composer, teaches World Folk Music in the graduate division of Hunter College, New York. She has also taught at Brooklyn College and the Philadelphia Dance Academy. She is the author of *The Music of Central Africa* and music and dance editor of the *Encyclopedia International*. Dr. Brandel was a student of Curt Sachs, who helped to launch her professionally.

The Commonwealth of Music

June 29, 1881 - February 5, 1959

The Commonwealth of

Music

EDITED BY GUSTAVE REESE AND ROSE BRANDEL

IN HONOR OF *Curt Sachs*

THE FREE PRESS, NEW YORK

COLLIER-MACMILLAN LIMITED, LONDON

Fp

For information, address:
The Free Press
A Division of The Macmillan Company
The Crowell-Collier Publishing Company
60 Fifth Avenue, New York, N.Y., 10011

Collier-Macmillan Canada, Ltd., Toronto, Ontario

Designed by Sidney Solomon

Library of Congress Catalog Card Number: 64-23082

PREFACE

*C*urt Sachs, in *The Commonwealth of Art*, produced one of those books in which the great breadth of his knowledge and of his interests was most brilliantly displayed. That work spans music and the visual arts. The present volume is mostly limited to music. But here too the area covered is large and diversified, and this has been possible because, in rendering homage to Sachs, the writers have been able to treat many different kinds of subjects and yet believe that all of them would have appealed to his wide-ranging and inquiring mind. It has been felt that a title patterned after the one Sachs gave to his great book would be suitable as suggesting the variety of the essays that are being offered—even if the collection does not present coverage of its field in the systematic way in which *The Commonwealth of Art* does of its bigger one—and that the title may be fitting especially for a book that is dedicated to his memory.

The collection, undertaken on the initiative of members of the American Musicological Society and the Society for Ethnomusicology, has taken form under the auspices of both organizations.

Those who have paid homage to Curt Sachs by contributing to the volume include, besides the authors of the articles, two former students of his: Dr. Mildred Pearl Parker and Dr. George C. Schuetze, Jr. The former has translated the essay by Professor Vetter, and the latter has discharged the considerable task of preparing most of the autography.

A special expression of thanks is due Mrs. Curt Sachs for the completeness and alacrity with which she responded to any requests for help that were addressed to her.

With regard to the "Fragment . . ." by the late Jaap Kunst, it should be explained that the author was, to his own knowledge, fatally ill when he received the invitation to contribute. However, because of his admiration and devotion to Curt Sachs, he wished to present an offering. Unable to prepare new material, he therefore culled from his diary certain passages whose content makes them, in combination, suitable for inclusion in a collection dedicated to Sachs.

Since Kurt Hahn's "Verzeichnis der wissenschaftlichen Arbeiten von Curt Sachs," *Acta musicologica*, XXIX (1957), 94-106, contains a comprehensive listing of Sachs's scholarly writings, no similar listing is provided in the present volume.

Gustave Reese

CONTENTS

PLATES

COMPOSITIONS *Printed Complete*

CURT SACHS AS

A HISTORIAN

Leo Schrade (Basle)

*C*urt Sachs began his scholarly career as a historian of art, and his doctoral thesis was on a theme chosen from the appropriate branch of knowledge: the so-called St. Thomas Group that Andrea del Verrocchio made for the tabernacle in Or San Michele in Florence.[1] For a few years after he received his doctoral degree, it seemed that he would continue to concentrate on the history of art. Although the definite turn toward music still came within the good season of youthful inquiry, the initial association with the history of art developed into something of considerable weight, a weight more significant than the study of a merely "additional" field can ordinarily be assumed to bear upon the basic principles of historical research; it may even be likened to a ferment that brought Sachs's intellectual pursuits into the shape of an ultimate philosophy.

It is this philosophy of history and historical explication rather than the various results of numerous studies that shall be our concern. The road toward the penetration of historiography by the philosophic idea— to be sure, a long and tedious road—crossed many a field of diverse subjects as well as vast ranges of human endeavor before the goal came within reach.

Since historiography as an independent science is bound to guard its own integrity by avoiding the pitfalls of a preconceived philosophy, the road begins where all historical research must do so: with the accurate study of the documents of history, whatever they may be. Fact-finding, the data of documentary historiography, forever the substance of historical description and eventual interpretation, guides the searcher on his protracted, if indeed not endless road. It is only after the gathering in of facts and data from the storage of history that the student can attempt to place the multitude of disconnected events, seemingly unrelated to each other, into a sensible whole, as detached pieces are fitted together into a mosaic. But the picture in the mosaic may well reveal a philosophic conception; for the manner in which the stones are pieced together must follow the historian's understanding of the pattern to which they belong. Though all of this is a well-worn truism, restated here not without a certain discomfort, it nevertheless reasserts its efficacy when applied to the method and scholarly performance of Curt Sachs.

The first major publications in the province of the history of music, concerned with the subject of musical life in Berlin and the conditions of music and opera at the electoral court,[2] purely and simply testify to the traditional procedures of positivistic historiography. That more or less brilliant sidelights of cultural history now and then flash up along-side reports of musical events illustrates incidentally the broad interests of the author without affecting his positivistic presentation. In this respect, the musical studies continue along the line of the dissertation, which held fast to the course of objective description, although it must be said that the thesis of stylistic verification carried the argument beyond the scope of documentary evidence; and it also may be added that Verrocchio's famous masterpiece fired the young scholar with an esthetic enthusiasm that does not necessarily lie within the nature of positivistic historiography. Three or four experiences, among others, appear subsequently to have had a decisive impact upon the forming of a philosophic conception of history: the co-operation with von Hornbostel, the exploration of the vast field of musical instruments, the contacts with Julius von Schlosser, the art historian, as well as those with the circle that existed around Max Dessoir, the esthetician.

To be sure, the investigation of musical instruments, particularly if a complete inventory had been the aim, imposed upon the author the pragmatic method, requisite for the description of the material condition of instruments. It nonetheless led the author also into the vast and various continents of culture, Eastern as well as Western, and thus revealed far-reaching relationships, both pragmatic and historical, which suggested the unifying idea of an all-comprehensive whole. Both the origin and, especially, the diffusion of a musical instrument set the historian upon those highways which connect not only neighboring countries, but also lands far distant and separated from one another by impassable mountains or enormous oceans. Even though the historian at times is wholly unable to show the route by which instruments traversed immense distances, he becomes aware of strange connections that mysteriously unite many peoples and many lands.

However deceptively the partially hidden ways in which separate objects seem to be joined together may sometimes insinuate mutual "influences," they may promptly suggest methods of constructing that all-embracing bond which assembles diverse parts into a homogeneous whole. In some respects, these circumstances, observable as the historical context within which musical instruments develop, greatly resemble the conditions surrounding the origin and dissemination of myths and legends.

Myths emerging as they do from the roots of local conditions seem to express all the special idiosyncrasies of national civilizations; thus they appear—now with, now without justification—to rest upon a certain uniqueness in each nation. But when comparative studies disclose similarities, if not identities, that link myths together into something in the nature of an intelligible organism, even though they belong to widely separated civilizations, it has been argued that "influences" traveling from one civilization to another must have brought about the affinities and so were responsible for the organic unity.

Reasonable as the theory of influences appears, it has been rejected partly because of lack of evidence of communication, a lack that is sometimes even total, partly because the organic unity contingent upon apparent similarities did not derive in certain demonstrable instances from mutual influences, but from the undivided nature of man. Human nature, i.e., a basically uniform mode of thought and aspiration, led to comparable results, to the affinities between various myths, while only the variations or modifications rested upon local or national conditions. To be sure, peoples of sundry civilizations differ from each other in varying degrees in the gift of imagination; but the distinction merely allots to various peoples a differing fecundity in the creation of myths. An altogether similar situation presents itself with regard to some aspects of the history of instruments.

Although Curt Sachs's historical studies of musical instruments were by their very nature of universal scope, they were, from the outset, intimately related to the author's interest in the history of art. As a matter of fact, the instrument as an entity ideally combines aspects of the visual arts and of music. The pictorial representation of an instrument is at times the sole evidence we have of it; instruments themselves, when extant, often qualify as artistic objects. Whether visually represented or physically preserved, the instruments as works of art yield esthetic satisfaction.

It is, surely, no accident that Curt Sachs, the historian of music, turned toward the history of instruments as his chosen field. And we find him as a result at the side of Julius von Schlosser who, historian of art by profession and director of the Kunsthistorisches Museum in Vienna, made musical instruments a part of his historical studies, undoubtedly because of his ardent musicianship. The highly competent descriptive catalogue of the Viennese collection of instruments[3] and the very valuable introduction to the history of musical instruments[4] were precious fruits of such studies.[5] The histories of music and the visual arts flow together in that harmonious alliance which attracted Curt Sachs to the same school of thought, as the two scholars shared a great many other views in the large domain of the history of art. Only one year after the appearance of von Schlosser's catalogue, Curt Sachs published the counterpart, a guide to the collection of instruments in Berlin,[6] and a descriptive catalogue as well.[7] But all the labors that had gone into the *Reallexikon der Musikinstrumente* (1913), a work that has proved its standard caliber ever since it came out, were crowned by those remarkable achievements which—together with a comprehensive treatment of the subject, but contrary to the design of a *Reallexikon*—admitted important views of historical interpretation; they are *Geist und Werden der Musikinstrumente*[8] and, lastly, *The History of Musical Instruments*.[9] And it is very characteristic of the author's outlook that he relegated the pragmatic, systematic arrangement of the instruments to a terminological appendix, where instruments are grouped according to the material formation of their sound as idiophones, aerophones, membranophones, and chordophones. The history itself, apart from the appended systematic list, disclosed the basic conceptions which, in the course of extended studies, had crystallized into a definitive shape of historical evolution. The idea of historical evolution, however, also reflected the results of new research in the field of musical ethnology, or rather the influence of the ingenious founder of such ethnology, Erich Moritz von Hornbostel. The views of ethnology and those of history begin to interpenetrate.

All kinds of experience in the vastness of the musical life of many peoples were brought to bear on a great variety of historical subjects. When Curt Sachs published his works on Greek music,[10] he for the first time drew Eastern elements into the investigation of the subject and uncovered relationships that had never before been observed. Familiar with tonal systems other than those of the Western world, he cast new light upon the vexing problems of both the tuning of Greek instruments and the Greek modes. And *The Rise of Music in the Ancient World* [11] expanded still further the theme of East and West in Antiquity.

The expansion, irrespective of its historical aspect, resulted from the attempt to reconcile the systematic and historical methods of approach. For ethnology, mainly given to systematic thought and classification, must, and does, seek agreement with history. But such an agreement is not to be had simply by identifying the ethnological phenomena of primitive peoples with early phases of history. Many an ethnologist has fallen victim to all too plausible, but nevertheless deceptive equations. Curt Sachs, however, fully aware of the fallacies and temptations of quick and general conclusions drawn from ethnological data, tried to impart the exactness of historical method and thought to the study of ethnology. A continual interweaving of two different approaches aimed at the union of two branches of knowledge.

In the meantime, Curt Sachs also strove for an ever closer union between the histories of the visual arts and music. As a matter of fact, the various objects of his research seem to have pertained to one broad, significant program. Although the combination of histories was to serve mainly to overcome the discrepancy that separated the historiography of music from that of the visual arts, it was also designed to counteract the overspecialization which, under the influence of the sciences, affected historical studies more and more deeply, with the result that the views of the historian became increasingly narrow and no longer allowed that comprehensive appreciation which understood all achievements to arise from one source, the one and indivisible human mind. By 1919, hopeful signs, posted alongside the seemingly parallel roads of scholarship, seemed to justify the expectation that the roads might yet converge at the end. Association of efforts among scholars of various fields, but also the union of all the arts, set up by concerted ideas, might rehabilitate faith in the integrality of mind.

A contribution to this effect made its appearance with the essay "Kunstgeschichtliche Wege zur Musikwissenschaft." [12] If the true comprehension of a musical art work, of a musical style, ultimately leads to the recovery of the intellectual and spiritual conditions, of the mode of life (*Lebensgefühl*), which brought the art work into being, the auditory organ, so we are told, is not capable of communicating such an understanding by itself; the organ of sight must render its assistance. "The route which must be taken" to reach the goal "cannot be prepared merely by the working tools of music history; the tools of art history are needed." The necessity of linking the two historiographies together rests on this premise. All the arts, and music more than the others, are said to be expressions of the "spiritual life" (*Seelenleben*), which changes with the passage of time, and the change is reflected in the succession of various styles. If the arts are born "out of an inner necessity," as indeed they are, and if they mirror "man's thought and aspiration, his attitude toward matters temporal and eternal, his tempo of life," as indeed they do, they all emerge from one and the same "fostering soil" (*Nährboden*), i.e. spiritual life. "Music and visual art are at every time children of one mother, just as flora and fauna, limited by region and time, are the children of one soil and one climate." The changes that we observe in the arts can well be compared with the changes in organic nature, as they are effected by similar laws. Thus, the author arrived at his theory of an all-comprehensive unity.[13]

With this in mind he characterized the affinities between music and visual art. "If the organ of hearing fails to lead to an understanding of a musical style, a careful comparison with the art style of the same period and the same region should seek common properties; it also should seek to comprehend musical attributes of style, previously lifeless materials only, as the living expression of a decisively directed artistic aspiration." As obvious as a comparison of music and the visual arts might be, it must not be carried out "superficially," lest it be more harmful than useful. "Only a methodical realization can be beneficial. First of all, the essentials on both sides, not just anything that strikes the eye, must be put in parallel position; one must proceed from the large artistic conceptions." [14]

After having sketched the stylistic "essentials" for the Orient, the Middle Ages, and the Renaissance, Curt Sachs two years later added the principles of the Baroque in another essay, "Barockmusik," [15] but not without placing new, and perhaps even sharper emphasis upon the cardinal problem. Here he states that the arts do not differ from one another except for the manner in which we perceive and receive them; the forms as well as the phases of growth are common to all. Musical phenomena failing, as they do, to result just from other musical phenomena, evolutionary precedence cannot be explained through music alone; any assumption to the contrary must be regarded as an error. Such fervor seems to fit the missionary spirit.

The new essay on Baroque music, however, went far beyond a programmatic statement, or restatement, of principle. It is here that Curt Sachs applied, point by point, the famous *Grundbegriffe der Kunstwissenschaft* of Heinrich Wölfflin to the historiography of music. These "fundamental ideas" are known to consist of contrasting pairs: the linear and pictorial, the plane and deep, closed and open form, the tectonic and atectonic, clarity and obscurity, and finally—besides the pairs—the idea of unity. With the gauge of Wölfflin's pairs in hand, Curt Sachs measured the musical style of the Baroque and found its characteristics to be identical with those of the styles of the visual arts. Actually, the identities corresponded to the ideas of Heinrich Wölfflin, even though Curt Sachs understood them to reveal the stylistic parallelism of the arts.

With the passage of time, the "program," or better the philosophy, was more and more reinforced as the veritable backbone of the scholar's historiography. When in 1927 he dedicated to Julius von Schlosser his contribution to the *Festschrift* in honor of that scholar, the chosen theme significantly expressed his old interest; it dealt with "Musik und bildende Kunst im Rahmen der allgemeinen Kunstgeschichte." [16] If the deep-seated conviction could be still more penetratingly expressed at all, it occurred in this essay. And it is unquestionably a merit that, in the course of treating his general idea, the author turned against the commonly accepted view that music historically has always limped behind the other arts—for instance, that the Renaissance commenced in music at a time when the period was all over in the visual arts. Although the view, inveterate but fallacious, could not be overthrown at once, the opposition of Curt Sachs played a remarkable part in depriving it of much of its force. "Music does not limp behind. In strict legitimacy (*Gesetzlichkeit*) it shares with the sister arts the great work allotted to all art. The arts do not stand independently apart from each other, but intimately joined together. For it is man who infuses blood and soul into the arts according to his law, who is the invariable, new creator." [17]

And from this association of music with the other arts arises, in the end, the concept of the "commonwealth of art" which, having pervaded like a leitmotiv the whole of Sachs's scholarship, culminated in the work that carries the name of the leitmotiv as its title.[18] All the individual studies or programmatic essays of previous years here operate to new advantage; they reveal their merits afresh as building stones in a large structure that has at last come to be erected.

Not only in the development of Curt Sachs as a scholar, but in musical historiography as a whole, here for the first time had a history of various arts combined been boldly attempted. Even though the sister arts were confined to architecture, painting, and sculpture, to the exclusion of poetry and literature, the concert of music, dance, and the visual arts could still be regarded as a "Commonwealth of Art." It is self-evident that the link which holds them all together could not be anything but style.

Yet if style works as the element basic to a common order, as the agent productive of coherence, what, then, is style? It cannot merely be manners, even less mannerisms, expressed in accordance with the accepted practices of an age or a person. Style must be more than a routine. And appropriately to his purpose, Curt Sachs finds it to be "the configuration of spiritual qualities that a certain man or age or country has created as the effigy of a certain will and emotion; and the easy characteristics that the handbooks teach are nothing but their outer marks." [19]

If so understood, style unites all that to a superficial view must appear to exist as separate components, as strangers side by side. Surely, such a concept of style must diminish, if not overthrow, modern specialization or "departmentalization," and Curt Sachs adopted the statement of Erich Kahler that "the autonomy of special departments of human activity is a disastrous phenomenon of modern times, and to extend the dividing lines backward into former ages is a falsifying interpretation of history." [20]

But style, the unifying element, has its link to generations as well as to larger units. Despite the differences apparent in the succession of generational styles and the "gigantic cycles" of broad epochs, an "eternal recurrence of general trends" makes itself felt as the law that brings to the fore its own inevitability with an almost deterministic force, as though it were set by an invisible "master." Man himself forever conducts the "gigantic fugue" with the individual arts serving as its voice-parts. "In however different ways they mirror the trends of ages and nations, they cannot get away from man or from each other. Springing from one urge, they are united in the one indelible commonwealth of art." [21]

On the whole and together with *The Commonwealth of Art, Eine Weltgeschichte des Tanzes* [22] and *Rhythm and Tempo* [23] likewise, but through a different approach and through specific elements as means of evidence, testify to the same unity, with man invariably as its maker. Thus, all the divergent aspects of music and history, more often than not apparently in desperate conflict, tend to combine in a coalition of components: of prehistory and history, of primitive man and man of culture, of ethnology and history, of systematic and historical methods, of folklore and art, of the relative and the absolute.

Notes

1. *Das Tabernakel mit Andrea's del Verrocchio Thomasgruppe an Or San Michele zu Florenz. Ein Beitrag zur Florentiner Kunstgeschichte* (Strasbourg: Heitz, 1904).

2. *Musikgeschichte der Stadt Berlin bis zum Jahre 1800* (Berlin: Gebrüder Paetel, 1908) and *Musik und Oper am Kurbrandenburgischen Hof* (Berlin: J. Bard, 1910).

3. Julius [von] Schlosser, *Die Sammlung alter Musikinstrumente. Beschreibendes Verzeichnis. Band III der Publikationen aus den Sammlungen für Plastik und Kunstgewerbe* (Vienna: Anton Schroll, 1920).

4. Julius [von] Schlosser, *Unsere Musikinstrumente. Eine Einführung in ihre Geschichte* (Vienna: Anton Schroll, 1922).

5. *Cf.* also Julius Schlosser, *Kleiner Führer durch die Sammlung alter Musikinstrumente* (Vienna: Verlag der kunsthistorischen Sammlungen, 1922) and "Musikinstrumente der Vergangenheit," in *Westermanns Monatshefte,* Jahrgang 66, Vol. CXXXI-CXXXII, fasc. 785 (1922).

6. *Staatliche Musikinstrumenten-Sammlung. Führer durch die Sammlung* (Berlin: J. Bard, 1921).

7. *Sammlung alter Musikinstrumente bei der Staatlichen Hochschule für Musik zu Berlin. Beschreibender Katalog* (Berlin: J. Bard, 1922).

8. Berlin: D. Reimer, 1929.

9. New York: W. W. Norton & Co., 1940.

10. *Musik des Altertums* (Breslau: F. Hirt, 1924) and especially *Die Musik der Antike* (Potsdam: Akademische Verlagsgesellschaft Athenaion, 1928).

11. New York: W. W. Norton & Co., 1943 (Italian ed., *La Musica nel Mondo Antico*, Florence: Sansoni, 1963).

12. In *Archiv für Musikwissenschaft*, I (1918-1919), pp. 451-464.

13. *Op. cit.*, pp. 451 f.

14. *Op. cit.*, p. 452.

15. *Jahrbuch der Musikbibliothek Peters für 1919* (Leipzig: C. F. Peters, 1920), pp. 7-15.

16. In *Festschrift für Julius Schlosser zum 60. Geburtstage* (Zürich, Leipzig, Vienna: Amalthea Verlag, 1927), pp. 31-34.

17. Cf. *Festschrift*, p. 34.

18. *The Commonwealth of Art. Style in the Fine Arts, Music and Dance* (New York: W. W. Norton & Co., 1946).

19. Cf. *Commonwealth*, p. 20.

20. Quoted in *Commonwealth*, p. 21.

21. *Commonwealth*, p. 391.

22. Berlin: D. Reimer, 1933; in English translation by Bessie Schönberg (New York: W. W. Norton & Co., 1937).

23. New York: W. W. Norton & Co., 1953.

CURT SACHS AS

AN ETHNOMUSICOLOGIST

Hans-Heinz Draeger (Austin, Texas)

*T*he most obvious way to characterize Curt Sachs as an ethnomusicologist might seem to be by means of an extended review of his last book, *The Wellsprings of Music.*[1] The student will rightly use the *Wellsprings* as a first guide in special problems of ethnomusicology. For Sachs it was an end, a survey of a lifelong work of research. The scope of his final contribution is clearly indicated on the last page. Here he states, with reference to the final chapter, that he has opposed a sketch of music in Western society to the fuller picture of primitive music, provided by the rest of the book. In an earlier work, however, he had very clearly described the subject matter of ethnomusicology as "(1) the high civilizations of the East, (2) the low and middle civilizations, (3) and the remainders of low and middle civilizations in rustic parts of our own civilization."[2] According to Sachs's own definition, therefore, the *Wellsprings* fits into only a part of the range of ethnomusicology—albeit an important part—and to characterize him as an ethnomusicologist will require reinvestigation of at least some of his other writings.

Other definitions of this field, even if picked at random, show the development of the discipline quite clearly: they become more and more comprehensive. Since Sachs's work reflects this development to a remarkable degree, it might be of interest to quote at least two such definitions. One of them—which is basic and widely accepted—is the recent one of Jaap Kunst:[3]

> The study-object of ethnomusicology, or, as it originally was called, comparative musicology, is the traditional music and musical instruments of all cultural strata of mankind, from the so-called primitive peoples to the civilized nations. Our science, therefore, investigates all tribal and folk music and every kind of non-Western art music. Besides, it studies as well the sociological aspects of music, as the phenomena of musical acculturation, i.e., the hybridizing influence of alien musical elements. Western art- and popular (entertainment-) music do not belong to its field.

Mantle Hood has characterized ethnomusicology in an all-embracing way. He draws upon a definition of musicology (in the broad sense) contained in a report of the Committee on Graduate Studies of the American Musicological Society, simply inserting the prefix "ethno" twice: [4]

> [Ethno]musicology is a field of knowledge, having as its object the investigation of the art of music as a physical, psychological, aesthetic, and cultural phenomenon. The [ethno]musicologist is a research scholar, and he aims primarily at knowledge about music.

Hood's deliberate borrowing emphasizes that there are parallels between ethnomusicology and traditional musicology, even though, as at present organized, they are disciplines with different topics. Not only are there parallels between the disciplines; they are tied to each other by strong links, a point to which Leonard B. Meyer has given thought: [5]

> . . . we can merely ask which features of music, if any, tend to be common to different cultures and which vary from culture to culture. The study and analysis of this material would presumably indicate which aspects of music are universal and which are culturally determined. . . . What we should ask is whether, beneath the profusion of diverse and divergent particulars, there are any universal principles functioning.

Mieczyslaw Kolinski has expressed the same idea as follows: [6]

> I wanted to emphasize the importance of the awareness of the existing links between the musical languages of the geographical populations around the world. These links are apparently due to basic similarities in the psycho-physical constitution of mankind and should, therefore, represent an essential factor in the evalua-

tion of the validity of ethnomusicological theories concerning cultural contacts or racial relationships.

In order to achieve this goal, Kolinski suggests that one should

> distinguish between descriptive, comparative and systematic ethno-musicology. Actually, this subdivision is not meant to be a strict classification but merely aims to stress the various facets of ethno-musicological research.

Unfortunately—or, in another way, fortunately—the same is true of musicology as a whole and, indeed, of other disciplines also. As a matter of fact, these three approaches provide the needed links between our two "parallels," particularly the systematic approach, described by Charles Seeger as "the system of history" [7] rather than "the history of system." It is precisely in the field of systematic research that some of Sachs's most challenging contributions are to be found. The present writer will, therefore, restrict himself to some of those "links between the musical languages of the geographical populations around the world" (Kolinski) that Sachs dealt with throughout some of his most prominent books. In other words, this article will lay less stress upon Sachs's factual, historical knowledge than upon his creative scholarship.

If this approach is justifiable, one may rightly omit from consideration here most of Sachs's works that refer directly to a more or less limited ethnomusicological topic. The same is true of his books and articles on specific exotic instruments.[8] There are, on the other hand, his "world histories," whether they bear this title or not: *Geist und Werden der Musikinstrumente*,[9] *The History of Musical Instruments*,[10] *World History of the Dance*,[11] *The Rise of Music in the Ancient World*,[12] and *Rhythm and Tempo*.[13] By the very nature of their subject matter, *Geist und Werden* and *The History of Musical Instruments* deal with only a part of ethnomusicology. The *World History of the Dance* is better left to the expert, because the relations between music and dance are extremely complex, at least in early society. Thus, the works to be discussed in this article, in addition to *The Wellsprings of Music*, narrow down to *The Rise of Music in the Ancient World* and *Rhythm and Tempo*. The phrase "narrow down," however, should not be given one of the interpretations of which it is capable. Actually, in these books Sachs not only epitomized his world-embracing historical knowledge, but presented it also in the light of his systematic findings, thus doing justice to the most comprehensive definitions of both historical musicology and ethnomusicology. In fact, *The Rise of Music* can be called a model of what a comprehensive book on ethnomusicology should be.

It corresponds to a high degree to Sachs's definition, covering, as it does, the high civilizations of the East, the low and middle civilizations, and the remainders of low and middle civilizations in rustic parts of our own civilization. Of great importance, in the present writer's opinion, are three "links between the musical languages of the geographical populations around the world," which have been discussed in these books and which are a challenge to the scholar: (1) vocal melodic styles, (2) musical systems in general, and (3) the main approaches of mankind to the problem of rhythm. Sachs devotes a special section or at least a special chapter to each of them and, in the process, demonstrates his brilliance as a creative musicologist. These three areas invite a grateful pupil to follow his lead into them, even if at a respectable distance. They may, therefore, justifiably become the central subject of this article.

Every musicologist, in fact every scholar, who tries to go beyond description and comparison, knows the danger of the next step, the systematic approach. It is here that the most important discoveries are made—and also the most embarrassing mistakes. Speculation and imagination too often replace history and facts. Sachs knew this danger, as he indicated in the opening section of his *Rise:* ". . . theories are futile unless solidly based on facts and their historical connection."

Vocal Melodic Styles

Sachs [14] defines "the primordial dualism of two different, indeed opposed singing styles" as logogenic and pathogenic; the higher, melogenic, forms arise from a mingling and mixing of the two basic styles.

"Logogenic" means primarily word-born, derived from cantillation. The evolution of the logogenic style was additive: more and more notes crystallized around a nucleus. The pathogenic style is derived from passion and motor impulse. Its evolution was divisive: "octaves were marked out, and after them, fifths and fourths, which, instead of a nucleus," such as exists in the logogenic style, "formed a solid skeleton." In the pathogenic style, " 'loud' and 'high-pitched,' 'soft' and 'low-pitched' are closely associated—so closely that the Romance languages have only one word for either couple of qualities: *alta vox* and *bassa vox*. . . . Melogenic music represents the wide middle area between the extremes of logogenic and pathogenic music"; its characteristic is a flexible melodic line.

Although this classification was developed with regard to music in primitive society, it is nevertheless applicable to any historical period or style. Thus, the three generally accepted designations of the Christian

chant as syllabic, neumatic, and melismatic have their place in this framework. The syllabic and logogenic are most closely related. The melismatic and the pathogenic, though far from being identical, nevertheless tend—at least within the stylistic frame of the chant—in the same
direction. The neumatic and the melogenic lie between the other pairs.

In *The Wellsprings of Music*, Sachs revised his former terminology
and applied the adjectives "tumbling" and "horizontal" to strains or
melodies. He writes: [15]

> For Tumbling Strains I once coined the term "pathogenic" or
> "passion-born." The name is still to the point and has generally
> been understood. But I hesitate to continue calling the usual hori-
> zontal melody "logogenic" or "word-born". . . . Indeed, the words
> themselves are often immaterial and little apt to shape a melody
> . . . we must realize that many melodies in this group are not word-
> born at all. Thus it might be better to drop the term "logogenic"
> and to speak of horizontal and of tumbling [i.e., pathogenic]
> melodies.

The present writer prefers Sachs's earlier terms "logogenic" and
"pathogenic" to "horizontal" and "tumbling" melodies. The former
words point to the underlying driving forces, whereas the latter are
mere descriptions of musical patterns. Furthermore, it does not matter
how "meaningful" syllables or other linguistic utterances are: nonsense
syllables often provide the text of primitive melodies (as Sachs points
out), and, if they are not "word-born," they are still "language-born."

It might be legitimate, however, to introduce here another pair of
terminological extremes that has been applied to language by Frederick
Dillistone [16] but that may as well be applied to music: "language-symbol"
and "action-sign." A language-symbol stands for articulate conceptual
thinking and is quite abstract, objective, and supra-personal; an action-
sign, on the other hand, a call of warning, of love, or of anger, is quite
concrete, subjective, and highly personal. Dillistone's classification, when
applied to music, considerably broadens the scope of Sachs's newer
scheme, because, like Sachs's older one, it shows not only the underlying
driving forces but also a more comprehensive formal relationship between
language and music—one that takes into account not just the word, but
language in a broader sense. The expansion encompasses, besides the
nonsense syllables already mentioned, the relationships within whole
groups of words—relationships that can be illustrated, for instance, by
means of the medieval chant. This music is not simply word-born, it
is language-born: it reflects the grammatical structure of a sentence
rather than just the structure of a single word.[17]

Expressed in the form of a tabulation, we have the following system:

language-symbol		action-sign
logogenic	melogenic	pathogenic
syllabic	neumatic	melismatic

It goes without saying that polyphonic music can also be properly fitted within this system. But a discussion of that subject would require another paper.

Musical Systems in General [18]

Sachs gives the following definition: "A system, generally speaking, is the specific organization of the musical space taken up by a certain national or epochal style." What he calls a presystematic trend is the tendency for a melodic flow "to crystallize in one or more of three consonant intervals innate in man: the fourth, the fifth, and the octave." Depending on whether the shaping force is a fourth or a fifth, a melody will be organized within a tetrachord or a pentachord. Two tetrachords can be combined, often in a conjunct way; the combination of two pentachords is rare; but the linking of one entity of each type is common "under the imperious sway of the octave." The result is "the most perfect form of organized scale," since it "unites the three innate intervals: octave, fifth, and fourth." (The reader may be referred here to the impressive tracing of the history of the seven-plus-one scale, namely, of the *octoechos*, in Eric Werner's book *The Sacred Bridge*.[19])

The organization devolving on any system is threefold, having regard to pitch, genus, and mode. Omitting pitch "as self-evident and irrelevant," Sachs gives the following definition: "A genus roughly denotes the (essentially) indivisible sizes of steps used." Thus he distinguishes the diatonic or heptatonic genus (which consists of whole tones and semitones), the twelve-tone genus (consisting of semitones), and the pentatonic genus (consisting of minor thirds and whole tones, or major thirds and semitones, or other combinations). A genus, being not yet a scale, yields "at least a steady circle of steps without a definite pitch, without a start, and without an end . . .

"A mode is brought about by selecting one note of the endless set as a starter or tonic. All modes of a genus, though following the same sequence of notes, differ in the tonal relations within the octave, since their tonics differ: each mode implies a structure and tension of its own." In its prevalent form, a mode tends either to descend or to ascend.

Scales "extend from the ground tone of a mode [at a certain pitch] to its octave and include all fully qualified notes, but leave out those due to casual alteration or modulation."

The relationship among the phenomena discussed above may be shown in the following chart:

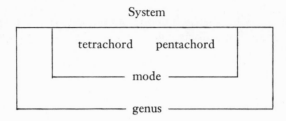

Undoubtedly belonging to this classification, though not dealt with by Sachs in the same chapter,[20] are two principles of system-building that pertain to tuning and that are of basic importance for wide areas and many cultures of the past and present. Sachs calls these principles cyclic and divisive. Starting from a string tuned to a medium-pitched note, the ancient players discovered the cyclic system by tuning a second string a fifth up, a third string a fourth down, and so on. "This is not just a circle or cycle of fifths, as it is generally called, but a continual, indeed cyclic, rising and falling, as $c\ d$ $\begin{smallmatrix}g\ a\end{smallmatrix}$. The *cyclic principle* might be an appropriate short name for it, or, less formally, the *up-and-down principle*." According to Sachs, this principle is related to "open-string" instruments, namely, harps and lyres. It is from the lute, on the other hand, that the divisive principle is derived.

> Struck by the fact that stopping at one half, one third, and one quarter of the entire length resulted respectively in the three principal intervals, they [the lutenists] logically went a step further and accepted the stopping at one fifth of the string as producing the major third and that at one sixth as producing the minor third. We call this victorious principle *divisive*.

A short reference may be allowed here to Sachs's repeated statement that there are three consonances innate in man, the octave, the fifth, and the fourth. The present writer believes, rather, that man has a general inherent capacity for distinguishing between intervals arising from simple ratios (usually considered consonant) and those arising from complicated ratios (usually considered dissonant). It depends, of course, upon the individual and upon his training whether or to what degree this capacity may be developed. Nevertheless, it remains true that the octave, fifth, and fourth are commonly accepted consonant intervals. This is clearly indicated by a comparison of Sachs's two principles—the cyclic and the divisive; each of these intervals has the same size under one of these principles that it has under the other.[21]

The basic difference between the two principles, from which all other differences can be derived, is, of course, that the thirds are not equal. The cyclic (Pythagorean) major third, the ratio of which is 81:64, is one syntonic comma higher than the divisive (just) third (ratio, 5:4). Thus, although there is only one type of perfect octave, fifth, or fourth in the two systems, there are two basically different major thirds, and their derivatives are different. This has had most important musical consequences, since historically monophony has generally called for the cyclic third, whereas part-music has generally called for the divisive third. To be sure, there have been exceptions. The just third has been used in melody, but usually only if supported by harmony. This has been true of thirds played by Indian lutenists and the thirds of Renaissance keyboard music. Moreover, as pointed out by Sachs, ancient Egyptian harpists, who used cyclic tuning, seem to have strummed some kind of chords when playing in the court orchestras in which whole groups of harps sometimes joined other instruments. Futhermore, a violinist may be inclined to use Pythagorean intervals in a solo concerto with orchestra (in which he is playing a melody), but in that case he acts against the intonation of the orchestra. It is well known that these deviations are very noticeable.

Although the point concerning the use of the two types of thirds is not being raised for the first time, it has been neglected in the interpreting of tone systems and in the formulating of rules of composition. The prevailing historical combinations, cyclic third with monophony and divisive third with part-music, would appear to have a psycho-physiological basis. The present writer, therefore, cannot agree with Fritz Kuttner's and J. Murray Barbour's statement concerning the major third in "just intonation": [22] "There are no *physiological* laws behind our reactions to certain intervals, and our response is entirely conditioned by psychological facts, or in plain language: by habit." The reasoning of Kuttner and Barbour is: "Most musical people, on concentrated listening to this narrow natural third of 386 cents, are dissatisfied and find the pitch offensively flat. . . . We found this view confirmed by about 90 per cent of roughly 120 listeners, all of them professional musicians or advanced music students." These authors do not say, however, whether the just third was presented successively or simultaneously. In any event, in many tests performed by the present writer a *simultaneous* cyclic (Pythagorean) third was never preferred to a *simultaneous* divisive (just) third, and a *successive* divisive (just) third was never preferred to a *successive* cyclic (Pythagorean) third. The medieval theorists and composers were correct in calling the simultaneous cyclic (Pythagorean) third a dissonance. As has been pointed out with regard to the 12th-century *Congaudeant catholici*, a three-part *Benedicamus domino* trope from Santiago de Compostela: ". . . thirds occur many times; but in almost every instance they appear between a unison and a fifth, and are the result of what we would today call passing-notes." [23] It is not the human ear that has changed down the years; it is the thirds. Now one can see clearly what is the outstanding character-istic of the octave, fifth, and fourth: typically, these intervals can be used both harmonically and melodically.

The fact that melodic progressions are linked with the cyclic values, whereas harmonic intervals are associated with divisive values holds good not only with regard to the simple ratios, but also with regard to the more complicated ones. The interval C-$F\sharp$, reached by a sequence of fifths, is available for melodic use, because the $F\sharp$ so reached is a cyclic value. If the interval is played harmonically, it is not only a dis-sonance, but it is wrong. On the other hand, the interval C-$F\sharp$, reached by two fifths and a just major third, should properly be played harmoni-cally, because this $F\sharp$ is a divisive value. If it is played harmonically it remains a dissonance, to be sure, but it is right.

There is not much evidence, as yet, why it has to be this way. It might, however, be helpful to refer here to a phenomenon that has become indispensable in the explanation of certain psychological data —namely, the nature of processes. Wolfgang Koehler writes in his book on *Gestalt* psychology: [24] "In any part of the visual field which is shaped, processes must have particular characteristics which are responsi-ble for the fact." We have only to replace the term "visual field" with the term "auditory field" in order to have a basic justification for the difference in use between the two kinds of thirds and their derivatives. In psychological terms, intervals can be called "dynamic structures," or processes. The explanation for their existence is the fact that from one process there always arises a complementary one. With regard to the time factor it is obvious that the sounding of tones successively is a more complicated process than a sounding of them simultaneously. The more complicated process in a given time-span therefore calls for the more complicated (cyclic) third. [25]

The above does not, of course, explain why octaves, fifths, and fourths are not subject to the same theoretical controls as the thirds. The present writer is Platonic enough to believe that the answer may be found in the theory of numbers. [26] In any event, much historical evidence and many tests point to the fact that the octave, fifth, and fourth are widely accepted consonances. It can at least be said that Sachs saw the basic importance of the two tuning principles, the divisive and the cyclic. His path-breaking investigation of the great musical cultures of the world in the light of these principles remains to be followed up.

Since the octave, fifth, and fourth are commonly acknowledged consonances, it seems somewhat paradoxical that parallel seconds are used in primitive polyphony "in a wide stretch from Micronesia to South Africa and the southeastern quarter of Europe." [27] Sachs's explanation is that "attention, strictly horizontal and focused on the re-entry of the theme in another voice . . . completely ignores the constant frictions on our vertically trained ears." However, he calls these seconds "innate" and "unconscious," and illustrates his point by referring to Chinese soldiers, recruits from primitive tribes in Inner China, who "were every morning on raising the flag compelled to sing the (westernized) national anthem." After a week or so, Walter Lurje reports,[28] "the men sang in parallel seconds. After a few more days, occasional fifths appeared, and about a week later, they sang in perfect fifths throughout. After a while, some octaves cropped up, and ultimately they sang in octaves throughout. . . . This happened again whenever a new batch of rookies came, and always in the same sequence." In addition to Sachs's interpretation, a previous statement made by the present writer may explain this phenomenon: there is a general inherent capacity in mankind to distinguish between simple and complicated intervals, and it depends on the individual and on training which intervals are to be used.

The Main Approaches of Mankind to the Problem of Rhythm

Sachs discussed the basic problem of rhythm twice: first in the fifth chapter of the section on the music of India in his *Rise of Music;* [29] then, of course, in his book *Rhythm and Tempo*. The two approaches are slightly different and may be compared here so that the problems involved may become more comprehensible. Sachs chooses the rhythm of India as the first subject for discussion because of its "marvelous wealth and importance" and because "it shows better than the system of the Western and the Eastern Orient the two basic forms of rhythmic organization: meter and time."

The following tabulation illustrates these basic forms:

time	meter
qualitative	quantitative
a series of stressed and unstressed notes whose lengths may vary but which are counted by regular beats	a series of long and short notes, in which a long note is counted as two shorts
numeric symbols that have the form of fractions: 4/4, 6/8, etc.	numeric symbols that have the form of sums: 2+1+1, 1+2, etc.

Needless to say, this tabulation shows polarizations: "Over and over the two forms of rhythm have overlapped—in modern Western music

no less than in ancient Oriental melody." An outstanding example of
this overlapping is "the most characteristic organization of Indian melody—the rhythmic patterns or tālas. The simplest explanation of tāla
might be: a rhythmic pattern that combines the essential features of
both meter and time. Its numeric symbols consequently are sums
of fractions."

The main reason why Sachs changed these definitions is a terminological one: he showed, in an amusing way, how the words "quantita-
tive" and "qualitative" were confused even by superior minds, and felt
that it was safer to abandon them. Moreover, in the process of modifying his terminology, Sachs enriches his definition by drawing upon the
theories of Werner Jaeger and others (cf. below).[30]

Sachs generally refrains from treating rhythm that can be seen or
felt. His book is "concerned rather with the steady, orderly recurrence
of audible impressions only, that is, with rhythmical sounds. And it is
concerned with rhythmical sounds exclusively as an element of art,
as an aesthetic experience."

Like Plato, he excludes kinetic chaos and kinetic continuum. He
finds Andreas Heusler's definition acceptable: "Organization of time in
parts accessible to the senses." Sachs, furthermore, accepts the "findings
of modern psychology that 'the maximum filled duration of which we
can be both distinctly and immediately aware' is twelve seconds, which
is the reason why the ancient Greeks limited the length of a verse
to twenty-five time units," that is, the Greeks limited the duration of a
line of poetry to approximately two time units per second.

Of more than philological importance is Sachs's discussion of the
Greek term rhythmos. This term "leads back to a verb for 'flowing'—
rheō, rhein, an early relative of the German Rhein or Rhine and even
of the English word 'river.' Thus Fowler could tersely state: 'Rhythm
is flow.' " An opposite, almost contradictory, definition that has become
famous has been provided by Werner Jaeger. He

> has made it convincingly clear that, far from denoting motion as
> such, the oldest use of the word indicated on the contrary a pause,
> a steady limitation of movement. Among his examples are a poetic
> monologue by Archilochos from the seventh century B.C., who
> urges himself to "understand the rhythm that holds mankind in its
> bonds" . . . ; and Aeschylos . . . whose Prometheus complains:
> "I am bound here in this rhythm."

It is on the basis of these fundamentally different approaches that
Sachs proposes his underlying definition of "rhythm" in general, as
being "kinetic, intermittent, and perceived through one of the senses."
With the realization that the many different forms of rhythm "overlap

enough to make the classifier's life uncomfortable," he then distinguishes man's two main approaches to rhythm:

divisive	additive
regulative function, showing how the parts are meant to be disposed	configurative function, showing how the parts are actually disposed
impulses at equal distances	impulses at different distances
once called qualitative) (by later called accentual) Sachs)	once called quantitative) (by later called metrical) Sachs)

As to the details: Divisive rhythm

> exists as a basic ruling pattern before the details of melody take shape in the head of the composer . . . Theoretically, the first beat of a group or bar is meant to carry the strongest accent or weight . . . What the ear perceives is often very different and con-tradictory: all accents, indeed all notes, may fall between the beats; and, ignoring the conductor's gesture, the composer might place a rest or else let die the fading remainder of a previous note tied over the bar line where properly the strongest beat should be. Actually, the rest is in this case not a repose, not a cessation of activity . . .

The characterization of additive rhythm reads:

> The regular recurrence on which such patterns rest is not a certain duration to be divided into equal parts, but rather a grouping . . . composed of longer and shorter elements . . . such as 2+1, or 3+3+2 units, or any other arrangement of shorts and longs. These rhythms are "additive." As a consequence, disturbing offbeats, ties, and rests in accented places are inadmissible in principle. They would destroy the identity of an additive pattern.

Sachs chooses the term "accentual" as the best antonym to "metri-cal," although "we accent very little unless there is a *sforzato* mark on a note" and although on the organ and the harpsichord accents are outright impossible. "The term 'accentual' is, however, acceptable as long as we keep in mind the basic fact that, as pointed out before, accent, albeit regulative, is not necessarily perceptible, provided that we ourselves project into music our awareness of an accentual pattern." "Metrical music, on the other hand, including the most metrical melodies from India and Greece, can seldom do without accents, even where stresses are not compulsory. . . .

"To sum up: pure accent and pure meter are mere extremes, not opposite classes. They meet and merge in ever new combinations."

Otto Gombosi, in his review of *Rhythm and Tempo* [31] objects to the terms "divisive" and "additive." Rhythm, he says, "may be divisible but not divisive." The present writer, however, is inclined to agree with Sachs because *every* rhythm is divisible. Therefore, the term "divisive" may well be the only one available to indicate the kind of rhythm to which Sachs applied it. But it may be useful to co-ordinate the definition of rhythm as a flow with divisive rhythm on the one hand, and the definition of rhythm as a bond with additive rhythm on the other.

Additive rhythm is characterized by Sachs as "a grouping . . . composed of long and shorter elements," such as $3 + 2 + 2$, in other words, a series of compound elements that are more or less independent of each other. Divisive rhythm certainly consists of compound elements too; however, an underlying controlling pattern makes the compound elements less self-sufficient. The basic difference between the two types of rhythm becomes evident when one observes their principles carried out in fullest form. The elements in additive rhythm may be of great variety and complexity; but they remain clearly outlined in their relative self-sufficiency. Even the less well-trained listener can recognize compound elements linked into a group, their diversity erecting border lines between them, no matter how relatively imperceptible the details within those elements may be. An overwhelming wealth of such elements is to be found in non-Western music, as well as in the scores of Bartók and Stravinsky.

Divisive rhythm, on the other hand, may be basically simple, even rudimentary. However, when its principle is carried out in fullest form, the result is not only complicated, but confusing. As the use of complicated divisive rhythm has become a special feature of Western music, and as Sachs himself refers to examples of Western music when he discusses the "elementary principles," the present writer may be allowed to cite such an example also. Let us take the beginning of the second movement of Beethoven's String Quartet in E-flat, Opus 127, as an illustration. The listener who does not know the score—and the following statement is the result of many tests—perceives the opening notes as in regular duple rhythm. As soon as the first violin plays the eighth-note *eb'*, however, he realizes that he was mistaken and has to correct his first impression; because what he believed to be notes in duple time are really in syncopation, and the underlying governing pattern is, rather, the 12/8 measure. We are not dealing here with compound elements that are rhythmically independent. No clearly defined link is present in the opening section. The underlying flow becomes the ruling pattern, but its effect is delayed. There cannot possibly be rhythmic principles more dissimilar than the additive and the divisive, unless they be kinetic chaos and kinetic continuum.

As with the vocal melodic styles, so with rhythm, Sachs suggests a third type between the two extremes—the numerical rhythm. This type is to be found in a "group of verses and melodies in which no metric organization and hardly any recurrence of accents are considered." He justifies the introduction of this category by the fact "that a feel of rhythm can doubtless be conveyed by an even or alternate recurrence of numbers, if they do not exceed the limit of easy perception." Examples are the *Rigveda*, the most sacred book of India, and the *Avesta*, the holy book of ancient Iran. Both are "uniformly composed of sixteen syllables in two equal half-verses, without any meter or accent." Other examples appear in Chinese, Korean, and Japanese verses, Byzantine chant, and Middle English, French, Spanish, Portuguese, and Italian poetry. Numerical rhythm has three qualities: "1) a counted number of syllables, 2) absence of meter, 3) absence, scarcity, or vagueness of accents. . . . While numerical rhythm is poetically a nuance of accentual organization, it is musically a shade of additive patterns." Sachs refers to modern composers, particularly to Stravinsky, and more specifically to works like *Les Noces*, in which he interprets the numerical rhythmic patterns as the "national heritage . . . of ancient Byzantium." [32]

Final Comments

In this article, an attempt has been made to show Sachs as a creative ethnomusicologist. He was, of course, more—he was a polyhistorian: first, because of his wide historical knowledge; but even more significantly, because of his ability to trace the links between the various musical cultures of the world, past and present. L. B. Meyer has asked the question, "whether, beneath the profusion of diverse and divergent particulars, there are any universal principles functioning." The vocal melodic styles, musical systems in general, and the basic types of rhythm are only a few of the subjects in the treatment of which Sachs gave answers to this question.

Moreover, he was able to find a "terminology and a method of handling it most suitable to the particular idiom under investigation." [33] His polar terms are "divisive" and "additive." Their application to the three topics discussed in this paper may be shown as follows:

divisive	*additive*
pathogenic singing style	logogenic singing style
divisive tone system	cyclic tone system
accentual rhythm	metrical rhythm

Again it goes without saying that this tabulation shows the theoretical extremes; the historical actualities lie in between. On the other hand, "divisive" and "additive" are not simply descriptive terms. They reveal, rather, two principles to which each musical concept is subject: additive —as an extreme—indicates a chain of structurally more or less independent compound elements; divisive—as an extreme—indicates an underlying ruling pattern that governs the details and that equally divides the structurally dependent parts. As far as this writer knows, Sachs nowhere suggested the tabulation given above. His terminology, however, clearly justifies it. He, himself, might have agreed to proceeding in this direction—a direction for which he opened the way.

Notes

1. Curt Sachs, *The Wellsprings of Music* (The Hague: Martinus Nijhoff, 1962).
2. Curt Sachs, "The Lore of Non-Western Music," in *Some Aspects of Musicology* (New York: The Liberal Arts Press, 1957), pp. 19-48.—The quote is on p. 46.
3. Jaap Kunst, *Ethnomusicology* (The Hague: Martinus Nijhoff, 1959).
4. Mantle Hood, "Training and Research Methods in Ethnomusicology," *Ethnomusicology Newsletter* No. 11 (1957), pp. 2-8, drawing upon *Journal of the American Musicological Society*, VIII (1955), p. 153.
5. Leonard B. Meyer, "Universalism and Relativism in the Study of Ethnic Music," *Ethnomusicology*, IV (1960), pp. 49-54.
6. Mieczyslaw Kolinski, "Ethnomusicology, its Problems and Methods," *Ethnomusicology Newsletter*, No. 10 (1957), pp. 1-7.
7. Charles Seeger, "Systematic Musicology: Viewpoints, Orientations, and Methods," *Journal of the American Musicological Society*, IV (1951), pp. 240-248.
8. For a comprehensive bibliography, see Kurt Hahn, "Verzeichnis der wissenschaftlichen Arbeiten von Curt Sachs," *Acta musicologica*, XXIX (1957), pp. 94-106.
9. Curt Sachs, *Geist und Werden der Musikinstrumente* (Berlin: Dietrich Reimer, 1929).
10. Curt Sachs, *The History of Musical Instruments* (New York: W. W. Norton & Co., 1940).
11. Curt Sachs, *World History of the Dance* (New York: W. W. Norton & Co., 1937).
12. Curt Sachs, *The Rise of Music in the Ancient World, East and West* (New York: W. W. Norton & Co., 1943).
13. Curt Sachs, *Rhythm and Tempo* (New York: W. W. Norton & Co., 1953).
14. Curt Sachs, *The Rise of Music in the Ancient World*, pp. 41 ff.
15. Pp. 68-70.
16. Frederick William Dillistone, *Christianity and Symbolism* (London: Collins, 1955).
17. See H. H. Draeger, "The Order of the Arts in the Catholic Service," *Paul A. Pisk, Essays in His Honor*, to be published by the University of Texas Press.

18. Curt Sachs, *The Rise of Music in the Ancient World*, pp. 64 ff.

19. Eric Werner, *The Sacred Bridge* (New York: Columbia University Press, 1959), pp. 373 ff.

20. Curt Sachs, *The Rise of Music in the Ancient World*, pp. 72 ff.

21. In the Pythagorean system, to be sure, the perfect octave (2:1) can never be attained by means of the cycle of fifths, since the twelfth fifth touches a note 24 cents (Pythagorean comma) above the perfect octave. However, a perfect octave may be obtained in the Pythagorean system by adding a perfect fifth (3:2) and a perfect fourth (4:3).

22. Fritz A Kuttner with the assistance of J. Murray Barbour, *Musurgia Records (Booklet)*, "The Theory of Classical Music" (1955).

23. Gustave Reese, *Music in the Middle Ages* (New York: W. W. Norton & Co., 1940), pp. 294-295.

24. Wolfgang Koehler, *Gestalt Psychology* (New York: Mentor Books, 1959), p. 110.

25. See H. H. Draeger, "Die Verbindlichkeit der mathematischen Inter-vall-Definition," *Musikalische Zeitfragen*, X (Kassel, 1962).

26. He hopes to give a possible answer to this question in the near future.

27. Curt Sachs, *The Wellsprings of Music*, pp. 179-181.

28. *Ibid.*, pp. 180-181.

29. Curt Sachs, *The Rise of Music in the Ancient World*, pp. 184 ff.

30. Curt Sachs, *Rhythm and Tempo*, pp. 11-34.

31. *Journal of the American Musicological Society*, VII (1954), pp. 221-228.

32. Curt Sachs, *Rhythm and Tempo*, pp. 372-373.

33. Charles Seeger, *op. cit.*

POLYPHONY IN

AFRICAN MUSIC

Rose Brandel (New York)

$\mathcal{A}$lthough the historical relation of polyphony to monophony is in many respects vague, there is no doubt concerning their cultural distribution. Polyphony, as the simultaneous sounding of more than one line of music, has existed in numerous areas of the world, both primitive and non-primitive, both Oriental and Western. While the emphasis within such music has generally been on the horizontal, namely, on the melodic rather than on the harmonic, it would be rash to state categorically that vertical awareness has been completely absent from all but Western polyphony. A more valid view would be that the sense of the vertical has been present in varying proportions in most polyphonic music, whether the polyphony be rudimentary or complex, inadvertent or deliberate. The moment two different pitches are sounded together, no matter what the context, the listeners or performers receive an impression of a totality, a Gestalt of sound involving the two notes as a whole, despite the fact that such an impression may be overshadowed by "single-line listening" and may even be subliminal. Vertical awareness, of course, reached an unparalleled peak of concentration in the West, where it crystallized in the unique form of functional harmony. In such harmony, horizontal motion is, in a sense, "stopped," so that simultaneous notes can be abstracted and viewed as integrated entities, or chords; these in turn are organized in a relational system involving concepts of tension and relaxation.

Western functional harmony is, to be sure, absent in the traditional music of Negro Africa. However, both horizontal and vertical manifestations of polyphony appear in this music, the former often of an elaborate nature and the latter hinting at times at the beginnings of a true harmony. Before discussing the polyphonic types found in traditional African music, the present author would like to say a few words about a methodological problem.

Because the West has contributed the most elaborate and systematic vertical polyphony in history, there is an underlying tendency to make this polyphony the focal point of all discussions of polyphonic music in general, to evaluate the world's varieties of polyphony from the point of view of the Western polyphonic "standard." At least two kinds of comparisons come to mind, both of which rest on postulates requiring some examination.

First, and most important, is the searching for the special characteristics of functional harmony in a non-Western polyphonic sample. The essential requirement, for a positive finding, is the presence of chords or chordal approximations functioning alongside each other as points of tension or relaxation within a pre-established tonal system. The tonal system belongs to the major-minor configuration, and the chords are "tense" or "relaxed" by virtue of their relative position within this configuration and their degree of dissonance or consonance.

For some four hundred years this harmonic system has held sway in the West, and for some four hundred years its basic postulates have been that certain vertical intervals are consonant and certain ones dissonant; that consonant chords function as magnets for dissonant ones; and that certain harmonic nodes, namely, the first, fifth, and fourth degrees of the scale, are in the order given the most important. However, if in what is probably the strictest area of human thought, mathematics, the 19th-century development of several non-Euclidean geometric systems [1] showed that certain postulates of Euclidean geometry were not, as had been thought for c. 2,000 years, "self-evident," it is surely possible that the postulates underlying Western functional harmony are not absolute, and that other harmonic systems based on other foundations may exist.

Actually, even in Western history the concept of dissonance and consonance has never been entirely fixed. It took at least two hundred years for the interval of the third, the *sine qua non* of Western functional harmony, to be firmly established in art music as a consonant rather than a dissonant interval. The first theorist known to call it consonant is the so-called Anonymous IV of the 13th century; [2] the idea was still highly controversial when Ramos de Pareja posited it in his *Musica practica* of 1482; and only when major and minor harmony was fully accepted by Zarlino in his *Istitutioni harmoniche* of 1588 were thirds

(both major and minor) officially deemed worthy of the designation
"consonant." [3] It is of interest to note that the third apparently fared
little better among the ancient Greeks, who, as Sachs points out, may
have been more concerned with polyphony [instrumental] than is
generally believed.[4] Plutarch, for example, speaks of the dissonance of
the vertical minor third d'-b, while Gaudentios seems to toy with the
concept of harmonic neutrality when he considers the major third, as
well as the tritone, to be neither consonant nor dissonant! [5] With respect
to the West again, in 20th-century art music many vertical intervals,
such as the second, have lost their previously dissonant character, functioning as harmonic points of "relaxation" as well as of "tension,"
depending upon the context. It cannot be said, in attempting to account
for this new attitude toward intervals, that vertical awareness has disappeared and that 20th-century polyphony is mainly contrapuntal, or
horizontal, in conception. Harmonic relationships still exist, and chords
still function with respect to each other, but the underlying perceptions
("postulates") concerning consonance and dissonance, harmonic focal
points in the scale, and the direction of harmonic movement, among
other things, have changed.

The second type of musical comparison which must be handled
with care involves the concept of predictability in history. Toynbee,
for example, sees parallel paths of development among civilizations, not-
ing a recurrent historical pattern, or "rhythm" of growth and disintegration. Although Toynbee's pattern is not inevitable, since he considers history *as a whole* moving in a spiral-like fashion, the "major
movement" being "not recurrent but progressive," [6] he does attempt to
define the cultural details, including the arts, at various stages of a
civilization's development. A sure sign, for example, of a declining civilization is what he calls "promiscuity" in the arts, which appears especially
as "vulgarity and barbarism." [7] Essentially this is the "deliberate abandon-
ment" of a long-established technique and style, a situation evident, for
example, in 20th-century Western music, the development of which
is due to our having "wilfully cast out of our souls the great masters,"
and which marks "some kind of spiritual breakdown. . . ." [8]

Toynbee belongs to a long and illustrious line of historical-pattern
thinkers, which goes back to Aristotle, Plato, and even earlier figures.
Many of them have dealt specifically with music, some, like Toynbee,
attempting to correlate its development with the progress-and-decline
stages of their respective culture cycles. Whether they can validly ascertain musical "progress" or not, and Toynbee's handling of 20th-century
art is certainly open to question, these thinkers have set up "laws" of
historical process in the fashion of natural science. Laws, by implication,
allow prediction, since they describe fixed patterns, although even physical laws, as pointed out since the days of David Hume and especially

emphasized by modern philosophers of science, indicate only a high degree of probability and are not absolute in predictive capacity.[9] Now the main problem is whether the historical laws governing cultures as a whole, assuming the existence of such laws, imply fixed patterns of development for all aspects of these cultures. It would be easy, for example, to set up a universal chronology of musical development, perhaps from monophony to polyphony, from symmetric rhythm to asymmetric rhythm, from chasmatonic (gapped) scales to diatonic scales, or perhaps from a "lesser" to a "greater" music or vice versa as Toynbee and Spengler would see it. The latter, for example, was convinced that "it is in string quartets and violin sonatas that it [Western music] has experienced its most transcendent and most holy moments of full illumination. Here, in chamber-music, Western art as a whole reaches its highest point." [10] Sachs, in his brilliant theory of musical cycles,[11] avoids the pitfalls inherent in the above approach by dealing with underlying human attitudes (ethos and pathos) in music history, and the variety of their realizations, and not with the historical inevitability of specific techniques and structures, or with value theories. He particularly disavows the last two themes in declaring that "the style of art . . . has unlimited freedom and never repeats itself . . ." and in pointing to the falseness of "the current trivial conception of eternal 'progress' to an ever greater mastership. . . ." [12]

Nonetheless, it is still important to ask, for example, what parallel thirds imply in African music. We are still concerned with historical sequence and have a right to deal with this problem. Our answer, however, must always involve awareness of at least two dangers, first, that of making inferential, predictive leaps from the historical music pattern of the West to African music history; and second, even if a uniform pattern of musical development could be shown for a large number of civilizations, the danger in assuming that inevitability is one hundred per cent absolute, for even in natural science a law is perhaps only contingent and not necessary.

The strongly polyphonic character of sub-Saharan traditional African music appears in several basic types—parallel intervals, overlapping choral antiphony or solo-choral response, ostinato or drone-ostinato, and double or triple melody (polymelody). The types are often intermingled, parallel intervals, for example, frequently appearing with overlapping response; furthermore, some of the types may fuse and lose their distinctiveness, so that double or triple melody, for example, may in certain cases also be considered as multi-ostinato (i.e., two or more simultaneous ostinatos); and finally, any of the types may run beyond two and three parts, a vertical density of four distinct pitches (excluding octave duplication) being a not uncommon achievement within a piece.

Of great interest, in the last respect, is that frequently three pitches form triads and four pitches produce chords revolving about a minor seventh [13] in which a tritone is often prominent, e.g., C-(D)-E-G-$B\flat$, E-G-$B\flat$-(C)-D, etc. (The notes shown in parentheses are sometimes used to enlarge the chord, as in Ex. 1, below.) The four-note chords are generally much more fluid than the triads, the notes of the former only momentarily converging, and simultaneity often being *implied* (in the manner of a broken chord) when only an echo remains of one of the rapidly moving tones. (Although not drawing parallels, the present author cannot resist pointing to the vertical "fullness" suggested by the arpeggios in Bach's works for unaccompanied violin, such as the famous Chaconne from the D Minor Partita.) The fluidity is in many instances due to the African propensity for melodic fragmentation, namely, hocket,[14] but hocket in which each player or singer holds part or all of his fragment (one or more notes) of the melody slightly longer than he would in strict hocket. Ostensibly, this overlapping of fragments makes a good case for asserting lack of vertical awareness, since the contributing "parts" of the polyphony actually comprise only one line of music. However, the overlapping, or sustaining of notes, may be quite deliberate and not inadvertent. It seems especially deliberate in Ex. 1, which illustrates a chord built on a minor seventh with tritone emphasis, the fluid five notes of which result from both melodic and harmonic hocket. The hocketing (executed by five ivory horns, each playing one tone, i.e., pitch) achieves harmony in two ways, through the overlapping of fragments in the main line (a very brief melody outlining three tones g'-f'-$e\flat'$) and through the presence of a second line, a little ostinato (moving through a-c'-a) also in hocket. Both lines may, in a sense, be seen as an example of multi-ostinato, since there is a third, vocal line, to which the others may act as "accompaniment." (The vocal melody, however, is closely related to the three-tone horn melody, lagging behind the latter in canon-like fashion.) The fluidity of the chord, a-c'-$e\flat'$-f'-g' (evident in the middle of the measure), which gives the effect of the first inversion of a Western "dominant ninth" chord, is further enhanced by the arpeggio effect mentioned above. This is realized here by the rapid hocket-exchange of a and c'. Simultaneity, therefore, is physically certain for four notes, but only aurally implied for all five:

Ex. 1 - Kukuya Ivory Horns (Congo Republic: Brazzaville) [15]

Transposed up minor second

The ostinato, one of the most important polyphonic types in African music, is generally short and of restricted range, averaging from two tones (often viewed as a drone-ostinato) to four tones and rarely spanning more than the interval of a fourth. The ostinato may be continuous or intermittent, vocal or instrumental, and may appear above or below the melody.[16] The one-note drone is less common, drones in general being more characteristic of Arabic (and Hindu) music.

Particularly interesting is the multi-ostinato, mentioned above. The combination of two or more ostinatos, a direct correlate of the African inclination for "orchestral" music, distinctly belongs to the contrapuntal, or horizontal, type of polyphony. That is, each ostinato moves in independent melodic and rhythmic patterns. Although strictly speaking the multi-ostinato (as well as the ostinato) is actually an accompaniment to a main melodic line, in many instances a main line is not apparent or almost as brief as the ostinato motifs (as in Ex. 1). Depending on the definition of "melody" (with respect to length, inner organization, etc.), the contrapuntal mosaic of multi-ostinato without a principal line may be seen either as a subdivision of polymelody or as a kind of accompaniment-standing-by-itself. The following extract (Ex. 2) from a bush-cutters' work song of the Kpelle people of Liberia illustrates this type of multi-ostinato without an apparent main line. The popular hocket style of execution, which seems to be allied to multi-ostinato, is also used here. However, the vertical columns (two and three tones) are not due to the holding over of hocket fragments (as in Ex. 1), but derive essentially from the coexistence of ostinato lines: [17]

Ex. 2 - Kpelle Bush Cutters (Liberia) [18]

Transposed down major third

Of the other contrapuntal types of polyphony, namely overlapping response (or overlapping antiphony) and double (or triple) melody, the type with overlap is definitely the more common. Polymelody is, of course, now being considered as involving melodies of some length and intricacy (beyond the fleeting two- or three-note ostinato motifs shown above). Long-lined melody, it should be understood, is certainly not a rarity in African music; it is the polyphonic combination of two or more such melodies which is unusual. Double melodies of four (assorted) measures each appear in a choral dance-song of the Babinga

Pygmies of the Congo Republic (Brazzaville), and double melodies of essentially six (assorted) measures in some royal horn music of the Banyoro of Uganda.[19] There are numerous instances of a type of independent-line movement which superficially appears to be polymelody. However, this is generally a case of heterophony in which a melody and its variants are contrapuntally juxtaposed. Such heterophony does not seem to be haphazard or fortuitous, for, despite the obvious derivation from and frequent merging with a main line, the variant lines often achieve a noticeable independence, usually at certain strategic points during the course of a piece.[20]

Responsorial and antiphonal overlapping provides one of the most important sources of African polyphony. As a formal device the alternation of a solo and chorus or of two choruses is, of course, not confined to Africa and is, in fact, almost universal.[21] Alternation leading to polyphony—i.e., overlapping alternation—is not as widespread,[22] however, and in Africa may, if taken together with other factors, be considered a sign of polyphonic consciousness. Such consciousness is perhaps weaker when the overlapping is canonic, i.e., when the chorus repeats the melody of the soloist (or of another chorus), since there is substantially only one line of music. Polyphonic consciousness seems to be stronger when the overlapping, answering section is different—when it is a refrain, an elongation of the first section, or perhaps a new melodic line. However, because of such factors as a chorus suddenly dividing or one or two subsidiary soloists interjecting additional notes, the result often being a greater vertical fullness of three or more notes, even the sparse, supposedly casual polyphony of the canon takes on a different hue and significance. In such instances polyphonic intent and awareness should not be underestimated, certainly not ignored. The following excerpts (Exx. 3 and 4) [23] illustrate responsorial overlapping giving rise to canon, in which added choral or solo fullness is apparent. The first example is from a banana-pounding song of the Bongili girls of the Congo Republic (Brazzaville), and the additional fullness (due to both solo interjection and choral *divisi*) appears in the last measure shown. In the second example, taken from an elephant feast song of the Mambuti Pygmies of the Congo Republic (Leopoldville),[24] the recourse to choral *divisi* is the source of the enlarged fullness:

Ex. 3 - Bongili (Congo Republic: Brazzaville)

Transposed up minor second

Ex. 4 - Mambuti Pygmies (Congo Republic: Léopoldville)

Although the types of part-music discussed above have been placed in the contrapuntal category, that is, the polyphony has been deemed primarily horizontal, or melodic, attention has nevertheless been drawn to polyphonic intent and awareness. The piling up of vertical sonorities in African music, through sustaining of hocket fragments in the multi-ostinato or interjection and *divisi* in overlapping antiphony and.response, does in fact point to something more than mere coexistence of independent lines. Even without the special devices of sustaining, interjection, and *divisi*,[25] any of the polyphonic types discussed thus far, despite their prominently linear structure may be associated with vertical attitudes of more than minimal level. The usually elaborate *motion* in African polyphony, in which melodies and also rhythms seem to be going their individual ways, does not in itself rule out harmonic consciousness. To what degree the African musician and audience hear independent line motions as integrated totalities cannot, of course, be exactly and incontrovertibly estimated. (Perhaps some future, rigidly controlled psychological tests may provide a complete answer.) However, the co-ordination required in intricate counter-motion, at least from the performer's point of view, certainly seems to imply a moderate, if not strong, awareness of simultaneity.[26]

As we look for "harmonic clues" again in the music itself, the African polyphony that especially draws our interest is the one deriving from parallel intervals. This type of polyphony is obviously not of the contrapuntal variety. The lines do not move independently, and the vertical sonorities, being more static, are more easily pinpointed. Certainly, it may be said that in parallel motion the columns of notes draw great attention to themselves and tend to lessen interest in the bare succession of notes. Such harmonic competition with the melodic is prominent in much African music, for parallel intervals are quite widespread. In no way does this statement cancel the previous reference to "elaborate motion" in African polyphony. The presence of both linear and vertical polyphonic types in a traditional musical culture is not startling: parallel intervals and rather involved counterpoint are both found, for example, in Italian and in Ukrainian folk music.[27]

Thirds, fourths, and fifths are the important parallel intervals in African music. In a discussion elsewhere,[28] the present author has pointed out the dubiousness of considering the third, as did von Hornbostel [29] and others, a later phenomenon than the fourth and fifth in African music history. Parallel thirds exist in many primitive areas in the Pacific,[30] and in Europe an older folk music was constructed on the interval of the third rather than on the fourth and fifth.[31]

The important problem with respect to parallel intervals in African music, however, is not that dealing with their chronology, but the one concerning their relationship to a functional harmony. Before discussing this we should like to consider some details of geographic distribution.

Parallel thirds are found throughout a large portion of sub-Saharan Africa, mainly in West Africa (Liberia, the Ivory Coast, Ghana, Nigeria), Central Africa (the Cameroons, the two Congo Republics, the Tanganyika Republic, Angola, Northern Rhodesia), and portions of Southeast Africa, including the Malagasy Republic. Among the tribes whose music contains parallel thirds are the Loma of Liberia;[32] the Baule of the Ivory Coast;[33] the Ga of Ghana;[34] the Ibo of Nigeria;[35] the Bulu of the Cameroons;[36] the Baduma, Mboko, Okandi, and Bungomo of the Congo Republic (Brazzaville);[37] the Mangbetu, Babira, Bapere, Bapende, Bapindi, Babunda, Bakwesi, Topoke, and Ekonda of the Congo Republic (Leopoldville);[38] the Wahehe of the Tanganyika Republic;[39] the Gangele, Luchosi, and Ovimbundu of Angola;[40] the Bemba and Baushi of Northern Rhodesia;[41] and the Acholi of Uganda,[42] a country where the usual parallels are octaves.[43] The following excerpt (Ex. 5) from a Bungomo song illustrates parallel thirds in the long-lined response of the chorus. The even longer soloist melody (of which only the opening phrase is shown here) prominently features the raised fourth of the scale, $f\sharp'$, as opposed to the $f\natural'$ of the choral line. Such fourth and raised-fourth scale fluctuation is not unusual and is also found among the Baduma (see below):

Ex. 5 - Bungomo (Congo Republic: Brazzaville)[44]

Transposed down minor third

Parallel fourths and fifths are prominent in East-Central and South Africa, but also appear in other areas. In the following excerpt (Ex. 6) from a song of the Zulu of Natal, South Africa, parallel fourths are sung by the male chorus in a rhythmic setting featuring the almost universal Greek dochmiac pattern $3 + 3 + 2$ (viz., 8/8). Of particular inter-

est is the song's unusual scale, *G-A♭-B♭-C-D♭-E♭-G*, which resembles the
Greek Hyperdorian, except that it is chasmatonic (gapped) at the top:

Ex. 6 - Zulu (Natal, South Africa)[45]

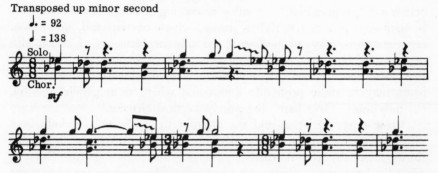

The geographic, and even tribal, mingling of parallel thirds, fourths,
and fifths may be greater than hitherto believed. Some interesting mixtures are evident as follows. The Wasukuma of the Tanganyika Republic seem to favor parallel fourths and fifths, but we find some parallel
thirds in one of their songs.[46] Parallel thirds and parallel fourths appear
among the Wahehe of the Tanganyika Republic.[47] In a song of the
Okandi of the Congo Republic (Brazzaville) there is a blend of parallel
thirds, fourths, and sixths.[48] It should be noted here that in the contrapuntal polyphony discussed above all kinds of harmonic intervals may
exist side by side in the same piece, but unless *full chords* are moving
in parallel motion, it is unusual to find a variety of parallel intervals in
a single work. In a related example from Ruanda, a Watutsi song, both
parallel sixths and alternately parallel fifths (i.e., separated by another
harmonic interval) appear in an overall form involving both contrapuntal and parallel motion. Especially noteworthy is the fact that the
ornamented Arabic vocal style, which is quite common in Watutsi singing, is also present in this particular song.[49] (Polyphony in Arabic music
is quite limited, the drone being the most important type.) Although
the evidence is far from complete, these and many other examples suggest caution in attempting to translate geographic distribution of interval-
types in terms of language areas, culture areas, or other categories.

Parallel seconds are not common in Africa; some isolated examples
appear among the Mambuti Pygmies (see Ex. 4, above) and the
Babira of the Congo Republic (Leopoldville) (the latter generally favor
parallel thirds), and among the Makwa of the Congo Republic (Brazzaville). In most of these examples the seconds, although parallel, are static,
i.e., instead of a succession of seconds at different pitch levels, the same
vertical second is repeated.[50] ("Repeated parallels," incidentally, occur in

a few of the examples of parallel thirds, fourths, and fifths given above.)

The question raised earlier as to the functional significance of parallel intervals in African music hinges on several issues: harmonic intent and awareness; tension and relaxation, or dissonance and consonance; and deliberate "progressions," or rules governing chordal succession, that is, harmony as a *system*. These issues, which overlap and, in a sense, represent three ways of looking at the same problem, are of course also pertinent with respect to the contrapuntal African polyphony (and the first issue was, in fact, already touched upon above). However, the issues may be more profitably considered when, as in parallel motion, the polyphony "lays bare" the purely vertical element.

Voice-range variation and the attempt to duplicate a melody at a different pitch level are obviously not valid explanations of parallel thirds, especially the alternation of major and minor thirds. Octaves, fifths, and fourths comprise the usual intervallic spacing between voice types, but in African polyphony parallel fifths and fourths are probably also beyond the purely biologic stage. (Needless to say, the biologic theory has no relevancy for parallel motion in instrumental music.) The structural setting, on the whole, is too complex for an easy explanation: parallel fifths and fourths often are sections of a piece also containing contrapuntal portions, and frequently the intervals appear in some "diluted" manner, such as a momentary divergence of one of the parallel lines in an opposite direction, perhaps at the cadence-like end of a phrase. Vertical intent and awareness can therefore be acknowledged, most strongly with respect to parallel thirds and perhaps moderately so where fourths and fifths are concerned. Furthermore, parallel triads, which are extensions of parallel thirds, are even more vivid expressions of harmonic attitudes, as are also other (non-contrapuntal) chords. The latter may be suddenly interjected and sustained at strategic points (note, for example, the chord $d\sharp'$-$f\sharp'$-$g\sharp'$-b' in the choral response of a Wameru war song of the Tanganyika Republic [51]), or they may be introduced in a recurrent pattern (such as the appearance of the chord e-$b\flat$-d'-e' on the first beat of every other measure in a Bapere horn piece [52]). Parallel triads (or any full chords in parallel motion), it ought to be pointed out, are not as common in African music as triads (and other chords) which are interjected, usually by means of a sudden *divisi*. Ex. 7 illustrates not only parallel triads, but also minor-seventh chords in a zither piece of the Mboko of the Congo Republic (Brazzaville):

Ex. 7 - Mboko Zither (Congo Republic: Brazzaville) [53]

By virtue of their obvious verticality, parallel intervals, notably thirds, and full chords provide positive structural clues to harmonic intent in African music, but harmonic tension and relaxation, also known as dissonance and consonance, are more difficult clues to deal with. The alternation of minor and major thirds in parallel motion or the succession of different chords obviously gives harmonic contrast, which is vital to harmonic tension and relaxation. If the contrast is seen in terms of dissonance and consonance, then either a "universal" classification plan must be superimposed on African intervals or the music itself and controlled estimation of mental attitudes must be considered in the attempt to determine what is consonant and what is dissonant in African harmony. Ideas of consonance and dissonance have undergone change even in Western music history (as pointed out at the beginning of this paper), and acoustic theory has been used by various thinkers (e.g., Pythagoras, Helmholtz, and Stumpf) for different "absolute" systems of consonance and dissonance. In effect, there seems, thus far, to be no universal classification plan.

Nevertheless, there is harmonic contrast in African music, although identification of the contrast in terms of consonance and dissonance is a difficult process, and there is harmonic tension and relaxation based on both the contrast (of chords and intervals) and the points of prominence within the various African scales. Thus, if a scale is constructed mainly on the notes a-c'-$e\flat'$-f'-g' (as in Ex. 4, above), the succession of the harmonic intervals f'-g' and d'-f' may provide harmonic relaxation and tension, but in the order given; that is, the major second may be the "relaxed" interval and the minor third the "tense" interval, because of the scale structure.

Hamonic tension and relaxation may also be influenced by other factors, such as a sudden, perhaps jagged, leap into a chord or vertical interval. The intermittent drone-note in a Bahutu (Ruanda) song, for example, gives the impression of great harmonic tension whenever it appears, regardless of the harmonic interval (fourth, major third, etc.) which it forms with the melodic line.[54] Furthermore, when a piece contains substantially only one type of chord, which sounds almost incessantly throughout, there is obviously no harmonic tension and relaxation. The lack of vertical contrast tends to counteract whatever tension may be present, for example, in the tritonic minor-seventh chord pervading pieces such as those played by the Kukuya horns (see Ex. 1, above) and the Mambuti Pygmy flutes.[55]

In some African music parallel thirds consist only of major thirds and hence in themselves offer no harmonic contrast. (The same may be said of the exclusive use of parallel fifths or of parallel fourths.) Parallel major thirds tend to be generated by scales featuring a lowered seventh, such as C-D-E-F-G-$B\flat$. The harmonic sequence $b\flat$-d', $b\flat$-d', c'-e', for

example, appears in the choral response of a song of the Baduma paddlers of the Congo Republic (Brazzaville).[56] (The Baduma also show a
propensity for scales with a raised fourth, as discussed below.) Parallel
major thirds in full triads (viz., parallel major triads) move in the
same stepwise manner in a song of the Gangele of Angola, an excerpt
of which is given in Ex. 8. The full triad, of course, with its major and
minor thirds, offers some inner compensation for the overall similarity
of chordal structure:

Ex. 8 - Gangele (Angola)[57]
Transposed up minor second

If we are looking for a functional harmony (not necessarily the
usual Western one), it is important to translate harmonic contrast in
terms of deliberate chordal progression. Do vertical sonorities succeed
each other in some planned fashion? Are they related to each other by
some rules of harmonic motion? There is obviously no written music
theory in tribal Africa, but harmony as a system may to some degree
be part of the oral tradition. Whether such a system is consciously
formulated, to the point where the introduction (composing, performing, teaching) of a new piece involves verbal articulation of harmonic
principles, is hardly likely. However, there do appear to be some guiding
principles, no matter how implicit, nonformulated, and embryonic. Certain chord clusters, certain combinations of vertical intervals are favored
by different tribes or even groups of tribes. There is great diversity, of
course, in the number of harmonic "patterns," for much of the harmonic
motion is influenced by the scale types, of which there are many
varieties in Africa.

The alternation of parallel major and minor thirds, the special combinations of parallel thirds, sixths, and other intervals may be considered
in a general sense as examples of the harmonic patterning indicated.
However, more specific patterns exist, such as the sequence e'-g', d'-$f\sharp'$,
which is used as a cadence-like formula in some music of the Baduma
paddlers of the Congo Republic (Brazzaville).[58] In this music the tonic
is C or A. In the C scale the $F\sharp$ is, of course, the raised fourth; furthermore, both C and A scales run the same gamut, namely, A-C-D-E-$F\sharp$-G-
A-(B)-C. Like the Bungomo example above (Ex. 5), the Baduma pieces
contain both $F\natural$ and $F\sharp$, which in one song gives rise to an interesting

fluctuation of parallel thirds involving d'-f' and d'-$f\sharp'$. Where the C or A scales contain an $F\natural$ only, a very common sequence involves alternate major and minor thirds moving through two basic areas, B-D-F and A-C-E-G, and coming to rest somewhere in the latter area (as in Ex. 7, above). Another example of harmonic grouping is the fluid pattern extracted from a contrapuntal (polymelodic) piece of the Babinga Pygmies of the Congo Republic (Brazzaville) as follows (the letters are to be read vertically):

$$a\text{-}d'\text{-}e'\text{-}g\sharp'\text{-}b',\ b\text{-}d'\text{-}f\sharp'\text{-}g\sharp'.$$

The bracketed notes are the most important and illustrate a chordal movement which in Western terms would be called "plagal." Many African octave scales are, in fact, constructed in a "plagal" manner, the interval of the fourth being below and that of the fifth, above a central pivot note. (This is the opposite of the traditional Western "authentic" scale structure, wherein the interval of the fifth is below that of the fourth.) As a result, the harmonic progression (not necessarily identical with the Babinga sample) involving root notes a fourth apart is not uncommon in African music.[59] (In the Babinga piece, incidentally, the notes e', $g\sharp'$, d', $f\sharp'$ often emerge through melodic and dynamic emphases, so that the last three frequently seem to give the chords an "inverted" character.) Finally, there is the harmonic sequence often implied in the motion surrounding the tritonic minor-seventh chord. As pointed out above, this type of chord makes numerous appearances in African music; furthermore, the chord was termed "fluid," for it generally appears in a contrapuntal setting, rarely in parallel or block formation. Such fluidity and the addition of a fifth note to the chord may, if the tempo is not too rapid, suggest a sequence involving the seventh-chord and its related ninth-chord, in root or in inverted positions. This is evident in Ex. 1, above, in which the motion exposes the chords a-c'-$e\flat'$-f' and a-c'-$e\flat'$-f'-g'.

Although it is admitted that chordal "progression" in African music is not standardized and far from elaborate, some rudimentary patterns are evidently part of the oral tradition. The chords do function, but the functioning is obviously not that of the full-blown Western tonic-dominant, major-minor system. Some of the African harmonic sequences point, in fact, to the possible evolvement of a variety of functional harmonies (were such historic evolvement presumably not to be interfered with). One can envisage systems based on "plagal" movement or on movement highlighting other scalar resting points, such as the whole tone or raised fourth above the tonic and the whole tone or minor third below the tonic. Depending on scalar emphases and on general scale structure (diatonic, chasmatonic, isotonic), such systems might feature minor-seventh chords, fourth-plus-major-second chords, and other chord types evident thus far in African music.

One of these possible harmonic systems may after all be like the traditional Western one. The African parallel thirds and, of course, the triads could be interpreted as precursors of such a functional harmony. This is a reasonable assumption, since parallel thirds in early European music were indeed important in the development of the triadically structured major-minor functional system. However, the assumption is fully reasonable only if Western music history is seen as an inevitable, universal pattern of development, or perhaps as a pattern applicable to African culture. These ideas have yet to be proved, although the rapid adoption of Western traditional harmony in the more sophisticated city life of Africa gives credence not only to the second idea, but also to the suspicion that the other types of embryonic harmonic systems may be pushed off the African scene.

Notes

1. Namely, the geometries of Lobachevski and of Riemann.
2. Anonymous IV in Charles E. H. Coussemaker, *Scriptorum de musica medii aevi nova series*, Vol. I, Facsimile ed. (Milan: Bollettino Bibliografico Musicale, 1931), p. 358.
3. Cf. Gustave Reese, *Music in the Renaissance* (New York: W. W. Norton & Co., 1954), pp. 377, 586.
4. Curt Sachs, *The Rise of Music in the Ancient World, East and West* (New York: W. W. Norton & Co., 1943), pp. 256 f.
5. *Ibid.*, p. 258.
6. Arnold J. Toynbee, *A Study of History*, Abridgement of Vols. I-VI (New York: Oxford University Press, 1947), p. 254.
7. *Ibid.*, pp. 465 f.
8. *Ibid.*, p. 259.
9. Cf. Hans Reichenbach, *The Rise of Scientific Philosophy* (Berkeley: University of California Press, 1951).
10. Oswald Spengler, *The Decline of the West* (New York: Alfred A. Knopf, 1926), Vol. I, p. 231.
11. Curt Sachs, *The Commonwealth of Art* (New York: W. W. Norton & Co., 1946).
12. *Ibid.*, p. 25. See also the chapter entitled " 'Progress'?" in Sachs's last work, *The Wellsprings of Music* (The Hague: Martinus Nijhoff, 1961), pp. 210-222.
13. Needless to say, many sizes of "minor" sevenths and of other intervals exist in African tuning, which is traditionally not based on the West's equal temperament. Details of African tuning are given in Rose Brandel, *The Music of Central Africa* (The Hague: Martinus Nijhoff, 1961), pp. 70-72.
14. Although hocket seems to be a specifically melodic phenomenon, it may rest basically upon rhythmic motivations, since the distribution of

bits of a melody among different performers results essentially in a rapid alternation of *timbres*. Rapid timbre contrast emphasizes rhythmic effects and is especially vital in hemiolic, or unequal-beat, rhythmic style (Sachs's "additive" style), which is highly characteristic of African music (cf. Brandel, *Central Africa*, pp. 73 ff). The possibly Oriental source of hocket and the importance of rhythmic color-contrast (for example, in *tāla* execution) are discussed in Marius Schneider, "Der Hochetus," *Zeitschrift für Musikwissenschaft*, XI (1927), p. 396.

15. The Kukuya excerpt in Ex. 1 is from Transcription 33, measure 3, by Rose Brandel in *Central Africa*, p. 192. Additional examples of the minor seventh with tritone emphasis (melodic or harmonic), as found among the Mambuti Pygmies and the Bapere of the Congo Republic (Leopoldville) and among the Mboko of the Congo Republic (Brazzaville), are printed *ibid.*, pp. 63 ff, 171 ff. Cf. also the vertical tritones and minor sevenths in John Blacking, "Problems of Pitch, Pattern, and Harmony in the Ocarina Music of the Venda," *African Music*, II, 2 (1959), pp. 15-23.

16. Examples of ostinato are given in Brandel, *Central Africa*, as follows: two-tone ostinato in Transcriptions 11, 34, 46, and 51, pp. 133 ff, 193 ff, 222 ff, and 241 f; ostinato of more than two tones in Transcriptions 14, 15, 29, 32, and 40, pp. 142 ff, 145 f, 180 f, 189 f, and 209 f; see also p. 88.

17. An excellent example of multi-ostinato in which the polyphony results not only from the simultaneity of independent brief motifs, but also from the holding over of hocket notes may be found in a ritual hunting song of the Babinga Pygmies of the Congo Republic (Brazzaville), in a recording of the Musée de l'Homme (Rouget-Didier Expedition, 1946), *La Boîte à Musique*, LD 325, Side II, Bd. 4. The Mambuti Pygmies of the Congo Republic (Leopoldville) also offer fine examples of multi-ostinato (with or without a longer, main line) in hocket; cf. the dance piece for flutes (Transcription 13) and the hunting song (Transcription 14) in Brandel, *Central Africa*, pp. 140-144. Cf. also the multi-ostinato in hocket in a Bamba (Uganda) flute ensemble, printed *ibid.*, Transcription 43, p. 216.

18. Ex. 2 gives measures 5 and 6 of a piece of Kpelle music transcribed by Rose Brandel from a *Folkways* recording, FE4465 (FP465), Side I, Bd. 2.

19. Brandel, *Central Africa*, Transcriptions 31 and 41, pp. 184 ff and 211 f; cf. also pp. 89-91.

20. See the Bechuana example (South Africa) on *Folkways*, FE4503, Side I, Bd. 8.

21. Alternation, which is highly prevalent in African music, is often pointed to as a feature distinguishing African from other traditional musics. The distinction is obviously dubious. For example, in the Middle East, which has shown a marked influence in several African areas, responsorial singing in folk music is not unknown. Edith Gerson-Kiwi, in "Halleluia and Jubilus in Hebrew-Oriental Chant," *Festschrift Heinrich Besseler* (Leipzig: VEB Deutscher Verlag für Musik, 1962), p. 45, considers it very common and points to its usage among many Oriental Jews as well as "in the so-called 'Ataba'-songs and in the narrative community songs" of the Arabs. See also the responsorial folk songs Nos. 173 (village of Ashmûn, Egypt) and 177 (Bedouins of Badracheîn) in Hans Hickmann, *Catalogue d'enregistrements de musique folklorique égyptienne* (Strasbourg: P. H. Heitz, 1958), pp. 66, 68; also *Folkways*, FE4480 (FP480), Side I, Bd. 6, and Side II, Bd. 1.

22. Sachs, in *Wellsprings*, p. 184, calls attention to overlapping alternation in Siberia, Malaya, Samoa, and Australia, among other places.

23. The Bongili and Mambuti excerpts in Exx. 3 and 4 are from Transcription 36, measure 7 f, and Transcription 12, measure 8 f, in Brandel, *Central Africa*, pp. 199 and 136.

24. Canonic imitation at the fifth appears in the ostinato accompaniment of another Mambuti Pygmy song and also in a responsorial song of the Babinga Pygmies: see Brandel, *Central Africa*, p. 87.

25. The devices, as well as the polyphonic types, may, of course, be intermingled within a piece.

26. With respect to the performance of polyrhythm, the present writer was once advised by Joseph H. K. Nketia of the University of Ghana that in West Africa the master drummer of an ensemble hears all the parts simultaneously, and, although it is difficult to gauge their listening habits, the other drummers are theoretically required to do so, as well. See Rose Brandel, "The African Hemiola Style," *Ethnomusicology*, III, 3 (1959), p. 114.

27. See, for example, the recording by *Columbia*, 5173, Songs 23 and 1, the first, a *canto a vatoccu* (bell-like song) of the fields, in which both parallel sixths and two-part counterpoint are apparent; the second, a Ligurian longshoremen's choral song ("trallalero"), which contains parallel thirds and also independent lines. See also the choral songs of the Ukrainian peasants on *Folkways*, FE4443 (FP443).

28. Brandel, *Central Africa*, p. 14.

29. Erich M. von Hornbostel, "African Negro Music," *International Institute of African Languages and Cultures*, Memorandum 4 (1928), p. 15.

30. Such as the Caroline Islands; see Sachs, *Wellsprings*, p. 179. Cf. also Jaap Kunst's mention of New Guinea, Flores, and Melanesia (e.g., the Solomon Islands) in his *Ethnomusicology* (The Hague: Martinus Nijhoff, 1959), p. 44.

31. See Sachs, *Rise*, p. 296; cf. also the parallel thirds of the medieval English *gymel*, discussed in Gustave Reese, *Music in the Middle Ages* (New York: W. W. Norton & Co., 1940), pp. 388 f. Note also Sachs, *Les Instruments de musique de Madagascar* (Paris: Institut d'Ethnologie, 1938), p. 53, in which attention is called to the tuning in thirds of an archaic tube-zither of Madagascar (the Malagasy Republic).

32. *Folkways*, FE4465 (FP465), Side I, Bd. 6.

33. *Folkways*, FS3855, Side II, Bd. 2.

34. Cf. Joseph H. K. Nketia, "Changing Traditions of Folk Music in Ghana," *Journal of the International Folk Music Council*, XI (1959), p. 33.

35. *Folkways*, FS3855, Side II, Bd. 4.

36. *Folkways*, FE4451 (FP451), Side I, Bds. 1, 4, 5, 8, 9; Side II, Bds. 1, 2, 4.

37. See Transcription 26 (Mboko), 37, 38 (Baduma); and 39 (Okandi) in Brandel, *Central Africa*, pp. 171, 200-207. For Bungomo see *Boîte à Musique*, LD324, Side II, Bd. 2.

38. Brandel, *Central Africa*, Transcriptions 1 (Mangbetu); 2, 3 (Babira); 7, 9 (Bapere); pp. 111-120, 126, 129-130. For Bapende, Bapindi, Babunda, and Bakwesi, see *Folkways*, FE4427 (FP427), Side II, Bds. 2, 6, 7, 8; Topoke: *Folkways*, FE4477, Side I, Bd. 1, Side II, Bd. 6; Ekonda: *Riverside*, 4002, Side II, Bd. 11.

39. Brandel, *Central Africa*, Transcription 52 (Wahehe), pp. 85, 244-245. Some of the Tanganyikan tribes around Lake Rukwa, near the Northern Rhodesian border, also use parallel thirds; cf. W. Heinitz, "Zwei Phonogramme aus Rutenganyo," *Vox*, XXII (Dec. 1936), pp. 50-56.

40. Gangele: *Folkways*, FE4503, Side I, Bd. 11; Luchosi: *Folkways*, FE4503, Side I, Bd. 10; Ovimbundu: transcriptions by George Herzog in Wilfrid Hambly, "The Ovimbundu of Angola," *Chicago: Field Museum of Natural History*, Anthropological Series, XXI (1934), pp. 217-223.

41. Bemba: African Music Society *(International Library of African Music)*, TR-65—see especially Side A, Bd. 2, and Side B, Bds. 4 and 5 (parallel thirds are evident on almost every band, however); Baushi: Trevor Cope, "African Music, a Lecture Given at Natal University," *African Music*, II, 2 (1959), p. 35. As for the Malagasy Republic, an excellent example of parallel thirds in a girls' song may be heard on *Folkways*, FE4504, Side I, Bd. 1.

42. *Folkways*, FE4503, Side IV, Bd. 31.

43. Note, for example, the lack of polyphony and the polyphonic restriction to parallel octaves in the respective harp musics of two Uganda tribes, as pointed out by K.P. Wachsmann in "Harp Songs from Uganda," *Journal of the International Folk Music Council*, VIII (1956), pp. 23-25.

44. Ex. 5 gives measures 13 to 19 of a piece of Bungomo music transcribed by Rose Brandel from *Boîte à Musique*, LD324, Side II, Bd. 2.

45. Ex. 6 gives the first statement of the choral theme in a Zulu piece transcribed by Rose Brandel from *Folkways*, FS3855, Side II, Bd. 8. Cf. also the Zulu on *Folkways*, FE4503, Side I, Bd. 1 (parallel fifths); the Bushmen of the Kalahari Desert on *Folkways*, FE4503, Side I, Bd. 5 (parallel fourths); the Watutsi of Ruanda on *Folkways*, FE4428 (FP428), Side I, Bd. 2 (parallel fourths); the Wakwavi (Masai) of the Tanganyika Republic on *Folkways*, FE4503, Side I, Bd. 4 (parallel fourths and fifths); the Wanyamwezi of the Tanganyika Republic: transcriptions in Brandel, *Central Africa*, p. 87 (parallel fourths) and in E. M. von Hornbostel, "Wanyamwezi-Gesänge," *Anthropos*, IV (1909), pp. 781-800, 1033-1052 (parallel fourths and fifths), and recordings on African Music Society *(International Library of African Music)*, GB1310, Side A (parallel fourths) and Side B (parallel fifths); the Banyoro and Baganda of Uganda in Brandel, *Central Africa*, pp. 209-210, meas. 12 f (occasional parallel fourths and fifths) and p. 218 (some fourths due to a repeated drone note); the Wolof of Senegal on *Folkways*, FE4503, Side IV, Bd. 38 (parallel fourths and fifths).

46. For Wasukuma parallel fourth and fifths, see Transcription 47, a wedding song, in Brandel, *Central Africa*, pp. 86, 225 ff; also, recordings of protective-spell songs on African Music Society, GB1324, Side A, Side B-Bd. 1. For Wasukuma parallel thirds, see African Music Society, DC158, Side A.

47. For Wahehe parallel thirds, see Transcription 52, an elephant hunting song, in Brandel, *Central Africa*, pp. 67, 243 ff; for Wahehe parallel fourths, see the agricultural work song on African Music Society, GB1331, Side B, Bd. 2.

48. Brandel, *Central Africa*, Transcription 39, pp. 86, 206 f.

49. *Folkways*, FE4503, Side I, Bd. 12. Cf. also the Watutsi parallel fourths mentioned above in note 45.

50. Mambuti Pygmies: In addition to Ex. 4 above, cf. also *Folkways*, FE4503, Side II, Bd. 20; Babira: Brandel, *Central Africa*, Transcriptions 2 and 3, p. 119, meas. 19 (repeated seconds) and p. 120, meas. 3 (repeated seconds); Makwa: *Folkways*, FE4503, Side IV, Bd. 34 (repeated seconds).

51. See African Music Society, GB1561, Side A; also the chord *a-eb'-g'* in a Wachaga (Tanganyika) chief-praise song in Brandel, *Central Africa*, p. 90.

52. Brandel, *Central Africa*, p. 64. The top two notes of the Bapere

chord result from overlapping hocket notes of the main melody, but the bottom two notes have no melodic function.

53. The Mboko excerpt in Ex. 7 is from Transcription 26, measure 6, in Brandel, *Central Africa*, p. 171. See also the parallel triads in a Baduma paddlers' song, *ibid.*, Transcription 37, measure 12, p. 201, and in a Gangele (Angola) song on *Folkways*, FE4503, Side I, Bd. 11.

54. Brandel, *Central Africa*, Transcription 17, pp. 150 f.

55. *Ibid.*, Transcription 13, pp. 140 f.

56. *Boîte à Musique*, LD324, Side I, Bd. 3, Song 1.

57. Ex. 8 gives measures 8 to 11 of a piece of Gangele music transcribed by Rose Brandel from *Folkways*, FE4503, Side I, Bd. 11.

58. See Baduma Transcriptions 37 and 38 in Brandel, *Central Africa*, pp. 200-205. (In No. 38 the harmonic sequence is also enlarged by a movement back to e'-g'.)

59. See Babinga Pygmies Transcription 31 in Brandel, *Central Africa*, pp. 184-186. A similar progression in reverse, involving movement from a minor triad (inverted) to the minor-seventh chord built on the scalar note a fourth above, may be found in some Venda ocarina music: see John Blacking, *op. cit.*, pp. 21 ff.

PHARAONIC JINGLES

Hans Hickmann (Hamburg)

Definition, Meaning, and Use of the Jingle

*J*ingles are often confused with other instruments, particularly with bells and rattles. The organological characteristics of these "idiophones" are, however, marked enough to allow an identification.

The receptacle of the jingle, often in the form of an open-work shell,[1] is generally closed on all sides, with the exception of a narrow slit that widens at its ends.

The majority of these instruments are provided with an ear. Some primitive jingles have, on the other hand, two holes pierced at their top, which serve to string the instruments together into a kind of necklace.

The interior of the jingle contains a pellet. The shock the pellet produces by knocking against the inside is another characteristic of this object. It is important to remember that we are dealing here with a single pellet, while rattles contain several of them, grains or shells,[2] a fact which naturally implies that rattles, in contradistinction to jingles, need to be carefully closed on all sides.

It is much easier to distinguish jingles from bells, of which the tongue (clapper) is one of the important criteria for their classification, apart from a number of other organological elements which it is unnecessary to specify in this study. It has been held that the African jingle gave rise to the African bell.[3]

Taken in a special sense, the jingle is, after a fashion, a more developed form of the rattle,[4] with a limited number of pellets. The single pellet of the jingle moves freely around the inside of the receptacle,[5] producing a sound the quality and timbre of which depend on the material of the shell.

The jingle has been defined, with regard to its form, as a spheric instrument, ovaloid or flattened on one side. The smallest examples have the size of a cherry, the biggest attain that of a fist. According to Curt Sachs,[6] the most ancient jingles were often pyriform (in the shape of a pear or a tear). We can add to this list some different forms of wrought jingles, known only in Egypt from the Middle Kingdom on, forms that may well cause us to extol the skill of the artisans, particularly that of the goldsmiths, of Ancient Egypt.

At all times this instrument has had an apotropaic meaning. Its role of protecting the bearer against the harmful influence of the malevolent spirit of some enemy or grudger, against the evil eye, is acknowledged and admitted wherever the jingle appears in the customs of peoples.

Like bells and cymbals, jingles serve to keep away evil spirits by the magic of sound or through the prophylactic virtues[7] of their material, if this is sounded when their possessors are exposed to dangerous influences.[8] Thus the jingle becomes a decoration or a pendant attached to the necklaces or leglets of persons particularly exposed to the dangers of supernatural influences because of their occupation. As for the sacred dancers, the rhythmic tinkle obtained from the instrument by imposing it upon the cadence of ritual dances and processions, associates quite naturally with its other qualities to make of the jingle the ritual appendage *par excellence* of diverse peoples. It is always for the same reason that jingles resound at the supreme moment of a rite, marking it by their rhythm, yet retaining their ancient meaning—that of protecting the shrine, the sanctuary, the presence of the divinity and its attendants.

The tinkling of the jingle, its musical and rhythmic functions, its role as a premonitor, are consequently of secondary importance. This statement is confirmed by the fact that certain votive jingles,[9] particularly those found in Egypt, produce a rather thin sound, wanting all of the qualities one would expect it to have if these instruments were invented and manufactured with the sole purpose of producing clearly audible rhythms.

In its capacity as an ornament and apotropaic warner, the jingle also serves to decorate domestic animals, in Egypt as well as all over the world. Its primary meaning is here again to protect the animals cherished by their owner against the malevolent envy of the neighbors.[10]

It is certainly owing to their protective virtues that so many jingles (as well as bells) are found in the tombs of Greece and Ancient Egypt.[11]

We are within the same range of ideas when we find that the Armenians of Cilicia "fix jingles to the garments of their children." And that is why jingles are suspended to this day from the girdles of children in the valley of Hérens (Valais) to keep them safe from snakes.[12]

Certain liturgical objects are also provided with jingles, such as a silver pyx in the abbey of Agaune [13] or the censers of the Armenian Orthodox Church, which have to be adorned with twelve jingles, three on each of the four chainlets.[14]

Jingles are sewed onto carnival dresses [15] and the costumes of folk dancers.[16] They belonged in ancient times to the attire of Hebrew priests to protect them against death when entering the sacrosanct place of the temple. [17] Curt Sachs, to whom we owe these details, mentions moreover the jingles of certain Indian dancers, instruments these artists would put on only after having pressed them against their forehead or eyes. No dancer would use them without saying a short prayer before decorating himself. According to the same authority, these jingles had become *the* particular symbol of the dance. The "Nâč" who has once put them on can no longer renounce the profession of a dancer.[18]

In Africa, jingles are used above all in the rites of initiation and circumcision. They keep the bearer in health; they serve to cast out devils and as a protection against the bite of serpents (Washambala).[19]

We have presented this brief survey of the meaning and use the jingle has had with various peoples, believing it conducive to a better understanding of the presence of jingles in Ancient Egypt, a rather frequent phenomenon, but one which, owing to the lack of publications in this field of Pharaonic musicology, is little known.

Summing up all of the non-Egyptian data, we come to the conclusion that the apotropaic role of the jingle is due to its timbre, its material, and its form. The last factor perhaps comes into question when we find Pharaonic jingles having the shape of a lion's head or that of a shell which vaguely resembles the human eye.

Let us add that the jingle, with its power to drive away evil spirits and to summon the good ones, has been used also in divination.

Attached frequently to the collars of dogs and, in the Saite period, to the harness of asses, the jingles seem to have played the role of warners or simply that of decorative objects. The animal, being moreover the property of its master, must be protected against the evil eye like any of his other possessions; the harmful glances of the eye must be averted from the object of greed.

Considering the Egyptian beliefs and particularly the role, similar to that of Typhon in Greek mythology, played in them by the ass—this animal *par excellence* in the cult of the god Seth—it seems legitimate to ask whether the meaning of the jingles hung around the neck of the creature was not quite the opposite—that of warning the surroundings against an eventual influence emanating from the beast, this symbol of the mischievous deity.

The history of civilization furnishes manifold examples confirming this hypothesis, and it is also substantiated by the folklore of diverse peoples. A legend told today in the town of Halle-on-the-Saale in Germany alludes to this function of the jingle. The building of the church of St. Moritz was undertaken by an extremely severe and cruel nobleman, who forced his workers to superhuman efforts to finish the work. It is told that the sister of this most exacting master had sewn jingles on his garments to announce by their tinkle his coming to the terrorized workers.[20] Of course, until the 15th century of the Christian era it was fashionable to adorn masculine garments with jingles.[21] It is of interest to note in this particular case the double meaning of the jingle, that of an ornament and warner, protecting the surroundings against its bearer.

The apotropaic virtues of certain objects manifest themselves in two ways, in a positive and a negative one. The object protects its bearer, but it can also be used to protect the surroundings against the bearer. Such is the role the jingle plays in the folklore of Morocco. A demon, precisely—a "jenniyah"—, appears to the people by taking the appearance of an ass. Its voice resembles that of the animal whose coming is always accompanied by the tinkle of silver or iron jingles bound around its neck.[22]

It is here that the combination, animal plus instrument, comes into special focus. According to Apuleius, jingles were an integral part of the harness of donkeys: the young girl, changed into a donkey and thus rescued by Lucius from the hands of brigands, promises her rescuer, as a mark of gratitude, to care for him and to adorn him with "golden balls," *bullis aureis*.[23]

Jingles are made of gold, silver, bronze, brass, iron, terra cotta, wood, and shells. The materials named first are used for their apotropaic virtues.[24] Shells are valued, on the other hand, for their prophylactic qualities.[25]

The Pharaonic jingles that constitute the object of our analysis correspond to this distribution. At least in this sphere the same conclusions regarding Egyptian jingles as compared to those of other peoples seem to suggest themselves.

Pharaonic jingles in the form of open-work shells, sometimes in the form of two adjusted hemispheric calottes, are usually made of bronze (except for a jingle of undefinable material). Ovaloid jingles are made either of gold, terra cotta, or natural shells. If we add to them, as a variant of the jingle, the balls or bullets that are found in great numbers in the Egyptological museums and were used as ornaments by the dancers of Hathor, faience could also be added to the materials used in the manufacture of jingles.

Description of the instruments preserved

The volume devoted to musical instruments that is included within the Catalogue Général of Egyptian antiquities at the Cairo Museum specifies only objects kept in the Museum, which possesses but a very limited number of jingles. It is therefore necessary to add here a detailed description of genuine jingles found in some private collections, a list that will round out the one in the General Catalogue. The jingles accessible to study may be classified as follows:

Spheric jingles in the form of open-work shells.
Spheric jingles without opening.
Pyriform jingles.
Wrought ovaloid jingles in the shape of a lion's head or shell.
Triangular jingles.

I. Spheric open-work jingles

Open-work jingle, plate 1 c.
Of strongly oxidized bronze (light green). The slit is short and irregular, the shell is cracked (by accident). The ear is asymmetric. The pellet seems to be of iron and has approximately the size of a cherry-stone. Its sound is dull.
Total height 4 cm., of which 0.9 cm. are for the ear.
Total width 2.9 cm.; width of the ear 1.9-2.0 cm.
Width of the slit 0.3-0.4 cm.; up to 0.8 cm. at its extremities.
Inner diameter of the ear 0.5 cm.
Provenance: unknown (purchase).
Date: probably from the Greco-Roman epoch.

Open-work jingle, plate 1 a.
Of strongly oxidized bronze (dark green). The slit is closed, the instrument having probably been compressed by accident. In good condition; only the pellet is missing. The ear and its opening are small. The instrument is decorated at the level of the rounded ends of the slit with two parallel bands running horizontally all around the shell.
Total height 4.9 cm. Height of the ear 0.9 cm.
Total width 3.9 cm.
Provenance: unknown (purchase).
Date: probably from the Greco-Roman epoch.

Open-work jingle, plate 1 i and j.
Of bronze. Made of a single piece. The slit is rather wide. On
the well-worn top of the instrument there is an ear; otherwise in
good condition. The shell is decorated with three horizonal lines
at the level of the extremities of the slit. Some remainders of
tissue are visible on the outside. (Plate 1 j shows a close-up of
them.) The custom of enveloping certain instruments in cloth
has been described elsewhere.[26] The same considerations can be
applied to bells as well as jingles. The pellet is of iron. It is
flattened on both sides and has the shape of a fruit-kernel.
The sound is bright and metallic.
   Height without ear 3.0 cm. Height of ear 1.7 cm.
   Total width 3.7 cm. Total width of ear 1.9 cm.
   Width of slit 0.4 cm. Thickness of the shell between 0.05 and
   0.2 cm.
   Provenance: unknown (purchase).
   Date: probably from the Greco-Roman epoch.

Open-work jingle, plate 1 b and f.
Of whitish terra cotta. The slit is rather wide and irregular, without the widenings characteristic of the ordinary jingle. Three
decorative lines embellish the shell of the instrument. Without an
ear, but having traces on its top that indicate the former existence
of an ear that could have been broken off by accident. The pellet,
probably a pebble, has the shape and size of a cherry-stone and
produces a clear sound, although without the typical metallic
timbre of the jingle.
   Total height 2.7 cm.; total width 2.7 cm.; width of the slit
   between 0.4 and 0.6 cm.
   Provenance: unknown (purchase), probably from Lower Egypt.
   Date: probably from the Greco-Roman epoch.

Open-work jingle (Rollschelle).
We know this instrument only from the description given by
Curt Sachs (Die Musikinstrumente des alten Ägyptens).[27] It is
more flattened than the jingles of the Cairo Museum. It is registered
under No. 16837 in the inventory of the Berlin Museum and is
made by two soldered hemispheric calottes.[28] The instrument
is provided with an ear and the usual slit.
   Total height 2.45 cm.; height without ear 1.86 cm.; diameter
   2.70 cm.
   Provenance: Abousîr el-Malaq.
   Date: probably from the Saite period or the Greco-Roman epoch.

Two open-work jingles.
Both of these objects are mentioned by Flinders Petrie (Objects
of Daily Use, pl. L, 301 and 302).

With the exception of the jingle at the Berlin Museum, the origin
of the instruments specified above is unknown, and the same holds for
the dates. Certain jingles in the museums of Switzerland can, however,

furnish some clues to their own date of origin. Thus jingle No. 18838 of the Historisches Museum in Bern is certainly from the Roman epoch. Its form and general aspect correspond perfectly to those of Egyptian instruments dating from the Greco-Roman epoch.

This date, however, is subject to modification. A representation of the jingle at the Louvre seems to indicate that the first appearance of this instrument is datable as far back as the close of the New Kingdom.

It seems that especially dogs were decorated with these spheric jingles. This fact is all the more surprising since writers of the Greco-Roman epoch often stated that jingles were suspended round the necks of asses.[29] To this literary testimony we can oppose some terra cottas of the Cairo Museum collection [30] representing dogs bearing one or several jingles.[31]

The limestone statuette of a dog with a jingle suspended from its collar at the Louvre [32] is an isolated example indicating the existence of the jingle at the time of the 19th or 20th dynasty.

Two terra cottas of the Greco-Roman epoch show that, at least at that time, horses and apes were sometimes decorated with jingles. Thus we can observe two jingles attached to the harness of a horse (a terra cotta in the possession of a dealer of antiquities in Cairo). The squatting monkey, pictured by the terra cotta of plate 2 a, is likewise decorated with a jingle hanging from its collar.[33]

II. Spheric jingles without opening

Jingles are often used as accessory *bruiteurs* comparable to the strung rattles. As such they are attached to other musical instruments to reinforce their sound by adding to it a new metallic resonance.

Among idiophones the marwahah (marawa sistrum), a liturgical object of the Byzantine, Syrian, and Armenian cults, known also in Egypt,[34] is decorated with jingles attached all around its circumference.[35] We referred above to a silver pyx hung with jingles and to certain censers bearing them. As further examples, we can mention the jingles of the *cai ban nac* (a sort of small clapper) of Tonkinese dancers,[36] those inside the tambourines of shamans, substituting for the strung rattles,[37] and those attached to the handles of crotales. Even some chordophones carry this appendage: certain musical bows [38] of South India are decorated with jingles, and the bows of certain Indian string instruments bear veritable grape-clusters of them.[39]

As for Africa, we can mention some harps from the Congo (Ubangi) that are provided with jingles,[40] as well as the harp-lute of the Dogon.[41]

To this list can be added various aerophones, trumpets,[42] and flutes, to show to what extent the custom in question has expanded.

Naturally, it is by no means surprising to find in Egypt also, from Antiquity to our own days, all sorts of small jingles attached as supplementary *bruiteurs* to other musical instruments. Just like the tambourines of the shamans, certain membranophones of Egyptian folklore have jingles inside them.

It is quite possible that the tambourines of the ancient Egyptians were constructed in the same manner. The rattle-drum, containing several pellets or grains between its two membranes, certainly existed in Greece. The musicians of Egypt, at least those of the Greco-Roman epoch, could have known the same custom, that of the rattle-drum or of the jingle-adorned tambourine.

The small jingle we present in plate 1 h (where it can be compared with larger instruments) cannot be dated with certainty. It may be Greco-Roman, or from the Coptic period, or of a still later date. If it did not join its tinkle to that of some little bell, it could perhaps have been attached to a tambourine or to some other instrument.

A. J. Arkell, during his excavations at Uri, Darfour, has found a bell with a jingle attached to its ear.[43] This could have been used as a decoration, suspended from anklets, as may still be observed today in the rural districts and oases of Egypt [44] and even in the streets of the towns.[45] Earrings and other similar appendages were also known in Pharaonic Egypt.

Like the jingle of the Berlin Museum, described by Curt Sachs, this little object [46] is made of two soldered hemispheric calottes. Having no slit, the general characteristic of the jingle, it is closed on all sides. Before the joining of the calottes, a hole was pierced from the inside through the shell, in which a wire was inserted, forming the ear. A single pellet produces a sound that is somewhat fainter than that of the open-work jingles.

Both the Cairo and the Coptic Museums possess certain wooden objects, the handles of which are carved out in the form of rectangular open-work receptacles, vaguely resembling a kiosk, which contain a wooden pellet. A description of the piece at the Cairo Museum has already been published.[47] The clapper No. 69502,[48] found at Kôm Aouchîm and dating from the 3rd or 4th century A.D., belongs to those percussion instruments whose sound is reinforced by the presence of a jingle, with the peculiarity that the handle of the clapper is transformed into a jingle, so that the latter forms an integral part of the clapper itself. It is therefore probable that clapper No. 69501 [49] once contained a pellet in the carved-out part of its handle.[50]

It is necessary to mention in a study dealing with jingles the faience balls that have been discovered in great number, but whose use has not yet been satisfactorily explained. The Cairo Museum possesses a certain number of them, and very beautiful examples can often be found in the shops of dealers in antiquities. Balls have come down to us that are made of materials other than faience, but those that do consist of it are at variance with the insubstantial claim that the objects were always meant to be used as playing balls or toys. Moreover, several of the balls— and these are formed of faience—are perforated on one side, as if their makers intended them to be suspended or attached somewhere.

Other balls, made almost invariably of wood or leather, are not perforated. In our opinion these could have been used as toys or for ball-playing. A spheric ball, ornamented with parallel lines and consisting of wood or some other indeterminable organic matter, has been described by M. Bénédite.[51] Other spheric objects, made of leather, straw, or twisted shreds, or fibers of papyrus, date from very different epochs.[52] Considering their form and material, they could be balls that were thrown in athletic and ritual games performed in honor of the goddess Hathor, games known by the Egyptian term rwj.t.[53] We are acquainted with them from representations and other sources. These objects were well-known in the Ancient World.[54] And they still exist today in the folk tradition of the peoples of White Africa.[55] However, even if used in play, these balls may have been intended primarily as jingles or rattles, at least according to the evidence of representations. Consistent with this view is André Schaeffner's description of "a musician . . . at the Court of the Sultan of Mandara (North-West Cameroon), who bounced a ball-like gourd filled with grains from one hand to the other." [56]

We of course believe that the solid objects of leather and wood at the Cairo Museum were used as balls, but we do not know whether the games were always played with such objects or whether hollow balls that were kinds of rattles or jingles may not sometimes have been employed.

It seems that the σφαῖρα used in the mysteries of Dionysus was only a symbolic ball, one, however, that produced sounds and rhythms.[57] In Egypt these balls should have had another symbolic meaning, associated with Egyptian religions, but this meaning has thus far evaded our knowledge. G. Lefèbvre discovered at Tehnah four resin balls, painted yellow and green, deposited at the foot of a sarcophagus with the head of a hawk, dating from the Greco-Roman epoch.[58] According to their inscriptions, they were consecrated to the four sons of Horus.

If the same objects we have supposed to be either balls tossed in play or balls having a symbolic significance were sometimes employed as "jingles," the faience bullets seem definitely to have been intended for rhythmic usage, serving at the same time as decorative appendages. Dancers, especially acrobatic dancers, were portrayed, from the Old Kingdom on, with bullets decorating their plaits of hair. The most striking representations may be found in the tombs of Mehou (6th dynasty, Saqqârah) and 'Ankhmahor (Saqqârah).[59]

Von Bissing [60] and after him Mrs. Brunner-Traut [61] have pointed out, as concerns the coiffure of certain dancers,[62] that here the question has been: Are the decorations in the hair rounded plates or are they balls? We can add that the objects contained probably one or several pellets and served both as a counterbalance to the coiffure and as rattles or jingles, marking by their rhythmic tinkle the cadence of the dance.

The two principal objections that could be raised against this hypothesis are the following: the balls preserved belong to a more recent epoch than those mentioned by the above-cited authors. Moreover, they are nearly always empty. Only a few of them contain some rustling elements which produce a clear and delicate sound when the objects are shaken.

As for the date (the most ancient objects date from the 18th dynasty; [63] another from Deîr el-Bahari belongs to the time of Queen Hatshepsout [64]) we know for definite reasons that in periods when an object no longer appears in representations, it may still be used as part of the folk tradition.

The oblique flute was no longer pictured during the New Kingdom. Yet we know it was played inside temples and by the people, because the Greco-Roman writers refer to it as characteristic of the ritual music of the Egyptians. The same flute exists in Egypt even today as a folk-music instrument.

With regard to the contents of the faience balls of which the Cairo Museum possesses a rather fair number, a cursory inspection has revealed that some of them are actually empty,[65] that some of the others contain a single pellet each [66] and should be classified as jingles, while a few contain several pellets (grains?), which characterizes them as rattles.[67]

The fact that there exist several such balls containing a single pellet led us to mention them in this study, although thus far nothing definite can be said about the real meaning of these objects. Of some interest is the fact that two of these balls, dating from the 17th dynasty, are tied up by a double string (*Journal d'entrée* No. 47674, a and b).[68] The design, the ornaments, the coloration of these balls, and the manner of appending them to the coiffures of the dancers appear especially distinct and instructive in the frontispiece of the work by N. and G. Davies, *The Rock Tombs of Deir el Gebrâwi*, London, 1902.[69]

The prehistoric jingles (plate 2 b) were probably made of terra cotta. They belong to the class of closed spheric jingles. We may ask whether the title of a book from the Pharaonic era, *Price of the Terra Cotta Balls* mentioned by S. Schott,[70] is not, in some way, an allusion to them.

III. Pyriform jingles

To complete our documentation, we indicate the existence of pyriform objects, shaped apparently like some fruit.[71] Are they rattles or jingles? A few of these objects contain one or several kernels that could have played the role of pellets. This question deserves more penetrating attention, especially since, in the opinion of Curt Sachs,[72] the most ancient jingles were pyriform. The fact that these objects represent fruits induces us to interpret them as rattles or jingles, as these instruments originally were the dried fruits of certain plants, the seeds of which functioned as pellets.

An examination of all these objects at the Cairo Museum [73] proved that they had no pellets, but something like a kernel could be found in other typical examples in the possession of dealers in antiquities in Cairo and Luxor. Similar objects in other museums should be examined before one forms an opinion as to whether these imitations of the fruits of the *Persea* classification may be regarded as musical instruments. They were found in the tombs of the New Kingdom. Some very interesting representations have been published and commented on by Louis Keimer.[74]

IV. Ovaloid jingles

The instruments we are classifying as ovaloid jingles often assume the form of a shell. Others are worked to represent the head of a lion; the modification, however, does not affect the general shape of the objects, which still remain ovaloid. Another organological detail is common to all these instruments: they are flattened on both sides, evidently in imitation of the natural form of a shell. With the exception of one unwrought object, all of them are made of one piece, chased probably from cold material; some of them are real masterpieces of the art of the goldsmith.

A. Shell-shaped jingles

The excavations at Dahshur in 1894 yielded rich finds in jewelry,[75] a portion of which is now kept at the Cairo Museum. These shell-shaped objects are of gold. They are parts of necklaces, which have been completely reconstructed.[76] In our opinion, they were the necklaces of dancers, necklaces that did not function solely as ornaments, but also marked the rhythms of the ritual dances. A description of them,[77] as well as some bibliographical references may be found in the *General Catalogue of Musical Instruments* (p. 69); [78] an excellent photograph

(j)

PLATE 1

Ten Views of Seven Pharaonic Jingles of Various Shapes and Materials
(a) Open-work spheric jingle of bronze, with closed slit (see p. 49); (b)
open-work spheric jingle of terra cotta, the pellet of which may be seen in
another view (f) (see p. 50); (c) open-work spheric jingle of bronze, with
asymmetric ear (see p. 49); (d) small shell-shaped jingle with pellet, from
Luxor (El-Aksur) (see p. 60); (e) shell-like terra cotta object with pellet,
used as an amulet or part of necklace (see p. 61).

(f) Terra cotta jingle with pellet, referred to above under (b); (g) another
view of terra cotta object (e) prepared for suspension (see p. 61); (h) small,
closed spheric jingle (see p. 52); (i) open-work spheric jingle of bronze,
with ear (see p. 50).

(j) Close-up of bronze jingle referred to above under (i) showing line
decorations (see p. 50).

(a)

(b)

(c)

PLATE 2

Jingles in Pharaonic Art

(a) Terra cotta figure of squatting monkey, with jingle suspended from its collar (see p. 51); (b) vase decorated with closed spheric jingles suspended from animals (see pp. 54, 64); (c) triangular jingles attached to ankles of Negro folk musicians of the temple of Luxor (El-Aksur) (see p. 62).

of one of the jingles has been published in *Die Kunst des alten Orients* by H. Schäfer and W. Andreas, Berlin, 1925, fig. 308. It seems certain that these necklaces of jingles had a sacral meaning. They were found buried separately, which evidently means that they were considered as objects of exceptional value.[79] It should be remembered that in more recent epochs sacred jewels were kept in specially constructed treasuries.[80]

The first of the necklaces excavated at Dahshur consists of six jingles [81] of average size. It ends on both sides with the halves of a catch, which together form the seventh piece. This necklace was part of the treasure of Princess Sat-Hathor. Each of the pieces has 2 perforations on each side, which served in stringing them together.

Another necklace, which belonged to Princess Merit, is composed of seven large and twelve small pieces of the same form, arranged in the following order (A and B are the halves of a catch and, when joined, form something like an eighth piece):

$$A_1 \; 1_2 \; 2^3_4 \; 3^5_6 \; 4^7_8 \; 5^9_{10} \; 6_{11} \; 7_{12} \; B$$

A similar necklace is preserved at the Metropolitan Museum of Art in New York; [82] another is in the possession of the British Museum.[83]

We can finally mention a single object (plate 1 d) [84] representing a small version of the same shell-shaped type.[85] However, the sound its pellet produces is rather loud. One can easily imagine that a whole string of these instruments could have produced beautiful rhythmic effects.

Most of the necklaces of shell-shaped jingles date from the same period. This kind of jingle was known from the Middle Kingdom on. It is consequently older than the spheric jingle. We think that the date of the first appearance of those jingles that form sacred necklaces should be set still further back, since, as has been conclusively proved by a fortunate discovery in the tomb of Remenwka (Guîzah), beads of shells were already known in the Old Kingdom; we counted eighteen pieces forming an ensemble.[86]

The same objects appear, as jingles and decorative appendages (necklaces and girdles), on feminine statuettes,[87] a fact of some importance, considering that the figurines or statuettes referred to are those of concubines. As their task was above all to entertain their master, it seems that we are dealing here with dancers wearing necklaces for rhythmic purposes,[88] with decorations made perhaps of natural shells (instead of golden jingles). [89]

It is obviously the ancient belief in the prophylactic efficacy of shells and their resemblance to the human eye [90] that lie at the bottom of the usage of wearing shell-shaped jingles. Protection against the evil eye through a magic act and by means of sound is an additional explanation of this strange custom, at least as concerns the peoples of North Africa.

As to Pharaonic Egypt, Elliot Smith has already emphasized, within the same range of ideas, that shells were set in the eye sockets of mummies because of their resemblance to semi-closed eyelids.[91]

Plates 1 e and 1 g represent a shell-like terra cotta object of dark color containing a pellet; the upper side of the object is pierced by several incisions, and it is provided at its top with a double hole for suspension. The object was strung with others or worn alone, as a necklace or an amulet.[92] Its pellet, the form and material of which we do not know, produces a clear sound, although a little muffled when compared with that of the golden jingles from the Dahshur finds.

An object of very similar form and dimensions, but showing a high finish and having no pellet, is preserved at the Cairo Museum, where it is registered under No. 69701 in the *General Catalogue of Musical Instruments* ("openwork cowrie amulet").

B. Jingles in the form of two lions' heads

These jingles are made of gold. Their dimensions, provenance, material, and date are similar to those of the shell-shaped jingles. They also form a necklace of seven pieces,[93] and everything said of the first category applies also to this one.[94] The idea of joining two lions' heads was not developed by Egyptian artisans and seems to be limited, at least as concerns necklaces of jingles, to the Middle Kingdom.[95]

C. Jingles in the form of a duck's head

There finally ought to be mention of a necklace consisting of several jingle-like pieces of jewelry.[96] These objects are of gold. Each piece encloses a "kernel," a sort of pellet. It is of secondary importance whether the contents of the jewels are a by-product of the manufacturing process or whether the artisan put them in with the intention of producing a jingle.

The presence of the "kernel" makes a jingle of each of the objects: every move of the bearer is accompanied by sounds that are more or less rhythmic, resulting from the concussion of the beads and their pellets. Thus we have every reason to classify these objects as *bijoux-bruiteurs*—more exactly, as jingles.

Some other golden objects may be classed with pyriform and ovaloid jingles.[97] Each of them consists of two adjusted shells (now opened). The pellets are lost. This simple form of jingle was probably used both as a decoration and as a rhythm instrument.

V. Triangular jingles

The jingles examined so far exist as museum pieces, while the following are known to us only from two representations. The more ancient document pictures a group of Negro folk musicians belonging to the great procession in the temple of Luxor (plate 2 c). One of the dancers and the drummer have a sort of vaguely triangular jingle attached to the left ankle.

Dancers wearing jingle-adorned anklets to mark the dance steps may be observed all the world over and especially in Africa. As to the form, we know but two varieties of sewed or basketwork rattles "in the shape of a pyramid," [98] used by Madagascan dancers, which have a strange resemblance to the jingle shown in plate 1 g. As we do not know whether they contain one or several pellets, the rhythm instruments of the Negroes of the temple of Luxor cannot yet be definitely classed as either rattles [99] or jingles.

The same observations apply to the dance instruments represented at Denderah, in the eastern crypt No. 1, on the western partition of the passage C-D.[100] The persons we can recognize in this scene wear a sort of jingle round their ankles. It seems to be fastened with a ribbon. These jingles are obviously of metal, perhaps of a precious one, as the artisans have managed to impart to them the character of real jewels, fashioned in a shape reminding one of a jackal's (?) head. Viewed at a distance these instruments again assume a vaguely triangular form.[101]

Conclusion

We do not know the term by which the jingle was called in Pharaonic Egypt. The Oriental languages show a certain logic in neatly distinguishing these instruments from bells and rattles. On the other hand, the Greek and Latin languages allude only to the jingle that has a spheric shell (σφαῖρα and *bulla*). While the Hebrew term *pa'amon* for the jingles of Aaron is not onomatopoeic,[102] our instrument is known in Arabic and Coptic [103] under several onomatopoeic names (cf. the English "jingle"): *al-qalâqîl*,[104] *al-khalkhâl*,[105] *al-hugûl, al-galâgil, al-ghirr, al-gingil, al-gülgül* (Arabic), *schkelkil* (Coptic.) [106]

The resemblance of these vocables is striking. A similar term should have existed also in Ancient Egypt, but no record mentions it. Yet it seems to be significant that the same vocable transformed into "dsanâd-sel" today means "sistrum" in the Coptic of Ethiopia.[107] Perhaps, reversing the principle "pars pro toto," we should search for the jingle's name among the terms for the sacred jewelry of the goddess Hathor, since the necklace *wśḫ* consisted of a string of jingles.

André Schaeffner was the first to emphasize that the jingle did not originate in the Bronze Age, as has been asserted, but that it certainly owes its diffusion to this age.[108] Considered from an organological point of view, this statement encompasses the spheric jingles with openwork shells and also, perhaps, some primitive forms in any material apart from metal. It should be extended to include the discoveries made in Egypt, especially the shell-shaped jingles that appear to date from a much remoter period.

The presence of spheric jingles—of bronze or gold—in the cultures of the ancient Orient, as well as in the folk culture of most contemporary peoples, seems to indicate that the jingle has had a very long history.

The most ancient records indicate its simultaneous function as an article of attire and as a rhythm instrument (or rather ritual and apotropaic instrument), a twofold role which the jingle has maintained to our day. The Old Testament (Exod. 28, 35) tells us of ancient jingles sewn on the sacred robes of the high priests; made of precious materials, these instruments were intended to protect those wearing them as they entered the Holy of Holies, guarding them against death.[109]

It should be remembered that the Chinese also knew votive jingles, whereas other Asiatic peoples have used them to decorate their horses. Thus, Tibetan festivals are enlivened by the merry tinkle of the numerous jingles suspended from the harnesses of horses.[110] Very curious are also the dances of the young people, wherein each dancer carries a little stuffed paper horse (in the Horse Dance). Here it is the "horseman" who is decorated with a broad waistband carrying a series of jingles.[111]

Contrary to the custom among the horse-breeding nomads, the jingle is used among the Hindus as a dancer's instrument. In this usage there survives the ancient meaning of the jingle as a ritual object. An ancient Georgian set of jingles, mounted on a handle, has even served as a mark of distinction or a kind of sceptre to a prince.[112]

Notwithstanding the formal ban by the Koran (24, 31), the jingle has never disappeared from the Islamic countries. Known since the pre-Islamic period [113] as the insignia of dancers,[114] jingles are mentioned in the tales of "A Thousand and One Nights" as decorations for horses and camels.[115] Finally, we can cite from H. G. Farmer (after Al-Maqrîzî) [116] a curious custom dating from the Mameluke period in Egypt, that of hanging jingles on the garments of criminals. The tradition of the jingle as an apotropaic and prophylactic object is best preserved in Africa. Wherever it is met with it serves as a decoration for domestic animals, as a ritual object of the sorcerer,[117] or to mark the time of dances and nuptial processions.[118]

Just as jingles have been used in the rituals of the Africans and in the rituals described in the Old Testament and in those of the ancient Chinese (and perhaps of even earlier people), so such instruments were used also in the rituals of the early Christians.

The Ethiopian priests, as well as the Eastern churches, use them even today.[119] The custom of sounding jingles has never disappeared completely, in spite of all bans against them in certain very strict cults.

This continuity is certainly due to the bridge provided by Greco-Roman antiquity, which has left abundant testimony concerning their use. The sarcophagus of Alexander the Great was decorated with jingles, the tinkle of which escorted him on his last procession through the streets of Alexandria.

The tradition of the Greco-Roman epoch was continued by the Copts, who use spheric jingles even today. On the other hand, the closed spheric jingle has been used in Egypt since prehistoric times (plate 2 b).[120]

The use of jingle-collars on dogs [121] and asses [122] is completely in keeping with the ancient tradition. The role of Egypt in this slow and continuous development is that of a country acting as intermediary between the ancient cultures and the Middle Ages, between East and West. After the adoption of the spheric open-work jingle toward the end of the New Kingdom, it was used more and more frequently in the Ptolemaic epoch.[123] Some documents of this epoch tell us of the silver jingles suspended on both sides of the gilded barge carried in procession by the priests of the ancient oasis of Siouah,[124] the sweet and pleasing sound of which accompanied the songs of women.

Jingles in the form of shells appeared in Egypt during the Old Kingdom. They were particularly in vogue in the Middle Kingdom, during which period the form of a double lion's head first appeared, and in the New Kingdom, when the duck's head originated. Later they existed as shell-shaped terra cotta jingles or were worked of natural shells. Today they are again what they were at the beginning: simple shells serving as *sonnailles* in the necklaces of dancers, that is, as decorative objects.

To both of these categories (spheric and ovaloid) should be added as a third that of the triangular jingles, which date from the New Kingdom (18th dynasty) to the Ptolemaic epoch.

Form:	Prehistory	Old King-dom	Middle King-dom	New King-dom	Late Period	Ptole-maic Egypt	Modern Egypt
Open-work sphere				⊢————	————	————	———⟶
Closed sphere	⊢————	————	————	————	————	————	———⟶
Ovaloid: shell-shape lion's head duck's head			⊢————	————	————	————	———⟶
				⊢—⟶			
				⊢—⟶			
Triangular				⊢————	————	———⟶	

Notes

1. André Schaeffner, *Origine des instruments de musique* (Paris: Payot, 1936), p. 45.

2. Hans Hickmann, *Catalogue général des antiquités égyptiennes du Musée du Caire, Nos. 69201-69852. Instruments de musique* (Cairo: Imprimerie de l'Institut français d'archéologie orientale, 1949), p. 69.

3. André Schaeffner, *op. cit.,* p. 49.

4. Curt Sachs, *Handbuch der Musikinstrumentenkunde* (Leipzig: Breitkopf & Härtel, 1930), p. 53.

5. The free mobility of the pellet is indeed an essential detail of the genuine jingle (André Schaeffner, *op. cit.,* p. 48).

6. Curt Sachs, *Geist und Werden der Musikinstrumente* (Berlin: Dietrich Reimer, 1929), p. 130, pl. 16 (figs. 120 and 122). In addition to the forms enumerated by Sachs, see the exceptional forms these instruments have assumed in Luristan (*La Musique, des origines à nos jours,* Paris: Larousse, p. 16: "Grelot en forme d'animal").

7. André Schaeffner, *Les Kissi. Une société noire et ses instruments de musique* (Paris: Hermann et Cie, c. 1951), pp. 19-25.

8. Eric Werner, "The Conflict between Hellenism and Judaism in the Music of the Early Christian Church," *Hebrew Union College Annual,* XX (1947), p. 412.

9. André Schaeffner, *Origine,* p. 116.

10. *Ibid.,* p. 102: "Le bruit d'un grelot indique le lieu où vague l'animal, mais a pu servir aussi à écarter les démons, et, plus immédiatement, à chasser les bêtes de proie."

11. *Ibid.,* pp. 111, 115, and 116 (citing Charles Victor Daremberg and E. Saglio, *Dictionnaire des antiquités grecques et romaines,* 5 vols. in 9, Paris: Hachette et Cie, 1877-1919, article entitled "Tintinnabulum," and Abbé L. Morillot, *Études sur l'emploi des clochettes* (Dijon: Damengeot, 1888, pp. 3 and 4).

12. André Schaeffner, *Origine,* p. 113.

13. *Ibid.,* p. 113, citing Morillot, *Études sur l'emploi des clochettes,* p. 129; Hans Hickmann, *Cymbales et crotales dans l'Égypte ancienne* (Cairo: 1949), p. 515.

14. Observation made in Cairo.

15. A. Fischer, *Villinger Fastnacht von einst und heute* (Villingen in Baden: 1922); Sir James George Frazer, *Der Goldene Zweig,* abridged edition (Leipzig: C. L. Hirschfeld, 1928), p. 443.

16. Curt Sachs, *World History of the Dance* (New York: W. W. Norton & Co., 1937): the *călușari* of Roumania, hobby-horse dancers (the legs of the dancers are overcharged with jingles).

17. Curt Sachs, *Die Musikinstrumente Indiens und Indonesiens* (Walter de Gruyter & Co., Berlin and Leipzig, 1923), p. 40; *The History of Musical Instruments* (New York: W. W. Norton & Co., 1940), p. 109.

18. Curt Sachs, *Die Musikinstrumente Indiens und Indonesiens,* citing P. T. French, *Catalogue of Indian Musical Instruments* (Calcutta: 1882), p. 245.

19. Curt Sachs, *Geist und Werden der Musikinstrumente*, p. 130. The Siberian shamans also use jingles, bells, and drums in healing (H. König, "Le Chamanisme," *Revue Ciba*, LX, 1947, p. 2150; see *ibid.*, pp. 2165-2167, for similar customs of the shamans of Sumatra, the information being taken from a study by Paul Schebesta).

20. The use of jingles is mentioned also in animal fables. For instance, in the Hindu version of the war between cats and mice, one of the ministers of the king of the mice proposes to bell the dangerous cats. (E. Brunner-Traut, "Altägyptische Tiergeschichte und Fabel" in *Saeculum*, X, 2, 1959, pp. 167-168.)

21. Curt Sachs, *Handbuch der Musikinstrumente*, p. 54.

22. Edvard A. Westermarck, *Ritual and Belief in Morocco*, Vol. I (London: Macmillan & Co., 1926), p. 405.

23. Apuleius, *Metamorphoses* VI, 28.

24. André Schaeffner, *Origine*, pp. 113 and 116 (ritual instruments are of metal); Edvard A. Westermarck, *Ritual*, Vol. I, p. 81.

25. Edvard A. Westermarck, *Ritual*, Vol. I, p. 439: ". . . the prophylactic virtue ascribed to cowries is probably in the first place due to their resemblance to an eye. In ancient Egypt, cowries, from their resemblance to semi-closed eye-lids, were often inserted into the orbits of mummies to represent the eyes (after Sir Grafton Elliot Smith, Introduction to John Wilfred Jackson, *Shells as Evidence of the Migrations of Early Culture*, Manchester: Manchester University Press, 1917, p. xix).

26. Hans Hickmann, *Symbales et crotales dans l'Égypte ancienne*, p. 467.

27. Berlin: K. Curtius, 1921, pl. 1 (50), No. 16837.

28. This object is again part of the Berlin collection.

29. Apuleius, *Metamorphoses* VI, 28; P. J. Faivre, *Canope, Menoutis, Aboukir* (Alexandria: 1917), p. 49. A representation can be seen in the *Dictionnaire des antiquités grecques et romaines* of C. V. Daremberg and E. Saglio, Vol. V, p. 341, fig. 6992.

30. C. C. Edgar, *Catalogue général des antiquités égyptiennes du Musée du Caire, Nos. 32001-32367. Greek Moulds* (Cairo: Imprimerie de l'Institut français d'archéologie orientale, 1903), No. 32199, pl. XXVII, p. 48; *Catalogue général*, Nos. 27216, 69219, etc. The dogs represented here carry one jingle or several jingles. Cf. Wilhelm Weber, *Die ägyptisch-griechischen Terrakotten* (Berlin: K. Curtius, 1914), pl. 38.

31. Cf. a terra cotta in the collection of Mr. G. Michailides, Cairo.

32. André Vigneau, *Encyclopédie photographique de l'art*, Vol. I (Paris: Éditions "TEL," 1935), pl. 82-83; Pierre Montet, *La Vie quotidienne en Égypte au temps des Ramsès* (Paris: Hachette, 1946), p. 70.

33. Cf. the statuettes Nos. 833 and 824 at the Pelizaeus-Museum, Hildesheim, representing a sacred monkey with a sun as head-dress, and a cat. Both animals have collars with jingles.

34. Hans Hickmann, "The Marawe Sistrum," *Journal of the Royal Asiatic Society* (1950), 1 and 2, pp. 4-6.

35. Hans Hickmann, *Cymbales et crotales dans l'Égypte ancienne*, p. 493, fig. 25.

36. Curt Sachs, *Die Musikinstrumente Indiens und Indonesiens*, p. 144.

37. *Revue Ciba*, LX (1947), p. 2148; Edith Gerson-Kiwi, "Wedding Dances and Songs of the Jews of Bokhara," *Journal of the International Folk Music Council*, II (1950), p. 18.

38. T. Norlind, *Geschichte der Zither* (Stockholm: Fritzes K. Hofbuch-

handlung, 1936), fig. 26; Curt Sachs, *Die Musikinstrumente Indiens und Indonesiens*, fig. 59.

39. Curt Sachs, *Die Musikinstrumente Indiens und Indonesiens*, p. 144.

40. Joseph Maes, "Sculpture décorative ou symbolique des instruments de musique du Congo Belge," *Artes Africanae* (Brussells: Commission pour la protection des artes et métiers indigènes, 1937), p. 7, fig. 7.

41. M. Griaule and G. Dieterlen, "La Harpe-luth des Dogon," *Journal de la Société des Africanistes*, XX (1950), p. 213.

42. Victor Charles Mahillon, *Catalogue descriptif et analytique du Musée instrumental du Conservatoire Royal de Musique de Bruxelles*, 5 vols. (Ghent: A. Hoste, 1893), pp. 125-126, fig. 62, shows a military horn (*rana-cringa*), the hollow rings of which "contiennent des ballettes de plomb qui résonnent bruyamment lorsque l'instrument est secoué."

43. A. J. Arkell, "Darfur Antiquities," *Sudan Notes and Records*, XXVII (1946), pl. XIX.

44. Brigitte Schiffer, *Die Oase Siwa und ihre Musik, Diss.* (Bottrop in Westphalia: W. Postberg, 1936), p. 106, fig. 17; cf. the similar attire of the Sumatran shamans (*Revue Ciba*, LX, 1947, pp. 2166 and 2167); cf. Edvard A. Westermarck, *Ritual*, Vol. II, p. 424.

45. Anklets with or without jingles, still mentioned in the Koran (24, 31), are widespread in North Africa (Edmond Doutté, *Magie et religion dans l'Afrique du Nord*, Algeria: A. Jourdan, 1909, p. 93) and Egypt الخَلخَال *al-khalkhâl*; in Egypt also الهُجُل *al-hugûl*, after Hans Alexander Winkler, *Bauern zwischen Wasser und Wüste*, Stuttgart: W. Kohlhammer, 1934, p. 164); cf. Edvard A. Westermarck, *Ritual*, Vol. II, p. 429.

46. 1.3 cm. x 1.5 cm.

47. Hans Hickmann, *Catalogue général des antiquités égyptiennes du Musée du Caire. Instruments de musique*, p. 31, pl. XVIII, A and B.

48. *Journal d'entrée* 65558.

49. *Journal d'entrée* 49882. Hans Hickmann, *Catalogue général*, p. 31, pl. XVIII, A and B; provenance: Kôm Aouchîm.

50. Hans Hickmann, "La Cliquette, un instrument de percussion égyptien de l'époque copte," *Bulletin de la Société d'Archéologie copte*, XVII (1950). p. 3.

51. *Catalogue général des jouets*, No. 68153.

52. The most ancient seems to be No. 68149 (12th dynasty), found at Meir.

53. Emma Brunner-Traut, *Der Tanz im alten Ägypten* (Glückstadt: J. J. Augustin, 1938), p. 80. In Arabia, certain rather curious games are performed at family gatherings. One of them, the *gimâl*, consists in the building up of a kind of human pyramid. Two men climb on the shoulders of four comrades. They are covered with a skin and hung with jingles (Solomon Dob Fritz Goitein, *Jemenica, Sprichwörter und Redensarten aus Zentral-Jemen*, Leipzig: O. Harrassowitz, 1934, p. 39).

54. E. Wegner, *Das Ballspiel der Römer*, Dissertation (Rostock: 1938).

55. Adolf Erman, *Die Religion der Ägypter* (Berlin and Leipzig: W. de Gruyter & Co., 1934), p. 179; Edvard A. Westermarck, *Ritual*, Vol. II, pp. 270-272; Edmond Doutté, *Magie et réligion*.

56. André Schaeffner, *Origine*, p. 39; quoted from the same author's *Notes sur la musique des populations du Cameroun septentrional*, p. 69.

57. George William Butterworth, *Clement of Alexandria* (London: W. Heinemann, 1919), Cap. II, 15 P.

58. G. Lefèbvre, "Sarcophages égyptiens trouvés dans une nécropole gréco-romaine à Tehnah," *Annales du Service des Antiquités,* IV (1903), p. 227.

59. Emma Brunner-Traut, *Der Tanz,* p. 23, fig. 8.

60. *Zeitschrift für ägyptische Sprache und Altertumskunde,* XXXVII (1899), LXXV (1939).

61. *Op cit.,* pp. 24 and 27; cf. Jean Capart, *Memphis* (Paris: Vromant & Co., 1930), fig. 388.

62. This fashion was in vogue during the 6th dynasty. It appeared again with the female acrobats of the Middle Kingdom, and once more with two harpists of the same epoch (Aylward Manley Blackman, *The Rock Tombs of Meir,* Vol. IV, London and Boston: Egypt Exploration Society, 1914-1953, pl. 9).

63. *Journal d'entrée,* No. 47674, a and b.

64. *Journal d'entrée,* No. 47718, diameter 4.3 cm., of blue faience, perforated on both sides for suspension and ornamented with eight light blue and dark blue segments. See a similar object in *Catalogue général,* No. 68179.

65. To the above-mentioned objects should be added *Catalogue général,* Nos. 68161-68166, 68169-68177, 68179-68182; *Journal d'entrée,* Nos. 45673 a, b, and 47674 a, b. Most of these balls are pierced on both sides. They are always of blue faience. Some are ornamented with segments of different colors (dark blue and light blue).

66. *Catalogue général,* No. 68167, and *Journal d'entrée,* No. 39183 *bis* (both objects come from Saqqarah).

67. *Catalogue général,* No. 68168. See Hans Hickmann, "Die altägyptische Rassel," *Zeitschrift für ägyptische Sprache und Altertumskunde,* LXXIX, 2 (1958).

68. The women of the Ababua tribe in the Congo Republic (Leopoldville) accompany certain songs with two hollow balls filled with grains and tied up by a string. They are obviously rattles (André Schaeffner, *Origine,* p. 44).

69. Cf. *ibid.,* pl. IX and X; Vol. II, pl. VII.

70. Who gives the title as *Preis der Tonkugeln.* See S. Schott, "Literatur," *Handbuch der Orientalistik,* Abteilung 1: *Der nahe und der mittlere Osten.* Bd. 1, *Egyptologie,* Abschnitt 2 (Leiden: E. J. Brill, 1952), p. 228.

71. *Mimusops schimperi (Persea),* after Louis Keimer, *Interpretation de quelques passages d'Horapollon* (Cairo: Imprimerie de l'Institut français d'archéologie orientale, 1947), pp. 34-36.

72. *Geist und Werden der Musikinstrumente,* p. 130.

73. *Journal d'entrée,* Nos. 39183 *bis* and 63816 (Deîr el-Medinah, 1933-1934).

74. *Op cit,* figs. 33 and 35.

75. Jacques Jean Marie de Morgan, *Fouilles à Dahchour,* 2 vols. (Vienna, 1894-1903).

76. *Ibid.,* pl. XVII. Other shells are strung as a necklace or have belonged to some appendage: pl. XXIII.

77. *Catalogue général,* No. 53074.

78. Some of the missing elements of these necklaces were identified by H. E. Winlock and are now kept at the New York Metropolitan Museum of Art (H. E. Winlock, "Elements from the Dahshur Jewellery," *Annales du Service des Antiquités de l'Égypte,* XXXIII, 1933, p. 135).

79. Iorwerth Eiddon Stephen Edwards, *The Pyramids of Egypt* (Middlesex and New York: Penguin Books, 1947), p. 186.

80. Other similar jewelry was found at Illahun (Fayoum). This is now preserved at the Metropolitan Museum of Art, New York.

81. Concerning a seventh piece belonging to this necklace, identified by Mr. Winlock, see note 78, *supra*.

82. J. H. Breasted, *Geschichte Ägyptens*, German transl. (Vienna: Phaidon-Verlag, 1936), fig. 326.

83. J. H. Breasted, *op. cit.*, fig. 330.

84. Provenance: purchase (Luxor).

85. Length, 2.1 cm.; maximum width, 1.2 cm.; maximum thickness of shell, 0.5 cm.

86. Selim Hassan, *Excavations at Gîza, 1930-1931* (Cairo: Government Press, 1936), pl. LXIII (beads of worked oyster shells).

87. H. E. Winlock, "Notes on the Jewels from Lahum," *Ancient Egypt*, III (1920), pp. 74-77.

88. Cf. the figurine of a woman wearing a girdle made partly of shells, Berlin Museum 9583 (Adolf Erman, *Die Religion der Ägypter*, p. 262, fig. 99).

89. For the Late Period, it is possible to document also cowrie necklaces. Cf. Marie Pouline Mogensen, *La Glyptothèque Ny Carlsberg (La collection égyptienne)* (Copenhagen: Levin & Munksgaard, 1930), p. 181 (A 392). It is significant that the sacred cat wears a collar of cowrie shells, on which is hung an amulet in the shape of the Holy Eye, as represented by a bronze statuette.

90. Edvard A. Westermarck, *Ritual*, Vol. I, p. 439.

91. Sir Grafton Elliott Smith, *op. cit.*, p. xix.

92. Length, 2.4 cm.; maximum width, 1.6 cm.; maximum thickness of shell, 1.1 cm.

93. Without the connecting link.

94. *Catalogue général des instruments de musique*, p. 69.

95. An excellent photograph of such objects is reproduced by Heinrich Schäfer and Walter Andrae, *Die Kunst des alten Orients* (Berlin: Propyläen-Verlag, 1925), pl. 308.

96. Berlin, No. 20786 (18th dynasty); after A. Hermann, "Das Motiv der Ente mit zurückgewendetem Kopfe im ägyptischen Kunstgewerbe," *Zeitschrift für ägyptische Sprache und Altertumskunde*, LXVIII, 2 (1932), p. 87.

97. *Catalogue général*, Nos. 53247-53254.

98. Curt Sachs, *Les Instruments de musique de Madagascar* (Paris: Institut d'Ethnologie, 1938), pp. 5-7, pl. II.

99. Hans Hickmann, "Die altägyptische Rassel," *Zeitschrift für ägyptische Sprache und Altertumskunde*, LXXIX, 2, (1958).

100. Émile Chassinat, *Le Temple de Dendérah* (Cairo: Institut français d'archéologie orientale, 1947), pl. CCCXXXVI.

101. Cf. the defile of Ogdoade where each person wears anklets provided with objects reminiscent of the triangular jingles (Gustave Jéquier, Neuchatel: *Considérations sur les religions égyptiennes*, 1946, fig. 56).

102. Fulcran Grégoire Vigouroux, *La Sainte Bible polyglotte*, Vol. I (Paris: A. Roger et F. Chernoviz, 1900) ; Franz Josef Dölger, "Die Glöckchen am Gewande des jüdischen Höhepriesters nach der Ausdeutung jüdischer, heidnischer und frühchristlicher Schriftsteller," *Antike und Christentum* (Münster: Aschendorffsche Verlagsbuchhandlung, 1935), pp. 233-242.

103. Walter Ewing Crum, *A Coptic Dictionary*, 6 vols. (Oxford: Clarendon Press, 1929-1939), p. 815.

104. Henry George Farmer, *The Minstrelsy of the Arabian Nights*, p. 8.

105. Hugo Gressmann, *Musik und Musikinstrumente im Alten Testament* (Giessen: J. Ricker, 1903), p. 32; Hans Hickmann, *Terminologie arabe des instruments de musique* (Cairo, 1947), p. 23.

106. Morocco (Edmond Doutté, *Magie et religion dans l'Afrique du Nord*, p. 93); cf. Henry George Farmer, *op. cit.*, p. 37. This term could mean jingles or *sonnailles* suspended from bracelets.

107. Hans Hickmann, "Äthiopische Musik," *Die Musik in Geschichte und Gegenwart*, ed. Friedrich Blume (Kassel: Bärenreiter Verlag, 1949), column 106; Curt Sachs, *Real-Lexikon der Musikinstrumente* (Berlin: J. Bard, 1913), p. 121; G. Barblan, *Musiche e strumenti musicali dell'Africa Orientale Italiana* (Naples: Edizioni della Triennale d'oltremare, 1941). The last-mentioned author uses the spelling "Tsanâtsel."

108. *La Musique, des origines à nos jours* (Larousse, Paris), p. 19.

109. Hugo Gressmann, *Musik und Musikinstrumente im Alten Testament*, pp. 5-6 and 11. Victor Charles Mahillon, *Catalogue des instruments*, p. 380, No. 285.

110. Sven Hedin, *Transhimalaya* (Leipzig: F. A. Brockhaus, 1909), Vol. I, p. 307, and Vol. II, pl. 213.

111. Sven Hedin, *op. cit.*, Vol. I, pl. 134 and 135.

112. *Vogue* (Édition de Noël, Dec. 1948).

113. Henry George Farmer, *A History of Arabian Music* (London: Luzac & Co., 1929), p. 6 (*al-galâgil*, الجلاجل).

114. *Ibid.*, pp. 16-27.

115. Henry George Farmer, *The Minstrelsy of the Arabian Nights*, p. 8.

116. *Ibid.*, p. 36.

117. Curt Sachs, *Real-Lexikon der Musikinstrumente*, articles "Edibu," "Enzonga," "Ndaku," "Nkenbi"; cf. the iron jingles of Cameroon (Ethnographic Museum, Basle); L. Frobenius, *Das sterbende Afrika*, Bd. 1 (Munich: O. C. Recht, 1923), pl. 35; St. Chauvet, *Musique nègre* (Paris: Société d'éditions géographiques, maritimes et coloniales, 1929), p. 78 (wooden jingles).

118. Souer Marie-André du Sacré Coeur, *La Femme noire en Afrique occidentale* (Paris: Payot, 1939), pl. VII; L. Levy-Erell, "Das Homowah-Fest in Accra," *Atlantis*, VI (1930), p. 346 (jingles suspended from rings).

119. Victor Charles Mahillon, *Catalogue des instruments*, p. 379, No. 280 (*Atâmo*).

120. Elise J. Baumgärtel, *The Cultures of Prehistoric Egypt* (London: Oxford University Press, 1947), p. 8, fig. 5.

121. C. V. Daremberg and E. Saglio, *Dictionnaire*, Vol. I, 2, p. 1290, fig. 1709 (from an ornamented terra cotta lamp).

122. Apuleius, *Metamorphoses*.

123. Hans Hickmann, "Ägyptische Musik," *Die Musik in Geschichte und Gegenwart*, col. 97, fig. 12.

124. Brigitte Schiffer, *Die Oase Siwa und ihre Musik*, pp. 6 and 41.

v

GREEK IDEAS ON

MUSIC IN JUDEO-ARABIC

LITERATURE

Eric Werner (New York)

I. Definition and Classification of Music

*T*he expression "Hellas in the Orient's embrace," coined by the art historian Strzygowski, well describes the pseudomorphosis of cultures in the Near East from the rise of Hellenism to the decline of the Arabic caliphate. Oswald Spengler has labored the point to its extreme consequences; and his less original but more careful confrère, Arnold Toynbee, has once more stressed the importance of this pseudomorphosis.[1] Thus the historian is now prepared to accept ancient Greek ideas in Islamic disguise. Toynbee's scrutiny of this intellectual superimposition merits citation for his discernment of the two antagonistic trends involved in it:

> The Islamic state, in the first chapter of its history, was up in arms against the political ascendancy of Hellenism in Southwest Asia and Egypt—an ascendancy that had been upheld there by Roman power since the last century B.C. On the cultural plane, on the other hand, Islam eventually equipped itself for playing its part as a universal religion by drawing on Hellenistic intellectual resources.

71

Thus its attitude towards Hellenism was the ambivalent one of attraction towards it on the cultural plane coexisting with hostility towards it on the political plane. . . .[2]

Toynbee, however, neglects all Jewish elements in Arabic philosophy, although he is quite familiar with some of its Christian components. In the Arabic literature on music, confluent Biblical, Hellenic, Hellenistic, and Islamic ideas form an impressive synthesis. The Jewish authors, writing under the spell of both Hellenic thought and its Arabic interpretation, attempted a reconciliation of this composite philosophy with Biblical and Rabbinic concepts. It is mainly in this respect that they deviate from their Arabic confrères and teachers. This is already evident in the definition and classification of music.

Here a word of caution may be appropriate. The following pages deal chiefly with the *concept of music* as expressed in Judeo-Arabic literature; they are less concerned with the actual performance or structure of Jewish or Arabic music. This kind of music was occasionally contrived at the courts of the caliphs and was mainly cultivated there.[3] In general, the musical culture of the Arabs reflects, in a different spectrum, another synthesis of Greek and Mesopotamian civilization—i.e., of the old Aramaean and Hebrew—just as early Christian songs represent a synthesis of Hellenistic and the newer Jewish-Syrian ideas and practices. Thus, for example, the mythical father of all music, called Yubal in the Bible, becomes Tubal in Islamic tradition; his sister, the Biblical *Na'amah*, is the Arabic Ḍilal (possible Delilah?).[4]

The older musical culture of Judaism did not develop in a steady, unbroken course: with the destruction of the Second Temple the further evolution of art music ceased for the next 1400 years. Still, the musical glories of the Temple cast a sunset glow over subsequent discussions of music among the Jews. Islam, on the other hand, could only look forward to attaining new heights and was less handicapped by either prohibitions or nostalgias.[5]

Yet even in the Islamic orbit the status of musical scholarship was by no means undisputed. The secular sciences (to which the study of music belonged), including all philosophical propedeutics, flourished under the Fatimide and Spanish caliphs, whereas they encountered considerable opposition in the northwest of Asia Minor. In fact, the influence of Hellenic thought on Islam was not equally distributed at any time or in any region.[6] The Hellenic component in Arabic musical speculation came to the fore only after a fierce battle with the puritans; it took place about the very same time as, in Judaism, a similar battle—out of which emerged the professional precentor (*hazan*) of the synagogue—was being fought for and against the newfangled metrical hymns or *piyyutim*. These initial disputes began in the 7th century and lasted until the 10th.

In examining the ways in which the Greeks, Arabs, and Jews *defined* music, we are at the outset confronted with a paradoxical situation. It is well known that the chief domain of the musical culture of the three nations was *vocal* practice, usually connected with a text. Yet the definitions that we shall quote show a remarkable neglect of music as a communication linked with words. Of the four Hellenistic definitions, namely those of Ptolemy, Aristides Quintilianus, Cleonides, and the Anonymus Bellermann, not one mentions the connection between tones and words. Ptolemy: Μουσική ἐστιν δύναμις καταλεπτική τῶν ἐν τοῖς ψόφοις περὶ τὸ ὀξὺ καὶ τὸ βαρὺ διαφορῶν —a definition that stresses the scientific aspect of distinguishing between high and low pitches. Aristides Quintilianus: Μουσική ἐστιν ἐπιστήμη μέλους καὶ τῶν περὶ μέλος συμβαινόντων —a definition that presents music as the science of melody and of matters pertaining to it. Cleonides: Μουσική ἐστιν ἐπιστήμη τῆς τοῦ ἡρμοσμένου φύσεως —a definition that regards music as the science of the nature of harmonic structure. Anonymus Bellermann: Μουσική ἐστιν ἐπιστήμη μέλους τελείου καὶ ὀργανικοῦ—a definition that treats of music as the science of perfect melody, including instrumental tunes.[7] Three of the four definitions term music a science, and one calls it a faculty(δύναμις). Three stress the melodic component in general, and only Ptolemy is concerned with intervals and pitches. Here already we encounter the distinction between music as science (ἐπιστήμη) and as skill, applied in performance (τέχνη), a distinction that later, in Arabic and Jewish literature, was stressed constantly.

The Greek ideas found their way into the Arabic realm through translations and paraphrases by Syrian scholars. Such texts were accessible to Muslims as well as to Jews. From the period when this transition from Hellenistic to Syro-Arabic culture was in progress, we encounter a fifth important definition, attributed to Euclid: "Music is a science [or profession] which connects every species [genus] with a thing pertaining to the same species [genus]. Subduing the nature (temperaments), music stirs up that which is at rest and brings to rest that which is restless." [8] The first part of this statement, transmitted to us by Ibn Honein, is not quite clear; the second part, however, combines elements of the "ethos-doctrine" with a kinetic approach.

In contrast with this speculative description, Al-Farabi's statement is pragmatic and straightforward: "Music is a science (theory) that occupies itself with melodies, not only with their arrangement and composition, but also with their practical performance.[9] This definition exceeds in its second part the scope of any of the statements quoted above: it refers also to the *interpretation* of melodies. Such a practical approach is not far from the Aristoxenian concept, which judges music almost exclusively according to acoustical and sensual criteria, relying upon the ear and its perception rather than upon mathematics. It was accepted by the Arabs rather than by the Jews. The latest classic theorists of Arabic civilization, such as Safiyu-D-Din (late 13th century) and his contemporaries, attempted a synthesis of the strictly mathematical approach of the Pythagoreans and the "practical" and phenomenological ideas of the Aristoxenians.[10]

Although the texts of Al-Kindi's definitions "are so sadly maimed by copyists that even a tentative reconstruction is unsatisfactory," [11] it is clear that this great Arabic theorist (c. 800-875?) was the first philosopher in the history of music to make an exact distinction between a sound, the result of a system of non-periodic vibrations (Arabic *saut*), and a note or tone, caused by periodic vibrations (Arabic *naghma*).[12] This distinction, generally neglected in musical theory (except in treatises on acoustics), has recently become very important; it represents the watershed between "traditional" or "conventional" music and "electronic music" or "*musique concrète.*"[13]

On the Jewish side, the first straightforward definition of music occurs in Spain in the writings of R. Moses Botarel (end of the 14th century). There we read: "The science of song and melody—this is music; the science of melody, i.e., of the motion of ascending and descending tones, as well as the study of intervals." [14] The late occurrence of the definition in Hebrew is somewhat puzzling; it does not, however, indicate a lack of interest in the subject, as we shall see. If anything, it betokens a certain reluctance to define an art, the value and religious importance of which was fully recognized by earlier Hebrew authors, even in Scripture. Those authors were more concerned with speculations on the psychological influence of music and its multi-valued functions, to borrow a mathematical expression, than with semantic problems.

The "science of music" has two aspects in Judeo-Arabic literature: applied music theory and esthetic-ethical speculation on the moral influence of music. This bipartition corresponds to a similar dichotomy within the general discussion of music.

Practical music

↓

calculation of pitches
and intervals

Theoretical Music

↓

theory applied to ethics
and esthetics

Turning to classifications of music, we encounter Greek ideas in profusion; the ones most frequently elaborated in the Arabic and Jewish orbit were those of Aristoxenos, Plutarch, Aristides Quintilianus, and Aristotle. In the subsequent tabulation we shall juxtapose each of the Greek systems with at least one Arabic and one Jewish counterpart, thus demonstrating the gradual metamorphosis of Hellenic ideas.[15]

The tabulation, on pp. 76-77, shows quite tangibly that the Greeks were the music-teachers of both Arabs and Jews; this much is well known.[16] But it is also evident that our Judeo-Arabic authors were not content with simply paraphrasing their Hellenic sources. In almost every case they elaborated upon the Greek ideas. In these elaborations, Arabs and Jews usually parted company. While we find that in the field of definition and in the division of the octave, etc., the Jewish authors clearly depend upon Arab sources, especially on Al-Farabi and Ibn Sina (Avicenna), the situation changes as soon as we examine ideas on the philosophy of music, i.e., its moral influence. Here we encounter sharp differences between Islamic and Jewish thought.

II. The Ethos Doctrine

Whatever the status of Greek speculations on the *ethos* of musical composition may have been—and it changed considerably from the Pythagoreans to Aristoxenos, Philodemus, and Ptolemy—neither the place nor the function of the *ethos* doctrine within the classic Greek system of musical thinking is comparable to the place and function of the fully developed doctrine as expressed by Arabic and Jewish authors. We encounter here a curious vacillation in the nature of the doctrine. The fact that music was embedded in the Quadrivium next to arithmetic, geometry, and astronomy, makes evident the recognition of its *rational* character as a science.[17] Yet all during the Middle Ages rational astronomy served as handmaid to superstition-ridden astrology; and speculation about the moral influence of music was tinged with astrological and alchemistic conceptions. The Arabs managed to link them even with physiological principles, following some of Galen's suggestions.

Where, finally, cabbalistic thought emerged powerfully in Judaism, it was applied to the philosophy of music. Cabbala, ethos-doctrine, alchemy, astrology, the therapeutic value of music, and the axiom of the harmony of the spheres formed an ideological compound, which it is difficult for anybody to unravel who is not familiar with late Gnosticism and Neo-Pythagoreanism.[18]

According to the Pythagoreans, the human soul is in constant motion. This motion is defined by certain numerical proportions that

DEFINITION

Greeks

1. Aristoxenos:
   Movement of Tones
2. (Pseudo)-Plutarch:
   Science pertaining to voice and tone [19]
3. Aristides Quintilianus: [20]
   Science of melody and of all things pertaining to it

Arabs

1. Al-Farabi: [21]
   Science of understanding harmony and harmonic species; also of melodies and their composition
2. Safiyu-D-Din: [22]
   Science of tones, whose height or lowness can be measured exactly; also of all compositions of such tones

Jews

R. Moses Botarel:
Science of song and melody; science of ascending and descending tones, also of intervals

CLASSIFICATION

Greeks

1. Aristoxenos:
   a) *Theoretical*
      Study of Intervals
      Harmony
      Melopoeia
   b) *Practical*
      Rhythmics
      (1) in speech (λέξις)
      (2) in melody (μέλος)
      (3) in bodily motion (κίνησις σωματική)

Arabs

1. Al-Farabi:
   a) *Speculative*
      (1) Principles
      (2) Intervals
      (3) Tone-word relationship
      (4) Rhythms
      (5) Melopoeia
   b) *Practical*
      Invention of harmonic species
      (1) in natural media (voice)
      (2) in artificial media (instruments)

Jews

1. Shemtob Ibn Falaquera: [24]
   a) *Theory*
      (1) Principles
      (2) Intervals
      (3) Consonances, instruments
      (4) Rhythms
      (5) Melopoeia of metrical texts
   b) *Practice*
      (1) Production and performance of tones
         (α) by natural means (vocal)
         (β) by instruments
      (2) Practical composition

2. Aristotle:
Ethical (ἠθικαί)
Expressing action (πρακτικαί)
Evoking enthusiasm (ἐνθουσιαστικαί)

3. (Pseudo)-Plutarch:
Harmonic-melodic (ἁρμονική)
Rhythmic (ρυθμική)
Metric (μετρική)

4. Aristides Quintilianus:
a) *Theoretical*
Acoustics
Arithmetic
Harmonic-melodic
Rhythmic
Metric
b) *Practical*
Melopoeia
Rhythmopoeia
Poetry
Vocal Training
Instrumental Training
Acting
Informative (ἐξαγγελτικόν)
Pedagogic

2. Al-Kindi:
Melody
Rhythm
Philosophy
Ethos of rhythmic melody:
(1) creating grief
(2) exciting delight
(3) producing veneration, honor, and praise (*muʾtadie*) [23]

3. Safiyu-D-Din:
a) *Theory*
Acoustics
Intervals
Groups, scales
Rhythms
b) *Practice*
Melopoeia
Compositions
c) *Performance*
Interpretation
Ornaments (vocal or instrumental)
Moral effects

2. Ibn Aknin: [25]
a) *Theory*
(1) Principles
(2) Numerical relations of intervals
(3) Harmonic-melodic composition
(4) Theory of rhythms and meters
b) *Practice*
(1) Melopoeia; practical composition
(2) Performance and interpretation
(3) Moral effects

attend the harmonic relations of the tones.[26] Therefore, certain tunes
evoke corresponding motions of the listener's soul. The mathematical
analogy linking the ratios of the soul's motion, the vibration of strings,
and finally the movements of the heavenly bodies, constitutes the basis
upon which rests the principle of ethical power—in Greek philosophy,
the ἐπανόρθωσις τῶνἠθῶν. The idea of the moral *katharsis* of the
emotions,[27] as proclaimed by Aristotle and his followers, is closely
related to the older Pythagorean ideology. The connection between
body and soul is improved and "harmonized" by properly selected tunes,
and this involves also the idea of music as effective medical treatment.
The motions of the celestial bodies, of the macrocosmos, are supposed to
be paralleled by those of the soul.[28] Thus a complicated numerical
calculation in musical astrology begins to take shape.[29]

Turning from the physical to the physiological, we meet the somewhat strange conception that music affects the "humors" or the human
body. Here the Arabs and the Jews went far beyond the original Greek
idea. The Greeks, as we have seen, asserted a close relationship between
music and medicine, ascribing to music a distinctly therapeutic effect
upon both body and soul. But while Plato, Aristotle, and the Neo-
Platonists were content to state the fact, explaining it by the cathartic
and sedative influence of the musical art, the Arabic and Jewish philosophers went boldly and almost materialistically into physiological
details. They emphasized the effect of music on the humors, blood,
phlegm, yellow bile, and black bile. Let us compare some of the most
significant statements on these points. Leaving aside the many legends
of the Greeks, Arabs, and Jews, telling how music cured some highly
fantastic ailments, we turn to the ideas that lie behind these stories.

The Greeks linked medicine and music in two different ways:

1. The Pythagoreans consider number and proportion as instruments
of the imitative principle (μίμησις), which prevails in all of the arts.
This is somewhat similar to the thought of the Aristotelians.[30] Thus
music, medicine, and mathematics employ the same fundamentals; music
does so in rhythms, intervals, and proportions, and medicine does so in
the proportion of the humors and medicaments and, particularly, in the
mysterious ratios of human pulsation,[31] whereas, in mathematics, number
and proportion are the working material itself. Plato expresses similar
ideas in his *Timaeus*.

2. The other link between music and medicine is more physiological.
It is based chiefly on the term *katharsis* in a medical sense. Aristotle as
well as Galen uses this word with the connotation of "purgation." Considering how Jacob Bernays has exhibited the predominantly medical
background of the entire cathartic idea, we could characterize this
principle as that of a treatment basically homoeopathic.[32] The Neo-Pla-

tonists Proclos and Jamblichos accepted Aristotle's explanation. Cure was accomplished, according to the Aristotelian prescription, by playing, before the insane corybantes, frantic melodies on the orgiastic instrument, the Phyrgian aulos. Thus *katharsis* was brought about homoeopathically. The Pythagoreans, however, preferred the playing of solemn, soothing melodies for the maniacal listeners in order to impress upon their disorganized souls the magically numerical and cosmic order, attuning them, as it were, to the proportions of the universe. This is the type of *katharsis* that is allopathic.[33]

The literature of the Arabs and the Jews discusses only the allopathic form of treatment, although in their philosophy cathartic elements still play a part. But for therapeutic purposes Arabs and Jews seem to have relied entirely on Pythagorean principles, which they stressed to the limits of the absurd. Being good physicians, keen observers, and consistent logicians, the Arabs zealously embodied everything in their Pythagorean concept. Accordingly, each musical mode, even each string of their chief instrument, the *'ud*, had to be seen *sub specie mundi*. The four seasons, the four humors, the four cardinal virtues, and the four elements had to be embodied in their music theory.[34]

We find in Honein-Alharizi's *Maxims of the Philosophers* a characteristic statement: "The reason for our making four strings is their correspondence to the four temperaments of which man is composed." [35] The author goes on to associate with every string of the *'ud* a special effect upon some special humor. No less specific is Falaquera, and also Saadya who, in his *Emunot wede'ot* (Beliefs and Opinions), Chap. 10 (end), connects every rhythmical mode (Arab. *naghama*, Hebr. *ne'imā*) with one humor and one virtue respectively. A highly important source for our subject is also the *Ikhvan es-Safa* ("Brethren of Purity"), from which Saadya may possibly have borrowed.[36]

We quote now a few sentences from the *Ikhvan es-Safa* by way of illustration:

The musicians restrict the number of the strings of the lute to four,[37] neither more nor less, in order that their work might resemble the things of sublunar nature in imitation of God's wisdom.

The treble string is like the element of fire, its tone being hot and violent.

The second string is like the element of air; its tone corresponds to the humidity of air and to its softness.

The third string is like the element of water; its tone suggests water-like moisture and coolness.

The bass string is like the heaviness and thickness of the element earth.

Subsequently the *Ikvan es-Safa* explains that the treble string cor-

responds to the yellow bile, the second string to the blood, the third
to the saliva, and the bass string to the black bile, as elaborately
explained.

Our source continues: "If one employs these tones in appropriate
melodies and uses these melodies at those times of the night or day,
the nature of which is opposed to the nature of a virulent disease . . . ,
they assuage the sickness, breaking up its force and relieving the sick
ones of their pains." [38]

Thus music was generally considered a strictly allopathic, pain-
relieving, or invigorating medicine, corresponding to the mixtures of
the humors or of the elements. Ibn-Sina refers to these matters
frequently in his al-Kanun.[39] Throughout Arabic literature, the Pythagorean relationship between astronomy, music, and medicine is consistently maintained.

Falaquera's *Mebhakkesh* ("The Searcher") closely follows these
ideas. This work is a poetic revision of an earlier work, *Beginning of
Wisdom*, with a stronger emphasis on the Pythagorean point of view.[40]

From here on it is only a short step, in fact an imperceptible gradation, to a detailed and elaborate theory of the influence of music upon
the individual emotions. It seems, however, that in this field the
Oriental nations preferred less of system and more of detail, fewer explanations and more plain statements. There are even more significant
differences, which we shall consider presently.

We are confronted now with a perennial problem of philosophy
and esthetics, a problem that concerns us today as much as it did the
people of three thousand years ago, a problem that is unlikely ever
to be solved objectively. It cannot be our task to discuss that problem
itself, and we shall only describe the different attitudes toward it found
in Greek, Arabic, and Hebrew Literature.

The problem to which we refer poses two chief questions, which
we shall formulate cursorily:

1. Does music express emotions and, if so, how?
2. Does music evoke emotions and, if so, how?

We may, again in a cursory way, classify the first question as one
relating to the expressive powers of music and the other as one relating
to the impressive powers. The very approach to these problems differs
among the Greek, Jewish, and Arabic authors and shows their unique
characteristics, although the answers frequently sound similar. But we
must not allow these apparently similar answers to deceive us about
the fundamentally different attitudes assumed. The Greeks consider
the issue either from the psychological-ethical side, exemplified by the
Pythagoreans, Platonists, and Aristotelians, or from the purely esthetic-

formalistic side, as exemplified by the Sceptics and the Sophists. Both questions are answered in the affirmative by the first group, while the Sophists give a negative answer to at least the first question and restrict their affirmative answer to the second one to a few cases. They explain the influence of music upon the emotions by a materialistic theory of the association of words and ideas.[41] Furthermore, the Greeks are far more interested in the second question than in the first. Both questions were answered in the affirmative by Aristotle. To the first he applied the principle of *mimesis*, i.e., imitation of the emotions. In dealing with the second, he modified and even contradicted Plato's explicit evaluation or disapproval of certain modes and their ethos.[42]

Very clear in this respect is the doctrine of Aristoxenos, a disciple of Aristotle, who probably gave the first characterization of the three τρόποι (styles), viz., the systaltic, the diastaltic, and the hesychastic. The first is described as paralyzing human energy. It includes love-songs as well as funeral lamentations. The second is strong and virile, spurs to action, and thus becomes the heroic style employed in tragedy. The last is in between. It indicates and at the same time stimulates balance of mind and feeling.[43] We notice here, as a decisive criterion, the effect that music allegedly has upon human will-power. *A priori*, Aristoxenos assumes that music expresses the same ethos that it is supposed to evoke in the listener. In all cases, only such music is considered good that arouses ethical powers and eventually dissipates emotions that are harmful or evil.[44] In short, the Greeks aim not to evoke stormy or violent feelings but to banish them, thus creating a happy philosophical balance of the soul.

Quite different is the Arabic approach, and different again the Jewish approach. It is here that we find perhaps the only really important departure of the Jewish attitude from Arabic influence in the entire realm of musical thought. The Arabic writers either consider music in its psycho-physiological, even in its materialistic aspect, or view it from the lofty tower of their metaphysical or mystical speculations.[45] If we ask which attitude in Arabia was not that of the esoteric scholars but that of the people in general, there can be no doubt that the materialistic concept represented the common outlook.[46] The Arabs in general prefer emotional excitement to eudemonic pacification. The philosophers discarded the sentiment of the masses and adopted much of the Greek ideology, even if with some change of emphasis. However, the question of expression in music is deemed important by Al-Farabi, though all but disregarded by the Greeks, whose distinction between "expressive" and "impressive" Al-Farabi adopted.[47]

Arabic thinkers raised no issue about harmful and unpleasant emotions: "Other good melodies evoke such emotions as satisfaction, ire, clemency, cruelty, fear, sadness, regret, and other passions." [48] The Jewish authors try to avoid anything violent, excessive, or even licentious.

While Arabic literature contains some genuinely esthetic speculations on music, Hebrew thinkers were all but indifferent to esthetics of any kind. This apparent disregard is well established in Scripture, and hence is not only traditional, but authoritative.

To Biblical literature the idea that music is beautiful is evidently alien; music had its place in the ritual of the Temple, or it served as a spontaneous expression of any individual or a group, but it did not have any direct connection with the "esthetically beautiful." That conception is linked to visual sensations only, as the Song of Songs and similar poems seem to indicate. Even so late a book as Ecclesiasticus, which describes in the most glowing terms the cult of the Temple, uses the word "beautiful" only where a visual sensation is involved.[49]

Otherwise the epithet "beautiful," when employed in Scripture, is always on the borderline between the esthetic and the ethical. A few examples will illustrate the point: "For it is a pleasant thing [the Hebrew word *na'im* indicates the pleasant, the agreeable, and the morally good simultaneously] if thou keep them [the words of the wise] within thee" (Proverbs 22:18); or: "Behold how good and how pleasant [*na'im*] it is, when brethren dwell together in unity" (Psalm 133:1). Here the Hebrew terms are *tob* (morally good) and *na'im* (pleasant, agreeable). A similar combination is found in the following verse: "The Lord is good [*tob*]; sing praises to His name; for it is lovely [*na'im*]" (Psalm 135:3). The juxtaposition of the "good Lord" and the fitting praises that are "lovely" is perfect.

In the entire lengthy description of the first Temple (I Kings, Chap. 5-8) the word "beautiful" does not occur; it does occur, however, in Proverbs 31:30, where it has a derogatory sense: "Favour is deceitful, and beauty [*yofi*, sensual prettiness] is vain."

The acoustical beauty of a voice or of an instrument is usually described as "sweet," "agreeable," "strong." Hence, the purely esthetic element in musical matters is not fully represented in Old Testament and early Rabbinic literature; these sources either stress the social point of view ("agreeable"), or the sensual ("sweet"), or the majestic. This type of description is found in Sirach and Josephus, perhaps under the influence of Hellenism.

Quite unlike the classic Greek estheticism with its sharp distinction —beautiful or ugly—Judaism poses another antithesis: sacred-secular. Two characteristic passages will clarify this. In the beautiful Psalm 23, the Psalmist concludes:

Thou anointest my head with oil;
My cup runneth over.
Surely, goodness and mercy
Shall follow me all the days of my life;
And I will dwell
In the house of the Lord for ever.

To the Jewish singer, the last prediction of the psalm promises happiness, bliss, and beauty all together. Similarly, with sharper emphasis, the concept is expressed in the following: "And they [my priests] shall teach my people the difference between the Holy and the Common and cause them to discern between the unclean and the clean" (Ezekiel 44:23).

From this passage the standard prayer has been derived that is recited at the end of every Sabbath: "Praised be Thou, O Lord our God, King of the Universe, who makest a distinction between the Holy and the Profane, as between light and darkness . . ."

In one respect, however, Jewish and Greek conceptions of the esthetically valuable are very much akin; just as in Platonic philosophy the truly Good is also the truly Beautiful, so in Judaism the genuinely Holy is also the Beautiful and the Good. Thus a resemblance to the concept of Plato's *kalokagathia* (the beautiful and good) is in evidence in Jewish thinking. We encounter it, for example, if we compare Plato's remarks about Socrates' ugliness with the Talmudic anecdote of R. Joshua ben Hananya and the king's daughter:

R. Joshua ben Hananya was an ugly hunchback. Once a king's daughter ridiculed him because of his ugliness and marvelled, rather dubiously, that a treasury of wisdom should be sheltered in so unattractive an abode. Whereupon R. Joshua asked her in what kind of vessels people preserve their best wines: in silver, gold, or clay. She replied that the best wines are kept in containers of simple clay. Then he asked her why she was so astounded that beauty of learning and wisdom should be sheltered in his—physically unattractive—person.

The core of the comparison of Socrates and R. Joshua may be expressed in the following statement: mere external pleasantness is, on the highest level of Greek and Jewish philosophy, spurned in preference to a "beautiful soul." In Scripture, the identity of beauty and holiness is best expressed in Psalm 29:2; 96:9 ("beauty of holiness").

This antinomy between the Arabic and the Jewish conceptions of music becomes most perceptible in Maimonides. What we have said about the state of Arabic music sheds a new light on his *Responsum* concerning music. It becomes clear that Maimonides had in mind chiefly the exciting and sensual songs of the Arabs and the Arabian Jews.[50]

Maimonides makes three distinctions: 1) He admits that there are some few connoisseurs who study music as a suitable means of reaching a higher wisdom (the Greek διανόησις). But, he continues, one must not base one's conclusions on these individual cases. The laws of the Torah were written not for exceptional people, but for the majority. 2) The prohibition of secular music is based on Hosea 9:1; Isaiah 5:12; Amos 6:5; and Babylonian Talmud, Tractate Berachot 24a, emphasizing that, in most instances, music does nothing but excite lust. It makes no difference whether the texts of the songs are in Arabic or in Hebrew; for not the language, but only the content of an utterance matters. The Jewish people must become a holy nation and must avoid everything that does not lead to perfection. 3) The music that is mentioned and even recommended by the proper spiritual leaders is of a purely religious character and consists of psalms, hymns, and songs of exultation. Secular music ought not to be tolerated; surely not when performed by a singing female. Elsewhere, however, music as a therapeutic measure [51] receives Maimonides' commendation.

All that separates the ideology of Jewish philosophers from the Arabic view is clearly recognizable in this *Responsum*. Maimonides endorses religious music. He wishes to eliminate all secular music, regardless of the few individuals who study such music in order to achieve a higher wisdom. He stresses the Biblical and Talmudic tradition and opposes the fashion of his time. In his preoccupation with the religio-ethical effects, Maimonides completely ignores esthetic appreciation. (The same is true, as we know, of his attitude toward poetry.)[52] On the whole, Maimonides faithfully reflects the Platonic and not the Aristotelian point of view. Like Plato he gives an ethical evaluation rather than an esthetic classification.[53] Still there are also some deviations. The highest aim of the Greek philosopher-artist is the world of ideas. Music is only an instrument for ethical education [54] and has all but lost its religious function. The highest goal of Maimonides, on the other hand, is the intellectual and ethical perfection that leads to the prophetic perception of the Divine. Music may, in some cases, conduct one to this goal. Nonetheless, music has no place in ethical training. Thus there are two different levels on which music appears as a spiritual force. It is hard to avoid associating the position of Maimonides with the function of music among the troops of ancient prophets, in whom it aroused the *nebuah*, the prophetic inspiration.[55] Maimonides refers, in fact, to the story of the prophet Elisha: "But now bring me a minstrel. And it came to pass, when the minstrel played, that the hand of the Lord came upon him." [56] This incident is mentioned in the philosophies of music throughout the ages, together with references to David, Miriam, and Asaph. The Church Fathers took over the story and passed it on to the philosophers as an irrefutable proof that music has divine potentialities.[57] Jewish literature also refers to this frequently.

We may regard the *doctrine of virtue* as an extension of the ethos-doctrine. Here the interrelationship between philosophy and music becomes even more articulate.

An almost mystical realm opens up before us when we consider the Neo-Platonic philosophy of the movements of the soul as affected by music. Here Greek, Arabic, and Jewish views converge. We confront an eclectic combination of ideas derived from Plato, Aristotle, Porphyry, and Plotinus. In one and the same Syro-Hebraic work,[58] we may find the views of all four philosophers reposing peacefully side by side. We give but one example: "Living in solitude, the soul sings plaintive melodies [emphasizing the vanity of the world] whereby it reminds itself of its own superior world. As soon as nature (the physical world) sees this . . . she presents herself in various forms, introduced one by one to the soul, until she finally succeeds in recapturing the soul. The latter, busy with worldly affairs, soon forsakes its own true essence and abandons that which is sublime in composition and in the rhythm of artistic melodies. At last . . . , the soul is entirely submerged in Nature's ocean." [59]

Very similar ideas may be found in Aristides Quintilianus, who describes the soul's solitude, the cathartic influence of music upon it, and the temptations, such as those offered by tawdry pleasures,[60] that keep it from perfection.

Alongside this grand and lofty vision, we find in Honein-Alharizi's work strictly Platonic theories, of which we quote only two examples:

Plato once said to a guitar-player who accompanied the music with his voice, "This voice is material, we do not need it." "Master," asked his disciples, "are you not material?" "Yes," replied Plato, "but my body is a servant of my intellect." [61]

This idea is directly borrowed from *Timaeus* 67; another thought, which has found its most articulate expression in the *Republic* III, 398 C, and also in *Laws* II, 669 C, is incorporated in the following as a legend of Alexander the Great, Aristotle's most celebrated disciple:

Alexander, when he was a young man, once sat with his father and his courtiers in a tavern. A musician sang a song of love and cohabitation between a courtier and a maid servant of the king. The king was angry and said to the musician: "Do you not know that it is written: 'Bodies of free men shall not be coupled with bodies of slaves, lest their offspring be bad ones'? And it is also written: 'You shall not drink wine, lest it alter your character and corrupt your mind.' "

Views more materialistic than those expressed in this story seem to have been characteristic of the Arabs.[62] In the Hebrew sources such views are almost totally missing.[63] Besides details about the individual virtues, so extensively pondered by the Greeks, are rarely found in Jewish literature. The Arabs, on the other hand, reared a considerable hierarchy of virtues that music was believed to evoke.[64] Al-Farabi and Ghazzali, in particular, stressed these speculations. Once more it is Saadya who followed the Arabic way. The virtues according to Saadya are power to reign, fortitude, humility, joy, and sorrow (!). In general, he follows the lines of Honein's work and shows striking resemblances to the *Ikhvan*.[65] He does not, however, refer to those virtues which Plato "standardized": [66] wisdom, moderation, justice, and courage. As for the Hebrews, their literature prefers to stress the virtues that are dianoetic or prophetic, apparently assuming that the practical virtues, the ordinary or civic ones, were already achieved by the performance of the Biblical commands.

If we ask which element of music was supposed to possess the greater ethical power, melody or rhythm, we must answer without hesitation: rhythm. On this point, Arabs, Greeks, and Jews agree completely. That this view was generally accepted, we can see from all of the later Greek and Arabic writers.[67] Saadya's entire theory is based on rhythmical constructions common in Arabic theory.[68]

III. The Harmony of the Spheres

Closely related to the ethos doctrine is the venerable principle of the harmony of the spheres.[69] This ancient and beautiful conception was, as we know, one of the keystones of Pythagorean cosmology. But today it has begun to appear that the idea of sounding spheres originated much earlier, in Egyptian and perhaps also in Babylonian culture. Apparently, it belonged to the esoteric doctrines of the priestly classes. Only in Greek philosophy does this conception emerge into the light of public and systematic discussion. The Greeks incorporated the idea into the general principle of harmony within the universe and within the human soul.

For Plato's cosmogony, harmony in its widest sense is an indispensable element.[70] Plato's allusion to the dance of the stars and to their perfect proportions represents a distinctly Pythagorean trend of thought. Aristotle was the only great philosopher of his time who energetically combated the idea, although he did acknowledge its fascinating beauty.[71] Of the later thinkers, the Neo-Platonists and the Pythagoreans again stressed this conception. Thence it found its way into the theories of astronomy and music of the dying ancient world.[72] Ptolemy and

Aristides Quintilianus fashioned very concrete and mathematically elaborate systems of cosmic harmony, developing some of the ideas of Nicomachus of Gerasa.[73] The last mentioned was one of the many Syrian writers who formed the bridge between Greece and Arabia over which Pythagorean doctrines traveled.[74]

The theory of cosmic harmony was not as popular with the Arabs or the Jews as it had been with the Greeks. Hence the concept of harmony of the spheres, which fitted so beautifully into the general ἀρμονία κόσμου of the Greek philosophers, while accepted and mentioned by the Arabs, was not greeted by them with much enthusiasm.[75] Al-Farabi, for one, opposed it. He vents his feelings against this doctrine in the words: "The opinion of the Pythagoreans that the planets and stars produce harmonious sounds in their courses is erroneous." [76] Nevertheless, most of the Arabic authors adhered to the ancient idea, notwithstanding Al-Farabi's great prestige. It became a cherished tradition, abandoned unwillingly even when not accorded much weight.

A different attitude is to be found in Hebrew literature. Allusions to the harmony of the spheres already appear in the Bible. The Talmud also accepts the theory, though not in a straightforward unequivocal way.[77] Jewish literature, accordingly, links the harmony of the spheres to Biblical and Talmudical authorities rather than to astronomical observation of the universe. If a Jewish writer was, in addition, inclined toward Pythagorean ideas, he could naturally support them with the available Biblical statements. Philo is the most vigorous advocate of the Pythagorean idea among the earlier Jewish philosophers. To him, the heavens are the archetype for all musical instruments. The purpose of the musical structure of the cosmos is to provide the accompaniment for hymns of praise. The seven planets are compared to the seven strings of the lyre.[78]

Among the Hebrew writers considered in this article, only Falaquera (in his Mebakkesh) and minor authors insist on the harmony of the spheres, though most of them support the theory by Biblical citations.[79] In his earlier work, Beginning of Wisdom, Falaquera follows Ibn 'Aknin almost verbatim, or rather Ibn 'Aknin's source, Al-Farabi's De scientiis, and does not even mention cosmic harmony.[80] It appears that Falaquera later became more friendly toward the old Pythagorean theory. As for Isaac Ben Abraham Ibn Latif, one of the lesser writers, it is characteristic that he constantly emphasizes the esoteric nature of his ruminations: "The psalmist has spoken cryptically . . . I can explain no more . . . This speculation can be grasped only by those who are initiated into both sciences." [81] The Neo-Platonists, Moses ibn Ezra and Abraham ibn Ezra, both accepted the doctrine. The former acclaims it in his poems; [82] the latter, less ardent, is content with one or two references to it. Strangely enough, of all Biblical passages alluding to cosmic harmony, Abraham ibn Ezra chooses Psalm 93:4, but misses such inviting opportunities as those offered by Job 38:7 or 38:37.[83] Simon Duran also broaches the ancient idea in the same connection.[84]

The most consistent and significant opponent of the entire doctrine is Maimonides; in his *Guide* he unequivocally expresses his antagonism.[85] Thus we arrive at the surprising conclusion that philosophers of the greatest consequence in their respective lands, viz., Aristotle, Al-Farabi, and Maimonides, were sceptical of or even inimical to the theory of cosmic harmony. To what extent the latter two did or did not follow Aristotle on that question is a problem with which we shall not deal. Yet the attitude of these thinkers did not deter later generations from returning to the old Pythagorean track. In Hebrew literature, however, Maimonides almost set a standard on this issue, so that the principle of spheric harmony was abandoned by most of his followers.[86] It appeared instead in the camp of his antagonists, i.e., in the literature of the Cabbalists. There it received the utmost elaboration throughout the following centuries. We cannot discuss these sources here, for the position of music in the esoteric literature of the Jews would require a special study.

A comparison of the Greek theories on the calculation of intervals, or even on the structure of melodies, with the Arabic and Jewish systems is a more difficult task than the examination of philosophical ideas. The crux here is the Arabic terminology employed in these writings. H. G. Farmer has shed a good deal of light on these problems, and d'Erlanger's editions of the main sources of Arabic applied theory of music has made available the most important writings.[87] Yet, until the Greek terms *tropos*, *nomos*, *eidos*, and *tasis*, which were used most perplexingly and perhaps promiscuously, are elucidated beyond any possible doubt, and until some Arabic terms, such as *lahn*, *'usul*, *ghina*, are also clearly explained, we must content ourselves with the words of Curt Sachs: "It would be a mistake to imagine that the intellectual processes of combining, permutating, and coupling [intervals, modes, tetrachords, etc.] were actually responsible for the motley diversity of Mohammedan music; in other words, that lifeless theory created living melody." [88] We are able to trace Greek ideas in the *literature* on music of Arabs and Jews; nor is it hard to find Aristoxenian methods in the calculation of intervals and the division of the octave as practiced in Islamic civilization: yet living music does not depend on philosophical or even mathematical ideas. They may serve as foundations, but the musical superstructure—composition and performance—, while partly determined by abstract conceptions, is in principal autonomous; the morphology and structure of Arabic or Jewish music draws its most characteristic traits from psychological and linguistic forces. Their interrelation with music and its theory forms a chapter hitherto neglected but fascinating nonetheless.

Notes

1. Arnold J. Toynbee, *A Study of History*, Vol. XII, "Reconsiderations," (New York: Oxford University Press, 1961), p. 450.

2. Toynbee, *op. cit.*, p. 466.

3. Cf. Julián Ribera, *Music in Ancient Arabia and Spain* (Stanford: Stanford Unversity Press, 1929), Chaps. III (end) and VI (end), p. 72, *et passim;* also Higini Anglès, "Hispanic Musical Culture from the 6th to the 14th century," *The Musical Quarterly*, XXVI (1940), pp. 503 f, where one reads: "The religious musical Christian culture of the 9th and 10th centuries could not compete with the musical culture of the Arabic courts."

4. H. G. Farmer, "The Music of Islam," in *New Oxford History of Music*, Vol. I, "Ancient and Oriental Music," ed. by Egon Wellesz (London: Oxford University Press, 1957), p. 423.

5. It should not pass unnoticed (and unreprehended) that H. G. Farmer in his fine essay on the music of Islam puts Ishtar and Yahwe on the same footing. This betrays an attitude which, as Martin Buber has pointed out repeatedly, is tinged with the Protestant prejudice that the God of the Hebrew Bible is a pre-monotheistic, tribal deity, who is best disposed of by referring to him by a name on a par with the names of other pagan divinities. Such remnants of the Lagarde-Wellhausen saga should no longer be seriously maintained.

6. Cf. H. G. Farmer in *New Oxford History of Music*, pp. 428 ff.

7. Cf. Eric Werner and Isaiah Sonne, "The Philosophy and Theory of Music in Judaeo-Arabic Literature," *Hebrew Union College Annual*, XVI (1941), pp. 251-319, and XVII (1943), pp. 511-573, Chap. I; also *Die Musik in Geschichte und Gegenwart*, ed. by Friedrich Blume (Kassel: Bärenreiter Verlag, 1949-   ), Vol. IX, col. 976-977.

8. Cf. Werner-Sonne, "The Philosophy and Theory of Music in Judaeo-Arabic Literature," XVII, p. 531.

9. Al-Farabi's definition is given in Rodolphe d'Erlanger, *La Musique arabe*, Vol. I (Paris: P. Geuthner, 1930), pp. 6-7, and Vol. III (1938), p. 191 (as quoted by Safiyu-D-Din); see also H. G. Farmer's edition of Al-Farabi's *Isha Al 'Ulum (De scientiis)* in Farmer's *Al-Farabi's Arabic-Latin Writings on Music* (Glasgow: The Civic Press, 1934).

10. Of early authors, only St. Augustine comes near this attitude in his celebrated definition "Musica est scientia bene modulandi" (if we are permitted to interpret *modulari* as referring to the production of tones). The assumption that Al-Farabi knew Augustine's definition is hardly tenable.

11. Cf. H. G. Farmer, *Sa'adyah Gaon on the Influence of Music* (London: A. Probsthain, 1943), p. 23.

12. *Ibid.*

13. The periodicity of vibration, which gives birth to tone, is a *necessary* condition for music in the traditional sense; the question of its being also a *sufficient* condition constitutes today a crucial problem of musical esthetics.

14. Cf. Moses Botarel, *Commentary on the Sefer Yetzira* (Mantua, 1562); see also Werner-Sonne, "The Philosophy and Theory of Music in Judaeo-Arabic Literature," XVI, p. 264, note 50.

15. A careful examination of the main sources shows the prevalence of a general ideological trend only in the realm of the applied and moralizing theory of, or speculation on, music; in the field of performance we encounter, of course, all sorts of regionally and temporally limited ideas, trends, fashions, and fads. The greatest authority in the field of Islamic music, Prof. H. G. Farmer, while fully familiar with this pluralism of musical customs, is perhaps sometimes inclined to overlook the pluralism for the sake of a clearer general picture. A characteristic symptom of this regionally "plural tradition" in the Islamic orbit is the muezzin's invitatory to prayer—a chanted passage from the *Kor'an*. Even this sacred call to worship irked the Islamic puritans and elicited a theological controversy. Finally, after the victory of the "populists" over the legalistic purists, "the cantillation [of the invitatory] itself was not confined to any fixed melodic contour, and so, from the shores of Morocco to the Oxus, one may hear this cantillation today in almost as many patterns as there are mosques." (H. G. Farmer in *New Oxford History of Music*, I, p. 439.) Again, there is a Jewish counterpart to this development: the Masoretic accents of the Bible were being introduced between the 6th and the 10th centuries, but they and their cantillation became a hotbed of theological controversy—a long and tedious struggle between puritanic legalists and a more democratically inclined group of scholars. Here the term "democratic" has no direct political significance, but has been chosen to indicate the rule of the majority, which *in this case* proved to be wholesome and wise.

16. We need only to quote the preface of Al-Farabi's second (lost) volume on musical instruments, in order to demonstrate that both Arabs and Jews were themselves aware of the Greek patrimony. There we read: "We treat here whatever came down to us of the writings of the celebrated Greek theoreticians. . . ."

17. Cf. Werner-Sonne, "The Philosophy and Theory of Music in Judaeo-Arabic Literature," XVI, p. 257 (Honein-Alharizi's ideas on the place and function of music).

18. Ibn Aknin finds a place for music after the study of Writing, Torah, Mishna, Grammar, Poetry, Talmud, Theology, Logic, Mathematics, Optics, and Astronomy. He remarks: "The practice of music precedes the theory. The former must come first, because its healing power cannot show itself except by actual performance . . ." (Werner-Sonne, "The Philosophy and Theory of Music in Judaeo-Arabic Literature," p. 255).

19. Cf. (Pseudo)-Plutarch, *De musica*, ed. by Robert Volkmann (Leipzig, 1856), p. 57.

20. Cf. Aristides Quintilianus, *De musica*, German transl. by Rudolf Schaefke (Berlin-Schöneberg: M. Hesse, 1937), p. 167.

21. Cf. Al-Farabi, *Isha Al'Ulum* (*De scientiis*) in H. G. Farmer, *Al-Farabi's Arabic-Latin Writings on Music*, pp. 21-31.

22. Cf. Rodolphe d'Erlanger, *La Musique arabe*, III, p. 192.

23. Cf. H. G. Farmer, *Sa'adyah Gaon on the Influence of Music*, p. 15.

24. Cf. Werner-Sonne, "The Philosophy and Theory of Music in Judaeo-Arabic Literature," XVI, pp. 269-270.

25. Cf. *ibid.*, p. 265.

26. Cf. Ptolemaeus, *Harmonica*, III, Chap. IV.

27. We are using in this study the term "emotion" in place of the more correct, but unusual, "affectus." The terms are not quite identical, however, and we apologize for this lack of precision.

28. Cf. Plato, *Timaeus*, 34B.

29. If Hermann Abert in his *Lehre vom Ethos in der griechischen Musik* (Leipzig: Breitkopf & Härtel, 1899) disposes of this entire system with the words "gelehrte Tifteleien" (learned hairsplitting), then let us remember the enormous influence of this great conception upon philosophy, esthetics, music, and astronomy up to Newton. Even in such sober books as those of the astronomer Eddington we may find speculations that are closely related to Pythagorean ideas. At any rate, Abert's rash statement could hardly be sustained in our times.

30. Cf. Aristotle, *Metaphysics*, I, 6, 987 b, 11.

31. Aristides Quintilianus elaborates upon the theory of pulsation in true Pythagorean spirit: "The pulsation that corresponds to normal circumstances—analogous to the octave 1:2, or to the fifth 2:3, or to the fourth 3:4—does not necessarily endanger life. . . . Those pulsations, however, that present themselves in an entirely non-consonant ratio . . . are dangerous and may bring death." (See *De musica* in Marcus Meibom, *Antiquae musicae auctores septem*, Vol. II, Amsterdam, 1652, p. 127.) The entire medieval theory is full of similar statements. Cf. Boethius, *De institutione musica* in J. P. Migne, *Patrologiae cursus completus. Series latina* (Paris, 1844-55), Vol. LXIII, 1170; Boethius is the chief source for all further speculation.

32. Aristotle, *Politics*, VIII, 1341 b 32. We give here part of his report: "We see that if those insane persons (ἐνθουσιαστικοί) listen to enthusiastic melodies which intoxicate their souls, they are brought back to themselves again, so that their catharsis takes place exactly like a medical treatment." He relates how corybantes were cured by listening to corybantic tunes. (*Ibid.*, 1340 b 8.)

33. Aristides Quintilianus, ed. by Marcus Meibom, pp. 103-107.

34. Although Greek literature offered the basis for the scheme, it was the more radical Arabs and Jews who tried to link anything and everything to their musical system. Whatever the Christian writers wrote in this fashion was always borrowed from the Arabs, even with the help of Arabic words. Thus, in Odo of Cluny's and in Hucbald's writings there occur words like *scembs, kaphe, neth*, and *caemar*, clearly recognizable as Arabic terms. Yet the Christian authors do not know their origin or their meanings. Cf. Martin Gerbert, *Scriptores ecclesiastici de musica sacra potissimum*, Vol. I (1784; facsimile ed., Berlin, 1905, also Milan: Bollettino bibliografico musicale, 1931), p. 249. Even in our own day it has been possible for a scholar like G. Lange (in his article on solmization, *Sammelbände der Internationalen Musikgesellschaft*, I, 1899-1900, pp. 539 ff.) not to recognize the Arabic origin of Odo's syllables. See especially H. G. Farmer, *Historical Facts for the Arabian Musical Influence* (London: W. Reeves, Ltd., 1930).

35. Cf. Werner-Sonne, "The Philosophy and Theory of Music in Judaeo-Arabic Literature," XVII, p. 530 (Honein, Chap. 20).

36. Cf. Jacob Guttmann, *Die Religionsphilosophie des Saadya Gaon* (Göttingen: Vandenhoeck & Ruprecht, 1882), pp. 287 ff, which stresses the almost verbal similarity of the *Ikhvan* with Saadya's text in the musical portion. Since Honein is older than both Saadya and the *Ikhvan*, we have to look for

a common (probably Syrian) source, from which all the three authors drew. Cf. Anton Baumstark, *Aristoteles bei den Syrern*, Vol. I (Leipzig: B. G. Teubner, 1900), pp. x-xii.

37. Cf. H. G. Farmer, *An old Moorish Lute Tutor* (Glasgow: The Civic Press, 1933), p. 38: "Ziryab claimed to have added a fifth string to the lute. . . . Naturally, he had to connect it with the cosmic scheme and hence associate it with a fifth nature—the soul. What would have prompted this association? In the Pseudo-Aristotelian *De mundo* (393a) we find a fifth element—ether, which occurs in the *De musica* of Aristides Quintilianus."

38. *Ikhvan es-Safa*, ed. by F. H. Dieterici, Vol. VI, *Die Propädeutik der Araber* (Leipzig: J. C. Hinrichs, 1872), pp. 126-128.

39. The medico-musical system, as accepted by Arabs and Jews, admits of this tabulation:

String	Element	Humor	Quality	Season
Zir (treble)	fire	yellow bile	hot	summer
Mathna (2nd)	air	blood	humid	spring
Mathlath (3rd)	water	phlegm	cold	winter
Bam (bass)	earth	black bile	dry	autumn

40. On the relation between Falaquera, Ibn 'Aknin and Al-Farabi, see H. G. Farmer, *Al-Farabi's Arabic-Latin Writings on Music* (cf. note 9 *supra*), pp. 6, 57, where a very clear picture is given; also Moritz Steinschneider, *Die hebräischen Übersetzungen des Mittelalters und die Juden als Dolmetscher* (Berlin: Bibliographisches Bureau, 1893), par. 12. Thus, Güdemann's assertion of an alleged Averroes influence is no longer tenable.

41. Cf. Hermann Abert, *op. cit.*, par. 4, 5, 9, 11. The problem itself has created an enormous literature, of which we cannot give a comprehensive bibliography here. We mention only the works in which such bibliographies may be found: Adolf Aber, *Handbuch der Musikliteratur* (Leipzig: Breitkopf & Härtel, 1922), pp. 470-490; Ernst Kurth, *Musikpsychologie* (Berlin: M. Hesse, 1931; Bern, 1947), Index. It was this perennial problem that created the famous struggle for and against Richard Wagner.

42. Cf. Plato, *Politics*, III, 398C-402; Aristotle, *Politics*, VIII, 7, 1342a, b.

43. Hermann Abert, *op. cit.*, pp. 67-69.

44. Cf. Plutarch, *Quaestiones conviviales* III, 8th question, c. 2. "The wailing-song and the funeral-flute excite pain and bring about tears, but afterwards attune the soul to compassion, gradually mitigating and annihilating the painful emotion."

45. Cf. *Arabian Nights*, ed. by E. W. Lane, p. 400: "Ibn Sina hath asserted that the lover's remedy consisteth in melodious sounds, and the company of one like his beloved . . ." *Ibid.*, pp. 129, 302, *et passim*. Compare with this Shakespeare, *Twelfth Night*, Act. I, Scene 1: "If music be the food of love, play on!"

46. Cf. Charles Montagu Doughty's statement, in his *Travels in Arabia Deserta* (London: J. Cape, 1936), about the polar nature of Arabic culture, which is both rude and refined, containing materialistic and mystic elements at the same time; also: "Music is in constant connection with everything intoxicating: wine, love, and ecstasy . . ." (Robert Lachmann, *Musik des Orients*, Breslau: F. Hirt, 1929, pp. 98-101.)

47. Al-Farabi, *Kitab* I, p. 13.

48. Al-Farabi, *Kitab* II, pp. 89 ff.

49. Ecclesiasticus, Chap. 48-50.

50. I. Goldziher, in "Das Gutachten des Maimonides über Gesang und

Musik," *Monatschrift für Geschichte und Wissenschaft des Judentums*, XXIII (1875), pp. 174-180, omits consideration of the tendency of Arabic music at the time of Maimonides.

51. Here it is the physician Maimonides who speaks, the faithful disciple of the great Arabic tradition of medicine. Cf. Maimonides, *Shmone Perakim*, in Joseph I. Gorfinkle, *The Eight Chapters of Maimonides on Ethics (Schmone Perakim)* (New York: Columbia University Press, 1912), p. 30.

52. Many centuries later, a truly Christian philosopher, a stranger to his own contemporaries, displayed a somewhat similar attitude toward music. In Kierkegaard's *Entweder Oder* we meet striking resemblances to Maimonides. But the Danish thinker grants us a choice only between the beautiful and the good, which makes it not a little difficult to lean in favor of the good when Kierkegaard makes Mozart his champion of beauty.

53. We set the typical statements of both Plato and Maimonides side by side:

Plato, *Laws*, II 668 A, *Politics*, III 398 C, *Politics*, II 376 E, *Laws*, II 669, etc.: Then, when anyone says that Music is to be judged by pleasure this cannot be admitted; and if there be any Music of which pleasure is the criterion, such Music is not to be sought out or deemed to have any real excellence but only that other kind of Music, which is an imitation of the good. The chief place of Music is in the *paideia* (transl. by B. Jowett, IV, p. 197).

Maimonides, *Responsum on Music:* Secular Music is to be prohibited, because it arouses lust and wickedness. Music of a religious character and Music leading to ethical wisdom are permitted. The only decisive criterion of Music's value is its religious-ethical essence. The chief place of Music is in the Synagogue, and generally, in worship.

54. At bottom, Plato seems to have cherished the same ideas as Maimonides regarding the religious functions of music, although he is not quite as outspoken on this issue and clothes his conception in the form of a historical report. He says: "Among us and our forefathers . . . Music was divided into various classes and styles; one class of song was that of prayers to the gods, which bore the name of hymns; contrasted with this was another class, best called dirges; paeans formed another; and yet another was the dithyramb, named, I fancy, after Dionysos . . ." (Plato, *Laws*, III, transl. by Bury, Vol. I, p. 245.)

55. Maimonides mentions the story of Elisha while discussing the nature of prophecy. Cf. *Guide of the Perplexed*, II, 32. Cf. also Plotinus' great conception of the chanted prayer: "The tune of an incantation, a significant cry . . . These two have a power over the soul . . . similarly with regard to prayers; the prayer is answered by the mere fact that one part and the other part (of the All) are wrought into one tone like a musical string which, plucked at one end, vibrates at the other also. . . ." (Stephen Mackenna, *Plotinus on the Nature of the Soul*, Oxford: P. L. Warner, 1924, p. 96.)

56. Dr. Morgenstern, in his illuminating "Amos-Studies III," looks upon the Elisha story from quite a different angle: "And in order to divine for them as requested Elisha proceeded to work himself into a state of ecstasy, in accordance with the customary technique of the professional prophets, by having a musician play in his presence. The significance of this procedure is unmistakable. Within two years after the death of Elijah Elisha had fallen from the high level of prophetic standards and technique of his great master

to the much lower level of the professional prophets . . ." (*Hebrew Union College Annual*, XV, 1940, p. 228.)

57. Of the innumerable references to the stories of David or Elisha, we mention here only three of the most characteristic ones from Christian sources:

(1) *Joanni Damasceni vita a Joanne Hierosolymitano conscripta* (J. P. Migne, *Patrologiae cursus completus. Series graeca*, Paris, 1857-66, Vol. XCIV, 473).

(2) Regino Prumiensis (d. 915) in J. P. Migne, *Patr. lat.*, Vol. CXXXII, 490.

(3) Roger Bacon in Robert Belle Burke, *The Opus Majum of Roger Bacon*, Vol. I (Philadelphia: University of Pennsylvania Press, 1928), pp. 259 ff. Here the philosopher confuses the name Elisha with Elijah!

58. Honein-Alharizi's *Maxims of the Philosophers* in Werner-Sonne, "The Philosophy and Theory of Music in Judaeo-Arabic Literature," XVII (cf. note 7 *supra*), pp. 513 ff.

59. This thought might in a more general form occur in Schopenhauer's *Welt als Wille und Vorstellung*. Cf. F. Rosenthal in *Hebrew Union College Annual*, XV (1940), p. 468.

60. Cf. *De musica* in Marcus Meibom, *Antiquae musicae auctores septem*, p. 184.

61. Honein-Alharizi, *Maxims of the Philosophers*, 19:15.

62. Cf. Friedrich Albert Lange, *The History of Materialism*, transl. by Ernest Chester Thomas, 3rd ed. (New York: Harcourt, Brace & Co., 1925), p. 177: "Mohammedanism is more favorable to materialism than Christianity or Judaism"; also, p. 181: "The Arabs set to work with an independent feeling for exact observation, and developed especially the doctrine of life, which stands in so close a relation to the problems of materialism."

63. The inklings of materialistic reasoning, which may be found in Falaquera and Saadya, are more than counterbalanced by a strong emphasis upon religious and theological principles.

64. Cf. Julián Ribera, *Music in Ancient Arabia and Spain*, 3rd ed., pp. 90 ff.

65. Cf. note 36 *supra*.

66. Cf. Plato, *Politics*, IV, 441 C.

67. Aristotle, *Poetics*, Chap. i; also, very clearly evident in Aristides Quintilianus' *De musica*, ed. by Marcus Meibom, p. 31.

68. This fact has been overlooked by all writers on Saadya except H G. Farmer; perhaps because the passage about music is a "rather dark one" (Steinschneider), "offers difficulties" (Guttmann), "has not been properly explained," Henry Malter, *Saadia Gaon, his Life and Works* (Philadelphia: The Jewish Publication Society of America, 1921). In view of Saadya's emphasis upon rhythm, the statement of P. Gradenwitz (in *Monatschrift für Geschichte und Wissenschaft des Judentums*, 1936, p. 463) that the rabbis unanimously objected to rhythmical music, cannot be upheld. Here Gradenwitz, or the rabbis, or both, confuse rhythm and meter.

69. How inseparably these two conceptions are connected may be seen in the following juxtaposition of sentences: "Coelum ipsum sub harmoniae modulatione revolvitur. Musica movet affectus." (Isadore of Seville in Gerbert, *Scriptores*, I, 20 b.)

70. Cf. Plato, *Timaeus*, 34 B ff; *Politics*, VII, 530. The word χορεῖον,

used in *Timaeus*, 40 c, can be understood only as the rhythmic motion of the heavenly bodies.

71. Cf. Aristotle, *De caelo*, Chap. ix, 290 b 12.

72. Cf. Sir Thomas Little Heath, *The Copernicus of Antiquity, Aristarchus of Samos* (New York: Clarendon Press, 1913), pp. 105-115.

73. Cf. Ptolemy, *Harmonics*, in Ingemar Düring, *Die Harmonielehre des Klaudios Ptolemaios*, III (Göteborg: Elanders Boktryckeri Aktiebolag, 1930), Chap. XVI-XIX, Aristides Quintilianus, *De musica*, ed. by Marcus Meibom, pp. 145-155; Nicomachus of Gerasa in Karl von Jan, *Musici scriptores graeci et melodiarum veterum quidquid exstat* (Leipzig: B. G. Teubner, 1895), pp. 230-43, 272, 276-80, *et passim*. A survey of the entire ideology is given in K. W. F. Piper, *Mythologie und Symbolik der christlichen Kunst*, I, pp. 245-75.

74. It is significant that three of the most important authors who wrote on music in Greek were Syrians, viz., Nicomachus of Gerasa (c. 100 A.D.), Porphyrius of Tyre (c. 260 A.D.), and Jamblichus of Coelesyria (Palestine, c. 310 A.D.).

75. Except in the *Ikhvan* which, being fervently Pythagorean, stresses to the utmost the conception of spheric harmony. Cf. *Ikhvan es-Safa*, ed. by F. H. Dieterici (see note 38 *supra*), pp. 162 ff. On Al-Kindi's attitude, see Moritz Steinschneider, *Al-Farabi* (St. Petersburg: Académie Impériale des Sciences de St. Petersbourg, Mémoires, Série 7, Tome 13, No. 4, 1869), p. 80.

76. Cf. *Kitab*, I, p. 28.

77. Psalms 19:1, 93:4, 96:11, 97:6; Job 38:7, 38:37; Ezekiel 1:4, 1:22; Babylonian Talmud, Tractate Joma 20b, 21a.

78. Ὁ τοίνυν οὐρανός, τὸ μουσικῆς ἀρχέτυπον ὄργανον ἄκρως ἡρμόσθαι δοκεῖ δι᾿ οὐδὲν ἕτερον ἢ ἵνα οἵ ἐπὶ τιμῇ τοῦ τῶν ὅλων πατρὸς ᾀθόμενοι ὑμνοὶ μουσικῶς ἐπιψάλλωνται. (*De somniis*, I., 37, in *Philo's Works*, ed. by Colson and Whitaker, Vol. V., p. 314 [Loeb Classics]). Elsewhere he states that the idea of cosmic harmony has been developed by the Chaldeans. See also Hermann Abert, *Die Musikanschauung des Mittelalters* (Halle: M. Niemeyer, 1905), pp. 39 ff. Also, I. Heinemann's article, "Philo," in August Friedrich von Pauly-Wissowa, *Realencyclopädie des classischen Altertumswissenschaft* (Stuttgart: J. B. Metzler, 1839-52).

79. Chiefly Psalm 19:1 and Job 38:7.

80. The decisive word on Al-Farabi's negative attitude toward the theory of spheric harmony has been written by H. G. Farmer in *Al-Farabi's Arabic-Latin Writings on Music* (see note 9 *supra*).

81. Here the esoteric influence of cabbalistic thought is clearly noticeable.

82. Moses ibn Ezra in a *piyut* for the New Year writes glowingly about the "sounding, revolving vaults of the heavens, their inaudible harmony . . ."

83. Cf. Abraham ibn Ezra's Commentary on Psalm 93:4. " 'The sound of great waters': More than the sound of great waters is the Great Name in the heights, and that in turn is surrounded by the orbits of the spheres and their sounds." Cf. also Abraham ibn Ezra's Commentary on Job 38:7. " 'Who can tell': Nothing in the celestial world is comparable to the power of the spheres and their sound and their mathematical relation." (Paraphrase.)

84. Cf. Simon Duran, *Magen Abot*, 52 ff.

85. Maimonides, *Guide of the Perplexed*, II, #8 (Chap. XXXII). We may realize here to what an extent the different translations of a single Scriptural verse have influenced philosophy. The passage, Job 38:37 says: "Who can number the clouds by wisdom . . . ?" Vulgate: "Quis enarrabit coelorum

rationem, et concentum coeli quis dormire faciat?" Authorized version: "Who can number the clouds in wisdom?"—or "Who can stay the bottles of heaven?" The interpretation of the Vulgate may be found also in Hebrew literature; cf. Abraham ibn Daud, Commentary on *Sefer Yezirah*, Chap. I, f. 27, col. 3. The Christian philosophers refer to the Vulgate version, which is their chief basis for the doctrine of spheric harmony. Cf Boethius, *De institutione musica*, in J. P. Migne, *Patr. lat.* LXIII, 1171. Also Aurelianus Reomensis, in M. Gerbert, *Scriptores* I, 32, who refers to the passage from Job and to the seven voices of the planets, linking them to the eight musical modes of the Church. This idea occurs also in cabbalistic literature in connection with Psalm 29:2-9, where the seven voices of God are interpreted in quite the same manner. Allusions to the astro-musical idea are very frequent. Kepler himself defended this theory in his *De harmonice mundi*, and Shakespeare refers to it in the beautiful passage, *The Merchant of Venice*, Act V, Sc. 1.

86. Cf. Moritz Steinschneider, *Al-Farabi*, p. 244 (note to p. 80).

87. H. G. Farmer, "Islamic Music" in *New Oxford History of Music* (see note 4 *supra*), I; *Historical Facts for the Arabian Musical Influence* (see note 34 *supra*); *A History of Arabian Music to the XIIIth Century* (London: Luzac & Co., 1929); *Al-Farabi's Arabic-Latin Writings on Music* (see note 9 *supra*); *The Sources of Arabian Music* (issued privately by the author, Bearsden, Scotland, 1940). Also, Rodolphe Baron d'Erlanger, *La Musique arabe*, 5 vols. 1930-49) (see note 9 *supra*).

88. Curt Sachs, *The Rise of Music in the Ancient World, East and West* (New York: W. W. Norton & Co., 1943), p. 281.

vi

WOMEN'S SONGS FROM

THE YEMEN: THEIR

TONAL STRUCTURE

AND FORM

Edith Gerson-Kiwi (Jerusalem)

𝒲omen's songs in folk societies have for a long time attracted ethnomusicologists in their search for more archaic strata of musical expression. This is true, for example, of the songs of women in Oriental countries, especially in Islamic civilizations. We may include, for present purposes, the Jewish women residing in Islamic countries, as their living conditions are not basically different from those of Islamic women. In the Jewish as in the Islamic folk communities, the social structure as a whole is built around the society of men, so that women are debarred from participation in social and, particularly, in religious ceremonies; as a result, they are excluded from literate and learned education, which in these Oriental-Jewish communities mainly serves the religious community life.

We are here primarily concerned with women's songs of the ancient community of Yemenite Jews, who lived in South Arabia for about

2,000 years, but were transplanted to Israel in their entirety about 1950. Thus, a unique opportunity presented itself for a close study of this ethnic group, which, as a whole, serves as an instance of rare stability and remoteness in all its folkways.[1] Here women's songs represent a genre of their own, apart from those of the men. This is mainly the result of the women's status in the greater family unit, which has imposed upon them a life of great seclusion. In their guarded precincts, a feminine musical culture has developed, which today reveals signs of greater antiquity than does the musical culture of the men. The men, obviously, have been exposed to the continuous influence of their environment, in spiritual matters as well as in material ones. Thus confined to their own little world, Yemenite women have developed unexpected abilities of their own. An amazing amount of handicraft, embroidery, story-telling, verse, and song has been produced by them. Their poetry, in the Arabic folk language, is oral and often improvised. It reveals a wealth of poetic types, from pure lyrics and shrewd proverbs to story-telling and the epic narration of historical or current political events.[2] The epic songs are especially featured in Yemenite Jewish women's songs, together with work- and love-songs, nursery rhymes, and dance and play tunes; foremost, however, are the various species of ceremonial wedding songs.[3]

The songs are performed in pure antiphonal style: two small groups of women, sitting huddled together, sing their way through the long epic songs by alternating with each other in half verses. This body of secular music, by the way, is one of the last strongholds of ancient antiphony, since in the liturgical music of the Yemenite Jews, as in most Western liturgical music, and especially in psalm-singing, the antiphonal manner of performance has given way to responsorial forms with their solo intonations.[4]

For purposes of accompaniment, only rhythmical instruments are used—the hand-drum and copper-plate—, in addition to the ever-present clapping of hands, the snapping of fingers, and the famous women's trills. Not one melody instrument seems to be known, and the absence of this type has helped to preserve in the women's songs some rare remnants of tone relations that are prerational, i.e., that are not determined by fixed ratios. Here, the human voice, unrestrained by the normalizing influence of melody instruments, still exercises its own laws. Such instruments, with their mechanical limitations and fixed tunings, eventually reduce the individual vocal inflections to measurable proportions. Owing to the absence of the melody instruments, any choice of intervallic combinations may be right on a given occasion. The multitude of non-standard tonal inflections undoubtedly indicates their original use as a direct means of expression and of textual or emotional characterization. The frequent return of certain tone clusters under similar conditions in the text works like a *Leitmotif* and thus prevents a state of tonal anarchy. There *is* a tonal order, but one that antedates the concept of fixed scale systems, of intervallic ratios, and also of the handling of *maqam*-models.

In the following, some examples of this prerational or prescalar music-making will be provided.[5]

The first example of Yemenite Jewish women's songs is a kind of bridal lamentation, sung by two young girls, with the accompaniment of a gong (copper plate). Speaking in terms of Western music history, we have here a bar-form (*AAB*), moving within the frame of a hexachord around a central tonic, a kind of *mesē-finalis* serving as a point of conjunction (see below). The two *A* sections are confined to the upper tetrachord, the *B* section to the lower region, thus providing excellent contrast. Melodic movement is mostly step by step, with microtonal inflections, and is built on small revolving motifs. Rhythmically, the melody proceeds in seven-beat periods (= patterns, transcribed in this article as single measures), but without any strong accents. The absence of such organizing accents facilitates the formation of ever new variants of melodic particles in the inner organization of each melodic period; the variants are produced through the stretching or contracting of the particles without change in the melodic pattern as a whole. As frequently observed in these pieces, the gong accompaniment is conceived independently: it proceeds in rhythmic periods of four beats. The constant crossing of the seven-beat period of the melody with the four-beat period of the gong part produces curiously overlapping accents. There is a kind of quarter-tone "leading"-note to the tonic-*mesē*. Here is one stanza taken out of the much longer song (as sung by Noemi and Yona Badichi):

Ex. 1: Yemen, Women's Song "Ya ualdi"   G-K 1747

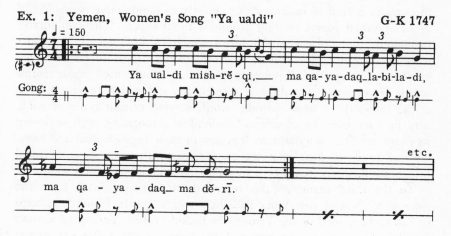

The melody of the second example comes from Northern Yemen, where the Jews were surrounded by a more primitive fellah culture. The piece is sung by two half-choirs of Jewish village women and is built on its own individual scale. We could call it a kind of Aeolian modal scale, with freely changing tonal inflections. But the song, taken as it is, with its unique melodic fluctuations, represents, rather, a melody type, which may itself be the starting point for a number of similar song types. Melodically, there is a broad up-and-down motion, within the wider span of an octave and more, in small diatonic and microtonic steps, without any leaps, but nevertheless with quite a variety of interval sizes. This early singing style does not rule out esthetic elaboration: thus, in true artistic fashion, a direct up-movement is countered by a down-movement that is retarded by small recurring down-up curves. The lack of dynamic accents in this type of song, with its broad melodic swing, is quite remarkable. There is an accompanying drum, again with its own rhythmic "ostinato," this time of seven beats, and, although the melody could also be divided into seven-beat periods, there is no fixed rhythmic coincidence between the two parts. It seems that melodic and rhythmic periods run along independently, with only the *chronos-protos* units (the eighth-note pulses) proceeding together:

Ex. 2:   Yemen, Women's Song "Ya Allah ana"(stanza no.4)   G-K 1239

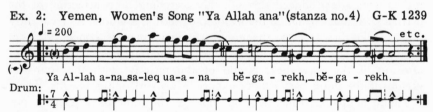

In the absence of a single organized tonal system, melodies tend to move in a kind of multimodality, mostly in conjunctive heptachordal or hexachordal forms circling around a tonal center. The conjunctive formations (i.e., "plagal" scalar forms which are built on two conjunct tetrachords and which feature a central tonic) seem to be of much greater age than the disjunctive ones (i.e., "authentic" scalar forms which are built on two disjunct tetrachords and which feature a tonic at the bottom). A small melodic motif, serving certain types of song, may be variegated by a series of individual intonations without losing its character as a melodic unit. It is just in these heptachordal and hexachordal types of song that we may discover the first signs of tonal organization, in the sense of a modality containing structural tones.

In the third example (also recorded and written down from the singing of Noemi and Yona Badichi), which comes from the ghetto of San'a, the capital of the Yemen, the melody reveals periods of various lengths. The periods are grouped by four, in the following order:

12/4, 10/4, 9/4, 9/4. The first three periods end with a different cadential tone. One of these tones, *e'*, may be regarded as the tonic of the entire piece. The other cadential tones are the supertonic, *f'*, which actually functions as the predominant, i.e., the melodic dominant, and the subtonic, *d'*. Thus, the melody starts on *c'*, the first line ends on *f'*, the second on *d'*, and the last two lines on the tonic, *e'*.

A further tendency to organize the melodic flow may be seen in the fact that all four lines are linked together through related initial motifs:

Ex. 3: Yemen, Women's Song "Sa'at ar-raḥman"   G-K 1745

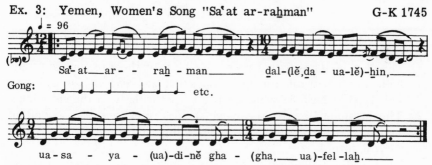

Quite different forms of modality are revealed in the next two examples, written down from the singing of Esther Yahud, an old woman from San'a. The first of them moves in the narrow space of a diminished pentachord, with the *finalis* on a quarter-tone, and with many repetitive variations in the numerous stanzas (not shown here):

Ex. 4: Yemen, Women's Song "Uttabina tabinati"   G-K 1993

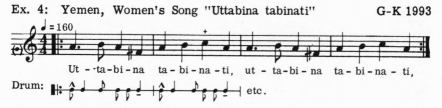

The next song follows along the same lines; it is built in two-part form, or modified bar-form (*AABB*), with the concluding part on the lower level of the pentachord. Indeed, we have here the conjunctive form of two neutral thirds (instead of a pentachord) revolving about a central tonic:

Ex. 5: Yemen, Women's Song "Ya etz marilon"   G-K 1994

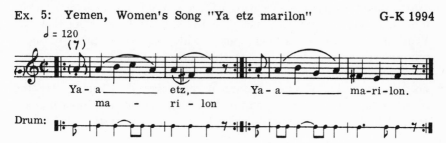

Side by side with these formations there are also partly pentatonic, i.e., gapped, structures:

Ex. 6: Yemen, Women's Song "Hubbak yebi"   **G-K 1991**

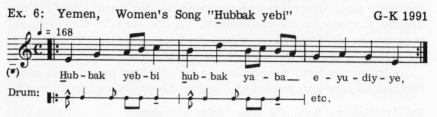

To these forms of multimodality many others could be added. Among all of them three main types are outstanding:

1) The class of songs with a narrow ambitus of three to four steps and with a symmetrical, songlike disposition and *ouvert-clos* cadenzas. This type of melodic structure is used particularly in the epic songs.

2) The hexachordal type revolving about a tonal *mesē* in a kind of bitonality, partly pentatonic and tending toward a more rational musical form.[6]

3) The broadly swinging type of diatonic melody, with a wider ambitus, though still in an unsteady, "prescalar" stage of intonation, and with a lack of dynamic accents.

The impression of archaism obtained from the Yemenite women's songs is further accentuated by the presence of the Biblical women's instruments, namely, the hand-played drum and gong (i.e., a copper-plate filled with some tinkling objects like rings or bracelets); these do not so much accompany the song as they accentuate the interludes between the stanzas, i.e., they act as pre- and postludes.

In many a way, these songs may be helpful in our renewed search for the primeval sources of musical forms and systems of tonal ratios. Since Erich von Hornbostel,[7] Robert Lachmann,[8] and Curt Sachs [9] called our attention to women's songs as sources illustrating early singing, others have joined in the collecting and study of such examples. Bartók's analyses of Croatian women's songs,[10] Kodály and Bartók's collections of children's songs,[11] Bence Szabolcsi's,[12] Constantin Brailoïu's,[13] and Walter Wiora's [14] studies of forms prior to pentatonality seem to indicate a general pattern of approach. In all probability there does not exist a simple gradation or "natural" evolution from two- and three-tone melodies to eight-tone melodies. Looking back, we note that our Yemenite women's songs built upon a wide diapason seem to be more primitive than those built on a narrow one, as the latter possess some distinctive qualities of tone relations and form. Perhaps the most developed of all early melodies—though never classified as such—were the one-tone lines of epic chant, and of Lamaistic, Vedic, and Biblical chant (i.e., of lection and psalmody), considering the great historical developments that were based on the same principle, namely, that of the spiritualized manifestation of speech melody.[15]

Notes

1. For general ethnological information, see Erich Brauer, *Ethnologie der jemenitischen Juden* (Heidelberg: C. Winter, 1934); Joseph Kafaḥ, *Jewish Life in Sanà* (Jerusalem: Ben-Zvi Institute, 1961), in Hebrew.

2. Shelomo D. Goitein, "Portrait of a Yemenite Weavers' Village," *Jewish Social Studies*, XVII, 1 (1955), pp. 3-26.

3. Johanna Spector, "Bridal Songs and Ceremonies from San'a, Yemen," *Studies in Biblical and Jewish Folklore*, ed. by Raphael Patai, Francis Lee Utley, and Dov Noy. (Bloomington: Indiana University Press, 1960), pp. 255-284.

4. For a discussion of the historical documents and forms of ancient Hebrew antiphony, see Hanoch Avernary, "Formal Structure of Psalms and Canticles in Early Jewish and Christian Chant," *Musica Disciplina*, VII (1953), pp. 1-13.

5. Additional examples and analysis appear in Edith Gerson-Kiwi, "Folk Music: Jewish," *Grove's Dictionary of Music and Musicians*, 5th ed., ed. by Eric Blom (London: Macmillan & Co., Ltd., 1954), Vol. III, pp. 304-313; and Edith Gerson-Kiwi, "Jüdische Musik," Section B, *Die Musik in Geschichte und Gegenwart*, ed. by Friedrich Blume (Kassel: Bärenreiter Verlag, 1949-   ), Vol. VII, col. 266 ff.

6. For interesting parallels of this modal type in African music, see Rose Brandel, *The Music of Central Africa* (The Hague: Martinus Nijhoff, 1961), Exx. 35 and 39, pp. 68-69.

7. Erich M. von Hornbostel, "Musikalische Tonsysteme," *Handbuch der Physik*, ed. by H. Geiger and K. Scheel (Berlin: J. Springer, 1926-29), Vol. VIII (1927), pp. 425 ff.

8. Robert Lachmann, *Jewish Cantillation and Song in the Isle of Djerba* (Jerusalem: Archives of Oriental Music, The Hebrew University, 1940), pp. 67 ff.

9. Curt Sachs, *The Rise of Music in the Ancient World, East and West* (New York: W. W. Norton & Co., 1943), p. 91.

10. Béla Bartók and A. B. Lord, *Serbo-Croatian Folk Songs* (New York: Columbia University Press, 1951).

11. Zoltán Kodály and Béla Bartók, *Children's Songs*, Corpus Musicae popularis Hungaricae I, 2nd ed. (Budapest: Academia Scientiarum Hungaricae, 1957).

12. Bence Szabolcsi, *Bausteine zu einer Geschichte der Melodie* (Budapest: Corvina, 1959), p. 16.

13. Constantin Brailoïu, "Sur une mélodie russe," *Musique russe*, ed. by Pierre Souvtchinsky *et al.*, Bibliothèque Internationale de Musicologie, Vol. II (Paris: Presses Universitaires de France, 1953), pp. 329-391.

14. Walter Wiora, Älter als die Pentatonik," *Studia Memoriae Belae Bartók Sacra*, ed., by Zoltán Kodály and L. Lajtha, 2nd ed. (Budapest: Aedes Academiae Scientiarum Hungaricae, 1957), pp. 185-208.

15. The present article is based on a paper read at the Eleventh Conference of the International Folk Music Council, Liège, Belgium, 1958.

A CHINESE PAINTING

OF THE T'ANG COURT

WOMEN'S ORCHESTRA

Shigeo Kishibe (Tokyo)

1

*I*n Curt Sachs's *The Rise of Music in the Ancient World,* *East and West,* the plate facing page 160 shows a Chinese painting that represents a women's orchestra.[1] The author borrowed this picture from Heinz Trefzger's article, "Das Musikleben der T'ang-zeit."[2] If it is true, as Sachs and Trefzger say, that the orchestra is performing for Emperor Ming Huang (Hsüan-tsung; reigned 712-756) and Empress Yang Kuei-fei, and if the picture does in fact depict an actual perform-ance by a women's orchestra of this time, the painting would provide one of the most important pieces of evidence for research in the music of the T'ang dynasty (618-907), which was one of the climaxes in Chinese music history.

In considering this apparently important evidence, we must first of all ascertain the reliability of the artist's testimony by determining the date of the painting. From the point of view of visual-art technique, it seems to have been painted in the Ming dynasty (1368-1662). But the subject matter, which has to do with musical instruments and also with instrumentation and musicians' costumes, seems, to a remarkable extent, to belong to the T'ang dynasty.

The theme of the painting, a nobleman and his wife listening to a women's orchestra composed of eighteen members, can also be found, to my knowledge, in three other paintings of the Ming dynasty and the Ch'ing dynasty (1616-1911):

1) "Ming Huang and Yang Kuei-fei Listening to Music" [3]

(see plate 1)

This is in the collection of the Worcester Art Museum, Worcester, Massachusetts. It is a silk scroll, in color, 52 inches in length and 11½ inches in height.

2) "Picture of Ming Huang Reviewing the Imperial Orchestra"

The owner of the painting is unknown. A photograph of it (in black and white) is owned by the Fogg Museum at Harvard University. The painting is accompanied by two scrolls of brush-written poems and comments by five Chinese of the Ming and Ch'ing dynasties.

3) "A Female Orchestra of the Han Court"

This is reproduced in color on page 88 of a novel, Chao Chün, Beauty in Exile, by Shu Ching (Mrs. Wu Lien-teh), Shanghai, 1934.[4]

However, another scroll painting, which seems to be much older than these four, is in the collection of the Art Institute of Chicago. (See plate 2.) Charles Fabens Kelly [5] has regarded this painting as a Sung dynasty imitation of an original painted by Chou Wên-chü, a famous painter of the Nan-t'ang dynasty (937-975), one of the "Five Dynasties" (900-975). Dr. Oswald Sirén [6] also regarded the painting as the Sung version of Chou Wên-chü's favorite motif, musical perform-ance by the palace orchestra. It seems to be true that the original paint-ing was done by Chou Wên-chü, since on the right end of the scroll there is a brush-written title, "Chou Wên-chü Ho-yüeh-t'u. Wu-shang-shên-p'in yeh" (Picture of an orchestra drawn by Chou Wên-chü. The most excellent masterpiece). Except for a color post card of part of the painting, which is printed by the Institute, the only reproduction of the scroll in color is in my book Tōdai Ongaku no Rekishiteki Kenkyū ("The Historical Study of Chinese Music in the T'ang Dynasty"),[7] where the entire scroll is reproduced to serve as the frontispiece of the second volume.

There are a number of paintings, sculptures, and clay figures of the T'ang dynasty that depict male and female musicians of the court and scenes that include musical ensembles and dancing. For example, wall paintings of the Buddhist cave temples of T'ung-huang in the northwest of China show dozens of scenes representing dancers and accompanying musicians in front of Buddha and Boddhisattvas.[8] There

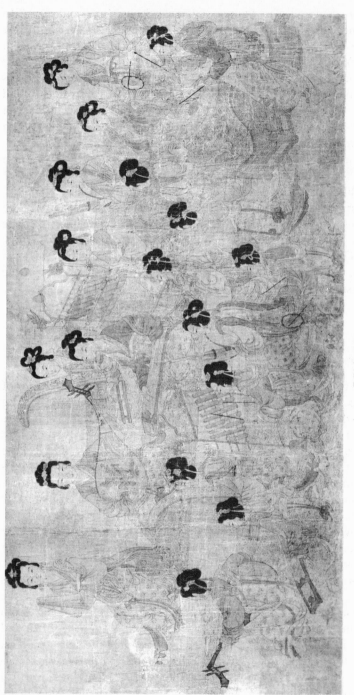

PLATE 1

Above: *Ming Huang and Yang Kuei-Fei Listening to Music* (Ming dynasty painting on silk), detail: left side of picture. (Courtesy *Worcester Art Museum, Worcester, Massachusetts.*)

Below : Detail: right side of same picture, showing eighteen instrumentalists.

are also many colored clay figures of female dancers and musicians.[9] In addition, the reliefs of twenty-four female musicians carved on the stone stand of the coffin of Wang Chien, the king of the Ch'ien-shu dynasty (901-925), offer us substantial information on seventeen kinds of instruments of the T'ang dynasty.[10] But in none of these art works is the representation of detailed aspects of the musical instruments and of playing techniques necessarily accurate. Detailed aspects of the instruments of the T'ang dynasty can, however, be judged with accuracy from the 75 musical instruments (which belong to 18 categories) preserved in the Imperial Treasury of Shō-sō-in. Most of these instruments were used in the ceremony celebrating Opening Eyes of the Great Buddha at the temple Tōdaiji in Nara, Japan, in 752 A.D.[11] But to certify that the instruments in the Shō-sō-in are of the same type as those of the T'ang dynasty, we must have detailed Chinese illustrations, concerning which there is ample information in literary sources.[12] The painting we discuss here, however, is the best of such illustrations, provided it be a true representation of the orchestra in the T'ang dynasty.

II

Because the Chicago copy (the Sung copy [13] of the Art Institute of Chicago) is far better than the four copies of the Ming and Ch'ing dynasties, which were referred to at the beginning of this paper, it is not necessary to consider the latter group in detail. However, since the Otto copy (the later Ming or early Ch'ing copy [14] in the Otto Collection), which is reproduced by Sachs and Trefzger, is now well-known through Sachs's book, it may be desirable to point out some of the reasons why the Chicago copy should be regarded as superior to the Otto copy.

It is obvious that the Chicago copy is older than the Otto copy from the standpoint of the visual arts, that is, with respect to painting technique and the representation of human figures and of costumes. The orchestra of the Otto copy consists of eighteen musicians. As Sachs pointed out, at the left end of the picture (i.e., at the right end of the orchestra itself) is a clapper (*p'ai-pan*) and at the right end, a big drum (*ta-ku*). The sixteen other instruments belong to eight categories and are present in pairs, from left to right, representing the lute (*p'i-p'a*), long zither (*chêng*), angular harp (*k'ung-hou* or *shu-k'ung-hou*), metallophone, or gong-chime (*fang-hsiang*), mouth organ (*shêng*), vertical flute (*ch'ih-pa*) or oboe (*pi-li*), transverse flute (*ti*), and side drum

PLATE 2

Chou Wên-chü: Picture of an Orchestra (Sung dynasty copy). (*Chicago Art Institute*; from Oswald Sirén, *Chinese Painting*, Vol. III, plate 126.)

(*chieh-ku*.) [15] The arrangement in the picture is shown in the following diagram:

```
            harp                    mouth organ        side drum
clapper                    gong chime
      lute                                        oboe
                  zither                  flute
                        oboe                          big drum
          harp              mouth organ      flute
lute              gong chime
      zither                    side drum
```

The clapper on the left and the big drum on the right are beyond the edges of two carpets, on each of which a group of eight musicians sits. As Sachs assumed, the clapper player seems to be the leader.

However, in the Sung copy of Chicago there are two clappers instead of one, just as the other instruments (excluding the big drum) are in pairs. The clapper players sit, not at the right end of the orchestra as does the single clapper player in the Otto copy, but at the left end of the other musicians (except for the drummer). This makes the total number of musicians nineteen instead of eighteen. No historical source from the T'ang dynasty refers to a clapper player as leader of an ensemble; on the other hand, in the Ming and Ch'ing dynasties the instrument did become more important, and its player did act as a leader. The change in the number of players and in the position of the clapper in the Ming and Ch'ing dynasty paintings, as compared to the Sung copy, obviously represents the corresponding historical modification in the status of this instrument.

The shape of each instrument is also slightly modified in the later paintings. The biggest difference can be found in the big drum. Although no illustration of a court orchestra of the T'ang dynasty shows the figure of the big drum depicted in the Sung copy, this type often appears among pre-T'ang archaeological materials, especially those of the Han dynasty. As for the kind of big drum shown in the Otto copy, this was common in the Ming and Ch'ing dynasties.

Other instruments in the later paintings also show small changes, which are not necessarily basic. It is admirable how well most of these instruments are illustrated in their older, T'ang dynasty forms. This becomes obvious when comparisons are made with similar instruments painted in other pictures of the Ming and Ch'ing dynasties. The best example may be found in the lute (*p'i-p'a*), which is illustrated with a much narrower body and more frets in the paintings of the Ming and Ch'ing dynasties than are evident in today's *p'i-p'a*.

III

The theme of the Sung painting in Chicago is more clearly apparent than that of the others. It illustrates the female orchestra performing for a nobleman who is in the company of his wife, five other ladies, five gentlemen, and a child. The nobleman sits on a platform surrounded on three sides by screens, and his wife sits on a chair to the right and front of him. The musicians of each group sit on a blue carpet, while the big drum player is on her own carpet. Another carpet, designed with a Chinese phoenix, the significance of which is unknown, is between the musicians and the platform. The performance is represented as being out of doors; behind the screens some trunks of large trees may be seen.

The content of the picture is organized in a way that easily reminds us of the *li-yüan*, a kind of music conservatory of the T'ang court, which was established by Ming Huang in 714 A.D., the third year of his reign.

The principal organization in charge of court music in this period consisted of two departments in the Ministry of Rites and Music (*t'ai-sh'ang-ssŭ*). One of these, the *t'ai-yüeh-shu* (department of music), was concerned with Confucian ceremonial music (*ya-yüeh*), native art music (*su-yüeh*), and foreign art music (*hu-yüeh*), while the other, the *ku-ch'ui-shu*, was concerned with military band music. The musicians in the departments were governmental slaves. In the period of Ming Huang, who was very fond of music and dance and was the greatest sponsor of music and dance in the history of Chinese music, another institution was established for the performance of music and dance mainly by female court musicians or singing girls. It was called *chiao-fang*. In this period, the *chiao-fang* had more than three thousand female musicians. In addition, Ming Huang built one more conservatory, the *li-yüan*, to teach himself his favorite music, called *fa-chü*. This consisted of native Chinese songs in a developed style that dated from the Han dynasty and had formerly been called *ch'ing-shang-yüeh*. Actually, the *fa-chü* was a style of music that resulted from a combination of Chinese songs with foreign music, mainly the music of India, which streamed eastward through Chinese Turkestan and became most popular. Ming Huang's new conservatory was located in a pear garden (*li-yüan*) in the courtyard, northeast of the palace in the capital Chan-an. Its staff consisted of three hundred excellent performers selected from the slave musicians of the *t'ai-yüeh-shu*, hundreds of female musicians from the *chiao-fang*, and over thirty child-singers. *Shin-t'ang-shu* ("The

New History of T'ang"), compiled by the governmental historians
under the emperor's order, states in the chapter on music (Chap. 22)
that the emperor himself taught the students and never overlooked their
errors.[16]

All of the nineteen instruments illustrated in the painting at the
Chicago Art Institute were utilized in the instrumental ensemble of
the li-yüan. Since more instruments (about fifty kinds) were in use in
the art music of the T'ang court, the ensemble seems to be rather small
in size. Nevertheless, the instrumentation is adequate for an ensemble
of the li-yüan. The fa-chü music, which was taught in the li-yüan, was
a most refined modification and blending of native Chinese and foreign
art music, a combination for which the more specifically native or
foreign instruments would not have been appropriate. The four-stringed
lute (p'i-p'a)—which had originated in Persia, but was regarded as a
Chinese instrument in the T'ang dynasty because it had been introduced
to China centuries earlier in the Han dynasty—was used instead of
the five-stringed lute (wu-hsien-p'i-p'a). The latter, which originated in
India, appeared in China only one century before the T'ang dynasty and
from then on was considered one of the most representative of foreign
instruments.[17] The situation with respect to the harp (k'ung-hou or
shu-k'ung-hou) was the same as that just described concerning the lute.[18]
The long zither (chêng) and the mouth organ (shêng) had long been
the representatives of instruments used for the art music of the court.
The transverse flute (ti) may have been either native or foreign. The
oboe (pi-li) and the side drum (chieh-ku) were representative of foreign instruments. The gong-chime (fang-hsiang), clapper (p'ai-pan),
and vertical flute (ch'ih-pa) were new Chinese instruments, constructed
in the T'ang dynasty or a little earlier. Finally, the big drum was the
contemporary modification of the big drum that had long been the
traditional drum of China.

In short, the size and the instrumentation of the orchestra shown
in the picture at Chicago seem to represent adequately that of the li-
yüan orchestra.

IV

Notwithstanding what has been said, we must not be too hasty to
accept the painting as representing a performance of the li-yüan female
musicians for Emperor Ming Huang. Caution is necessary, because the
custom of giving outdoor concerts with this type of ensemble may
have existed also in other places and times, for example, in the T'ang
dynasty after Ming Huang, in the Five Dynasties when the original

painting was made, and even in the Sung dynasty when a remnant of T'ang court music was in fashion at the Sung court. Dr. Sirén has made two assumptions in his book, *Chinese Painting:*

The main person of the audience is a distinguished-looking gentleman with a long pointed beard and a high cap, who resembles Han Hsi-tsai (as he is represented in Ku Hun-chung's picture) so closely that one is tempted to conclude that the minister is also the principal personage in this picture. Yet it must be admitted that certain other figures make it more probable that the entertainment takes place in the garden of the imperial palace in Nanking, in which case the august person who is seated isolated on the daïs would be the "puppet" emperor Li Yü (Hou-chu).[19]

There is no reason to deny these assumptions, which are made mainly from the point of view of the visual arts. But no direct proof can be found to sustain them.

The bibliographies of paintings compiled after the Five Dynasties need to be checked. For instance, in *Hsüan-ho-hua-fu*, the most comprehensive bibliography written in the period of Emperor Hui-tsung (1101-1125) of the Northern Sung dynasty, paintings with the following titles are attributed to Chou Wên-chü:

1) *An-yüeh-kung-nü-t'u* (Picture of Court Ladies Playing Music)
2) *An-yüeh-shih-nü-t'u* (Picture of Court Gentlemen and Ladies Playing Music)
3) *Ho-yao-shih-nü-t'u* (Picture of Court Gentlemen and Ladies Collecting Medicines)
4) *Ming Huang Ho-ch'i-t'u* (Ming Huang Watching a Group at Chess)

Neither in this bibliography nor in any other can we find an entry that reads *Ho-yüeh-t'u* (Picture of an Orchestra), which is the title of the Chicago copy. Possibly No. 1 had the original title *Ming Huang Ho-yüeh-t'u* and was the model from which the Chicago picture was copied. But this is no more than an assumption.[20]

A question is raised by the symmetrical arrangement of the two groups of musicians in the Chicago picture. Is the symmetry present only for pictorial purposes? This question reminds one of a short account in the chapter on music in *Shin-t'ang-shu*, in the section on Ming Huang. It states that when the emperor began his reign he ordered a prince to organize the musicians in his private household into the system known as the *t'ai-ch'ang-ssŭ* (Ministry of Rites and Music) and to divide the musicians into two parties so that they could compete with each other. Another example of the idea emphasizing contrast between two groups is the system of *Erh-pu-ch'i* (Two Kinds of Music), which is an organized repertory of fourteen dance tunes that are divided into two groups: the *li-pu-ch'i* (the group of musical works performed by musicians standing), and the *tso-pu-ch'i* (the group of musical works performed by musicians sitting). The concept of standing and sitting musicians comes from the *ya-yüeh* (Confucian ceremonial music), which divides the music into two groups, performed under and upon the stage. Naturally, this Confucian concept is based on the philosophical idea of "Yang and Yin" (male and female). In spite of these concrete examples of the principle of organizing music in two sections, we are still without a direct explanation for the symmetrical arrangement of the female orchestra in the Chicago picture.

One might look in certain other directions for help, but unfortunately they too will fail to provide evidence resolving the problem of whether the painting represents Ming Huang and Yang Kuei-fei reviewing the female orchestra in the court garden or merely a nobleman and his wife listening to his private female orchestra.[21] As a conclusion, one might, in common with most post-Sung commentators on the copies, resolve the problem in the affirmative. Furthermore, it might be presumed that the orchestra consists of members of the *li-yüan* (conservatory) and that the outdoor concert is held in the *li-yüan* (pear garden). However, as I have stated above, this conclusion is no more than an assumption, which rests only on circumstantial evidence. But the greatest importance of the painting lies in its not only illustrating a female orchestra owned by a nobleman (emperor, aristocrat, or high-class official) of the T'ang dynasty, but in its doing so with remarkable attention to detail. An extended discussion of this point, which involves a comparison of the instruments in the Chicago picture with those concerning which we have evidence in other archaeological and literary sources, will be published by the present author in the near future in the next volume of his work on the historical study of Chinese music in the T'ang dynasty.

ADDENDUM

Trefzger, in his *Die Musikleben der T'ang-Zeit*, assumes that the Otto copy represents the occasion described in *Shin-t'ang-shu*, Chap. 22, in the section on Emperor Hsüan-tsung (Ming Huang), when the emperor listened to a new tune performed by child-musicians of the *li-yüan* at the palace of Chang-shêng-tien at Li-shan on a birthday of Yang-Kuei-fei. Trefzger might not have understood the real meaning of the term "hsiao-pu" in the account in *Shing-t'ang-shu*, for the term applies to the section of child-musicians belonging to the *li-yüan* but no child-musician is shown in the painting. Cf. Kishibe, *The Historical Study of Chinese Music in the T'ang Dynasty*, Vol. I, Chap. 3, pp. 469-471.

Notes

1. Dr. Sachs's comment below the picture reads: "Chinese women's orchestra performing before Emperor Ming Huang (713-756 A.D.). From a silk scroll in Dr. Otto's collection, Canton. After Heinz Trefzger.—The conducting lady agitates a clapper, and in the rear a girl strikes a big drum; the other instruments—harps, long zithers, lutes; transverse flutes, oboes, mouth organs; metallophones and hourglass drums—are played in pairs."

2. In *Sinica*, XIII (1938), p. 58.

3. See George Rowley, "A Chinese Scroll of the Ming Dynasty, 'Ming Huang and Yang Kuei-fei Listening to Music,'" *Worcester Art Museum Annual*, II (1936-37), pp. 63-79.

4. The comment below the picture reads: "A female orchestra of the Han Court, from an ancient painting in the author's possession." Of course, "Han Court" in this title is a mistake. I thank Mr. Robert Garfias, School of Music, University of Washington (Seattle), who has called my attention to this book.

5. Charles Fabens Kelly, "Chinese Painting," *The Art Institute of Chicago Quarterly*, XLV, 4 (1951), pp. 67-74.

6. Oswald Sirén, *Chinese Painting, Leading Masters and Principles*, Vol. I (New York: The Ronald Press Co., 1956), pp. 169 and 170.

7. 2 vols., Tōkyōdaigaku Shuppan Kai (Tokyo: University of Tokyo Press), 1960 and 1961, 1,000 pages in Japanese, with English summary (46 pages) in the second volume. A black and white photograph of the painting is printed in Oswald Sirén, *Chinese Painting*, Vol. III, plates 126-127.

8. Sir Mark Aurel Stein, *The Thousand Buddhas: Ancient Buddhist Paintings From Cave-Temples of Tun-huang at the Westmost Border of China* (London: B. Quaritch, Ltd., 1921); Paul Pelliot, *Les Grottes de Touen-huang*, 6 vols. (Paris: P. Geuthner, 1920-24).

9. Oswald Sirén, "Über die Stilentwicklung der chinesischen Grabfiguren," *Wiener Beiträge zur Kunst- und Kultur-Geschichte Asiens*, VI (1931), pp. 3-29.

10. Shigeo Kishibe, "Zenshoku Shiso Ōken Kanza Sekichō no Nijūshi Gakugi ni tsuite" (Twenty-four Female Musicians Carved on the Stone Coffin of Wang Chien in the Ch'ien-shu Dynasty), in *Kokusai Tōhōgakusha Kaigi Kiyō* (The Transactions of the International Conference of Orientalists in Japan), No. 1 (Tokyo: Institute of Eastern Culture, 1956), pp. 9-21.

11. Sukeyasu Shiba, Kenzō Nagaya, Ryōichi Taki, and Shigeo Kishibe, "Shōsōin Gakki Chosa Gaihō" (Preliminary Report on the Survey of Musical Instruments of Shōsōin), in *Shoryōbu Kiyō* (Bulletin of the Archives and Mausolea Division, Imperial Household Agency), Nos. 1-3 (1951-53), pp. 10-26, 28-53, and 74-88.

12. *Sui-shu* (History of Sui Dynasty), compiled by Wei Chêng, 629 A.D. (Shanghai: Kai-ming-shu-tien edition, 1934), chapters 13-15, music; *Chü-t'ang-shu* (Old History of T'ang Dynasty), compiled by Liu Hsü, 945 A.D. (Shanghai: Kai-ming-shu-tien edition, 1934), chapters 28-31, music; *Shin-t'ang-shu* (New History of T'ang Dynasty), compiled by Ou Yang-hsiu, 1060 A.D. (Shanghai: Kai-ming-shu-tien edition, 1934), chapters 21-22, music; *T'ung-tien* by Tu Yu, 801 A.D. (Shanghai: Wan-yu-wên-k'u edition, 1935), chapters 141-147, music; *T'ang-liu-tien*, compiled by Emperor Hsüan-tsung, 739 A.D. (Kyoto: Konoe edition, 1724); *T'ang-hui-yao* by Wang P'u, 961 A.D., chapters 32-34, music; *Yüeh-fu-tso-lu* by Tuan An-chieh, later T'ang (Shanghai: Ts'ung-shu-chi-ch'eng edition, 1936); *Chiao-fang-chi* by Ts'ui Ling-ch'in, middle T'ang (Shanghai: Ts'ung-shu-chi-ch'eng edition, 1936); *Chieh-ku-lu* by Nan Cho, 848 A.D. (Shanghai: Ts'ung-shu-chi-ch'eng edition, 1936); *Yüeh-shu* (Book on Music) by Ch'en Yang, 1101 A.D. (Sung dynasty edition).

13. Beside Dr. Kelly's thorough discussion of the date of the imitation, we need further investigation, from the musical point of view, to determine this date. I would point out here only that the whole treatment of the painting, including the details of the musical instruments and of the instrumentation, shows what must be a modification of the original, a modification in keeping with the Sung style; this means that the Sung copy reflects the state of musical instruments in the Sung dynasty, which is slightly different from that in the Five Dynasties, the period of the original painter, Chou Wên-chü. The state of instruments in the Five Dynasties is the same as that in the T'ang dynasty.

14. The Otto copy is closest to the Worcester copy (being a little earlier or later than the latter), which was done in the later Ming dynasty. It is obvious that the Otto copy is an imitation of the Worcester copy or *vice versa*. But it is difficult to determine which is earlier, since the photographs of both Sachs and Trefzger are not clear enough to make a decision possible.

15. For discussion of these instruments and of musical instruments of the T'ang dynastry as a whole, the reader is referred to the following writings: Shigeo Kishibe, *Tōyō no Gakki to sono Rekishi* (Musical Instruments and Their History) (Tokyo: Kōbundō, 1948), in Japanese, illustrated, 270 pp.; "The Origin of the P'i-p'a (Chinese Lute)," *Transactions of the Asiatic Society of Japan*, Second Series, XIX (1940), pp. 259-304; "The Origin of the K'ung-hou (Chinese Harp)," *The Journal of the Society for Research in Asiatic Music*, No. 9 (1954), pp. 1-51; "Twenty-four Female Musicians Carved on the Stone Coffin of Wang Chien" (cf. note 10 above); Shiba, Nagaya, Taki, and Kishibe (cf. note 11 above); Kenzo Hayashi (Nagaya), *Tung-ya-yüeh-ch'i-k'ao* (Studies on Asian Musical Instruments) (Peking: Yin-yüeh-ch'u-pan-she, 1962), in Chinese. Except for the clapper, all of the instruments in the painting were brought to Japan in ancient times. Seven of them, namely, the lute, zither, mouth organ, oboe, transverse flute, side drum, and big drum, are still in use in the Gagaku ensemble today, although some of them have been slightly changed. In the comment by Dr. Sachs, the term, "hourglass drum," requires modification. The *chieh-ku* is a cylindrical drum placed on a stand horizontally and played with two sticks on both heads. The picture is not clear enough to permit identification of the vertical pipes. There are two possibilities, oboe and vertical flute. In the Chicago copy it is obvious that both are represented—one pipe is an oboe and the other a vertical flute. In the comment by Li Wen-

tien that accompanies the painting of which the Fogg Museum owns a photograph (see p. 105), there are a few errors. He mistakes the *chêng* for the *sê* (a 25-stringed long zither used in the *Ya-yüeh*, the Confucian ceremonial music), and he names the big drum *chang-ku*, although it would have been named *ta-ku* in the T'ang dynasty. He mistakenly suggests that the side drum, which is a barrel drum and should be called the *chieh-ku*, has another name, *ti-êrh-ku* (the second drum), which is actually the name of one of four big and small hourglass drums. Two vertical pipes are not clear enough in the picture to enable one to decide whether to apply the name oboe (*pi-li*) to them, as Li Wen-tien does, or the name vertical flute (*ch'ih-pa*). Also, a few names of instruments given by Dr. Rowley in his article on the Worcester copy (see note 3 above) should be corrected: *p'i-p'a* (mandolin) on page 74 to *p'i-p'a* (lute); *ch'in* (psaltery) on pages 76 and 77 to *chêng* (long zither). In comments by Dr. Sirén on page 170 of his *Chinese Painting*, Vol. I (cf. notes 6 and 19), "chi" should be corrected to "chêng" and "hu-ch'in" should be taken out.

16. Shigeo Kishibe, *The Historical Study of Chinese Music in the T'ang Dynasty* (cf. note 7 above). The two volumes of this work are mainly concerned with detailed research into the various musical organizations at the court of the T'ang dynasty.

17. Kishibe, "The Origin of the P'i-p'a," pp. 288-301.

18. Kishibe, "The Origin of the K'ung-hou," pp. 33-41.

19. Vol. I, p. 170 (cf. note 6 above).

20. There is a Sung dynasty painting that represents a banquet attended by ten court ladies, some of whom play instruments, namely, a lute, *chêng* (long zither), *shêng* (mouth organ), *pi-li* (oboe), and *p'ai-pan* (clapper). The subject seems to be an imitation of Chou Wên-chü's idea of a female orchestra. Cf. Oswald Sirén's *Chinese Painting*, Vol. III, plate 132.

21. a) The position and the order of the instruments do not help us to determine the kind of music.

b) The organization of "The Ten Kinds of Music" (*Shih-pu-ch'i*), which consisted of an organized repertory of ten kinds of Chinese and foreign music and was established at the beginning of the T'ang dynasty, has no relation to the structure of this female orchestra.

c) The organization of "The Four Groups of Musical Instruments" (*T'ai-ch'ang-ssŭ-pu-yüeh*) has a direct relation to the instrumentation of the female orchestra in that all of the instruments except the vertical flute (*ch'ih-pa*) are the most basic and common instruments of the four groups: the lute, long zither, harp, oboe, transverse flute, gong-chime, and clapper belong to the *hu-pu* (or *fa-chü-pu* in the Sung dynasty); the oboe, transverse flute, clapper, and side drum belong to the *kuei-tsu-pu*, and the big drum belongs to the *ta-ku-pu*. The fourth group was not concerned with the art music of the court, but with the instrumentation of the accompaniment for theatrical performances. Cf. Kishibe, *The Historical Study of Chinese Music in the T'ang Dynasty*, Vol. II, chapter 7, pp. 439-500.

MODAL VARIANTS

IN MEDIEVAL

SECULAR MONOPHONY

Theodore Karp (Davis, California)

$\mathcal{W}$hile studying the chansons of the Châtelain de Coucy (c. 1170-1203), I observed that the modal structures of many melodies vary—sometimes widely—from one MS reading to another. In the literature dealing with medieval secular monophony, there are occasional bits of information regarding the lack of consistency in the preservation of modal structures, but, on the whole, the entire area of modal analysis is treated in such cavalier fashion that one might assume it to be devoid of worthwhile subjects of inquiry.

Some modern treatments of mode in troubadour and trouvère music leave the impression that all of these melodies are either in one of the church modes or in major or minor. Other possibilities, though not ruled out, are not actively considered. Since the combined resources of this proposed dichotomy provide for finals on six of the seven white keys, and since the MSS indicate relatively few accidentals, a reasonable case may be made for such views provided that the definition of mode comprehends only a characteristic scale formation and final.[1] However, there is no universal agreement regarding the proper usage of the term,

118

"mode." The problem of definition is one that has engaged the attention of many eminent scholars, including Curt Sachs. The present writer has been much influenced by his remarks on mode in *The Rise of Music in the Ancient World, East and West*, particularly in the section on "Musical Systems in General." For purposes of this article, mode is to be defined as a pattern which may be expressed in terms of a characteristic scale formation and which, in addition, exhibits specific interval relationships between salient notes. These notes, which I shall call focal centers, are to be established by cataloguing the most prominent notes of each phrase: the first and final, the peak and nadir, repeated notes, and notes reached or left by skips. Under this system, melodies with the same underlying scale formation will receive different modal classification if they vary significantly with regard to interval relationships between focal centers. Thus, the changes in modal structure to be discussed may: 1) emphasize a difference of scale pattern; 2) emphasize a difference in the relationship between focal centers; 3) affect both characteristics equally.

The first of these three varieties of mode change occurs among the different readings of *L'an que rose ne feuille* (R. 1009), by the Châtelain de Coucy. In the *MS du Roi* (M²) and the *MS de Noailles* (T), the final of the piece is *f*. *B♭* is indicated consistently in the M reading; although this accidental is absent from T, one may reasonably assume that it was added in performance. The scale pattern to be derived from these two readings is thus identical with major. In the *Chansonnier de l'Arsenal* (K) and in MSS P and X, the range lies a fifth higher than in M and T; in other words, the final falls on *c'*. All three MSS use *b♭* consistently. The scale to be derived from these readings is the equivalent of Mixolydian. The *Chansonnier Cangé* (O) contains two readings of the piece, and these employ a third range, with a final on *g*. These readings use both *b♮* and *b♭*; in addition, the second employs *f♯* twice. Thus there is an alternation, curious for the time, between "major-" and "minor-sounding" passages. It is, of course, conceivable that the differences in scale patterns indicated in the notation of these three families of readings were resolved by the addition of further accidentals in performance. However, the written use of both *b♮* and *b♭* in O would, if applied to the other MSS, require an alternation between *e♮* and *e♭* in K, P, and X, and an alternation between *a♮* and *a♭* in M and T. The written use of *e♭* in the sources is rare, and I have not yet encountered the written use of *a♭*. The adoption of both would represent an extreme course, which, in my opinion, is not justified by data at present available.

In examining the different readings of *Quant voi esté* (R. 1450), an *opus dubium* attributable to the Châtelain, we find the second variety of mode change, in which the interval distances between focal centers vary. Again there are three different types of readings. One occurs in the *Chansonnier de Saint-Germain-des-Prés* (U); the second, in the *Chansonnier Cangé* (O); the third, in MSS K, N, and X. The ranges of the last two types are identical; that of U is lower. However, the interval relationship between the U reading and those of the other MSS does not remain constant throughout. In lines 1 and 3, the reading of U is a fourth lower than those of the other sources, while in the remaining lines it is a fifth lower. A further complication arises from the fact that the last three notes of lines 2, 4, and 7 are a second lower in O than in K, N, and X.

Ex.1. Quant voi esté et le tens revenir   (R. 1450).[3]

Line 4

Line 5

Line 6

Line 7

The sudden shifts in pitch shown in this example cause the intervallic relationship between focal centers to vary from one of the above-mentioned three types to another, even though corresponding intervals between successive notes of the melody are normally the same. The opening note of the K-N-X reading is a fourth above the final, whereas it is a fifth above the final in the O and U readings. The opening note is clearly established as a focal center because it is also the first note of lines 2-6 in K, N, and X, while it is the first note of all lines in O. Whereas the O and K-N-X readings differ in this one respect, they are similar or identical in most others. On the other hand, the similarity between the O and U readings in this detail is only superficial; the differences between the two, as shown above, are more basic. The melody of *Quant voi esté* is in bar-form and may be described as a rounded chanson according to Gennrich's terminology. Because the variants discussed remain constant in repetition, they are apparently the result of intent rather than of oversight.

The third category of mode change appears in *A vous, amant, plus qu'a nule autre gent* (R. 679), also by the Châtelain de Coucy. In this work there are two main focal centers, the final and the recitation tone. In the readings of MSS K, P, X, and O, these centers are a major second apart. In the readings of MSS M, T, A, R, and V, the centers are a major third apart, while in U the interval in question is sometimes a major third and sometimes a minor third. If we turn our attention to the interval pattern of the scale, we find the following. In MSS M, T, A, R, and V, the interval between the tonic and the degree below is a minor second. In MSS U, K, P, and X, that interval is a major second. In MS O, the interval quality varies: at first it is major; later, a sharp ($f\sharp$) indicated at the cadence of line 7 changes it to minor. In MSS M, T, A, R, and V, the interval between the tonic and the third degree is major; in MSS K, P, and X, the interval is consistently minor; in MSS O and U, the interval is sometimes major, but more often minor. One therefore finds a melody with a distinctly major cast in one group of MSS, with a distinctly minor feeling in a second group of MSS, and with a strangely ambivalent feeling in the remaining two sources (O and U).

From among the 19 melodies attributable to the Châtelain that survive in more than one MS family, 12 present changes of mode of one sort or another in various readings.[4] Admittedly a few of these examples are not as strong as the ones chosen for discussion; some readers may cavil at their inclusion in the above summary. But even if the weaker examples are omitted, the proportion of the remaining ones to the total is disturbingly high.

Mode change between readings is by no means restricted to the output of this one trouvère. Random findings—based both on secondary literature and on primary sources—show clearly that mode change occurs not only in other trouvère works,[5] but in the troubadour and Minnesinger repertoires [6] as well. However, its normal rate of occurrence in the trouvère repertoire as a whole may well be lower than the one cited with regard to the works of the Châtelain and borne out by the data given in note 5.

One readily available example of mode change appears in Friedrich Ludwig's contribution to Guido Adler's *Handbuch der Musikgeschichte*. Ludwig gives first the well-known chanson by Raimbaut de Vaqueiras, *Kalenda maya*, and then an anonymous trouvère contrafactum, *Souvent souspire* (R. 1506).[7] The troubadour melody is substantially modified in the contrafactum version, and this modification affects modal characteristics. The two pieces end on the same final, but the first eight phrases of the contrafactum are for the most part a second lower than the corresponding phrases of the model.

A second example is provided by J. A. Westrup in his chapter on "Medieval Song" in the *New Oxford History of Music*. In discussing *A l'entrada del tens clar*, Westrup states:

> More than one editor has suspected an error in the latter part of the song; and this supposition is confirmed by a three-part setting of the tune to the Latin words 'Veris ad imperia,' which shows that from bar 13 onwards the solo version is a tone too low. The mistake may have arisen because at the right pitch the melody requires both F$\sharp$ and C$\sharp$.[8]

Westrup then gives an emended transcription. It should be noted, parenthetically, that his main point of discussion concerns form rather than mode. By carefully stating both the evidence and his train of thought, Westrup guides the reader and yet permits full exercise of individual discretion.

This writer would prefer a slightly different description of the modal problem encountered in *A l'entrada del tens clar*. It is obvious that each medieval melody originally had only one musical text. Any departure from that text—intentional or otherwise—may be described as an error or mistake if we use these words in their widest senses. Nevertheless, in view of the number and significance of the variants among different readings of medieval monophonic pieces, it seems essential that we differentiate as far as possible between inadvertent slips and intentional changes. The former may undoubtedly be disregarded. The latter, however, should be carefully studied for they may yield valuable insight into medieval musical concepts. With regard to *A l'entrada del tens clar*, there is no particular reason to ascribe the variants in the monophonic version to carelessness; indeed, Westrup cites one reason for believing them to be the result of deliberate change.[9] Before reaching our main conclusion, one further example may not be amiss.

The original melody to *La douce vois du rossignol salvage* (R. 40) by the Châtelain de Coucy survives in nine sources.[10] All readings except one end on *d* and are clearly in the Dorian mode. The one exception is the reading in V. The first five phrases of this reading lie a fourth higher than their counterparts in other sources. However, the reading does not end on *g*, as one might expect, but on *a*. To facilitate comparison between the V reading and a more representative one, that of the *Chansonnier Cangé* (O), the former is transposed down a fourth in the following example.

Ex. 2. La douce vois du rossignol salvage (R. 40).

Line 6

Line 7

Line 8

The variants before the end of the fifth phrase are not particularly important. However, the two readings fail to agree in any of the last four cadences; the variants here affect the analysis of mode. This example differs from others, such as *A l'entrada del tens clar*, in that one can with ease assess the dependability of the conflicting variants. Because V has a very poor reputation with regard to the authenticity of its musical readings in general and because this reading in particular is not corroborated by any other, one can promptly label the V variants as corrupt. It is possible to speculate that the variants involving the last two musical units of line 6 and the first of line 7 arose because of a slip in clef reading. The material in V from the penultimate unit of line 7 to the end is obviously placed a second too high. However, taken together, these variants exhibit a certain musical logic. Each of the last three lines ends on *a*, the last two ending with the ternaria, *g-f♯-e* (that is, according to the transposition adopted in the example). While the V ending is unusual, it is nevertheless well prepared; it seems to be the result of a deliberate plan.

A prime object of this paper was to demonstrate the existence of a sizable body of melodies surviving with intentional modal variants. The exact proportion existing between this body and the surviving repertoire, as well as the specific limitations of the former, can be determined only after further research. Nevertheless, the sampling of evidence now at hand seems enough to permit one to conclude that the medieval secular musician did not feel bound to adhere to the original mode of a melody. Apparently he was free to alter mode provided the melodic outline was retained.

Before closing, I should like to return briefly to a topic touched upon in passing, namely *musica ficta*. The addition of accidentals in performance may, of course, alter modal characteristics. I have previously had occasion to point out how incorrect suggestions concerning accidentals can produce a misrepresentation of mode.[11] The paucity of information at present available on the application of *musica ficta* to secular monophony can only be deplored. While this deficiency cannot be remedied in these pages, two remarks may furnish a pertinent addendum to the preceding inquiry.

> 1. Inasmuch as the sources show divergent usage of written accidentals, there is no reason to postulate that the medieval musician treated unwritten accidentals in a fixed and consistent manner.
> 2. It is poor policy to disregard written accidentals that do not fit into present conceptions of medieval modal practices.

A comparison of the readings of line 6 of *Mout ai esté longuement esbahis* (R. 1536)[12] in the *Chansonnier Cangé* (O) and the *Chansonnier de Saint-Germain-des-Prés* (U) may serve to clarify the first of these points. The former specifies $b\flat$ for the eighth musical unit, whereas the latter indicates $b\natural$.

Ex. 3. The O and U readings of Mout ai esté longuement esbahis, line 6.

Another example of flexibility in the treatment of accidentals may be observed in the first of the two readings in the *Chansonnier Cangé* of *L'an que rose ne feuille* (i.e., the one on fol. 74).

Ex. 4. L'an que rose ne feuille, MS O, fol. 74r.

Line 2

The first b, placed between two a's is provided with a flat; the second, in almost identical circumstances, is marked with a natural. Further examples of divergent usage could be marshalled were this necessary.

The second point may be illustrated by comparing Jean Beck's transcription of Thibaut de Navarre's well-known chanson, *Pour conforter ma pesance* (R. 237), with the facsimile of his source, the *Chansonnier Cangé*.[13] Beck's transcription presents a work in a diatonic, plagal mode, ending on *f;* he indicates *b♭* in lines 1 and 3, but not in line 5. Consulting the facsimile, one finds that the MS does not indicate any *b♭*, but does indicate *f♯*, not merely for line 1, but for line 3 as well. The reading yields the following, curious result.

Ex. 5. Pour conforter ma pesance, MS O, fol. 95r.

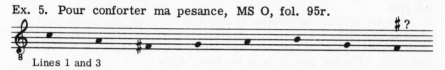

Lines 1 and 3

An outline of a diminished fifth has been created by a chromatic alteration of the tonic degree. Comparison with other sources shows that Beck's recommendations are well founded and that the Cangé version is inferior. However, by failing to provide any explanatory note, Beck is, in effect, suppressing a problem worthy of some attention. We cannot ignore the *f♯* on the ground that it is the result of mere carelessness; the fact that it occurs twice rules out any such assumption. Furthermore, this is not the only example in the trouvère repertoire of either the chromatic alteration of the tonic degree [14] or the creation of unusual melodic outlines through the use of written accidentals.[15] I do not suggest that this example furnishes a guide to the normal addition of unwritten accidentals in medieval performance. However, if each of these examples is suppressed in turn, if we fail to take note of their existence, then our overall impressions of mode in secular monophony will surely be inaccurate.

This article is, of course, in the nature of a preliminary report. I have sought to outline a long-neglected problem and to present initial conclusions. If this serves to promote an awareness of the need for more penetrating melodic analysis, my major purpose will be accomplished.

Notes

1. Even within this limited definition one may find examples that are difficult to account for under this proposed dichotomy. In the *MS du Roi*, *Ainc ne fis chançon jour de ma vie* by Gautier de Dargies—No. 1223 in Raynaud's numbering (I shall indicate such numbering hereafter simply by "R" plus a number)—is written in such a fashion that the final falls on *a;* the MS indicates seven accidentals: *b♭* (four times), *e♭* (once), and *f♯* (twice). The mode is related to Phrygian, once transposed; indeed the only

other surviving reading—that in the MS de Noailles—may be described as being in untransposed Phrygian. However, the presence of f♯ in the Roi version (i.e., the equivalent of c♯, allowing for the transposition) is contrary to present conceptions of Phrygian usage.

2. The MS symbols used in this article follow the Schwan system: A: Arras, Bibl. munic. 657; K: Paris, Bibl. de l'Arsenal 5198; M: Paris, Bibl. nat. f.fr. 844; N: Paris, Bibl. nat. f.fr. 845; O: Paris, Bibl. nat. f.fr. 846; P. Paris, Bibl. nat. f.fr. 847; R: Paris, Bibl. nat. f.fr. 1591; T: Paris, Bibl. nat. f.fr. 12615; U: Paris, Bibl. nat. f.fr. 20050; V: Paris, Bibl. nat. f.fr. 24406; X: Paris, Bibl. nat. n.a.fr. 1050; a: Rome, Bibl. Vat. Regina lat. 1490.

3. Notes within parentheses in the transcriptions are represented by plicas in the MSS.

4. These are R. 40, 209, 634, 679, 700, 1009, 1010, 221, 882, 1450, 1754, and 1876a. (The last five of these are opera dubia.)

5. Among melodies attributable to Hugues de Berzé, for example, four out of the five that survive in more than one MS family present mode changes in various readings. (These are R. 238, 1297, 1821, and 2071.) Among a similarly constituted group attributable to the Vidame de Chartres, four out of seven present mode changes—R. 130, 421, 502, and 14, the last being an opus dubium. With regard to works by Conon de Béthune, the proportion is at least three out of six—R. 1125, 1314, and 1960; an additional two pieces might be grouped with these, but they would furnish only weak examples. Still further documentation of this practice may be obtained by comparing the two readings in M of R. 1880 (Thibaut de Navarre's Costume est bien) and the M and K readings of R. 1727 (Thibaut's Dame l'on dit) and R. 2063 (Raoul de Soissons's Rois de Navare et sire de Vertu).

6. One example from the Minnesinger repertoire is discussed by Heinrich Husmann in his article, "Minnesang," in Die Musik in Geschichte und Gegenwart, IX, col. 357-358. Another example is mentioned in my review of Friedrich Gennrich's Troubadours, Trouvères, Minne- und Meistergesang (Journal of the American Musicological Society, VI [1953], p. 180).

7. Second ed. (Berlin: Max Hesses Verlag, 1929), p. 190f.

8. P. 241.

9. With regard to Westrup's argument, it may be pertinent to note that the monophonic source, U, has thus far a much better than average record for the reliability of its readings. Inasmuch as only two sources are available for comparison, the judgment that the polyphonic version is superior rests on purely subjective grounds. One cannot rule out the possibility that this version represents a late adaptation influenced by polyphonic requirements. If, however, we assume for the moment that the polyphonic version does represent accurately the original mode of the piece, we should still note that, by beginning a second lower, the scribe of the monophonic version could easily have preserved all of the modal characteristics while avoiding the use of f♯ and c♯.

10. A tenth source, Bern Stadtbibl. MS 389, preserves the poem without music, while an eleventh, London Brit. Mus. Egerton 274, preserves the poem in conjunction with another melody.

11. "Borrowed Material in Trouvère Music," Acta Musicologica, XXXIV (1962), 91.

12. The authorship of this work is credited in the sources mainly to the Châtelain de Coucy, but there are two conflicting attributions.

13. *Le Chansonnier Cangé* (*Corpus cantilenarum medii aevi*, Numéro 1, Philadelphia: University of Pennsylvania Press, 1927), Vol. I: facsimile, fol. 95; Vol. II: transcription, p. 222.

14. See the O reading of *A vous, amant, plus qu'a nule autre gent.*

15. The outline of a tritone is to be observed in two readings of *Fine amours et bonne esperance* (R. 221), attributed variously to Pierre de Molins, Gace Brulé, and the Châtelain de Coucy. In the *MS du Roi* one finds the progression, *c-d-e-f♯-d;* its counterpart in the *Chansonnier Cangé* is *f-g-a-b-g.*

ix

LORENZO MASINI'S

DEER HUNT

Alexander Main (Columbus, Ohio)

$\mathcal{T}$he Italian *caccia* of the 14th century is an appealing genre, remarkable as an early and systematic embodiment of the imitative contrapuntal principle and fascinating as a musico-textual expression of that period's new urge to celebrate man and his earthly surroundings. But the number of surviving examples is small. Even if one applies the term *caccia* so broadly as to include all the canonic pieces in the Italian repertoire from the 14th and early 15th centuries, as Marrocco has done in selecting the works for inclusion in the second edition of his well-known *caccia* collection,[1] the number is just 26, not a large one compared with 177 for the non-canonic madrigals,[2] or with 419 for the non-canonic *ballate*,[3] belonging to the same repertoire. But if one restricts the term to canonic settings of poems that employ dialogue in the realistic portrayal of lively outdoor scenes, as Marrocco rightly does in classifying the pieces within his volume,[4] the number is reduced to fifteen. And if one further restricts the term to what is presumably its original musical meaning, that is, to canonic settings of poems that portray hunting scenes, the number drops to a mere seven. Thus any canonic piece in the repertoire, and especially one in the smallest class, is a precious relic. Such a piece is *A poste messe*, by Lorenzo Masini da Firenze, a composition that seizes our attention for several other

130

reasons as well. It is one of the fairly small number of works by which we may come to know this illustrious predecessor of Landini, as we have only seventeen pieces definitely ascribed to Lorenzo.[5] Furthermore this is the only *caccia* we have from him, in fact the only canonic piece, though imitation appears occasionally in seven of Lorenzo's eleven other polyphonic compositions.[6] *A poste messe* is also one of the few *cacce* with texts whose authors we can name, and the only one we have with a text definitely attributable to the Florentine poet Niccolò Solda-nieri, who is little known today but who was important enough for his madrigals and *ballate* to appear in settings by Lorenzo and no fewer than five other composers of the period.

In modern times the history of Lorenzo's *caccia* has been something like that of *epigaea repens*, the trailing arbutus, a treasured wild plant that is much sought after but hard to discover and harder to domesticate. *A poste messe* has enjoyed the attention of distinguished scholars from Ludwig and Wolf to Fischer and Pirrotta, and it has appeared in five notable modern editions. But to date it has never, I think, been restored properly. Its editors have produced the *stanze* variously for two voices or for three, and the *ritornello* always for one voice. I am convinced that *A poste messe* is a canonic piece in three voices throughout, and that the transcription offered on pp. 148-161 below marks its first correct appearance in print.

The difficulty has been caused partly by the two primary sources transmitting the music, but perhaps more, as we shall see, by our imperfect understanding of them. Both in the Squarcialupi Codex [7] and in the Florentine Ms. Panciatichi 26 [8] the piece is set forth merely as a single voice-part. A canonic intention for the *stanze* is made clear in the Squarcialupi Ms. by a large, cross-shaped sign, placed above the point in the music at which an imitating voice is to begin. In the Panciatichi Ms. the same thing is accomplished by a series of rests inserted at the very beginning. For the *ritornello* there is no such sign in either source.

Looking at the music in either place, the modern reader receives the impression of a two-voice canonic *stanza* setting followed by a mono-phonic *ritornello*. Wolf listed this as a two-voice composition when, with his *Geschichte der Mensuralnotation* of 1904, he blazed his now well-known trail into the Italian *trecento* repertoire.[9] Ludwig must have been satisfied with that description, for he did not dispute it in his invaluable review [10] of Wolf's work, though he did correct Wolf on many other points. And both Marrocco and Husmann followed suit. The first edition of Merrocco's *caccia* collection, published in 1942, presents *A poste messe* as a two-voice canonic setting of the *stanze*, with a monophonic *ritornello*.[11] So does Husmann's anthology of medieval compositions, which appeared in 1955.[12]

But Wolf himself had second thoughts. In his posthumously published edition of the Squarcialupi Codex, issued in 1955, our *caccia*
appears with the *stanza* setting not in two canonic voices but in three.[13]
Wolf simply introduces an additional canonic entry, which follows
the second voice at the same time-interval as that at which the second
voice follows the first. As far as I can tell from the microfilms at my
disposal, there is no special sign, either in the Squarcialupi Ms. (Wolf's
only source for the piece) or in the Panciatichi Ms., that calls for a
third voice. Nor does Wolf state that he has discovered such a sign.
By way of justification for a three-voice reading he only cites "the
harmonic poverty" that results from a realization in only two voices.[14]
Certainly this is not enough to settle the matter, especially since Wolf
also mentions that there are many "hardnesses" (that is, dissonances) in
his transcription. We are still in the process of arriving at definitive
readings of the compositions in this repertoire. Our knowledge of its
harmonic style remains a little vague—too vague, I think, to support
a quick judgment concerning either harmonic poverty or dissonance.
Wolf's flash of intuition has called attention to an interesting possibility.
But can it be shown that a three-voice realization is actually the correct
one?

Marrocco apparently thinks not. The second edition of his *caccia*
collection, which appeared in 1961, sticks to a two-voice realization of
the *stanze*.[15] On the other hand Pirrotta, in the third volume of his
edition of 14th-century Italian music, published in 1962, produces the
stanze in three voices.[16] The question remains open, because neither Marrocco nor Pirrotta discusses it.[17]

No such dissension has divided the editors concerning the *ritornello*
of Lorenzo's *caccia;* all four have presented it as a monophonic appendage to an otherwise polyphonic piece. But Fischer has had a different
idea. In a review of Wolf's edition he remarks, "Possibly this *ritornello*
also is, despite some hard dissonances, to be sung as a three-voice
canon." [18] Here was another interesting possibility, and a likely-looking
one. After all, we have no other *caccia* with a monophonic *ritornello;*
it was reasonable to wonder if something had not gone wrong with
this piece. But the problem here was harder than the one Wolf had
faced in the *stanze*. Wolf knew from his source that he was dealing with
a canon, and he knew its time-interval. But before one could prove that
the *ritornello*, too, was canonic, one would first have to resolve it as
a canon. That meant finding the right time-interval. In his later work,
the valuable *Studien zur italienischen Musik*,[19] Fischer proposes a time-
interval of twelve imperfect longs. He expresses doubts about it, however, especially with regard to "the dissonances and fourths" it produces
in a three-voice reading. Pirrotta, in a short footnote to his edition, men-

tions the "harmonic shortcomings" of this proposal and rejects it.[20] He is, I think, quite right in doing so. For the worst of the shortcomings the reader may examine the closing measures of the transcription that results from the proposal. Granting that only in part do we as yet know the harmonic style of the period, still it is hard to be enthusiastic over a passage (judged within the framework of that period) containing nine dissonances in direct succession:

Ex. 1

Before leaving this questionable passage let us note that, although Fischer is especially doubtful about a three-voice rendition according to his proposal, actually a two-voice rendition is even more clearly wrong. Omit the bottom staff in the example just shown, and you have the two-voice realization. It ends on the interval of a fourth; and that, it seems safe to say, simply does not happen in two-voice compositions of the period. The two-voice version of this proposed solution can thus be ruled out at once. And there are reasons in addition to harmonic ones for ruling out the three-voice version as well. For one thing, it introduces a caesura immediately before a canonic entry:

Ex. 2

The effect is odd and unpersuasive in itself, as it weakens the canonic entry; and the like of it does not occur in any of the 25 other canonic pieces in this repertoire. Furthermore there is, as we shall see, a still better reason for rejecting Fischer's proposal altogether: a different time-interval produces far more convincing results.

Returning now to the *stanze*, we take up the question whether a three-voice realization is demonstrably correct. We recall that Wolf himself calls attention to "many hardnesses." Perhaps Wolf was particularly disturbed by this passage, which strikes me as, from the standpoint of harmonic usage, the only really unlikely one in his transcription:

Ex. 3

The note d' sounding against the e' would be perfectly acceptable as a suspension, but presumably both the e' and the f' would then have to be regarded, in some sense, as "harmonic" tones. Actually, however, the problem does not exist, because Lorenzo did not write the passage. Wolf's transcription is incorrect at this point, as the vertical alignment of the parts has been put out of joint by a misreading of two note-values earlier in the piece.[21]

But the fact remains that, concerning one section or the other of Lorenzo's *caccia*, three authorities have raised the question of harmonic propriety; yet no one has specified his objections. We might ask, then, what sort of harmonic usage is to be expected of Lorenzo. Let us remind ourselves not only that the harmonic thinking of the period is intervallic rather than chordal, but also that on the whole the perfect fourth is theoretically a consonance, even though composers and theorists of the time generally assign a lower consonant value to it than to the unison, fifth, and octave;[22] that dissonances are frequent and sometimes rather freely treated; and that, especially in rapid ornamental passages, melodic considerations sometimes take precedence over harmonic ones, producing dissonant clashes in direct succession. With respect to the latter two points, for example, I know of no reason for doubting the correctness of Pirrotta's transcription of these two passages from another of Lorenzo's compositions:[23]

The piece, by the way, is the madrigal *Dolgom' a voi*. Aside from *A
poste messe* it is the only one of Lorenzo's surviving works to employ
a three-voice texture; thus it is the one most appropriate to explore
in connection with our question. It also sheds a little light on our point
concerning the perfect fourth. The piece shows Lorenzo handling this
interval with some caution, for it does not contain an unmistakable
instance of a fourth above the lowest voice being treated as a con-

sonance.[24] But on the other hand it does offer a passage in which Lorenzo makes very clear that he likes the interval: [25]

Ex. 5

But the freedom of 14th-century dissonance treatment is, of course, not absolute. An important restraining principle of the period is readily apparent in Lorenzo's polyphonic music. In general each measure (to use the modern term [26]) begins with a consonant combination.[27] This principle can be brought to bear on our problem; that is, it can be applied to test the validity of the three-voice realization of the *stanze*. An examination reveals that at no point does the three-voice reading violate the rule; every measure begins with a consonance. It hardly needs to be added that this cannot be mere accident. Shift the third canonic entry in either direction, for example, and the rule is transgressed by the polyphonic result. The same is true if one adds a fourth canonic entry. Obviously, then, Lorenzo intended a three-voice canon.

This piece does contain one harmonic peculiarity that I have not found elsewhere in Lorenzo's music: a perfect fourth involving the lowest voice, introduced at the beginning of a measure and unmistakably treated as a consonance. The reader who wishes to examine this in measure 18 of the transcription may note that this particular detail would not occur in a two-voice realization, as it is the third voice that produces the interval of a fourth. But that is no argument against the three-voice realization, because the beginning of measure 57 presents the opposite situation: a fourth that in a two-voice reading would be similarly unusual, but that is rendered completely unexceptional by the third voice. The explanation seems to be that Lorenzo regarded the fourth, even when it involved the lowest voice, as a kind of consonance. Certainly he cannot have thought it as consonant as the fifth, say, or even the third, else we should find similar uses of the interval in his other works. But neither can he have considered it a dissonance, or he would not, I think, have employed it so prominently as in measure 25: [28]

Ex. 6

The three-voice rendering is also perfectly convincing with respect to another harmonic trait that is discernible elsewhere in Lorenzo's music. In the three-voice *Dolgom' a voi,* cited earlier as the composition most likely to furnish us with relevant information, even the most dissonant passages present no more than four or five dissonant combinations in direct succession; after five clashes at the most a consonance intervenes. The same holds for our *stanza* setting realized in three parts.[29]

To these observations we may add that even the structural scheme points to the rightness of the three-voice solution. The last eighteen measures (that is, of the first voice, the only voice written in the sources) clearly are laid out in three periods of six measures each, the length of the canonic time-interval. The function of this three-fold periodic design is to create convenient stopping-places for each of three canonic voices. The same purpose is evident in the handling of the text; in both Mss. the last line is written out three times, making it possible for the three voices to unite convincingly in the last syllable on the last note. And finally we may observe that the closing polyphonic cadence is perfectly normal for the period. Quite certainly the *stanza* setting is a three-voice canon.

But how is the *ritornello* to be solved as a three-voice canon? Searching for clues, one notes that the *stanza* setting opens with a long melisma on the first syllable of the text; that the second syllable appears (in both sources) at the point of canonic entry; and that at that moment the first voice is an octave below its initial note. The *ritornello* also opens with a long melisma on the first syllable. In both sources the second syllable appears just as the melody has reached an octave below its starting point. This occurs after precisely the equivalent of eight imperfect longs. I believe that here, too, the second syllable marks the point of canonic entry, and that both scribes simply neglected to provide an additional sign. Perhaps, indeed, neither scribe felt that another sign was necessary, since this opening pattern was so much like that of the *stanze*.

I am not the first to consider this solution in print. Pirrotta proposes it in his excellent edition,[30] although without explaining why he chose this particular time-interval. Then, with no explanation beyond the simple mention of "harmonic shortcomings," he rejects it. Here, I think, he is mistaken. Let it be noted at once that one of the harmonic principles we mentioned earlier tends to confirm our solution; nowhere in this canon do even as many as five dissonances occur in a direct succession. And in general the canonic resolution is in agreement with our other principle; of the forty measures of polyphony, twenty-seven begin with normal consonant combinations. Yet the remaining thirteen begin either with dissonances or with fourths that are sounded fleetingly in the manner of dissonances. Even if most of these can be explained as arising from appoggiaturas (that is, from mere ornaments applied to clearly consonant combinations), we may wonder how Lorenzo can be so much more daring here than in the *stanze*, for we recall that there every measure begins with a consonant combination. The answer probably lies in the fact that, except for the opening melisma, the entire *ritornello* is built on an organpoint; beginning with the onset of the first imitative entry, the note *a* is sung on almost every beat. The repetitions are so persistent that in a sense the note is continuously present, even though the printed page does not show it at every instant. The result is an effect of continuous tonic harmony, against which dissonances can occur with unusual freedom, without obscuring the consonant foundation. As a matter of fact, harmonically the *ritornello* amounts to little more than an extended polyphonic embellishment of an *A* minor triad. With the tonic organpoint in mind one can satisfactorily explain nine of the thirteen problematical clashes as arising from appoggiaturas.[31] The four remaining ones (in measures 94, 98, 102, and 106) require a different explanation. All four arise in the same way. Here is the first one in its context:

Ex. 7

The emphatic dissonance introduced by the note g' at the beginning of measure 94 is certainly unusual for Lorenzo. Here again, though, the organpoint seems to justify it. I submit that, to the ear, the passage essentially amounts to this:

Ex. 8

The dissonance arises from a passing tone, whose venturesome appearance at the beginning of a measure is made possible by the stationary bass note. The same is true for the other three cases. And elsewhere in this canon I find nothing that seems to lie outside of Lorenzo's normal harmonic practice.

In the end, though, the conclusive proof for the validity of our canonic solution lies not in the explanation of a few exceptional harmonic details but rather in an examination of the structural plan. It will be remembered that in the *stanze* the latter part of the written melody consists of three distinct periods, whose lengths agree with that of the canonic time-interval. The same is true in the *ritornello*. Again the special canonic purpose of the divisions is obvious, because Lorenzo does not as a rule compose in short, symmetrical blocks; except at the end of the *stanze*, he does not even do so elsewhere in this piece. We note also that this canon ends, like the *stanze*, in a standard 1-5-8 chord.[32] Of course the tonic organpoint shuts out the possibility of a normal ending cadence. But, recalling the notable array of parallel fourths in *Dolgom' a voi*, we cannot but welcome as characteristically Lorenzian the parallel fourths with which our *caccia* comes to a close. I think there can be no doubt that this canonic solution is correct.

Nor do I think that a musician of Lorenzo's time or soon after would have taken half a century to arrive at the correct reading, as we have done. Aside from this piece there are fourteen *cacce* known to us. All are three-voice compositions.[33] I submit that our musician would have recognized *A poste messe* as a *caccia* from its text, and that, finding only one voice-part written down, he would have suspected at once that a three-voice resolution was required. I venture to say that after a few moments' perusal of the textual repetitions and the musical form he would have been ready to produce it, even if the scribes had neglected to indicate the point of canonic entry in the *stanze* as well as in the *ritornello*. And if our musician had had the Panciatichi Ms. in his hands he would have understood the piece even before glancing at the text, because in that volume the scribe wrote the designation *Caccia* at the top of the leaf. It must have been an intention to ensure a three-voice realization that led him to do so. There are fourteen canonic pieces in this Ms. and thirteen in the Squarcialupi, but Lorenzo's is the only one in either source to be prominently labeled in this way.[34] None of the others required it, because none of them involved the canonic derivation of three voices from one.

That *A poste messe* is canonic in three parts is in itself an interesting point. The *ritornello* of Giovanni da Firenze's *Nel bosco senza foglie*[35] twice engages briefly in three-voice imitation, and the short *ritornello* of Landini's *Deh! dimmi tu*[36] is a three-voice canon. But Lorenzo's is the only known *caccia* that is canonic in three voices throughout. Its correct and authenticated restoration not only forces us to expand our notion of the *caccia* as a type but also provides us with a new link between the *caccia* and the French *chasse*. The piece also tells us something noteworthy about its composer's artistic personality, since, by comparison with other Italian pieces of the era, it reveals a turn of mind that we are accustomed to thinking of as more typically northern than southern. Pirrotta comments that ". . . Lorenzo's was a speculative mind . . . ,"[37] and the structural rigor of this work seems to support the observation. Yet in performance the piece is far from seeming austere, for it proves to be a rousing and brilliantly effective composition. And quite the opposite of speculative is the unmistakable gusto with which Lorenzo seizes upon the opportunities that Soldanieri offers him for spirited musical description. Not only does he render convincingly the cries of the hunters, the barking of the dogs, the song of a cuckoo, the racket of the beaters, and the call of the horn, all of which are present in the poem itself. He also adds remarkable descriptive touches of his own. The last syllable of the poem is turned into a repeated-note figure that could again represent the noise of the beaters but which in its poised, fairly deliberate rhythmic character seems rather more like drumbeats. Apparently Lorenzo's hunting party, like the one shown in a 14th-century Italian drawing owned by the Oppenheimer Collection in London (plate I), has brought along a band of musicians. And perhaps the band includes a bagpiper. Certainly the *zampogna* must have been known in Florence in Lorenzo's day, for Giotto or an assistant had depicted one in an Epiphany scene now owned by the Metropolitan Museum of Art in New York; later the sculptor Nanni di Banco was to place the instrument over a doorway of the cathedral, in the hands of an angel at the apex of his now famous Assumption of the Virgin. This possibility is suggested by the drone-like organpoint in the *ritornello*, a feature that is not to be found in any of the other

PLATE 1

Hunting Party, including two wind players and two drummers. (14th-century Italian drawings from Raimond van Marle, *Iconographie de l'art profane* [2 vols., The Hague: Martinus Nijhoff, 1931-32], Vol. 1, Fig. 222.)

known *cacce,* nor in any of Lorenzo's other compositions.[38] Also representational in its effect is the memorably abrasive suspension that in the first *stanza* twice accompanies the word *grido* (shriek).

Ex. 9

But perhaps Lorenzo's most imaginative pictorial stroke is the way the scene is brought to a close. One at a time the first and second voices depart from their incisive syllabic declamation and engage in melismas,[39] while the third voice ends with its own turn at the drumbeat repetitions of the poet's last syllable. Little by little the excitement of horn calls and textual narrative fades away in a kind of composed *diminuendo.* Unmistakably, I think, Lorenzo's hunting party vanishes into the distance. At its core this idea was a bold, illusionistic representation of physical space. We are reminded that it had been another Florentine, Giotto, who had revived the lost art of representing space on a flat surface, and that it was to be still another, Brunelleschi, who would give to painters the mathematical formulation of linear perspective.

Certainly Lorenzo possesses a remarkable ability to combine ingenious structure and vivid descriptiveness in a compelling synthesis. Nowhere is that ability more clearly demonstrated than in the dialogue portion of each *stanza* (measures 22 to 51).[40] Lorenzo sets these verses to a five-measure period; each voice-part traverses it three times, inserting a three-measure melisma before the last time. Thus the six-measure periodicity inherent in both the opening and the close of the *stanza* is completely overthrown. In effect the imitative relationships among the parts are changed, not only once but several times. There are two strettos with a one-measure time-interval, the first involving two voices (measures 27-28 and following), the second three (measures 33-35 and following); a third stretto follows, with a two-measure time-interval (measures 39-41 and following). Most interesting of all, each line of text is sung nine times altogether, every time to the same melody but every time with a different polyphonic accompaniment. The result is a superb example of controlled confusion. One hears all of the turmoil, unpredictability, and hullabaloo of the hunt, yet everything is held in check by the inexorable logic of the canonic structure. In a way this is the most arresting of all of Lorenzo's descriptive strokes, because it is description not superimposed on canonic structure but built into it. No other *caccia* that is known contains an episode so imposing.[41] In his complex manipulation of the canonic structure itself for the sake of description, Lorenzo in an extraordinary way penetrates to the heart of the *caccia* as a musico-textual idea and gives us what may therefore be our finest example of the type. Happily *A poste messe* is not the only one of his pieces to survive. But even if we had no other works from him, this composition alone would require us to rank Lorenzo among the great musicians of the 14th century.

Notes

1. W. Thomas Marrocco, ed., *Fourteenth-Century Italian Cacce*, 2nd edition (Cambridge, Mass., 1961).
2. For a list, see Kurt von Fischer, *Studien zur italienischen Musik des Trecento und frühen Quattrocento* (Bern, 1956), pp. 18-34.
3. For a list, see *ibid.*, pp. 38-72. Fischer's tabulation of 420 *ballata* titles includes the canonic *Dal traditor* by Andrea da Firenze.
4. See Marrocco, *op. cit.*, pp. xix-xx, xxii.
5. The works are printed in Nino Pirrotta, ed., *The Music of Fourteenth-Century Italy*, American Institute of Musicology, 1954- , Vol. III (1962), pp. 1-21. P. 46 of the same volume presents an anonymous *Sanctus* that Pirrotta (see pp. ii-iii) thinks may also be Lorenzo's. Sixteen of Lorenzo's compositions are printed in Johannes Wolf, ed., *Der Squarcialupi-Codex*, Lippstadt,

1955, pp. 77-96. Since Wolf's edition is unreliable, however, it is now not as useful in relation to Lorenzo's compositions as it is in relation to other works of the period that are still unpublished elsewhere.

6. In Pirrotta, *op. cit.*, Vol. III, the seven compositions are numbers 1-3, 5-7, and 10.

7. Florence, Biblioteca Laurenziana, Palatino 87. The music appears on fol. 49ᵛ-50ʳ.

8. Florence, Biblioteca Nazionale Centrale, Panciatichiano 26. The music appears on fol. 76ᵛ-77ʳ.—I wish here to express my gratitude to Dr. Dragan Plamenac, who, kind and generous as always, provided me with microfilm copies of the two Florentine sources.

9. Johannes Wolf, *Geschichte der Mensuralnotation von 1250-1460*, 3 vols. (Leipzig, 1904), Vol. I, pp. 234 and 245.

10. Friedrich Ludwig, review of Wolf, *Geschichte*, published in *Sammelbände der Internationalen Musikgesellschaft*, VI (1904-05), pp. 597-641.

11. W. Thomas Marrocco, ed., *Fourteenth-Century Italian Cacce*, 1st edition (Cambridge, Mass., 1942). The piece is No. 1 in the volume.

12. Heinrich Husmann, ed., *Die mittelalterliche Mehrstimmigkeit* (an unnumbered volume in the series entitled *Das Musikwerk: Eine Beispielsammlung zur Musikgeschichte*), Cologne, 1955, pp. 52-54.

13. Wolf, *Der Squarcialupi-Codex*, pp. 84-87.

14. *Ibid.*, *Revisionsbericht*, p. xix (unnumbered).

15. This edition is cited in note 1. The piece is No. 1 in the volume.

16. Pirrotta, *op. cit.*, Vol. III, pp. 17-19.

17. Nor does Fischer, who states (*op. cit.*, p. 35) that the music is *a 3* but offers no explanation.

18. Kurt von Fischer, "Zu Johannes Wolfs Übertragung des Squarcialupi-Codex," in *Die Musikforschung*, IX (1956), pp. 77-89. The quotation is from p. 85.

19. Fischer, *Studien*, p. 35.

20. Pirrotta, *op. cit.*, Vol. III, p. iv.

21. The passage is quoted from Wolf, *Der Squarcialupi-Codex*, p. 85, mm. 59-60. In his m. 49, in the first voice, Wolf renders as quarter-notes (the second and third in the measure) two breves that should have been rendered as half-notes. The parts are therefore misaligned from there to the end of Wolf's m. 67, by which point the same error duly repeated in the second and third voices has restored the correct alignment.

22. Of course there was considerable disagreement over this troublesome interval. Marchettus of Padua repeatedly and unreservedly describes the harmonic perfect fourth as a consonance; see his *Lucidarium in arte musicae planae*, printed in Martin Gerbert, *Scriptores ecclesiastici de musica*, 3 vols., (St. Blaise, 1784; facsimile ed., Milan, 1931), Vol. III, pp. 64-121 (the fourth is discussed in *Tractatus* III, cap. 1; *Tractatus* IV, capp. 3 and 11; and *Tractatus* VI, cap. 2). On the other hand the writer of the *Ars discantus secundum Johannem de Muris* classifies the perfect fourth as a dissonance; this work is printed in Edmond de Coussemaker, *Scriptorum de musica medii aevi nova series*, 4 vols. (Paris, 1864-76; facsimile ed., Milan, 1931), Vol. III, pp. 68-95 (dissonances are listed on p. 75). Nevertheless two theorists as widely separated in time and point of view as Jacob of Liège and Prosdocimus de Beldemandis are alike in presenting ambivalent accounts of the fourth that closely correspond to Lorenzo's treatment of the interval in practice (soon to be discussed

above). Jacob states that the perfect fourth is a "true consonance," but he emphasizes that it does not sound as good when placed below a perfect fifth as when placed above; see Book VII of his *Speculum musicae*, printed in Coussemaker, *op. cit.*, Vol. II, pp. 383-433 (the interval is treated in capp. 5-8). Prosdocimus lists the fourth among the dissonances, but adds that it is not as dissonant as the other dissonant combinations—that in a way it lies "between the true consonances and the dissonances"; see his *Tractatus de contrapuncto*, printed in Coussemaker, *op. cit.*, Vol. III, pp. 193-199 (the fourth is described in *Tractatus* II, cap. 1).

23. Pirrotta, *op. cit.*, Vol. III, p. 6, mm. 20-26; p. 7, mm. 40-43.

24. The composition does contain three passages in which a perfect fourth above the lowest voice seems to be treated as a consonance, but since all three cases are at least questionable they do not supply positive information concerning Lorenzo's attitude toward the fourth. One such case occurs in the first of the two passages just cited above, on the third beat of the fourth measure. If the editorial flat over the following note is wrong, then the *a* might be regarded as merely a dissonant appoggiatura; and even if the flat is correct, the *a* can be regarded as an appoggiatura that, after an inserted returning-note, proceeds to *g* as the consonant note of resolution. Another doubtful case appears in the second of the two passages just cited above, on the third beat of the third measure; if the *b* in the lowest voice is really *b*-natural, as the editor quite reasonably suggests, then the *e'* occurring above it must be a consonance, because the *f'* with which it is decorated is dissonant. But if, as seems possible though unlikely, the *b* ought to be left flat, then no perfect fourth occurs. Further on in the piece, in the two-voice *ritornello* (see Pirrotta, *op cit.*, Vol. III, p. 7, m. 48), there is a perfect fourth that at first glance seems unquestionably to be treated as a consonance. But the *ritornello* must, I think, be considered incomplete (see below, note 33) and therefore unreliable as a source of information on such a matter; the presumable missing third voice may have sounded the lowest note at this moment in the composition.

25. Pirrotta, *op. cit.*, Vol. III, p. 6, mm. 13-14.

26. I mean each breve (or its equivalent in other note-values) in the case of the earlier Italian notation, or each long (or its equivalent) in the case of the later, "manipulated" notation found in most of Lorenzo's works. On this point, see *ibid.*, especially p. iii.

27. Essentially the principle had been set forth by Franco of Cologne: ". . . concords are always to be used at the beginning of a perfection. . . ." See his *Ars cantus mensurabilis*, printed in Coussemaker, *op. cit.*, Vol. I, pp. 117-136; English translation in Oliver Strunk, *Source Readings in Music History* (New York, 1950), pp. 139-159 (the passage quoted is in cap. 11).—In Lorenzo's polyphonic works other than *A poste messe* there are, to be sure, a number of exceptions to the rule. They amount to about five per cent of the total number of measures if the interval of a fourth involving the lowest voice is counted as a dissonance, and to about three per cent if the fourth is counted as a consonance. But even in the exceptional cases Lorenzo exercises restraint. If one counts the fourth as a consonance (and, as we shall soon see above, there is some justification for doing so) there are 22 measures that begin with dissonances. (If one were to count Pirrotta, *op. cit.*, Vol. III, p. 16, mm. 61 and 66, there would be 24 measures beginning with dissonances. But in m. 66 the dissonant diminished fourth is produced by a sharp that seems to me dubious, since I do not find it in either the Panciatichi Ms. or the Squarcialupi, though

I assume it appears in either or both of Pirrotta's two other sources. And in m. 61 the dissonance is treated so strangely that I think the passage must be wrong, even though both the Mss. just mentioned present the dissonance exactly as Pirrotta shows it. There are three other sources for the passage, and I have so far been unable to consult them. Either the upper voice should be a step lower at this point or the lower voice a step higher. Wolf, *Der Squarcialupi-Codex*, p. 80, m. 66, elects the latter solution; the result is perfectly convincing, but, since he gives no account of the passage in his *Revisionsbericht*, one does not know just how much evidence Wolf found to support it.) In 21 of the 22 cases the dissonance treatment, whether it involves a suspension or an appoggiatura, is identical in several respects: the dissonance occurs between two consonant combinations, and while it is being resolved by stepwise motion in one voice (almost always the upper) the other voice remains stationary. (In Pirrotta, *op. cit.*, Vol. III, p. 16, m. 67, the dissonance seems to be preceded by a diminished fourth; but if the doubtful, earlier-mentioned sharp in m. 66 is struck out, the fourth is perfect and therefore, according to our assumption, a consonance.) In the remaining case (*ibid.*, p. 3, m. 46) the treatment is the same, except that before it is resolved the dissonance is first adorned by a consonant returning-tone that is approached and left by leap.

28. For other striking uses of the fourth as a consonance see mm. 31, 33, and 39.

29. For the longest chain of dissonances in *Dolgom' a voi*, see the penultimate measure of the second of the three passages from that composition that have been shown. For the longest chain in *A poste messe*, see the passage last shown.

30. Pirrotta, *op. cit.*, Vol. III, p. iv.

31. See mm. 1, 74, 76, 79, 82, 84, 95, 101, and 103. In m. 1 the note d' could be considered a more or less consonant fourth above the a; but I think the effect is actually that of an appoggiatura whose note of resolution, c', occurs in the lower voice. In m. 79, similarly, the d' is an appoggiatura resolved in the lowest voice.—If it is conceded that the pedalpoint supplies a stationary bass, six of these appoggiaturas are treated according to the description given in note 27. The other three are treated differently in one respect, as they are preceded by dissonances (see mm. 84, 95, and 103; the last of these is preceded by a g' that is consonant on paper, but that in relation to the pedalpoint has some dissonant effect).

32. The reader may note that the three-voice solution ends in a simple, direct manner, requiring only that the singers come simultaneously to a halt. A two-voice solution would require, if it were not to end on a perfect fourth, some special adjustment that is not called for in the sources. Furthermore, in a two-voice reading the organpoint that thitherto had given cohesion to the polyphonic web would illogically disappear eight measures before the end. These observations confirm that the *ritornello* is to be rendered in three voices, not two. Thus they also still further confirm the three-voice reading of the *stanze* (see note 33).

33. Except that the *ritornello* of Jacopo da Bologna's *Per sparverare* comes down to us in only two voices. But this must be by accident, because change in the number of voice-parts within a composition is not a stylistic trait of this repertoire. *Per sparverare* must originally have had a three-voice, non-canonic *ritornello*, as has Jacopo's canonic madrigal *Useletto selvaggio*. We may add that the tabulations in Fischer, *Studien*, pp. 18-73, list only one other

composition within which there is a change in the number of voice-parts. Sad to report, it is Lorenzo's *Dolgom' a voi*, aside from *A poste messe* the only three-voice composition we know from him; in the form in which we see it in Pirrotta's edition, with a *ritornello* in only two voices, it is obviously a torso.

34. In three pieces (*Per sparverare* in the Panciatichi Ms., and *Dappoi che'l sole* and *Passando con pensier* in the Squarcialupi) the name *chaccie* (or *caccie*) appears beneath the beginning of the tenor part. There, however, the label serves merely to identify the textless tenor as a part of the composition.

35. Printed in Pirrotta, *op. cit.*, Vol. III, No. 19; Marrocco, *op. cit.*, 2nd edition, No. 15 (1st edition, No. 11).

36. Printed in Marrocco, *op. cit.*, 2nd edition, No. 10; Leo Schrade, ed., *Polyphonic Music of the Fourteenth Century* (Monaco, 1956-), Vol. IV (1958), pp. 216-218; Wolf, *Der Squarcialupi-Codex*, pp. 206-208; Harold Gleason, ed., *Examples of Music Before 1400* (New York, 1942), pp. 108-112.

37. Pirrotta, *op. cit.*, Vol. III, p. ii.

38. Of course it may be that Lorenzo means only to imitate the tunelessness of beaters and drummers; this interpretation would not make Lorenzo's descriptive use of organpoint any the less remarkable.—The only other *caccia* to contain a passage even remotely comparable is Gherardello's *Tosto che l'alba* (printed in Pirrotta, *op. cit.*, Vol. I, No. 33; Marrocco, *op. cit.*, 2nd edition, No. 25 [1st edition, No. 19]; Wolf, *Der Squarcialupi-Codex*, pp. 47-48; and in six other works listed in Fischer, *Studien*, p. 39). The short *ritornello* of Gherardello's *caccia* holds fairly insistently to repetitions of the note *g*, mainly in order to provide an effective accompaniment for some horn signals. There again the insistent repetitions are brought about, though indirectly in that case, by a descriptive intention.

39. The shift to melismatic style is called for by the introduction of ligatures. They are used so consistently as to make their meaning clear enough in the Squarcialupi Ms. and absolutely unequivocal in the Panciatichi, which is the earlier source.

40. Pirrotta, *op. cit.*, Vol. III, p. iv, draws attention to this episode and sets forth an interpretation somewhat different from the one to be offered above.

41. The only *caccia* to contain a passage that is even comparable is *Cacciando per gustar* (printed in Marrocco, *op. cit.*, both editions, No. 2; Wolf, *Der Squarcialupi-Codex*, pp. 328-332; Johannes Wolf, "Florenz in der Musikgeschichte des 14. Jahrhunderts" [in *Sammelbände der Internationalen Musikgesellschaft*, III (1901-02), pp. 599-646], pp. 618-625), by Zaccaria, who is, we should note, of a later generation than Lorenzo's. Zaccaria sets four virtually identical lines of dialogue to four virtually identical phrases. While the second canonic voice is singing the first two of these, the first voice breaks in with the third and fourth phrases, so that three imitations occur in rapid succession. The essential idea is the same as in Lorenzo's piece, but Zaccaria carries it out on a far smaller scale.

Caccia

Poem by Niccolò Soldanieri

Lorenzo Masini
Edited by Alexander Main

148

ril! chia - man - - -
can, gri - da, de' gri -

po - ste_____
scia - ti i_____

A_____
La -

mes - se_____ vel - tri e gran_____ ma -
ca - ni_____ a lei si fèr_____ vi -

do, Ciof, ciof, qui, qui, ciof!
da! Ve' là, ve' là, ve'!

sti - ni: Te', te', Vil-lan! te', te', Ba-
ci - ni: A - i ca - ne! O tu del

Brac - chi e se - gu - gi
Pas - san - do il pog - gio,

ril! chia - man -
can, gri - da, de' gri -

po - ste
scia - ti i

per bos-ch'a-i - zan - do, Ec - co,
al - lor fu - ron le stri - da: Cu cu -

mes - se vel - tri e gran ma -
ca - ni a lei si fèr vi -

ec - co - la, ec-co-la! Guar-da, guar-da qua!
cu, cu-cu, cu cu-cu! Dal-li, dal-li, o tu!

do, Ciof, ciof, qui, qui,
da! Ve' la, ve' la,

sti - ni: Te', te', Vil-lan!
ci - ni: A - i ca - ne!

la, ec-co-la! Guar-da, guar-da qua! Las-sa, las-sa,
cu, cu cu-cu! Dal- li, dal-li, o tu! Che è, che è,

Ec - co, ec - co - la, ec-co-la!
Cu   cu - cu,   cu-cu, cu cu-cu!

Ec - co - la,   ec - co - la! Guar-da, guar-da
Cu   cu - cu,   cu cu - cu! Dal - li, dal-li, o

las-sa! O tu, o tu, o tu! Pas-sa, pas-sa,
che è? L'uc-cel, l'uc-cel, l'uc-cel! Che me, che me,

Guar-da, guar-da qua! Las-sa, las- sa, las - sa! O
Dal - li, dal-li, o tu! Che è, che è, che è? L'uc-

qua! Las-sa, las-sa, las-sa! O tu, o tu, o
tu! Che è, che è, che è? L'uc-cel, l'uc-cel, l'uc-

pas - sa!
che _____ me!

tu, o tu, o tu! Pas-sa, pas-sa, pas -
cel, l'uc-cel, l'uc-cel! Che me, che me, che ____

153

154

- io.____
- lo.____

____ a l'a-ba - -
____ap-pio me - -

la! Guar-da, guar-da qua! Las-sa, las-sa, las-sa! O
cu! Dal-li, dal-li, o tu! Che è, che è, che è? L'uc-

- io,____
- lo,____

tu, o tu, o tu! Pas-sa, pas-sa, pas -
cel, l'uc-cel, l'uc-cel! Che me, che me, che____

Bian - ca lat-
Per-ch' el-la in

Bian - ca lat- ta - ta, col col-lar di va -
Per-ch' el-la in ma-no a me la-sciò del pe -

sa! La cer-bia u-
me! Uc - cel - la e

Bian - ca lat - ta - ta, col col-lar di va - io.
Per - ch'el-la in ma-no a me la-sciò del pe - lo.

lar di va - io.
sciò del pe - lo.

- - io.
- - lo.

A

ri - col-ta bu bu bu bu bu bu bu bu bu

A

bu bu bu bu bu bu bu bu bu bu bu bu bu bu bu bu bu bu

no no no no no   no no no no no no no no

tim, ta -tim, ti-ton, ti-ton, ti - ton, ta -tim, ta-

no no no no no no no no

tim, ta-tim, ta-tim so-na - va per i - scor - no.

no no no no no no no no no no no no no no no no

no no no no no no no no no no no no no no no

161

Editorial Report

Sources: 1. Florence, Biblioteca Nazionale Centrale, Panciatichiano 26,
               f. 76ᵛ-77ʳ.
           2. Florence, Biblioteca Laurenziana, Palatino 87, f. 49ᵛ-50ʳ.
The transcription is based on both sources. In the tabulation of variants
that follows, the transcription is the standard of reference. Variants are
accounted for only in the first voice-part, but of course they apply to
the second and third as well. References are made by measure-number
and by note-number within the measure (a note tied to a preceding note
is not counted).
Source 1: m. 15, n. 6— ♩♪ ; m. 43, n. 1-2—no ligature; m. 51, n. 8—
           ♩♪ ; m. 56, n. 1—not in ligature; m. 57, n. 2—no sharp
           visible, at least in microfilm; m. 57, n. 3—not in ligature; m.
           78, n. 3— ♪♪♪ ; m. 79, n. 5—ditto; m. 81, n. 3—ditto; m. 82,
           n. 5—ditto; m. 83, n. 1— ♩♪ ; m. 92, n. 2— ♩ (quarter-rest
           omitted); m. 100, n. 4—ditto.
Source 2: m. 10, n. 2-4— ♪♪♪ ; m. 11, n. 6-8—f′, g′, g′ (I have chosen
           the reading in the other source because the other source
           is the earlier, but I am not at all sure that its version of the
           passage is the correct one; the version in Source 1 produces
           consonant results in all three occurrences, while the version
           in Source 2 does not; on the other hand the version in
           Source 2 seems a little more convincing melodically); m. 54,
           n. 1— o ♩ ♮ ; m. 57, n. 3— ♩ ♮ (the rest falls in the follow-
           ing measure); m. 58, n. 6—no sharp; m. 98, n. 1—not in liga-
           ture; m. 102, n. 2— ♪ ⁊ (not in ligature); m. 104, n. 2—ditto;
           m. 106, n. 5—ditto; m. 107, n. 6—ditto.

THE TWO-PART

QUODLIBETS IN THE

SEVILLE CHANSONNIER

Dragan Plamenac (Urbana, Illinois)

$\mathcal{A}$s a modest contribution to a posthumous offering in homage to Curt Sachs, the pages that follow derive their primary justification from being an addition to a study that was dedicated to the great scholar on the occasion of his seventieth birthday.[1] The writer deeply regrets that Sachs's death made it impossible for him to follow up the earlier dedication with another one on Sachs's eightieth birthday. There is, however, a recent * circumstance that makes a publication of the four pieces printed below appear particularly opportune at this time. At the last New York Congress of the International Musicological Society, a special Round Table discussion, held at Yale University on September 7, 1961, was devoted to a consideration of the "Origins and National Aspects of the Quodlibet." It is felt that the pieces printed here should add welcome illustrative material to the basic paper written for that Round Table session by Professor Kurt Gudewill [2] and to the condensed account of the discussion itself, published in Vol. II of the Congress Report.

As expounded in detail in the author's study mentioned above, the late 15th-century Chansonnier of the Biblioteca Colombina at Seville

* One of the first to respond to the invitation to contribute to this volume, Professor Plamenac sent in his article as long ago as November 1961. —*Editorial Note*

was subjected in 1884 to barbarous treatment, in the course of which four fascicles, numbering altogether forty-two leaves, were detached from the volume. These fragments, subsequently joined with fragments of other manuscripts, eventually landed in the Bibliothèque Nationale at Paris, where they now constitute Part I of MS Nouv. acq. fr. 4379. The four two-part quodlibets with which we are concerned here were to be found in the Seville volume before its mutilation in the very spot where the first fascicle consisting of ten leaves was torn out of the binding.[3] This act of vandalism was accomplished in such a way that the superius of the first piece was left behind in Seville, whereas the tenor and the three pieces that follow came to be included in the fragments now at Paris.

The four quodlibets occupy in the Codex the folios e1^v to e5^r in old signature foliation; they bear in the index of the reconstituted Chansonnier the current numbers 26 to 29. In the quodlibets Nos. 27 and 28, the straight voice-parts of the superius and tenor, respectively, from Dunstable's (or Bedingham's?) immensely popular O rosa bella are combined with chains of incipits (centos) in the other two voices. These chains of incipits are made up of quotations taken, in No. 27, from the stock of Gregorian chant melodies, in No. 28, from the French chanson repertoire. As for the remaining two quodlibets, No. 29 again combines a straight voice-part, the superius of Mon seul plaisir (ascribed in one contemporaneous source to Dufay, in another to Bedingham) with another chain of chanson fragments, while in No. 26 the "composer" did not scruple to patch together the straight superius of Binchois's Pour prison ne pour maladie—accompanied by its full text!—with a section of a Gregorian Passion as the tenor.

It appears from what has been said that the four quodlibets in the Seville Chansonnier, if we apply to them the classification suggested in Professor Gudewill's New York Congress paper,[4] fall into the sixth category, the "Cantus firmus-Cento" variety, with the distinction that a third, freely composed part is wanting here. With respect to the various component parts of our quodlibets, let us point out that the tenor in No. 26 is in the main a composite of passages extracted from the setting that has evolved from the application of the several Passion Tones to the Passion according to St. Matthew, but in an order different from the liturgical one.[5] The Gregorian cento occupying the place of the tenor in No. 27 will be found to be a medley of plainsong melodies of the most disparate liturgical character; bits of antiphons, hymns, communions, litanies, sections of the Ordinary, etc., follow one another in it in odd succession. As regards the chains of secular chanson incipits in the cento parts of Nos. 28 and 29, some of the quotations derive from pieces that have come down to us in complete polyphonic settings and at times accompanied by the names of their composers; others are known only by their texts, which have been preserved in literary sources; and of a third group neither text nor music seems to have survived. It should be pointed out that scraps of characteristic but otherwise unknown chanson melodies found in quodlibets may prove useful in identifying polyphonic settings of the same tunes if those settings have reached us either without any text or under the guise of *contrafacta*. The secular centos in the Seville Chansonnier use indiscriminately incipits of songs of the conventional, lover's-plaint type and tunes of clearly popular, street-song character; but it is interesting to note that tunes belonging to the first group, when included in song collections, ordinarily appear in regular polyphonic garb with the same text used in all parts, whereas tunes of the latter, popular type, if traced in polyphonic sources, are usually found relegated to the lower parts of quodlibetic structures, for the most part double or triple chansons.

Examples of incipits taken from chansons preserved in straight polyphonic settings are in Quodlibet No. 28: *Seule esgarée* (by Binchois; Rehm edition, No. 42); *Le maleureux habandonné* (anonymous; concordance in my study on the Seville Chansonnier, under No. 68); *Bon vin, je ne te puis laissier* (anonymous, found in Copenhagen, Ny kgl. Sg. 1848, 2°; evidently a parody of *Bon temps, je ne te puis laissier*. Cf. also the monophonic version in the Bayeux Chansonnier, Gérold edition, No. 43); *Par le regart de vos biaux yeulz* (by Dufay; concordance as above, but under No. 59); *Terriblement [suis fortunée]* (anonymous; concordance as above, under No. 65); *Puis que je vis* (possibly by Dufay; concordance as above, under No. 70). *Adieu tant que je vous reveoie* is not derived from Binchois's *Adieu jusques je vous revoye* (Rehm edition, No. 2), in spite of the near identity of the text opening, but from another setting not yet identified. *Resposons nous*, as already pointed out in my Seville study, Part I, p. 520, is the beginning of *Reposons nous entre nous, amoureux*, a poem written—and most probably also set to music—by Busnois. In this case, as in those of *Au sault du baing* [6] and *Par trop vous amer je me tue*, we are in possession of the complete texts, but the music of these pieces has so far become known only through the scant quotations in the Seville quodlibet. Another piece, *Gente de corps, belle aux biaux yeulz*, is found in a monophonic source, the Bayeux Chansonnier (Gérold edition, No. 47). There are three incipits in Quodlibet No. 28 that strongly suggest popular or dance-song origin, both in their texts and in the melodic and rhythmic alertness of their tunes. The pieces are *Quant j'estoie sur le pont a Paris, Amez moy belle Margot*, and *Gardez vous des leux waroux*. The last of these melodic fragments appears with its text, not as an incipit but at the end of the superius in Seville No. 130, *La belle fille par matin s'est levée;* the text is given also in two other parts.

Taking now a look at the other Seville quodlibet with a secular cento, No. 29, we find that the chain of incipits, which has been moved here to the lower voice, is put together in much the same way as its equivalent in No. 28. Six themes are taken from polyphonic chansons: *La dolour que je rechoy* (anonymous; for sources, see my Seville index); *Doel angoisseux* (by Binchois; Rehm edition, No. 50); *Franc cuer gentil* (by Dufay; published in *Denkmäler der Tonkunst in Oesterreich* XI [1]); *Mon seul plaisir* (as a consequence, not only does the chanson provide the straight superius to this quodlibet, but its opening theme takes an active part, as a chain link in the lower voice, in engaging the superius in a bit of witty imitation in meas. 15-16); *O rosa bella* (the tune reappears here in a cento after supplying the straight parts of the superius and tenor to quodlibets No. 27 and 28); and *O dona gentile* (by Dufay; found in the Mellon Chansonnier). Two other incipits, *Leal en amours* and *Hellas quel doel*, are obviously taken from songs of the conventional amorous type; they are not known to me from other sources. As in Quodlibet No. 28, one theme can be traced to an item in the Bayeux manuscript: *Beuvons fort* (Gérold edition, No. 48). As the first two words of the opening reveal, it is an honest, unadulterated drinking song. There are in this cento several themes that no doubt belong to popular and dance-songs: *Va l'ententu, Garde la garde, Povres gens ne sont pas rices, Ma courte houcette, Hove sur la mer*. For the most part, songs of this type are difficult to trace in complete form in sources of the period. But there are two exceptions: *Marchiez laduriau ladure ho* and *Hellas la fille Guillemin*. The first of these tunes turns up in the Dijon Chansonnier in the contra I and the tenor of a four-part piece with the superius *Puisqu'aultrement ne me peut estre*, and in the tenor and contra of a three-part piece with the superius *Ma dame de non* in Escorial IV.a.24.[7] It appears with slight variants in *La durium dure* in Seville No. 22 and *Ladurion dure* in Florence, Banco rari 229, 191ᵛ-192ʳ. It is also found as a *basse dance, Marchon la dureau*, No. 45, in the Brussels MS 9085.[8] The second tune, *Hellas la fille Guillemin*, performs a similar function in a three-part piece preserved in two manuscripts, El Escorial IV.a.24 and Montecassino 871 N, in which it assumes the parts of the contratenor and tenor with *A Florence la joyeuse cité* in the superius.[9] And just as *Marchons ladureau* was used as a *basse dance* at the Burgundian court, so *Hellas la fille Guillemin* was picked by one of the great Italian dancing masters of the 15th century, Domenico da Piacenza, to serve his choreographic purposes. As we learn from Domenico's dance treatise in Paris, Bibliothèque Nationale, MS ital. 972, this tune, the only one he used that he did not invent himself, was drawn upon by him in composing the choreography for two *balli*.[10]

This, of course, reaffirms the widespread popularity enjoyed by such songs and the close connection that existed between them and instrumental music-making. It seems also useful to point to the nonsense syllables and onomatopoeic features in these pieces, which stamp them from the outset as popular and street-songs. I rather like to think that their freedom from mawkish sentimentality and their straightforward-ness would have endeared them to the man to whose lasting memory the present volume is dedicated.

Notes

1. "A Reconstruction of the French Chansonnier in the Biblioteca Colombina, Seville," *The Musical Quarterly*, XXXVII (1951), 501-542; XXXVIII (1952), pp. 85-117, 245-277.

2. Printed in *International Musicological Society—Report of the Eighth Congress, New York 1961*, Vol. I (Kassel: Bärenreiter, 1961), pp. 30-43.

3. See "A Reconstruction . . . ," *The Musical Quarterly*, XXXVIII (1952), p. 100.

4. *Report . . .* , pp. 32-33, 35-36.

5. As a result of continuing attempts to restore the chant melodies to their pristine purity, the readings of the Passion Tones, like those of other portions of the repertoire, may, in modern or fairly modern editions of the chant books, be found to differ considerably among themselves as well as from the readings incorporated in polyphonic settings of the Renaissance period. The following passages, as given in *Cantus ecclesiasticus sacrae historiae Passionis D. N. J. C.* (Ratisbon: Pustet, 1868), are found in our quodlibet tenor, with larger or smaller discrepancies: *Passio . . . suis* (p. 1), *Amen . . . negabis* (p. 6, omitting the words *quia in hac nocte*), *Quid vultis . . . argenteos* (p. 3, omitting the word *Exspiravit* in the quodlibet), *Dixerunt . . . perditio haec* (p. 2; *dixerunt = dicentes*), *Dicebant . . . in populo* (p. 1, omitting the word *forte*).

6. There can be little doubt that this text is identical with *Au sault du lit*, preserved in the Rohan Chansonnier (Löpelmann edition [*Die Liederhandschrift des Cardinals de Rohan* in *Gesellschaft für romanische Philologie* XLIV, Halle-an-der-Saale: Max Niemeyer, 1923], No. 393). *Par trop vous amer* is found in the same literary source (Löpelmann, No. 321).

7. Dijon, f. VIII^{xx} V^{v}-VIII^{xx} VI^{r} (168^{v}-169^{r}); El Escorial, f. 119^{v}-120^{r}.

8. Jean Molinet, in his *Chroniques*, calls it "une chanson vulgaire, qui lors [i.e., in 1492] estoit en bruit." Cf. A. van der Linden, "La Musique dans les Chroniques de Jean Molinet," in *Mélanges E. Closson* (Brussels: Société Belge de Musicologie, 1948), pp. 176-177.

9. El Escorial, fol. 60^{v}-62^{r}; Montecassino, fol. 3^{v} (p. 252). In the Escorial MS, the text of the contratenor opens with "En ma chambre apprendre latin." In Montecassino the text is hopelessly corrupt.

10. The passage in MS ital. 972, fol. 7^{r}, reads as follows: "Le infrascripte dançe sono composte cusi il canto come le parole per lo spectabile & egregio cavagliero Misser Domenico da piasença salvo che il canto de la figlia guilielmino che e Ballata francese, et sopra esso canto el domenico cavaglier ha composti i doi balli." On fol. 18^{v}-19^{r} follows the music, superscribed "la fia guilmin in canto" and accompanied by a detailed account of the two dances composed upon it by Domenico.

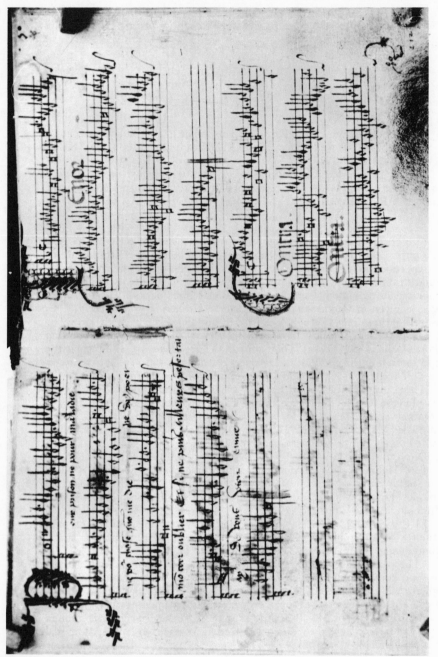

PLATE 1

Superius part (shown at left) of the Quodlibet, *Pour prison—Passio Domini nostri* (Seville Chansonnier).

I. Pour prison—Passio Domini nostri

Seville No. 26

Pour pri - son ne__ pour__ ma - la - di - e Ne__ pour cho - se qu'on____ me__ di - e Ne vous__ poet__ mon____ coer__ ou - bli - er;

Pas - si - o Do - mi - ni no - stri I - he - su Chri - sti se - cun-dum Mat - the - um. In il - lo tem-po-re di - xit I - he-sus di - sci-pu-lis su - is: A - men di-co ti - bi; an - te-quam gal - lus__ can-tet ter__ me ne - ga - bis.__ Ex - spi - ra -

169

Et si ne___ puis ail - leurs___ pen -

vit: Quid vul - tis mi - hi da - re et e - go e - um vo - bis tra -

ser Tant ay___

dam. At il - li con - sti - tu - e - runt e - i tri -

de___ vous ve - oir___ en -

gin - ta ar - gen - te - os. Di - xe - runt e - i: Ut__ quid per -

vi - e.

di - ti - o haec.__ Di - ce - bant au - tem: non in di - e fe - sto_

__ ne tu - mul - tus fi - e - ret in po - pu - lo.__

170

PLATE 2

Tenor part of the Quodlibet, *Pour prison—Passio Domini nostri* (Paris, Ms. n.a.f. 4379).

171

PLATE 3

II. O rosa bella—In pace

Lau - da - mus te A - ve ma-ris stel-la De-

i ma - ter al - ma at - que sem - per vir-go fe -

lix coe - li por - ta Pa-ter no-ster Pla - ce -

- bo O - mnes san - cti et san - ctae o - ra-te

pro no - bis Ky - ri - e e - lei - son

Pas-si-o Do-mi-ni no-stri I-he-su Chri-sti se-cun-dum Mat-

the - um A - gnus De - i

Per o-mni-a sae - cu-la sae-cu-lo - rum A - men

Ju-be Do-mi-ne be-ne-di - ce-re Te De - um te

ae -ter-num pa-trem o-mnis ter-ra ve-ne-ra - tur.

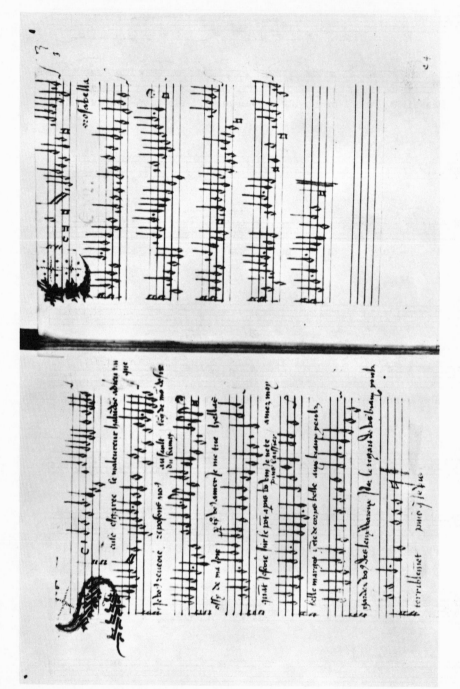

PLATE 4

III. Seule esgarée—O rosa bella

Hel - las. Quant j'es-toie sur le pont a Pa - ris Bon vin je ne te puis lais-sier A-mez moy bel-le Mar-got Gen-te de corps, bel-le aux biaux yeulz Gar-dez vous des leux wa-roux Par le re-gard de vos biaux yeulz Ter-ri-ble-ment Puis que je vis.

IV. Mon seul plaisir—La dolour que je rechoy

Mon seul plai - sir,⎯ ma doul -

La do-lour que je re-choy Le - al en a-mours Beu -

- ce⎯ joy - - -

vons fort Me-re don-nez moy ma - ri Doel an-gois-seux

- - - e, La

ra-ge des-me-su - ré - e Va l'en - ten - tu va l'en-ten-tu

mais - tres - se de⎯ mon es -

Franc cuer gen-til⎯ Mar -chiez la - du-riau la du-re

poir,

ho Gar-de la gar-de gar-de la gar-de Mon seul plai-

1) The ♭ in the key-signature is dropped from here to the end.

179

PLATE 5

The Quodlibet, *Mon seul plaisir—La dolour que je rechoy* (Paris, Ms. n.a.f. 4379).

THE SCHOOL OF

GAUDENZIO FERRARI AND

THE EARLY HISTORY OF

THE VIOLIN

Emanuel Winternitz (New York)

*O*ne of the great lacunae in the history of musical instruments is the question of the origin of the violin. This seems absurd, considering the increasing importance of this instrument for more than three hundred years. How different was the treatment accorded by musical historians to that other ruler among the tools of music, the pianoforte! We know almost everything about its origin and evolution, as it has been recorded in minute detail. True enough, the history of the pianoforte posed a much easier problem: one man, after a few years of experimentation, produced what the fashion of his time demanded—a keyboard instrument with a hammer action that enabled the player to perform crescendos and decrescendos, simply by modifying the pressure of his fingers on the keys. Thus a new keyboard style was at once made possible.

The violin, however, was not an "invention." Rather, it was the

final product of a long and variegated process of development, a combination or fusion of many patterns and elements contributed by a
number of different bowed instruments. Only when the great Lombard
instrument-makers in Brescia and Cremona took over, after the middle
of the sixteenth century, did something like a standard form emerge—
standard, it is true, only in the sense of adherence to basic characteristics
that still admitted countless variations of proportion, curvature, tonal
quality, and so on. From that time on, we have something like a
coherent history of the violin, told, if not in treatises, then by a considerable number of wonderful specimens that have survived to the
present day.

A reliable account of the pre-history of the violin, and by that I
mean the process of development mentioned above, has not yet been
written, and a consultation of the modern books on the history of this
instrument proves disappointing—they are vague or incorrect, or they
simply avoid the problem.[1] So the origin of the violin is still obscure.
Neither the alleged strict distinction between the families of the viola
da gamba and the viola da braccio, nor the supposed direct evolution
of the violin from the lira da braccio, conforms to its actual evolution,[2]
and some attempts at condensation of its complex story have resulted in
oversimplification. One cannot even blame the simplifiers, for the history of the violin is a process emanating from wide and wild experiments towards standardization, a standardization which is, in fact,
almost unparalleled in the history of instruments. According to pictorial
evidence, and contrary to the neat and departmentalized *Syntagma* of
Praetorius, there were lire da braccio with "violin" scrolls, violins with
exuberant rebec sickles, violins with *C* holes, viols with bulging sound
boards, and near-"violins" still with the flat peg-leaf or peg-box of the
lira da braccio.

The situation is further complicated by the predilection of the curio
collectors of the 15th and 16th centuries, who liked to commission unique
and fantastic shapes as worthy additions to their *Kunst- und Wunder-
kammern* or *Musikkammern*. The only straight and clear evolution in
Renaissance string instruments, as far as I can see, was the gradual
transformation of what pre-16th-century Italy called the "viola" (a
fiddle with a flat head and frontal pegs, with or without drones, such
as was depicted, for instance, by the school of Giotto) into the full-
fledged lira da braccio of about 1500, as shown in countless representations by Carpaccio, Giovanni Bellini, Cima da Conegliano, and others.

The veil that covers the origin of the violin may be lifted, at least
a little if not wholly, by the evidence of pictures, and specifically by
pictures that pre-date the time when the Cremonese masters created
what appears in retrospect to be the first "standardized" pattern of the

violin. The first outstanding painter we have to consider in this connection is Gaudenzio Ferrari, whose creative years filled almost the
whole first half of the 16th century. Very close in time and place to
the great giants, Leonardo and Bramante, he achieved and maintained
an astounding originality and independence. His frescoes and other
paintings are characterized by vivacity and a great ease and variety of
composition. His art is deeply rooted in his native soil, and many of
the faces, figures, and gestures that he depicted can still be found
today in Lombard and Piedmont villages.[3]

Apart from his glory as a painter, Ferrari was deeply interested in
the other arts, including music. Several of his chief works contain representations of musical instruments, including violins: the Sacro Monte
in Varallo; his altar-piece, "La Madonna degli Aranci," in the Church
of San Cristoforo in Vercelli; the cupola fresco in the Santuario in
Saronno; and others. A detailed study of these representations seems
indispensable for the history of Renaissance instruments, and it is hardly
too much to say that Gaudenzio's name is inseparable from the early
history of the violin.

Now we turn to Ferrari's gigantic cupola fresco in the Santuario at
Saronno,[4] one of his most important and original works. He received
the commission for it in 1534 and worked on it throughout 1535. His
idea of representing a large angel concert in a cupola had only one
forerunner, Correggio's famous fresco of the "Assumption of the
Virgin" in the cupola of the cathedral in Parma. We do not know
whether Gaudenzio knew Correggio's fresco, which had been finished
only a few years earlier, in 1530. In any case, Gaudenzio's composition
is quite different and original; it represents the arrival of the Blessed
Virgin in Heaven. Mary appears at the outer rim of the cupola, flanked
by puttini; God the Father, in glory, is represented in stucco relief in
the center of the painting. The whole enormous, shallow, and circular
vault between these two main figures is filled with angels, arranged
in four concentric circles: the innermost circle next to God consists
of thirty-one dancing putti; the other three circles are comprised of
numerous large figures of angels, sumptuously clad in flowing robes.
Some of them pray, some adore and exalt, but most of them play
instruments. Of the eighty-seven large angels, no less than sixty-one
play or assist in playing instruments.[5]

There are, in all, fifty-six instruments. Among the bowed instruments we find several viols, several lire da braccio, rebecs, a Sicilian cane
violin, a bizarre compound of fiddle with recorder, to be blown and
bowed at the same time,[6] and, last but not least, a number of instruments
that show most if not all of the basic characteristics of the violin.

But before concentrating on the violins, we should say something in general about the perspective in this fresco. The linear projection is far from being optically exact or—should we say?—pedantic. Even a quick glance convinces the beholder that most stringed instruments appear to be asymmetrical, with the bouts on either side not corresponding to each other. Also, the necks of instruments curve slightly upward so that their strings could not run parallel. Some of these irregularities are explained by the unevenness of the stucco surface in the cupola, and many spots are warped by fissures. But apart from that, Gaudenzio, with all his love for fancy detail, was not aiming here at photographic precision. He would, for instance, show the neck of an instrument with its sickle-head or scroll at a slightly different angle from that of the body, in order to insure identification of the instrument by its most characteristic feature. The scholar must be aware of this freedom in handling perspective, "con alcune licenze"; only then will he justly interpret the painted shapes, or rather "reconstruct," as it were, the actual instrument from its fanciful appearance in the painting. There is also another "unrealistic" feature in the fresco: none of the stringed instruments, not even the lutes, citterns, harps, or psalteries, has its strings painted in. The suggestive position of the stopping, plucking, and bowing hands was evidently sufficient for the onlooker far down below.

To the left of a beautiful positive organ are four angels with bowed instruments (plate 1). The one on top, which certainly has nothing to do with the violin, we may in the main disregard here. The angel plays a bizarre three-stringed instrument of very complex shape. Its curves project and, again, cut in deeply toward the center of the body; its back is strongly bulging; and its broad rim is profusely decorated with intarsias. Its heart-shaped head with frontal pegs is typical of the contemporary lira da braccio.

The three other instruments, however, different as they are from each other, all have some features that can be related to the violin. Closest to our present-day, standard violin is the alto-sized instrument played by a feminine angel at the right (plate 2). There are the typical upper, middle, and lower bouts, and a shallow body with a bulging sound board and projecting edges. There is also the narrow neck and finger board, and an elegantly shaped scroll. Inside the peg-box, four pegs are clearly visible.[7] Beside all these typical violin traits, however, there are other features that would perhaps seem abnormal today: the sound holes, although they correspond fairly well to standard f holes, are placed very high, at the height of the middle bouts, which are extremely short and deep; the lower part of the body is much wider than the upper; and there are no purflings.

The bass (or tenor) instrument nearby, played by the sitting angel at the lower rim of the cupola, shares some elements of the violin with the alto instrument to its right: the outline, consisting of three bouts; the strong molding of the sound board; the shallowness of the body in comparison with that of a regular viola da gamba; the projecting edges; the long thin neck; and the scroll. On the other hand, there are many differences: the proportions of the body; the much less-marked angle at which the shoulders meet the neck; the position and reversed shape of the sound holes; the leaf-shaped string holder; and the position of the bridge, between the sound holes and therefore much higher up. In fact, the differences are so remarkable that one hesitates to regard this second instrument as belonging to the same whole consort. The pegs are not clearly visible in the deep shadow, and the strings, as usual, are not drawn. The narrow finger board would probably not allow more than four strings, a number not contradicted by the position of the stopping fingers.

The smallest of our three pre-violins is somewhat hidden between the lute player and the player of the richly curved string instrument with the lira da braccio head. We see only half of its body, in a three-quarter back view, and the sickle-shaped peg-box, without scroll, is turned with some freedom of perspective so that we can look into it. The middle bouts are obscured by the peg leaf of the lira da braccio in front of it but, as far as we can see under these circumstances, the proportions have some similarity to those of the alto instrument. The head, however, is much more primitive than the elegant scrolls of the other two instruments; it resembles, in fact, that of a rebec (which, by the way, is twice represented in this fresco). Three pegs are indicated.

In short, our three instruments, although they have several common features, are so different in proportions and in other respects that one again hesitates to consider any of them as part of one set or consort.[8] Certainly, if Gaudenzio had wished to design three sizes for one homogeneous set he would have expressed his intention more clearly. He actually did so in a drawing of playing angels (now in the Staatliche Graphische Sammlung in Munich), which is probably a study for the Saronno fresco and which shows an actual set of three musical instruments that differ only in size, from treble to tenor (plate 3).[9] They are instruments of fantastic shape with extremely long necks terminating in flamboyant sickle heads. Their bodies are of such complex curvature that one does better to avoid the danger of verbalizing a description. Out of their shoulders grow projections in spiral shape, similar to those on many Renaissance citterns—projections that were, in fact, a last atrophic reminiscence of the arms of ancient and Carolingian lyres and kitharas.[10] And even these fantastic instruments are not the last word in Ferrari's exuberant fantasy of form: among his many beautiful sketches of musical putti and amorini, there is one that is even richer in curves, a veritable orgy in spirals (plate 4). The body is spade-shaped —its tail decorated with sculptured leaves (a frequent ornament not only of Gaudenzio's instruments but also of real instruments of the Renaissance); and the long neck ends in a giant spiral. The shoulders not only continue in side spirals, but also carry double scrolls that imitate, in reverse shape, the form of the *f* holes.

Oddly enough, since Karl Geiringer's reference to the Saronno fresco and Curt Sachs's pointing out the three angels (as playing *"violette da braccio senza tasti* with three strings in the true shape of the present violin family"), there has been no analysis of these representations, but only passing remarks, by historians of musical instruments. It is even more curious that attention has never been called to another violin in the same fresco (plate 6). This violin is in a section quite remote from the instruments mentioned before and is also somewhat obscured there by the surrounding instruments, two psalteries, a harp, a Platerspiel, and a lira da braccio. Our violin is shown face forward, presenting a top view of the sound board, whose bulge is strongly marked by shading. The middle bouts are precisely in the center of the sides—a position quite different from that on the alto instrument above; the sound holes correspond in shape to those of the "bass violin" but are much more finely drawn, terminating in delicate spirals; and there is a three-pronged string holder. The bridge is placed between the lower parts of the sound holes, just where their curve affords maximum width; this arrangement is different from that on the alto instrument, on which the sound holes converge toward the bottom of the instrument causing the bridge to be placed extremely low. The neck is narrow, and the head, to the dismay of the organologist, is covered by the arm of an angel playing the lira da braccio. But from the small width of the neck it is quite clear that no lira da braccio was intended here, since that instrument had to accomodate five melody strings on its fingerboard, to say nothing of the two bourdons running outside.[11] The bow may seem short at first glance, but part of it is actually covered by an angel wing. From the position of the stopping fingers it appears that the angel is not playing at the moment, but is awaiting his turn.

We now turn from these violins in the Saronno fresco to one appearing in an altarpiece painted by Gaudenzio for the Church of San Cristoforo in Vercelli, in oil on wood. It is called "La Madonna degli Aranci" because of the beautiful orange grove that forms its background, and it is reliably dated 1529, that is, six years before the Saronno fresco (plate 7). But we have chosen to defer discussion of it until now, since the variety of shapes and the free style of drawing and perspective apparent in the Saronno fresco have sharpened our eyes for the appreciation of the "Aranci violin." This violin differs in many ways from the Saronno instruments. Most striking are the proportions: its body is compact, very wide, and its upper half is almost mirrored by its lower, slightly wider half; also, the double curve of the shoulders is repeated at the bottom of the body. This is a shape as different from all the Saronno fresco violins as it is from the modern violin. The marked bulge of the sound board does not begin near the edges, but is confined to a rather narrow middle section. The *f* holes slightly diverge towards the neck; they are cut precisely into the rims of the strong middle bulge of the sound board. There is a heart-shaped string holder. The long finger board terminates in a long peg-box with a scroll and three pegs. The instrument is played with the head pointing downward, the bow is short, and the bowing and stopping hands, with the thumbs visible, are depicted most carefully and convincingly.

The execution of the whole painting reveals the master's hand. There is no question here of assistants. The two putti, and especially the violin player with his tender and meditative expression, are of exquisite workmanship. The instrument itself appears in perfect perspective in front view, and is turned just a little to make one side wall and the projecting edges visible.

That the shape of this instrument was not just a passing idea of Ferrari's appears from the repetition of the same shape in his sketch for an Adoration of the Child, in the Palazzo Reale in Turin (plate 5), although there the contours appear rather sketchy and perfunctory. It seems also significant that this same shape was taken over by Gaudenzio's school, especially by his long-time pupil and assistant, Bernardino Lanini.

There is no doubt that Gaudenzio had more than a profound interest in musical instruments; he must have been an expert player and, I am convinced, also a builder of instruments. His paintings reveal not only a deep familiarity with the forms of instruments (although there are occasional slips, probably committed by assistants), but also with their function, that is, their practical use. The attitudes of the musicians' bodies, the positions of arms and shoulders, the embouchures and finger positions in the wind instruments, and the truthful, lively rendering of hands and fingers in bowing, stopping, or plucking on the string instruments, are based on sharp observation. Telling, also, is the great variety of instruments shown, unsurpassed in any other angel concert and approximated only, perhaps, in a Northern painting: Geertgen tot Sint Jans' *Virgin and Child*, which shows virtually all the instruments existing in his time.[12]

Still more strikingly, Gaudenzio's profound acquaintance with instruments reveals itself in his crossing of the borderline between reality, that is, the exact portrayal of existing instruments, and free imagination —creating shapes that are functional enough but divergent from tradition even in a period that was remarkably little restricted by standardization. But in these fantastic instruments, such as a double bagpipe and a fiddle that could be both blown and bowed at the same time, Gaudenzio was not merely making wild creations of the brush for the sake of visual beauty; his instruments are functional—they could have been constructed and perhaps even were, for the fun of it, in a playful mood. In this they differ fundamentally from the many fantastic and scurrilous instruments that were created with sinister fantasy—the bird monsters with oboe beaks, etc., which a Northern contemporary of Gaudenzio's, Hieronymus Bosch, used in his hell scenes. But, of course, hell admits more of the grotesque than does heaven!

There is, finally, another fact that makes it seem probable that Gaudenzio built instruments himself: he was not only a painter, but also a sculptor, as we know from his expressive life-sized figures at Varallo peopling many scenes from the New Testament.

Vasari (ed. Milanese, IV, 652, and VI, 518) mentions Gaudenzio in a few laudatory words without going into detail; he was evidently not directly acquainted with Gaudenzio's work. Strangely enough, then, in the evaluation of the musical subjects painted by Ferrari, the most important biographical source has been entirely neglected, although it exists in a book often quoted by art historians: Lomazzo's *Idea del Tempio della Pittura* (1590?). Lomazzo, a painter and poet, was a nephew of Gaudenzio's and his superlatives, with which he was never thrifty, should perhaps be taken *cum grano salis:* in his account of Gaudenzio's works in the *Trattato dell'Arte della Pittura Scultura ed Architettura*, he calls Gaudenzio (p. 185) *"il mio vecchio precettore Gaudenzio, non solamente saggio pittore . . . ma profondissimo filosofo, e matematico . . ."* But he is more precise, at least as far as Gaudenzio's musical activities are concerned, in his *Idea del Tempio*. There, in Chap. IX, entitled "Fabbrica del Tempio della Pittura, e dei suoi Governatori" (p. 37ff.), he establishes an analogy, in his fanciful poetic way, between the seven planets and the seven governors in the Temple of Painting, whose statues are to be erected in the temple. The governors are to be Michelangelo, Gaudenzio, Caravaggio, Leonardo, Raphael, Mantegna, and Titian (in that order). Of Gaudenzio, second only to Michelangelo, Lomazzo says: *"Nacque costui in Valdugia, e fu pittore, plasticatore, architetto, ottico, filosofo naturale, e poeta, sonator di lira e di liuto."* The "lira" was no doubt the lira da braccio.[13] Thus, on the basis of this information, Gaudenzio played the most noble and difficult bowed instrument of his time, a fact quite significant in view of his inclusion of violins in his pictures.

The basic shape of Ferrari's violin in the altar painting of "La Madonna degli Aranci" was retained by his followers, especially by Bernardino Lanini. Lanini, who lived from about 1510 to 1583, had joined Ferrari's workshop in 1530 and was probably still assisting the master in the work on the Saronno fresco. As we shall see, Lanini was not deeply interested in musical instruments. Yet, since his many altarpieces included numerous representations of the Adoration of the Infant, the Sacra Conversazione, and the Assumption of the Virgin, the musical angels traditionally connected with these themes had to be represented.

Lanini repeated the broad and short pattern of the Aranci violin in his altarpiece of the "Assumption" in the Church of San Sebastiano at Biella, in 1543, and also in his "Madonna with Saints and Angels" in the church of San Paolo, Biella, and the "Adoration of the Infant" in San Magno, Legnano. A surprising difference appears, however, in another instrument painted by him in the Sacra Conversazione (from the Cook Collection in Richmond, which later came to the Kress Collection in New York and is today in the Raleigh Museum in North Carolina; plate 8).[14] There, one single putto plays a fiddle before the throne of the Virgin. At his feet are lying a lute, a recorder, and a jingle drum. The fiddle, although unmistakably a violin, with four strings and a strongly marked bulge in the sound board, does not repeat the broad pattern of Lanini's other violins mentioned above, nor of Ferrari's Aranci violin, but is of an extremely long and narrow shape and shows purflings which, to my knowledge, had not been represented before. The painting reveals that Lanini, for all his good intentions and neat drawing, was not a player or connoisseur. The representation of the bridge disregards perspective to such an extent that it appears to be upside down, and the positions of the stopping and bowing fingers are so lifeless and perfunctory that they could have been drawn only by a musical ignoramus. But for just this very reason we must assume that this violin did not spring from Lanini's imagination, but portrayed an existing instrument; and this makes the painting an important record, especially since it is dated. To the left of the bow handle we read "B.nardinus Laninus . Ucellen . F . 1552" (that is, thirty-two years after Ferrari's "Madonna degli Aranci").

Most treatises on the violin have pointed to Brescia and Cremona as the cradles of this instrument. But the great Brescian master, Gasparo da Salò, was only born about 1540 and would not have been constructing violins before the 1560's. And Andrea Amati, the founder of the

Cremonese dynasty of Amatis, was born about 1535 (according to Lütgendorff, *Die Geigen und Lautenmacher*); his earliest known violins are dated about 1564, according to *Grove's Dictionary of Music and Musicians*, although some instruments dated "1551" are listed as authentic by Franz Farga (in *Violins and Violinists*).

But the violins represented in the paintings of Gaudenzio Ferrari and Bernardino Lanini point to another and considerably earlier root west of Milan or even to the Piedmont. They also add another little bit of information to the complex and fascinating story of the early violin: they show such a bewildering variety of shapes and proportions that one almost directly senses the morphological fermentation of which they were a part and which had not yet reached the point of crystallization into the more or less standardized patterns later created in Brescia and Cremona.

Notes

1a. George Hart, *The Violin* (London: Dulau & Co., 1884), pp. 24-25, refers to manuscript notes by Vincetto Lancetti that mention a three-stringed violin in the collection of Count Cozia di Salabue, in the form of the Italian viola, dated 1546 and attributed to Andrea Amati, but "altered in the 19th century"! Then Hart continues: "When or where the four-stringed Violin, tuned in fifths, first appeared in Italy is a question, the answer to which *must ever remain buried in the past.*"

b. Alexander Hajdecki, *Die italienische Lira da Braccio* (Mostar: The Author, 1892), p. 50, says: "Die italienische lira da braccio . . . ist die Mutter unserer Violine . . ."

c. Laurent Grillet, *Les Ancêtres du violon* . . . (Paris: C. Schmid, 1901), p. 9, refers to Lanfranco's *Scintille*, published in Brescia, 1533, and to an account from the same year of the "dépenses secrètes" of Francis I, which mentions "tous vyolons et joueurs d'instruments du Roy" and some later French sources (from after 1550), including Rabelais, that refer to "joueurs de violon," but is silent about Italians before Andrea Amati, 1572.

d. The article in the *Encyclopedia Britannica* (11th ed., 1911) refers to a tenor viola "bearing in general outline the typical features of the violin," exhibited in 1872 in the Loan Exhibition of Musical Instruments at South Kensington, with the label "Pietro Lanure, Brescia, 1509."

e. W. Leo von Lütgendorff, *Die Geigen und Lautenmacher* . . . (Frankfurt-am-Main: Frankfurter Verlags-Anstalt, 1922), cautiously credits Gasparo da Salò with "the merit of having built the first violins and of having given them their definitive (*endgültige*) form" (Vol. I, p. 31).

f. Gerald R. Hayes, *Musical Instruments and their Music*, II: "The Viols and other bowed instruments" (London: Oxford University Press, 1930), clearly reflects the embarrassing situation of the historian when he says (p. 160) that "the violin is one of the very few important instruments of which it can be said that at a given date it was not at all, and that shortly afterwards it is found full-fledged in active life." He very prudently refuses to decide whether

Lanfranco's reference to the "Violetta da Arco senza tasti" (*Scintille di Musica*, 1533) means rebecs or violins (p. 169).

g. Edmund van der Straeten, *The History of the Violin* (London: Cassell and Co., 1933), p. 35, refers to the well-known print showing a portrait of Gasparo Duiffoprugcar, dated 1562, which shows two early violins; and also to the description of a "violin" in Philibert Jambe-de-Fer's *Epitome Musical*, published at Lyons in 1556, which mentions tuning in fifths, but does not say anything about the form of the instrument.

h. Francis Farga, *Violins and Violinists* (translated by Egon Larsen; London: The Macmillan Company, 1950), regards Tieffenbrucker as the "probable inventor of the violin" (Illus. XXVII) and says on p. 32: "The violin is depicted in the paintings of some Bolognese masters towards the middle of the 16th century, for example, in a picture by Giulio Romano (c. 1550). There is also a picture by Pellegrino Tibaldi in the Vienna State Gallery which portrays St. Cecilia with two violin-playing angels. It is possible, therefore, that the violin originated in Bologna in the third or fourth decade of the 16th century." He considers two violins by Andrea Amati with the year 1551 on the label as unquestionably authentic.

i. David D. Boyden, in his article on the violin in *Musical Instruments Through the Ages* (ed. by Anthony Baines, London: Penguin Books, Ltd., 1961), carefully and prudently formulates the problem (pp. 110, 111): "It is fruitless to try to attribute the 'invention' of the violin to any one man or country . . . The most impressive contributions were those of northern Italy where, shortly after the middle of the 16th century, the Italian school of violin-making dominated all others."

2. In my article on the "Lira da Braccio" in *Die Musik in Geschichte und Gegenwart*, VIII, I have discussed these problems in detail.

3. This article is not the place for an evaluation of the importance to history of this great Lombard-Piedmontese painter, but I should like to refer here to one of the most lucid and concentrated studies of Ferrari's importance, recently written by Anna Maria Brizio, as the introduction to the unforgettable "Mostra di Gaudenzio Ferrari" in Vercelli, 1956.

4. It was Karl Geiringer who first drew the attention of musical historians to this fresco, in 1927, in an excellent article, "Gaudenzio Ferraris Engelkonzert im Dome von Saronno," in the *Kongressbericht der Beethoven-Zentenarfeier* (Vienna: Universal Edition, 1927).

5. It was thanks to the late Fernanda Wittgens, the director of the Brera and the *Soprintendente delle Gallerie di Lombardia*, that numerous detailed photographs of my favorite angels were made. I had visited the Santuario of Saronno so often that I was called by the sacristan and his family, "questo Americano pazzo," and when, soon after World War II, I noticed rain damage in the cupola, "La Fernandissima" lost no time in effecting repair and restoration. It was on that occasion that the photographs were taken from which illustrations 1, 2, and 6 are made.

6. On this and other "fantastic" instruments and their interpretation, see my articles, "Instruments de Musique étranges . . .", *Les Fêtes de la Renaissance* . . . I, Centre National de la Recherche Scientifique (Paris, 1956), and "The Visual Arts as a Source for the Historian of Music," *International Musicological Society, Report of the Eighth Congress, New York, 1961* (Kassel: Bärenreiter Verlag, 1961).

7. I am aware of the fact that Curt Sachs, who referred to Ferrari's depiction in his *History of Musical Instruments* (New York: W. W. Norton & Co.,

1940), p. 357, calls this violin three-stringed, and there are indeed only three peg-heads visible. A close scrutiny, however, reveals that these heads do not precisely coincide with the four visible stems and that the somewhat shoddy perspective, attributable to quick fresco painting, or perhaps to a careless assistant, was intended to suggest a fourth peg hidden behind the juncture of the finger board and the sickle-shaped peg box. Certainly the painter would hardly have depicted the four stems without a factual base.

8. Cf. Curt Sachs, *op. cit.*, p. 357.

9. I should like to express my thanks to Prof. Degenhart, the director of the Staatliche Graphische Sammlung, for kindly providing me with a photograph of this drawing.

10. See my article, "The Survival of the Kithara and the Evolution of the English Cittern," *Journal of the Warburg and Courtauld Institutes*, XXIV (1961), Nos. 3-4.

11. This can be seen, for instance, in the lira da braccio to the right of our violin. Illus. 6 shows only the bowing hand and a small section of the contour of the body.

12. See my article, "On Angel Concerts: A Critical Approach to Realism and Symbolism in Sacred Painting," *The Musical Quarterly*, XLIX (1963), No. 4.

13. In my article on the "Lira da Braccio" in *Die Musik in Geschichte und Gegenwart*, VIII, col. 936, I have investigated the various names applied to this instrument and the resulting confusion, especially with reference to Vincenzo Galilei's explanation that the viola da braccio had begun to be called "lira" only in what for him were modern times.

14. I am grateful to the Kress Foundation and Dr. Alessandro Contini-Bonacossi, who have made photographs of this picture available to me and permitted me to use them.

PLATE 1

PLATE 2

Enlarged detail of plate 1.

PLATE 3

Gaudenzio Ferrari: Study for an Angel Concert. (Courtesy *Staatliche Graphische Sammlung, Munich.*)

PLATES 4 AND 5

Left: Gaudenzio Ferrari: Putto with Bowed Instrument. (*Collection E. Schweitzer, Berlin.*) *Right:* Gaudenzio Ferrari: Sketch for an *Adoration of he Child. (Palazzo Reale, Turin.)*

PLATE 6

Gaudenzio Ferrari: Detail from the Fresco at Saronno.

PLATE 7

Gaudenzio Ferrari: Detail from *La Madonna degli Aranci*. (*Church of San Cristoforo, Vercelli.*)

PLATE 8

Bernardino Lanini: Detail from *Sacra Conversazione.* (Raleigh Museum, Raleigh, North Carolina.)

THE REPERTOIRE

OF BOOK II

OF ORTIZ'S *TRATADO*

Gustave Reese (New York)

*D*iego Ortiz's *Tratado de glosas sobre cláusulas y otros géneros de puntos en la música de violones* (Rome, 1553) [1] has become fairly well known since its publication in modern form by Max Schneider.[2] The pieces that Ortiz presents in it as illustrations are played with some frequency by groups that specialize in the performance of early music, and a fairly large number have been made available on recordings. Apparently the earliest of these was one that Curt Sachs included in his pathbreaking *Anthologie Sonore*. This was a lively recording by Van Leeuven Boomkamp and Erwin Bodky, playing the viola de gamba and harpsichord, of the attractive *Recercada quinta* in the last group of compositions in the treatise, and this performance may well have been influential in calling to the attention of musicians the intrinsic merits that qualify these pieces to serve as more than illustrations in a treatise. Otto Gombosi managed to compress a remarkable amount of information about a substantial part of this repertoire into a brief footnote,[3] but no attempt seems to have been made to publish a description of it in more detailed form.

The treatise is divided into two books, in the first of which Ortiz, by means of many brief examples, teaches the performer systematically how to ornament and vary cadences. It is in Book II that he provides extended pieces, and these, besides serving a pedagogical function, are of interest by reason of their musical organization. The pedagogical aim, in this book, is mainly to teach the player on the viola da gamba how to improvise in the company of a harpsichordist; he may do this in three *maneras*, but the repertoire itself is divided into four sections.

The pieces in the first section provide less occasion for discussion about content than do the ones in the other three. Ortiz prefaces the section as follows:

> This second Book deals with the way in which one may play the viola da gamba with the harpsichord; there are three kinds of [such] performance; the first is *fantasía*, the second [is playing] over a *canto llano* [= *cantus firmus*], the third [is playing] over a composed [polyphonic] piece. I cannot demonstrate *fantasía*, because each person plays it in his own way; but I shall say what is required when one plays it. The [part of the] *fantasía* that the harpischord is to play should consist of well ordered chords [*consonancias*], and the viola da gamba should enter with elegant passages; and when it tarries on some sustained notes, that is an appropriate time for the harpsichord to respond to it. Some points of imitation [*fugas*] may be played, one player waiting upon the other in the manner in which concerted counterpoint is sung. . . .
>
> It seems suitable to me to set down in free and untrammeled form [i.e., without a harpsichord part] the four *recercadas* that here follow, in order to exercise the hand and in part to give out knowledge of the procedure to which one should adhere when one plays a viola da gamba alone.

Ortiz threupon provides the four *recercadas* for viola da gamba solo, pieces that consist mainly of runs, ornamental figures, and leaps, that of the twelfth being not uncommon. Motivic development (if this term may be applied) takes the form of melodic sequences. The second *recercada* begins with several presentations in sequence of a motive which, whether by design or not, consists of an ornamented form of the opening of the *passamezzo antico* bass (Ex. 1b), thereby foreshadowing the procedures Ortiz is to follow in two of the remaining sections of the Book.

Ortiz shows taste and skill in the second section, which consists of six pieces. (The numbering, *Recercada prima*, etc., begins over again in each of the three later sections.) These examples provide the violist with models, showing him how he can fashion six different solo parts over a single *cantus firmus*. Ortiz does not name the *cantus firmi* that he employs in his second and fourth sections, but this one was identified by Manfred Bukofzer, in his essay, "A Polyphonic Basse Dance of the Renaissance," [4] as the once popular *Spagna* melody. The form in which it is applied by Ortiz is shown in Ex. 1a; it agrees with the original form, except that it omits repeated notes.[5] Ortiz's added parts for the first pair of *recercadas* move mainly in minims and semiminims, with a few semibreves; those for the second pair move mainly in semiminims and fusas; those for the third pair do much the same thing, but only half as much (so far as time-value is concerned) is pitted against each *cantus-firmus* note.

Although in this section, unlike the first, Ortiz indicates that his illustrations are for a violist performing in duo with a harpsichordist, he actually provides for the latter only the bare notes of the *cantus firmus*. But the comments that precede the section show that the keyboard player is expected to round out his part with "chords [*consonancias*] and some counterpoint fitting the *Recercada* that the viola da gamba plays."

In the third section, Ortiz first presents, in its basic unadorned form, Arcadelt's famous four-part madrigal, *O felici occhi*. He then proceeds to show how the composition may be reworked, by means of four *recercadas* for the same two instruments. As he points out in his introductory comment, the madrigal is to be played on the harpsichord as it is "ordinarily" performed, and "he who plays the viola da gamba may play two or three or more variations" upon the individual parts. The remark, incidentally, seems to provide evidence contradicting the view sometimes expressed by present-day writers, to the effect that Renaissance music was so often executed with ornamentation that a modern performance without it presents only a skeleton of what Renaissance listeners normally heard. Certainly the many manuals on ornamentation show that it was common enough,[6] but what Ortiz gives to the harpsichord—the madrigal as it is "ordinarily" performed—is the music in its undecorated form. In the first *recercada*, the viol doubles the bass, but adds to the melody a considerable amount of ornamental passage-work. In the second *recercada*, it is the superius that is assigned to the viol, diminutions again being added, but this time there is no doubling. Not only does Ortiz omit the superius from the keyboard part, but he remarks that the music sounds better (*tiene mas gracia*) if the harpsichord does not play the top part under the circumstances. He states that the third *recercada* is like the first, except that it is harder, because it requires more manual skill. However, examination shows that, while the viol does indeed decorate the bass line much

Ex. 1

a) La Spagna

b) Passamezzo antico

c) Passamezzo moderno

d) Folia

e) Ruggiero

f) Romanesca

of the time, it sometimes shifts its attention and decorates the tenor instead. In the fourth *recercada*, the viol adds a new, fifth decorated part to the four basic parts in the harpsichord.

Ortiz turns next to that great international favorite of the time, Sandrin's four-part *chanson, Doulce mémoire,* and treats it in virtually the same general way, the only difference of any consequence being that in the third *recercada* of this series the viol is more consistent in elaborating the bass than it is in the third piece of the Arcadelt series.[7]

At the end of his comment before the second section, Ortiz promised that he would provide, later on, further examples of *recercadas* over *cantus firmi,* and this he does in the whole of the fourth section, in which the *recercadas* are based "on *cantus firmi* which in Italy they commonly call tenors." This section consists of nine examples, the first eight of which are numbered. The last one is headed *Quinta Pars,* and the original table of contents points out that this piece includes a fifth voice. However, the purpose of the indication is not entirely clear, since other *recercadas* in this section assign to the viol fifth parts that are equally independent. Some modern writers refer to the final section as consisting of eight *recercadas,* thereby implying that the *Quinta Pars* is a portion of the *Recercada Ottava.* However, the *Quinta Pars* is based on a different tenor and, as already indicated, receives a separate entry in the table of contents.

The Italian tenors that appear in the keyboard bass of the *recercadas* in this portion of the *Tratado* are those shown in Ex. 1b-f. Unlike the *recercadas* in section 2, in each of which the *Spagna* melody is presented only once, the pieces in section 4 repeat their tenors, the results being sets of variations.[8] In every piece, many of the *cantus-firmus* notes are immediately repeated one or more times, to produce rhythmic patterns. Some of the individual features of the nine pieces may be described as follows, the details being neatly illustrative of the way in which these traditional ground-basses could be adapted in the course of composition as well as of improvisation:

1. This presents seven variations over the *passamezzo antico.* Note 4 lies a minor third lower than in Ex. 1b—a common variant. An extraneous note is inserted before the penultimate one.
2. Six variations are constructed over the *passamezzo moderno.* In the first leap, the bass rises a fourth instead of descending a fifth; note 6 lies a fourth higher than in the normal form.
3. The *passamezzo moderno* is again used (this time for seven varations), but the penultimate note is supplemented by its upper and lower neighbors.
4. The *cantus firmus* here is a variant of the *folia*—actually a three-fold statement of it, no two statements being alike rhythmically;

the first note is omitted; B-flat is approached and quitted by leaps of a fifth down and up rather than by leaps of a fourth up and down; the optional C shown in Ex. 1d appears only in statement 3. The complete *cantus firmus* is presented twice.

5. This consists of nine variations over the first half of the *passamezzo moderno*.[9]

6. Ortiz provides three variations over the first three and a half measures of the *Ruggiero* tenor, to which he adds a cadence.[10] He lowers by a minor third the second note in (complete) measure 3. In the first leap, the bass rises a fourth instead of descending a fifth; the octave leap is replaced by a repetition. The frequency with which the direction of the leaps is changed in the application of the stock tenors, incidentally, helps to emphasize the extent to which they are not so much melodic formulas as harmony-generating formulas.

7. Ortiz employs the common variant of the *romanesca*, in which a C is inserted before the penultimate note. He turns the first and fourth leaps into ascents of a fifth instead of descents of a fourth, and the third leap into a descent of a third instead of a rise of a sixth. The *cantus firmus* in each of the three variations consists of the resulting modified tenor, extended by two restatements of the last three notes (each restatement containing immediate repetitions of the first and last notes).

8. Like Number 4, this is based on the variant of the *folia* that omits the first note and treats the B-flat in the way described above. The *cantus firmus* for each of the two variations consists of six statements of the tenor in three rhythmic patterns, each pattern being presented twice successively; the last pair uses the second ending shown in Ex. 1d.

9.[11] Nine variations unfold over a considerably modified form of the *passamezzo moderno*. Most leaps of fifths and fourths become leaps of fourths and fifths, respectively, in the opposite direction; the first pair of leaps is repeated; the fourth pitch element is decorated by its upper neighbor; the antepenultimate note is lowered a third.

To his own application of the procedures that he was aiming to teach, Ortiz was able to bring the exercise of a considerable creative gift, especially a fine gift for rhythm, so that, in illustrating his treatise, he simultaneously brought into being an attractive body of viable compositions.

Notes

1. The work was also published in the same city, and probably in the same year, with Italian text.

2. First edition, 1913; second, revised edition, Kassel: Bärenreiter, 1936.

3. Note 3 in his "Zur Frühgeschichte der Folia," *Acta musicologica*, VIII (1936), pp. 119-129.

4. In *Studies in Medieval and Renaissance Music* (New York: W. W. Norton & Co., 1950), pp. 190-216. In a music example on p. 208, Bukofzer makes the differences in the added *recercada* melodies strikingly clear by placing their openings in vertical alignment over the first four notes of the *cantus firmus*.

5. Ortiz's notes 1, 6, 9, 14, 17-19, 24, and 37 are repeated in the original.

6. Cf. Imogene Horsley, "Improvised Embellishment in the Performance of Renaissance Music," *Journal of the American Musicological Society* IV (1951), pp. 3-19.

7. The *chanson* and the four *recercadas* may be easily compared in the composite score in which they are printed (together with an ornamented version of the bass by Vincenzo Bonizzi, 1626) in Ernest Ferand, *Die Improvisation in Beispielen aus neun Jahrhunderten abendländischer Musik* (Cologne: Arno Volk Verlag, 1956; English ed., 1961), pp. 38 ff.

8. In the sense in which one may apply the term "variation" to chaconnes or passacaglias.

9. I.e., on the "in den Studententänzen vorkommende Halbform" (Gombosi, *op. cit.*, p. 128; see also *ibid.*, p. 120, about what Gombosi calls the bastard forms of the standard basses).

10. John Ward's article on the *Ruggiero* in *Die Musik in Geschichte und Gegenwart* includes examples of it in a generous number of variant forms.

11. I.e., the *Quinta Pars*, discussed on p. 205.

PARODY TECHNIQUE

IN 16TH-CENTURY

INSTRUMENTAL MUSIC

John M. Ward (Cambridge, Massachusetts)

$\mathcal{T}$he aim of this paper is to state in sharper terms and with the help of new evidence one aspect of an earlier study, "The Use of Borrowed Material in 16th-Century Instrumental Music." [1] For this purpose I propose to define parody technique as *free (often random) variation of an autonomous thematic complex,* a definition that can be glossed as follows:

1. In variation properly speaking (i.e., in the diferencia, partita, modo, variatio, etc.) the theme normally determines the length, in measures at least, and, generally, the musical events—of harmony, melody, phrasing—of each variation; no such predictable relationship exists between a parody and its theme. Parody is *ad libitum* variation.

2. The thing parodied (i.e., the theme) must exist independent of the parody; and the relationship between the two must be, if not that of equals (I think, e.g., of such an extreme case as the song Mahler turned into symphony movements), at least that of self-contained entities. A theme expressly created for variation lacks the independence requisite for parody.

3. Though the drawing off of individual voices from the theme is common enough in parody, the theme itself cannot be monophonic (i.e. a *cantus firmus* like *La Spagna* or public-domain tune like *Walsingham* or the single voice-part of a madrigal or motet), since an essential

feature of parody technique is the quotation—often literal—of vertical slices of the thematic complex, i.e., of chords and intervals.

4. For the same reason, the theme must exist already fully realized and not be, like the great skeletal patterns of the 16th century—*folia, romanesca, passamezzo antico,* etc.—a harmonic plan whose melodic and other details are to be worked out in each variation.[2] In other words, the theme must exist complete in all particulars, though the composer is under no obligation to use all or even much of it.

Three examples, each making use of the same borrowed music, but only one satisfying the proposed requirements for parody, will further clarify the distinctions involved.

One of the dances in John Dowland's *Lachrimae* is entitled "M. Buctons Galiard"; it is, in fact, nothing more than three sections of Lasso's well-known chanson *Susanne un jour* cast in galliard time and arranged for instrumental ensemble.[3] Dowland has done little beyond selecting the passages, if, indeed, the selection is his.[4] The first strain derives from measures 1-6 of the chanson, then skips to the cadence in measures 13-14.[5] Similarly, the second strain derives from measures 28-34, then skips to the cadence in measures 47-48. The third strain quotes the end of the chanson, measures 53-58. Departures from Lasso's original amount to isolated chord changes, the juggling of inner voice-parts, an occasional octave displacement of the bass. The piece is, in short, an arrangement, similar to the many chanson arrangements in the *danceries* of Attaingnant, Susato, and others, more a product of scissors and paste than of composition.[6]

Four *glosas* of the same Lasso chanson are included in the *Flores de Música* (1617) of the Portuguese Manuel Rodrigues Coelho.[7] All four reproduce, chord by chord but not note for note, the entire Lasso piece, including sectional repetition. Over the familiar bones is draped a tissue of tired *Spielfiguren: cantus-firmus* technique applied to a *corpus firmus*. The *glosas* are four figural variations of Lasso's chanson, direct descendants of the so-called "colored transcriptions" made by generations of keyboard players.[8]

Quite different is Giulio Severino's *Fantasia . . . sopra Susane un jour* included in Simone Molinaro's *Intavolatura di Liuto* (1599).[9] With the chanson's 58 measures (really 44, since he ignores the repetition of the first section) the lutenist creates 112. Like Coelho, he proceeds systematically through the chanson; but instead of setting up, like corset stays, one chord of the theme on the first beat of each measure, he quotes short patches of the borrowed music, sometimes a phrase, sometimes less, and surrounds the more or less exact quotations with sections in which he freely develops motives drawn from the chanson. Most of the Lasso piece is appropriated; a few small spots are left out or only hinted at. Some idea of the technique employed can be gained from study of the fantasia's opening section.

Ex. 1.

Lasso: Susanne un jour

Severino: Fantasia sopra Susanne un jour

Severino's quotations of the chanson are variously exact (e.g. m. 2-3), transposed (m. 1-2, down an octave; m. 8-13, down a fourth), altered slightly (m. 13-14, with voices omitted) or significantly (m. 4-6, the cantus and alto exchanged; m. 25-26, passing notes added); snippets of the chanson are omitted (e.g. m. 23 and 25); and most of the chanson's motives are led through imitations far more ambitious and lively than the modest few of Lasso's text-inhibited music; in this way Severino produces two sections, respectively 13 and 14 measures long, to Lasso's one of 15 measures. The added length is achieved largely by means of paraphrase of the theme: i.e., by using borrowed motives, chord sequences, structural plan in a manner different from that found in the theme, the parodist expressing borrowed ideas in his own music. The "second exposition" in Ex. 1, m. 8-13, provides an instance; another occurs in m. 13-22, where a brief passage of no great moment in Lasso's piece is developed at length in the lutenist's.

Unlike the Dowland arrangement and the Coelho glosas, Severino's fantasia *sopra Susane un jour* is a relatively free variation of an autonomous thematic complex, i.e., a parody in the light of the definition proposed at the beginning of this paper.

Pieces making similar use of borrowed music include Alonso de Mudarra's glosa of the "Cum sancto Spiritu" section of Josquin's *Missa de Beata Virgine;*[10] Andrea Gabrieli's three ricercars on chansons and one on a madrigal;[11] an anonymous *Report upone* [Tallis's] *quhan sall my sorowfull sighing slaik;*[12] a fantasia on Palestrina's *Vestiva i colli* by John Bull;[13] etc. The way parodies of the same music can differ may be seen, e.g., in the opening measures (given in Ex. 2) of three fantasias on Cipriano de Rore's popular *Anchor che col partire*, one by Vincenzo Galilei,[14] a second by Melchior Neusidler,[15] the third by Nicolas de la Grotte.[16]

Having defined the species, I now propose to describe the varieties of parody. For how much of the theme is incorporated, which parts are chosen, where they appear, how they are varied, differs considerably from piece to piece. The close exegesis of a text, of which Severino's fantasia and the other pieces just cited are illustrative, contains, in diluted form, most of that text's respective thematic complex; the parodies now to be cited contain something less.

Antonio de Cabezón mixes quotation and paraphrase in nearly equal parts in his *Tiento sobre Qui la dira.*[17] Proceeding punctiliously through the whole of Willaert's chanson, he borrows, first motives only, then brief patches of two- and three-voice writing, finally all of the chanson's last 14 measures. Most of the theme is drawn upon in some manner, but only 26 of its 46 measures are actually quoted and many of these are somewhat elaborated.

Less overt use of the theme occurs in Claude Le Jeune's great two-

Ex. 2.

Cipriano de Rore: Anchor che col partire

Vincenzo Galilei: Fantasia sopra Anchor che col partire (Fronimo, 1568)

Melchior Neusidler: Fantasia super Anchor che col partire (Intabolatura, 1566; Munich Ms.1627, ff.15^V - 16^V)

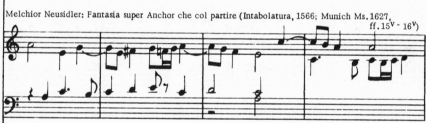

Nicolas de La Grotte: Fantasia sopra Anchor che col partire (Vienna, N.B., Ms.10110, fol. 32)

This example is continued on p. 214.

part *Fantasia ad imitationem moduli Benedicta es coelorum Regina*.[18] Doubts have been expressed concerning the presence of parody throughout the piece; and the fact that Josquin's motet and the fantasia both paraphrase the plainsong melody has encouraged this doubt. However, quotation of vertical, albeit freely handled, slices of Josquin's motet

are met with in most parts of Le Jeune's piece. In a few places he
quotes four of the motet's six voice-parts; more often he quotes short
snippets of two- and three-voice writing; and at times a single, *cantus-
firmus*-like line supplies the point of contact between theme and
parody. Quotations are usually brief, often varied, therefore not always
easily located in the motet. No matter how extensive or full a quotation,
Le Jeune adds something of his own, be it new material or a paraphrase of Josquin's; the emphasis is on variation rather than on quotation.

Only at the beginning of each *pars* are the motet quotations easily heard by the "naked" ear.

Whatever the amount of borrowed music present and however extensive its paraphrasing, each piece thus far named or described has faithfully reflected the sequence of musical events found in its respective theme. The pieces next to be cited exmplify *random* borrowing, a quite different kind of variation. If one likens the former variety to interlinear commentary, the latter is more like the homiletic use of Scripture.

In the first 35 measures of his tiento on *Malheur me bat,* Cabezón paraphrases in a number of ways Ockeghem's first 8; and in the remaining 22 he treats in a similar way the last 5 measures of the chanson, omitting all the rest of Ockeghem's—for Cabezón rather old-fashioned—chanson.[19] How the borrowed material is freely elaborated can be seen in the following transformations of the chanson's closing measures.

Ex. 3.

Ockeghem: Malor me bat (Odhecaton, No. 63)

Antonio [de Cabezón] : Tiento sobre Malheur me bat (Venegas de Henestrosa, Libro de cifra nueva, No. 43)

In Enriquez de Valderrábano's fantasia on certain passages of Gombert's *Aspice Domine*, 29 measures are heard before any part of the
motet appears.[20] At this point the vihuelist quotes, with varying exactness, 34 measures of the theme (m. 8-41), beginning in the middle of the
first point of imitation and breaking off in the middle of another—an
indifference to imitative proprieties characteristic of the composer.
After an 8-measure development of a just-quoted Gombert motive, there
comes an almost uninterrupted mosaic of motet passages: m. 49-50, 54,
57-61, 68-69, 80-87. Another brief passage of Valderrábano's, followed
by a second quotation of m. 32-42, and the fantasia ends. In summary:
52 measures of the theme are used, 10 twice, and 57 not at all. Ex. 4
(on p. 217) presents an excerpt, which, in passing seamlessly from quotation to paraphrase to quotation, is typical of Valderrábano's parodies.[21]

Parodists sometimes use very little indeed of their themes. For
example, in a fine piece described in one source as the *Galliard upon the
Galliard before*, John Dowland borrows little more than the first half-
strain of a popular dance by Daniel Bacheler, and passes quickly from
quotation to vigorous development of the galliard's *C B*-flat *A*-flat *G*
opening motive.[22] Particularly striking are Dowland's 9-measure strain
and 10-measure varied reprise in place of Bacheler's neat strain and
reprise of 8 (4 plus 4) measures. Francis Cutting's parody of the same
galliard is at once freer and more indebted to the theme than
Dowland's.[23]

In these and other parodies actual quotation of the thematic complex
is of less significance than other types of borrowing. The opening 26
measures of Giovanni Paolo Paladino's fantasia on *Quand' io pens' al
martire* presents a continuous discourse on Arcadelt's opening motive,

Ex. 4.

Gombert: Aspice Domine (Opera Omnia, V, 88)

Enriquez de Valderrábano: Fantasía remedando en algunos pasos al Aspice de Gombert (Silva de sirenas, fol. 66ᵛ-67)

including ten statements to the madrigalist's epigrammatic three; in the
course of the first 17 of these 26 measures Paladino also includes, in
two-, five-, and three-measure bits, free but unmistakable quotations
of four-voice texture from the madrigal's first 6 measures.[24] No other
vertical quotations occur. Other of the madrigal's motives as well as
new ones by Paladino are developed; and toward the end of the fantasia the lutenist imitates a bit of the madrigal texture, thus:

Ex. 5.

Archadelt: Quand' io pens' al martire (Il Primo Libro di Madrigali a Quatro)

Paladino: Fantasie sur la ditte chanson (1553/60)

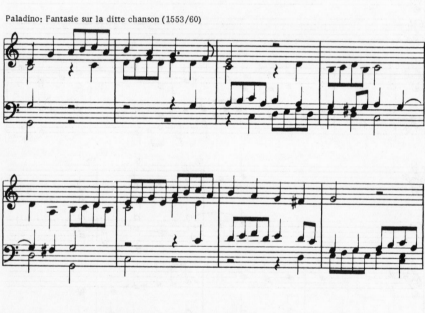

Equally restrained in its use of the theme is Francesco da Milano's *Fantasia De mon triste*.[25] Beginning with the first two measures of Richafort's chanson, he continues in brisk two- and three-voice imitative music to explore for 27 measures various permutations of the tones and intervals in the passage quoted. In other words, Francesco borrows just enough of the theme to allow composition in his usual, highly analytical, thematically parsimonious style.

Subtle to the point of debate is the relationship between Spinaccino's *Recercare a Juli amours and Recercare de tous biens* and their respective chanson themes, both of which appear, intabulated, elsewhere in the same *Libro Primo* of 1507.[26] It has been argued by those who find no palpabale relationship between the two that the recercars must be some kind of prelude or postlude or even ritornello to the chanson arrangements, the relationship analogous to the one between Bossinensis recercars which were expressly made to be played before (possibly after) frottola arrangements, Dalza's *Recercar detto Coda* which follows one of his *calate spagnole*, or others.[27]

I am not convinced the analogy is relevant or that the musical facts of the case have been exhausted. Spinaccino's recercar style is difficult to summarize: a seemingly casual mixture of activated two- and three-voice homophony, laced with one-voice rhapsodies, short sequences, an occasional bit of imitation, the latter more often suggested than realized. He was concerned, not with melody *per se* or with rhythm or repetition as begetters of form, but rather with abstract (an emergency word, alas!) elements—an interval, a modal segment, a trivial figure—, which he exploited with the practised hand of the improvisor. What would such a composer extract from a Ghiselin or Hayne van Ghizeghem chanson? Ex. 6 on pp. 220 and 221 shows m. 6-9 of the 28-measure *Recercare a Juli amours* and below the passage a few of the possible sources that lie at the bottom of it in the 83-measure Ghiselin song. (The music on the two facing pages should be read straight across.) Comparable resemblances between the *Recercare de tous biens* and Hayne's chanson can be shown. In neither instance is the borrowing more random, the treatment of borrowed material freer than that in several of the pieces described earlier; pieces, be it noted, in which the discrepancy in length between theme and parody is not so great. Neither extended or exact quotation nor exhaustive use of the theme is essential to parody. The requirements set forth at the start of this paper are satisfied when part (or all) of an autonomous thematic complex is freely varied. I propose that Spinaccino has satisfied these requirements.

Thus far the parodies mentioned have in some way declared in their titles one composer's indebtedness to another. There are as well parodies in no way identified as such. Their discovery is made with luck and their number is anybody's guess. Edward Lowinsky has found an instance

Ex. 6.

Francesco Spinacino: Recercare a Juli amours (Intabolatura de Lauto, Libro Primo, 1507)

Ghiselin: Joli amours (Petrucci, Canti C, 1505)

in the opening section of Master Newman's *Fancy*, the Englishman having drawn on the first measures of Marco Antonio (Cavazzoni) da Bologna's *Salve Virgo*.[28] Another instance is the—for the moment—inexplicable appearance midway through one of Albert de Rippe's fantasies of the Josquin *Cum Sancto Spiritu* also parodied by Mudarra and Cabezón.[29] And one of Mudarra's most elegant fantasias parodies another by Narváez.[30] Why composers, editors, publishers, copyists—it is impossible in most cases to know on whom to fix responsibility—failed sometimes to make known the presence of borrowed music is matter for speculation.[31]

In dealing with these "secret" parodies one must be prepared to discover that their mystery is not unlocked with a single key. Luys de Narváez's *Fantasia del primer tono por ge sol re ut* offers a cautionary example.[32] In its opening measures the Granadine vihuelist parodies the beginning of Josquin's *Adieu, mes amours* and in its closing measures Gombert's *Tu pers ton temps*,[33] though no hint of these borrowings is given in the three 16th-century prints in which the piece appears. Between parody sections the music is presumably Narváez's, though one cannot rule out the possibility of further chanson quotations and the discovery that the whole fantasia is a quodlibet, though I doubt that this is really the case.

The end of the mystery is not yet. Among the Albert de Rippe works published posthumously by Le Roy and Ballard is a fantasia that begins with parody of Josquin's *Adieu, mes amours* and later includes parody of Gombert's *Tu pers ton temps*. Further, there occur sufficient other references to Narváez's fantasia in de Rippe's to make obvious what the title of the latter piece does not: the lutenist has parodied the vihuelist's parody. (I assume this order of events, though it might be argued that the relationship was the other way about.[34]) Two musical styles could hardly differ more: the Spaniard's tight, lithe, balanced, in a word "classicistic"; the Italian's diffuse, asymmetrical, devious—I am tempted to add "manneristic." In Ex. 7 on pp. 224 and 225 (here again, as in Ex. 6, the music should be read straight across the facing pages), note, for example, how Narváez transforms the Gombert passage, compressing, adding a few of the striking cross-relations for which he had such a penchant, and how de Rippe follows Narváez for a moment, then strikes off on his unpredictable own.

Much remains to be learned about parody. This much is certain: it is an important type of 16th-century variation, differing from other types in the free (often random) handling of a composed theme. Parody is, indeed, the first of the variation types to make consistent use of a composed theme—i.e. a theme made by a particular composer (allowing, of course, for the common accident of his name having been lost in the transmission of his work)—instead of   an anonymous theme, often shaped through popular use.

Use of a composed theme suggests one way in which the two quite distinct meanings of the term parody—the one, satirical imitation; the other, the musical technique described in the preceding pages—can be reconciled. (I ignore for this occasion the *contrafactum*, which involves words, not music.) Parodists, whatever their purpose or esthetic means, create something new out of something already in existence, something that leads a life of its own. Chabrier's *Quadrille* for piano four-hands on "thèmes favoris" from *Tristan und Isolde*, for example, parodies the music drama without, to my knowledge, employing the musical technique described in the preceding pages.[35] Cavazzoni's recercar on *Faulte d'argent*, so far as we know, pokes no fun at Josquin's chanson, but draws on it for musical parody only.[36] It is in the technical use of the theme that the two parodies differ. But both works are at the same time variations of pre-existent, independent, composed—in the sense of the word employed above—themes, and herein they are kin; between each parody and its theme exists a clear if ambivalent relationship which encourages the informed listener to remember one musical passage even while his ear is concerned with another.

Notes

1. *Journal of the American Musicological Society*, V (1952), pp. 88-98.

2. It is commonly observed that 16th-century variation sets begin, not with the theme but with a variation. It should rather be observed that most 16th-century themes were monophonically or skeletally received and that a composer had perforce to begin with a setting, i.e., a variation, of the theme.

3. See P. Warlock's edition of the *Lachrimae* (London: Oxford University Press, 1927), p. 34. A different arrangement *a 5* by Dowland is in the Füllsack and Hildebrand *Ausserlesener Paduanen* (Hamburg, 1607), No. 18, paired with a Paduana of Joh. Sommer that makes use of the same Lasso music; see B. Engelke, *Musik und Musiker am Gottorfer Hofe*, I (*Schriften der Baltischen Kommission zu Kiel*, XII, 1; Breslau: Hirt, 1930), pp. 110-112. An arrangement of *M. Bucton's Galiard* for lute, also by Dowland, is *The Right Honourable the Lord Viscount Lisle, Lord Chamberlaine to the Queenes most Excellent Maiestie, his Galliard*, which opens Robert Dowland's *Musicall Banquet* of 1610.

4. Two different, anonymous lute arrangements of the same chanson excerpts are known: Cambridge University Ms. Dd. 2.11, fol. 52, *Susana Galliard*, and Nuremberg, Bibl. des Germanischen National-Museums, Ms. 33748/I, fol. 14, *Gall: Susanne*.

5. In this and subsequent references to music, one mensurally notated 16th-century semibreve (normally binary) equals one measure.

6. See, e.g., the similarly procrustean handling of a Josquin chanson in Susato's three-strain pavan *Mille regretz* in his *Danserye* of 1551, ed. F. J.

Ex. 7.

Gombert: Tu pers ton temps (Attaingnant, Vingt et six chansons, 1534)

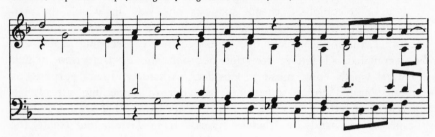

Narváez: Fantasía (Delphin de Música, 1538)

de Rippe: Fantasie (Quart livre de tabulature, 1553)

Giesbert (Mainz: Schott, 1936), I, p. 42. F. Blume, *Studien zur Vorgeschichte der Orchestersuite* (*Berliner Beiträge zur Musikwissenschaft*, 1; Leipzig: Kistner & Siegel, 1925), *Anhang* B, includes several examples of this common practice.

7. Ed. M. S. Kastner, *Portugaliæ Musica*, Series A, Vol. I (Lisbon: Fundação Gulbenkian, 1959), pp. 250-279; also separately under the title *4 Susanas* (Mainz: Schott, 1955).

8. There are similar keyboard glosas of Lasso's chanson by Ammerbach, A. Gabrieli, and Correa de Araujo in the Panmure Ms. 10, the Suzanne van Soldt Ms., etc.

9. G. Gullino's almost unreadable transcription of Severino's fantasia is included in his deceptively entitled *Intavolatura di Liuto di Gio. Battista Dalla Gostena* (Florence: Maurri, 1949), pp. 69-72. Gostena's glosa of the Lasso chanson is also included, pp. 65-68.

10. Ed. E. Pujol, *Monumentos de la Música Española*, Vol. VII (Barcelona: Consejo Superior de Investigaciones Cientificas, 1949), pp. 59-61.

11. Ed. P. Pidoux, *Orgel- und Klavierwerke* (Kassel: Bärenreiter), Vol. IV (n.d.), pp. 17-20, 24-26, 29-31; Vol. V (1953), pp. 36-39.

12. Ed. T. Dart and W. Coates, *Musica Britannica*, Vol. IX (London: Stainer & Bell, 1955), pp. 46-47. According to K. Elliott, *Music & Letters*, XXXIX (1958), p. 423, the piece is by John Black, though on what grounds the attribution is made he does not say.

13. Ed. J. Steele and F. Cameron, *Musica Britannica*, Vol. XIV (1960), pp. 25-26. Bull's second fantasia on the same madrigal is more random in its use of the theme.

14. *Fronimo* (Venice, 1568), pp. 94-96.

15. *Teütsch Lautenbuch* (Strasburg, 1574), No. 45.

16. Ed. J. Bonfils, *L'Organiste liturgique*, Vols. XXIX-XXX (Paris: Schola Cantorum, n.d.). The first page of the source, a Ms. in the Nationalbibl., Vienna, is reproduced in *Die Musik in Geschichte und Gegenwart*, Vol. III, col. 1769.

17. Ed. M. S. Kastner, *Tientos und Fugen* (Mainz: Schott, 1958), pp. 7-8, with the chanson-theme attributed to Janequin.

18. Ed. J. Bonfils, *Orgue et liturgie*, XXXIX (Paris: Schola Cantorum, 1956), pp. 15-22.

19. Ed. H. Anglés, *Monumentos de la Música Española*, II (1944), pp. 74-75.

20. *Silva de sirenas* (Valladolid, 1547), fol. 66'-67.

21. Libro V of Valderrábano's tablature contains at least 19 fantasias based in some way on borrowed material. According to the prevailing treatment of the themes, they can be divided roughly into quotation and paraphrase parodies, and *cantus-firmus* fantasias, the last-named conjectural since none of the themes has been found. Those of the first sort include: (1) the *Aspice Domine* parody, fol. 66'-67, described in the text above; (2) *Fantasía . . . contrahecha a otra estrangera*, fol. 68-68', on a fantasia by Alberto da Mantua (= da Ripa) first published in Casteliono's often reprinted anthology of 1536, fol. 5-6'; (3) *Fantasía . . . contrahecha a la del milanes*, fol. 70-70', on a fantasia by Francesco da Milano published in the same Casteliono anthology, fol. 55-56'; (4) *Fantasía . . . remedando de la mitad adelante* [= m. 23-46] *a un benedictus de la misa de Mouton tua est potentia*, fol. 71'-72; (5) *Fantasía sobre la entrada* [= m. 1-17] *de la gloria de la* [Lupus] *misa de panis quem ego dabo*, fol. 72-73, a parody of a parody; (6) *Fantasía remedada al chirie postrero de la misa de Josquin, de beata virgine*, fol. 73'-74; (7, 8) two fantasias on the *prima pars* of Mouton's motet *Quaeramus cum pastoribus*, fol. 79'-80'.

Probably similar to these but with themes I have either not found or not seen are: (9) *Fantasía . . . remedando a una magnificat de Morales que es al primer verso y al tercero*, fol. 67'-68 (according to H. Anglés, *Monumentos de la Música Española*, XVII [1956], p. 44, "es la versión del Magnificat, hasta aquí desconocido, concervado incompleto en Toledo, manuscrito 18 de Libros Polifonía"); (10) *Fantasía . . . remedando a un Pleni de contrapunto*, fol. 68'-69; (11) *Fantasía remedando a un pleni de una misa de Bauldoin*, fol. 74-74', whose theme is not to be found in any of the Masses listed in Schmidt-Görg's article on Bauldoin in *Die Musik in Geschichte und Gegenwart;* (12) *Fantasía . . . remedando a un quia fecit de contrapunto*, fol. 77-77'; (13) the *Fantasía . . . contrahecha a otra de Francisco milanes*, fol. 78'-79', for whose theme extensive search in the works of Francesco has proved fruitless.

(14) The *Fantasía . . . sobre la entrada de una baxa*, fol. 64-65, may parody the opening measures of Narváez's *Baxa de contrapunto;* however, the resemblance is slight, and the entrada may be that of the monophonic basse danse tenor on which Narváez's piece is based and on which Valderrábano also composed a duet for two vihuelas, *Sobre el tenor de la baxa*, fol. 58'-60. Other fantasias composed on themes probably monophonic include: (15) *Fantasía sobre un Benedictus*, fol. 64; (16) *Fantasía . . . remedando a una entrada de ave maris stella*, fol. 69-69'; and (17) a *Fantasía sobre una entrada de una canción*, fol. 74'-75.

(18) The fantasia described in one place as *remedando a algunos pasos de la misa de Josquin de Ave maris stella*, and in another as *acomposturada de cierta parte de la missa*, fol. 75'-76, draws very slightly on the second Kyrie and, perhaps, bits of the Credo. Problematic is the fantasia (19) described as *alguno tanto acomposturada del motete de Gombert, que se dize Inviolata*, fol. 71-71', whose use of the theme is difficult to discover and may not exceed certain stylistic and structural similarities.

22. Dowland's galliard appears in Cambridge University Ms. Dd. 5.78.3, fol. 35'-36; Fitzwilliam Museum Ms. 3-1956 (Lord Herbert of Cherbury's Ms.),

fol. 54'-55; British Museum Add. Ms. 38539, fol. 15'-16; Glasgow University Ms. R.D.43, fol. 20'-21; and Fuhrmann's *Testudo Gallo-Germanica* (Nuremberg, 1615), pp 108-110, *Galliarda incerti Authoris 2*.

Bacheler's galliard is found in Cambridge University Mss. Dd. 2.11, fol. 99'; Dd. 4.22, fol. 6'-7; Dd. 9.33, fol. 4; British Museum Add. Ms. 38539, fol. 15'; Glasgow University Ms. R.d.43, fol. 21; Trinity College, Dublin, Ms. D.1.21, p. 17; the Welde Ms., fol. 7'. An anonymous arrangement *a 5* is in Füllsack and Hildebrand, *Ausserlesener Paduanen*, ed. Engelke, *Musik und Musiker am Gottorfer Hofe*, p. 104.

Bacheler's galliard is based on his own lute song, *To plead my faith*, found in Robert Dowland's *Musicall Banquet*, sig. D2'-E, and, arranged *a 5* by W. Wigthorp, in British Museum Add. Ms. 17786, fol. 12'-13; and *a 2*, with the melody embellished, in Add. 24456, fol. 48'-49 (the Giles Earle Ms.). Dowland's *My thoughts are winged with hope*, from *The First Booke of Songs* (1597), No 3, and its instrumental form, *Sir John Souch his Galiard*, in *Lachrimae*, No. 13, are indebted to the first strain of Bacheler's song (unless the indebtedness runs the other way).

23. Cutting's piece occurs in Cambridge University Ms. Dd. 9.33, fol. 10'.

24. The fantasia is on fol. 16-17' of the *Premier livre de tablature de luth* (Lyons, 1560 on the title-page; 1553 in the colophon). Paladino's work also contains another madrigal and two motet parodies, one of the latter on Jacotin's *Proba me Domine*.

25. Richafort's chanson is reprinted in Commer's *Collectio*, Vol. XII (Berlin, 1858), 13. Francesco's fantasia is in his *Intabolatura de Lauto . . . Libro Terzo* (Venice, 1547), sig. B4-B4', which also contains a straightforward intabulation of the chanson on sig. B3'-B4.

26. The recercars are on fol. 37'-38 and 38-38' of Petrucci's first *Intabulatura de Lauto* (Venice, 1507); the two chansons, arranged for lute duet, are on fol. 11-18'.

27. The arguments are summarized by Otto Gombosi, *Compositione di Meser Vincenzo Capirola* (Neuilly-sur-Seine: Société de Musique d'Autrefois, 1955), pp. xxxii-xxxiiii.

28. Contrary to the opinion expressed in a contribution to *La Musique instrumentale de la Renaissance*, ed. J. Jacquot (Paris: Centre National de la Recherche Scientifique, 1955), p. 229, n. 9, I now find myself in agreement with Professor Lowinsky concerning Newman's indebtedness to Cavazzoni; see "English Organ Music of the Renaissance," *The Musical Quarterly*, XXXIX (1953), pp. 389-391. Whether Newman's *Fancy* was originally composed for keyboard or lute remains in question. The Archbishop Marsh's Library Ms. Z3.2.13 contains two versions of the piece for lute: one, on p. 49, similar to the keyboard version in the Mulliner Book; the other, on pp. 230-231, more elaborate and a full section longer than either of the simpler versions. Which is the original form of the piece is difficult to guess.

29. Further concerning this popular Josquin excerpt, see "The Use of Borrowed Material in 16th-Century Instrumental Music," pp. 90-91, 94-95. In a similarly puzzling fashion, a piece by John Blow (see W. Shaw's edition of the *Complete Organ Works* [London: Hinrichsen, 1958], pp. 2-3) begins with 9 bars of a Frescobaldi toccata (*Orgel- und Klavier Werke*, ed. P. Pidoux [Kassel: Bärenreiter, 1949], Vol. III, p. 43), and another piece (Shaw's ed., pp. 59-63) incorporates, m. 45-57, part of another Frescobaldi toccata (Pidoux's ed., Vol. III, pp. 29-30). In both instances the borrowed music is more quoted than parodied.

There are, of course, works of composite authorship acknowledged to be such, of which the Sweelinck-Scheidt variations of the *Pavana Hispanica* (ed. M. Seiffert, *Werken van J. P. Sweelinck*, Vol. I, rev. ed. [Amsterdam: Vereeniging voor Nederlandsche Muziekgeschiedenis, 1943], pp. 248-251) is the best-known instance; but see also *Io mi son giovinetta del Ferrabosco diminuito per sonare da Scip[ione]. Stella, Gio. Dom. Montella, Ascanio Mayone* in Mayone's *Secondo Libro di Diversi Capricci* (Naples, 1609), pp. 68-78; the two *Passomezi variorum Authoram* in Fuhrmann's *Testudo Gallo-Germanica* (Nuremberg, 1615), pp. 75-85; the tiento "de varios autores" published by Kastner, *Monumentos de la Música Española*, Vol. XII (1952), pp. 256-261, from the Ms. additions to the Real Biblioteca da Ajuda, Lisbon, exemplar of the Correa de Arauxo *Facultad Orgánica;* etc.

30. Compare, e.g., m. 6-17 of No. 35, *Monumentos de la Música Española*, Vol. VII, with m. 65-67 of No. 4, Vol. III of the same series.

31. I have discussed a related problem in "The Editorial Methods of Venegas de Henestrosa," *Musica Disciplina*, VI (1952), pp. 105-113.

32. Ed. E. Pujol, *Monumentos de la Música Española*, Vol. III, No. 1.

33. Josquin's chanson is reprinted, e.g., in A. Smijers, *Van Ockeghem tot Sweelinck*, Vol. V (Amsterdam: Alsbach, 1949), pp. 156-157. J. Schmidt-Görg, *Nicolas Gombert* (Bonn: Röhrscheid, 1938), p. 227, prints the incipit of *Tu pers ton temps.*

34. Narváez's fantasia was first printed in 1538 and reprinted, translated into French lute tablature, in both 1546 editions of Phalèse's *Livre deuxième.* De Rippe died before February 1552; his fantasia was printed for the first time in the *Quart livre de tabulature de luth* (Paris: Le Roy and Ballard, 1553), fol. 2-5; it does not appear in the Fezandat-Morlaye edition of de Rippe's *oeuvre.* We cannot enter into the vexing question of who is responsible for what appears in these posthumous publications of the *feu Maistre;* e.g., the very next fantasia in the *Quart livre* is a disarranged version of one by Francesco da Milano. Both the date of publication and the musical style of the two pieces argue for Narváez's as the theme and de Rippe's as the parody.

35. *Souvenirs de Munich: Quadrille pour piano à quatre mains sur les thèmes favoris de Tristan & Iseult,* in *Revue musicale S.I.M.*, VII (1911), pp. 33-44. Chabrier's irreverent attitude can be seen, e.g., in the third of the five pieces, entitled "Poule," in which he uses the tune the shepherd plays in Act III when Isolde's ship is finally sighted.

36. The Josquin chanson and Cavazzoni recercar are both reprinted in the *Historical Anthology of Music* of A. T. Davison and W. Apel, Vol. I (Cambridge, Mass.: Harvard University Press, 1946)), pp. 93-95, 126-127.

ADDENDA TO THE

BIOGRAPHY OF

JACOBUS VAET

Milton Steinhardt (Lawrence, Kansas)

Since the publication of my book on Jacobus Vaet [1] in 1951, our scanty knowledge of the composer's life has been augmented by a number of discoveries. Of these, the most notable is undoubtedly a letter that Vaet wrote to Ferdinand II, Archduke of the Tyrol, for it is his only known autograph. Other documents are equally valuable, however, and one should now incorporate all of them into the biography of the composer. In eventually doing this, I shall take the opportunity to add certain emendations to my previous account of his life.

As has been known, Jacobus vander Vaet (to use the original family name) was a choir boy of the church of Notre Dame in Courtrai in the 1540's. According to the *Acta capitularia* of that church, his father, Egidius, petitioned the Chapter to accept his son on February 17, 1543, and Jacobus is referred to as being thirteen years old at the time.[2] It follows then that he was born between February 18, 1529, and February 17, 1530, with 1529 the more likely birth year.

In the same entry of the *Acta*, Vaet's father is called "magistro Egidio vanden Vaet custode de huele." The previously puzzling word, "huele," has been found to be the old form of Heule, a village near Courtrai. By "custode" (*custos*) is meant a sacristan or sexton of the church. Since the sexton's duties often included the accompanying of the religious singing on some instrument (an organ if available), it is probable that Egidius possessed musical talent.

The Vander Vaet family seems to have been fairly new to Courtrai and Heule, according to the evidence of the archives of those communities.[3] It appears that it came from Harlebeke, for this town, some five kilometers from Courtrai, has recently been established as the birthplace of Jacobus.

An inquiry directed to the University of Louvain has brought to light the fact that, in its matriculation records for August 29, 1547, a "Jacobus Vat de Arlebeka" is listed. Since Jacobus vander Vaet had received from the Chapter of Notre Dame of Courtrai a subsidy for two years to be spent "in learning letters diligently wherever he will" on June 28, 1546, the matriculant named is undoubtedly our composer. This entry, in addition to designating Vaet's place of birth,* informs us of his educational background and fills in part the biographical gap between his departure from Courtrai and his first known connection with the Hapsburg court, in 1553. The Courtrai archives record that Jacob's grandfather, like his father, was named Gillis, the Flemish equivalent of Egidius. There are references also to an uncle, Joos vander Vaet, and to a brother named Jan (=Johannes).[4] The latter apparently had seven children, of whom one, Maximiliaen, might have been named after Maximilian II, his uncle's royal patron. The nature of frequent references to the Cokere family in connection with those relating to the Vaets indicates that Elizabeth de Cokere became the wife of Egidius and was Jacob's mother.

By the middle of May, 1547, both of the parents had died. The subsequent settlement of the estate was recorded in the *Hane*, or "Rooster," as the register devoted to affairs of orphans of the citizens of Courtrai was called:

Joos vander Vaet Dieric de Cockere in Huele ende ———— als voochden van Hannekin ende Coppin vander Vaet filii Me Gillis bringhen over by huerlederen eede up den XXVIIᵉⁿ in Meye XVᶜXLVII het goedt den weesen toecommen ende verstorven byden overlydene vanden vaedere ende moedere Te wetene een behuusde hostede groet acht hondert ofte daer ontrent noch twee huusen staende ter plaetse te Huele met zulcke renten als eer de heere up heeft Item noch een vyverkin groet een hondert ende half in Huele.

Joos vander Vaet, Dieric de Cockere, in Huele, and————, as guardians of Hannekin [Johannes] and Coppen [Jacob] vander Vaet, sons of Master Gillis, on their oath transfer on May 27, 1547, the estate to which the orphans are entitled in consequence of the death of the father and mother. This comprises a farm with a house on it, measuring some 800 *roeden* [about 1.8 acres or 8/11 of a hectare] and two more houses situated on the town square in Huele, together with such rents as the lord has a right to; also a small

* See ADDENDUM at end of article.

Den VII^{sten} in Hoymaendt XV^C-XLVII zo certifierde Jacop Josep stedecnape dat de voochden consent hebben van Ghyselbrecht Crommelinc Adriaen de Crytsche Joos de Hane ende Andries de Pratere als scepenen te mueghene vercoepene al tlant ende huussen ende catteilen daer up staende omme daer mede schulden te betalene ende rekeninghe ende bewys te doene.

Den VIII^{sten} in Mey XV^CXLVIII was by Maerten vander Beke inghebroch de somme van XXIIII lbs grooten commende vanden vercochten lande up idem uut ghegheven an Jan Stuvaert in Lee ende staet inden hane.

Den XXVIII^{sten} in Ougst XV^C-XLIX zo brochte Maerten vander Beke noch over commende vanden vercochten lande de somme van XII lbs grooten up idem uut ghegheven an Alaert de Persyn in Curtricke ende es ghestelt inden hane.

Den eersten in Ougst LI compareerde hier Jan vander Vaet ghehuudt zynde ende Jacop zyn broeder zyn selfs zynde alzoo Me Joos vanden Berghe certiffierde ende hilden hemleden content van huerleder goede ontsloughen huere voghden ende allen anderen.[5]

pond of 150 *roeden* [about ⅓ of an acre or 13 ares] in Huele.

On July 7, 1547, Jacop Josep, the town messenger, certified that the guardians had received permission from the aldermen, Ghyselbrecht Crommelinc, Adriaen de Crytsche, Joos de Hane, and Andries de Pratere, to sell the whole of the land together with the houses and chattels upon it, to pay the outstanding debts, and to make a full accounting.

On May 8, 1548, Maerten vander Beke brought in the sum of 24 great pounds [one great pound equalled 12 Parisian pounds] received from the sale of land and committed it to Jan Stuvaert in Lee, as is recorded in the *Hane*.

On August 28, 1549, Maerten vander Beke brought in an additional 42 great pounds realized from the sale of land, and on the same date this sum was committed to Alaert de Persyn in Courtrai, as is recorded in the *Hane*.

On August 1, 1551, there appeared here Jan vander Vaet, being married, and Jacob his brother, having reached his majority, as Master Joos vanden Berghe certified, and they declared that the estate was settled to their satisfaction and that their guardians and all others were free of further obligation.

The mention of Jacobus Vaet as having reached his majority would in those days have meant that he was twenty-five years old, whereas we have reason to believe that he was only twenty-one or twenty-two. However, majority was sometimes granted by special dispensation before attainment of legal age, and this may well have been done for Jacobus in view of his status as an orphan.

The heretofore circumstantial evidence by which Jacobus Vaet, the Hapsburg court composer, has been identified with Jacobus vander Vaet, the choir boy of Courtrai,[6] is confirmed elsewhere. It is now made conclusive by the aforementioned entry in the *matricule* of the University of Louvain, wherein the name, for the first time, appears as "Vat," without the prefix. Additional evidence can be deduced from an item in the *Acta capitularia* of the church of Notre Dame dated January 19, 1557: "Vocarunt coram se magistrum Franciscum Hemum capellanum huius ecclesiae paedagogum privatum et privatim docentem

. . ." [7] Thus we learn that the poet François Haemus, who devoted a number of his works to people from Courtrai and its environs, and who wrote an elegy on Vaet's death, was himself a chaplain of the church of Notre Dame.

The death of Vaet was recorded not only in the Hapsburg court records, as has been previously known, but also in the private diary or memorandum book kept by Emperor Maximilian II. In this document, which is made up mostly of notations concerning political or family affairs, there are only two references to musicians. One of them, written in 1567, reads: "Den 8, Januarij ist main capelmaister Jacobus Faet in gott verschiden." [8]

Maximilian's brother, Ferdinand, had a high respect for Vaet's judgment and ability. When he wished to form his own court chapel, in 1564, he therefore turned to Vaet, among others, for help in obtaining singers and music. On August 30th of that year, he wrote from Prague to thank Vaet for sending him some of the singers from the disbanded choir of his father, Emperor Ferdinand I, who had recently died. [9] A few months later, on November 2nd, he wrote again to Vaet, as follows:

Getreur lieber Nach dem wir un-längst wie dir gehorsamblich wohl bewusst ein Cantorey bestellt und aufgenomben haben, so ist unser gnediges anliegen an dich du wellest zu desto pesserer fürsehung solcher unser Cantorey zwei oder dreierley guete Compositiones Missae (ausser der Confundantur genannt, so der Orlando komponiert und unser Capellmaister zuvorhin hat) gehorsamblich mittheilen und mit dem ehendisten überschicken . . . [10]

Faithful and Well-beloved: As you are dutifully well aware, we have recently appointed and established a chapel choir. So it is now our gracious desire that you inform us concerning two or three good Masses for its better provision (other than the *Missa Confundantur* composed by Orlando, which our Kapellmeister already has) and send them to us as soon as possible.

Vaet was quick to accede to this request, for on December 5th Hans von Welsberg, a member of Ferdinand's court, wrote to his patron from Vienna: "So hat mir der Rö. Kay. May. etc. Capellmeister drei neigesezte oder componierte Messen mitler weil zuegestellt." [11] ("In the meantime the imperial choir director has delivered to me three newly composed Masses.")

The letter that Vaet addressed to Ferdinand II is dated November 21st of the following year, 1565. In a beautifully clear and graceful script the composer wrote as follows:

Allerdurchleüchtigister Gross-mechtigister Fürst und Herr etc. allergnedigist Herr.
Euer Für. durch. meinem aller-

Most illustrious, mighty sovereign and lord, most gracious lord:
My obedient, diligent, and loyal service has at all times been at the

gnedigisten Herrn sein mein gehorsam
geflissen und underthennigist dienst
alzeit zuvor berait. Wievol ich Euer
Für. Durch. bissherr mit meinem geringen vermügen hab wenig diennen
khünnen. Yedoch dieweil ich unver-
dienter bissher ieder Zeit bei Eurer
Für. Durch. allen gunst und gnad ge-
spürt, wil es sich nit unbillich ge-
tzümen das ich mich widerumb gegen
Euer Für. Durch. wo nicht nach gepür
jedoch sovil imer müglich mit diesem
geringsten dankhpar ertzaig.

Schikh derwegen Euer Für. Durch.
ein Motetam die ich die verschinnen
täg Euer Für. durch. zu ehren gesetzt
hab. Bit underthennigist E. Für.
Durch. wellens gnedigist und mit frö-
lichen gemüet von mir annenemen and
zu glegener Zait anhören.

Daneben bit ich underthennigist
Euer Für. Durch. wellen meinen Dis-
cipulum mit namen Gregorium den
ich Eueren Für. Durch. zugeschikht,
wofer er anderst tauglich ist, in dersel-
ben Capellen zu einem Singer aufne-
men oder aufs wenigist mit im ver-
suechen ob er sich mit der Zeit mit
der stimb pessern wurd. Im faal aber
das es ye nit sein khund, so bit ich
nochmals underthennigist Euer Für.
durch. wellen seiner doch mit einem
gnadengelt auf das er widerumb ins
Niederland zu seinen Eltern ziehen,
und dasselbs etwo ein Condition uber-
khumen müg, allergenedigist nit
vergessen.

Diss alles wil ich selbs nach meinem
geringen Vermügen umb Euer Für.
durch. meinen allergnedigisten Fürsten
und Herrn widerumb zuverdiennen
jeder Zeit underthennigist geflissen
sein. Thue hiemit Euer Für. durch.
mich underthennigist und gehorsamist
bevelhen.

Datum Wienn den 21. Novembris
65 Jars.

Euer Für. Durch. Underthennigis-
ter gehorsamister diener,
Jacobus Vaet.
Röm. Kay. mt. Capelmaister.[12]

disposal of your highness, my most
gracious lord. Nevertheless, I have
thus far been able to serve your illustrious highness but little with my
meager talents.

Inasmuch as I have at all times in
the past received undeserved favor
and grace from your highness, it is fitting that I in turn show my gratitude,
if not as much as is due, at least insofar as lies within my power.

I therefore send your highness a
motet that I have recently composed
in your honor. I humbly beg that
your highness accept it graciously and
in joyful spirit, and that at some convenient time you listen to it.

At the same time, I humbly beg
your excellency to accept into your
chapel as a singer, if he be qualified,
my pupil named Gregory, whom I
have sent to your highness; or at least
to try him to see if his voice will
improve in time. In case this cannot
be done, I humbly ask that your highness graciously remember him and
give him an allowance so that he may
return to his parents in the Low
Countries and may secure a situation
there.

I shall try, insofar as it lies within
my poor powers, to merit all this and
to serve your highness most humbly
and diligently. Herewith I commend
myself to your highness most loyally
and obediently.

Vienna, the 21st of November, the
65th year.

Your highness's most loyal and
obedient servant,
Jacobus Vaet
Kapellmeister to his Imperial
Majesty

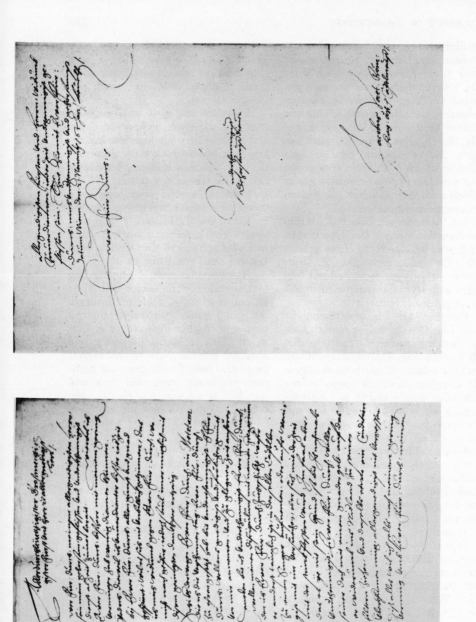

PLATE 1

Holograph Letter from Vaet to Maximilian II dated November 21, 1565. (Innsbruck, Landesregierungsarchiv, Hofregistratur.)

This document is valuable on three counts. First, it provides us with an autograph of the composer, the only one known. Second, it enables us to date one of Vaet's motets, *Ferdnande imperio princeps* (for this is undoubtedly the work referred to), some three years prior to its first published appearance, in the Joanellus *Novus thesaurus musicus*. And finally, by showing Vaet's solicitude for the welfare of one of his pupils, it adds a warmly human element to the factual data on his life.

ADDENDUM

According to a communication from the author, received after the above article had already been typeset, a visit to the archives of both Courtrai and Harlebeke made in July 1964 has led him "to the conclusion that Vaet's birthplace can only be designated as 'Courtrai or Harlebeke.'" The author also found, in the "notes de Pinchart" at the Bibl. Royale de Belgique at Brussels, evidence that Vaet served as a tenor in the Flemish chapel of Charles V for some time (or perhaps continuously) between 1551 and 1554.—G. R.

Notes

1. Milton Steinhardt, *Jacobus Vaet and his Motets* (East Lansing: Michigan State College Press, 1951). Subsequent references to this work will be by the short title, *Jacobus Vaet.*
2. On fol. 99v. The entry is quoted and translated in *Jacobus Vaet,* p. 1 f. The *Acta* are now in the Episcopal Archives in Bruges.
3. I am deeply indebted to the late Dr. J. Soete, Municipal Archivist of Courtrai, for having undertaken the necessary investigations in my behalf.
4. It is noteworthy in this connection that Vaet set the text, *Misit Herodes* (from Acts, 12), with its reference to "James the brother of John." By curious coincidence, the first tenor part of Vaet's motet, *Miser qui amat,* is ascribed to "Joannes" Vaet in the *Thesaurus musicus* of Berg and Neuber.
5. *Den Hane,* "Huelle" LIII, fol. 2v.
6. In *Jacobus Vaet,* p. 3 f.
7. Fol. 191r and 191v.
8. Vienna, *Haus- Hof- und Staatsarchiv, Familienakten,* Kart. 88, fol. 72r, item 5. The second reference is to Gabriele Martinengo, who had sent a gift of his works to the emperor in the hope of becoming court composer.
9. This letter is quoted in Walter Senn, *Musik und Theater am Hof zu Innsbruck* (Innsbruck: Oesterreichische Verlagsanstalt, 1954), p. 66.
10. Innsbruck, *Landesregierungsarchiv, Hofregistratur,* B., Fasz. 4. The parenthetical reference to Lasso's *Missa Confundantur* establishes conclusively the authorship of this work, which was considered doubtful by Joachim Huschke, writing in the *Archiv für Musikwissenschaft* in 1940. More recently, Wolfgang Boetticher has attributed the Mass to Lasso, though unaware of this evidence. See his *Orlando di Lasso und seine Zeit* (Kassel: Bärenreiter, 1958), pp. 316 and 856.
11. Innsbruck, *Landesregierungsarchiv, loc. cit.*
12. Innsbruck, *Landesregierungsarchiv, loc. cit.* For photographic reproductions of the letters quoted in this article, I am indebted to the *Landesregierungsarchiv* and to Dr. Walter Senn of Innsbruck.

TABLE BLESSINGS

SET TO MUSIC

Carleton Sprague Smith (New York)

*T*he custom of giving thanks or asking a blessing at meal times goes back thousands of years and was practiced in the Orient as well as in countries bordering on the Mediterranean. Dietary laws have played an important role in Judaism, and blessings connected with certain days were early introduced. The writings of Homer, Plato, and Virgil indicate the universality of remembering divine benevolence while eating and drinking. Moses, Joshua, and David praised God for food partaken, and when Jesus fed the multitudes he "looked up to Heaven and blessed and brake the loaves." (St. Matt. 14:36.) St. Paul approved of the custom, and Clement of Alexandria (A.D. 192) observed: "As it is meet that before taking food we bless the Maker of all these things, so also does it become us, when drinking, to sing psalms unto Him; forasmuch as we are partaking of His creatures." (*Paedagogica*, lib. ii, cap. iv. par. 44.)

It is difficult to determine when graces were spoken and when they were sung, but we know that blessings were associated with music from earliest times. As an example of an early Western table blessing, let us cite from the *Apostolical Constitutions* a prayer for the midday meal: εὐχὴ ἐπ᾽ ἀρίστῳ (lib. vii, cap. 49):

Blessed art Thou, O Lord, who dost nourish me from my youth, who givest food to all flesh. Fill our hearts with joy and gladness, that, having always what is sufficient for us, we may abound to every good work, in Christ Jesus, our Lord; through whom glory, honor, and power, be to Thee for ever. Amen.

This grace in a slightly modified form achieved great popularity by being included in the homilies of St. Chrysostom (c. 347-407). It is indeed so similar that the two can be translated in almost identical words. The Latin version of the modified form, the one that became familiar in the Western world, reads:

Benedictus Deus qui me pascis a juventute mea, qui cibum praebes omni carni; repli laetitia et gaudio corda nostra, ut assatim quod satis est habentes, abundemus in omne opus bonum, in Christe Jesu domino nostro; cum quo tibi gloria, honor et imperium, cum Sancto Spiritu in omne et unum. Amen.[1]

The *Oratio ante cibum* (Prayer before Food) of both the Gelasian and Gregorian rites was *Benedic, Domine, dona tua quae de tua largitate sumus sumpturi*, which is practically the same as that used today. The *Bobbio Missal* which, however, is no earlier than the 7th century, gives *Benedicantur nobis Domine dona tua, quae de tua largitate sumpturi sumus, qui vivis et regnas*.

The *Post cibum* texts were quite different from those in common use now, save for the words *tibi gratias agimus*. The Bobbio *Benedictio post mensam levantam* read:

Gratias tibi agimus, omnipotens, aeterne Deus, qui nos de tuis donis satiare dignatus es, per famulos ill[os]. Redde illis, Domine, pro parvis magna, pro temporalibus praemia sempiterna, qui vivis et regnas.[2]

Two long graces were written by the Roman-Spanish-Christian poet Aurelius Clemens Prudentius (348-c. 405) in his *Cathemerinon Liber* ("Daily Round"), and both have enjoyed considerable popularity. The first has forty, the second thirty-four stanzas. In a Gradual of the 13th century in the Archiepiscopal Library of Udine, there are four verses of *Hymnus III*, *Ante cibum*, beginning *O Crucifer bone, lucis sator*, and four of *Hymnus IV*, *Post cibum*, commencing *Pastis visceribus, ciboque sumpto*.

Ex. 1   *Ad mensam dicatur*

Some of the verses of *Hymnus III* specifically mention singing.

Te, Pater optime, mane novo,
Solis et orbita cum media est,
Te quoque luce sub occidua
Sumere cum monet hora cibum,
Nostra, Deus, canet harmonia.

Quod calet halitus interior,
Corde quod abdita vena tremit
Pulsat et incita quod resonam
Lingua sub ore latens caveam
Laus superi Patris esto mihi.[3]

The monastic orders made grace a cardinal part of daily worship,
St. Martin (d. 580), Bishop of Braga in Portugal, insisting

Non oportet clericos vel laicos religiosos ante sacram horam diei
tertiam inire convivia, neque aliquando clericos nisi hymno dicto edere
panem, et post cibos gratias auctori Deo referre.[4]

Alcuin of York (d. 804) mentions singing in the grace:

Christi Deus nostrae benedic convivia mensae
Quaeque Tuis servis, mitissime, dona dedisti,
Per Te sint benedicta quidem. Tu largiter almus
Omnia Tu dederas nobis; jam quidquid habemus
Sunt bona quippe Tua, quia Tu bonus omnia condis;
Vos quoque, convivae, laudes, rogo dicite Christo
Semper in ore sonent pacis vel verba salutis.[5]

The Rule of St. Benedict (d. 543) prescribed penalties for those who
were late for meals:

Ad mensam autem qui ante versum non accurrerit (ut simul omnes
dicant versum et orent, et sub uno omnes accedant ad mensam qui per
neglegentiam suam aut vitium non occurrerit) usque secundam vicem
pro hoc vitio corripiatur: si denuo non emandaverit, non permittatur
at mensae communionis participationem: sed sequestratus a consortio
omnium reficiat solus, sublata ei portione sua de vino usque ad satis-
factionem et emendationem. Similiter autem patiatur, qui ad illum
versum non fuerit praesens, qui post cibum dicitur. Nec quisquam
praesumat ante statutam horam, vel postea quidquam cibi, aut potus
praesumere.[6]

On fast days the monks were limited to a single meal, and one
medieval inmate waggishly noted in his edition of Cassian (*Patr. lat.*,
XLIX, col. 151-152):

Confiteantur amo, quia coenam vespere clamo;
Odi *Memoriam*, quia tollit vespere coenam.[7]

The explanation is that on fast days, at the end of the single meal permitted (the evening *coena*), the monks customarily sang *Memoriam fecit mirabilium suorum*, while on normal days, when a substantial *prandium* was served, the main repast was followed by the *Confiteantur tibi, Domine, omnia opera tua*, etc. This particular priest extolled the Lord enthusiastically when chanting the *Confiteantur* after eating his full, but hated the melody associated with disciplining the body.

The words for table blessings that came to be most accepted in the Middle Ages were a combination of the 145th Psalm (144th in the Vulgate) and extracts from the Gelasian and Gregorian sacramentaries. For the blessing *Ante prandium* it was usual to hear:

Benedicite, oculi omnium in te sperant Domine
Et tu das escam illorum in tempore opportuno.
Aperis tu manum tuam, et imples omne animal benedictione.

Sometimes the *Gloria Patri*, *Kyrie*, and *Pater Noster* were inserted after it, followed by: *Benedic, Domine, nos et haec tua dona, quae de tua largitate sumus sumpturi.*

The *Post prandium* chant began:

Tu autem, Domine, miserere nobis. Deo gratias.
Confiteantur tibi Domine omnia opera tua.
Et Sancti tui benedicant tibi.

Occasionally the *Gloria Patri* was inserted before the standard text:

Agimus tibi gratias omnipotens Deus,
Pro universis beneficiis tuis
Qui vivis et regnas in saecula saeculorum.[8]

In a short paper of this sort, it is not possible to discuss the various ways in which the plainsong formulas have been combined with the several texts. The Benedictines and the Augustinians, for instance, do not sing precisely the same melodies. They chant words, however, that are basic for most of the graces we have. Since the table blessings of the order to which Luther belonged are less familiar, being adopted from two 14th-century manuscripts, they are given here as found in the *Proprium Missarum et Officiorum Ordinis Eremitarum Sancti Augustini:* [9]

Ex. 2 *Lector mensae, vadens ad medium Refectorii, ad signum Prioris incipit, dicendo :*

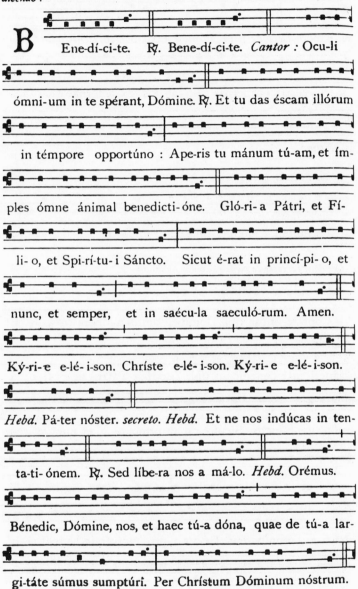

B Ene-dí-ci-te. ℞. Bene-dí-ci-te. *Cantor :* Ocu-li

ómni- um in te spérant, Dómine. ℞. Et tu das éscam illórum

in témpore opportúno : Ape-ris tu mánum tú-am, et ím-

ples ómne ánimal benedicti- óne. Gló-ri- a Pátri, et Fí-

li- o, et Spi-rí-tu- i Sáncto. Sicut é-rat in princí-pi- o, et

nunc, et semper, et in saécu-la saeculó-rum. Amen.

Ký-ri-e e-lé- i-son. Chríste e-lé- i-son. Ký-ri- e e-lé-i-son.

Hebd. Pá-ter nóster. *secreto. Hebd.* Et ne nos indúcas in ten-

ta-ti- ónem. ℞. Sed líbe-ra nos a má-lo. *Hebd.* Orémus.

Bénedic, Dómine, nos, et haec tú-a dóna, quae de tú-a lar-

gi-táte súmus sumptúri. Per Chrístum Dóminum nóstrum.

This example continues on p. 242.

    The universities early accepted the practice of praising God both *ante* and *post cibum*, and there are numerous Latin graces still in use at Oxford and Cambridge that continue the medieval tradition.[10]

    About the turn of the 15th century, we find the vernacular em-

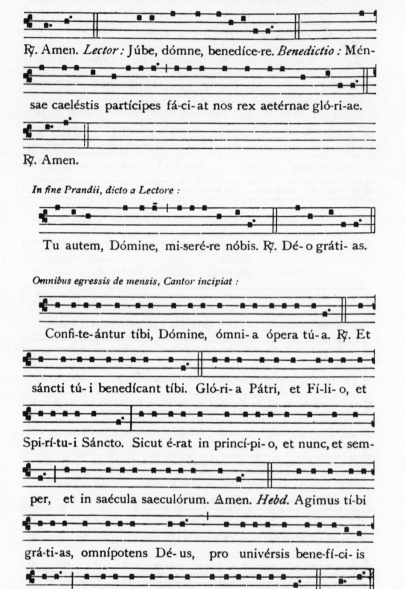

℟. Amen. *Lector :* Júbe, dómne, benedíce-re. *Benedictio :* Mén-

sae caeléstis partícipes fá-ci- at nos rex aetérnae gló-ri-ae.

℟. Amen.

In fine Prandii, dicto a Lectore :

Tu autem, Dómine, mi-seré-re nóbis. ℟. Dé- o gráti- as.

Omnibus egressis de mensis, Cantor incipiat :

Confi-te-ántur tíbi, Dómine, ómni- a ópera tú- a. ℟. Et

sáncti tú- i benedícant tíbi. Gló-ri- a Pátri, et Fí-li- o, et

Spi-rí-tu- i Sáncto. Sicut é-rat in princí-pi- o, et nunc, et sem-

per, et in saécula saeculórum. Amen. *Hebd.* Agimus tí-bi

grá-ti-as, omnípotens Dé- us, pro univérsis bene-fí-ci- is

tú- is, qui ví-vis et régnas in saécula saeculórum. ℟. Amen.

ployed for religious purposes, and English, German, French, and Dutch
table blessings begin to appear. Hermann, the monk of Salzburg (c. 1370),
is responsible for at least the text of *Almechtiger Got, Her Jesu Crist,*

and the melody asociated with it is found in half a dozen versions, one of which is in the *Lochamer Liederbuch*. There are also organ variations on the tune in Paumann's *Fundamentum organisandi* and in the *Buxheimer Orgelbuch*, as well as vocal *cantus-firmus* settings elsewhere.[11]

Two charming table blessings are attributed to Oswald von Wolkenstein, "the last of the Minnesinger," the first, *Benedictus: Gesegnet sei die Frucht, Trank, Essen, Wein und Brot;* the second, a *Gratias: Wohlauff als das zu Himel sei*, also sung to *Danck sag wir dir umb alles, das wir yn speisz und tranck genossen haben*.[12] This famous Minnesinger led an extravagant life, traveled to Russia, Persia, Greece, and Spain, and visited northern Italy with King Rupprecht in 1401. He is a transitional figure representing both monophony and the sort of polyphony that was to flower in the *Lochamer Liederbuch*.

The 16th and 17th centuries marked the zenith of musical table graces. The historically important Huguenot composer, Louis Bourgeois, published a collection of Psalm settings in which *bénédictions à table* are specifically mentioned on the title page:

Pseaulmes•LXXXIII de David, Le Cantique de Siméon, Les Commandementz de Dieu, l'Oraison dominicale, Le Symbole des Apostres, Les Prières devant et après le repas . . . Lyon, Chez Godefroy Beringen, M.D.LIII.

In most harmonized Huguenot collections the *Prière avant le repas* and *Prière après le repas* were given a distinct place, the special texts beginning *O Souverain Pasteur et Maître* and *Père éternel qui nous ordonnes*. Both are by Clément Marot, the versatile court poet who also put the psalms of David into a metrical version for the use of the French reformers.[13]

As a result of the wide dissemination of these two special prayers and of the practice of drawing upon part of Psalm 145, there are various settings of graces in the collections of Claude Goudimel, Claude Le Jeune, Paschal de l'Estocart, Jan Pieterszoon Sweelinck, and others. Since Goudimel and Le Jeune each produced several versions, whose contents were similar to those described in the above title, we have half a dozen harmonizations by these great composers, some in note-against-note style, others in the form of more elaborate motets. There is considerable variety in the treatment of harmonizations "*a trois, à quatre, et à cinq parties, et aussi à voix pareilles*."

Probably the most frequently sung table blessings in the Protestant world were the simple harmonizations made by Claude Goudimel for

Prière après le repas

Clément Marot

Claude Goudimel

the two special prayers at the end of the Huguenot Psalter. These first appeared in 1564-65 in Paris and Geneva, and the number of editions in French, German (the text translated by Ambrosius Lobwasser), and Dutch (the text translated by Petrus Dathenus) was legion. Since these graces are relatively unknown today, the opening part of the *Prière après le repas* is given as an illustration on the opposite page.

Graces were not confined to the religious collections, and Tylman Susato, among others, published a group of love songs introduced by and concluded with table blessings of his own composition.

> L'unziesme livre contenant vingt et neuf chansons amoureuses à quatre parties . . . avec deux prières ou oraisons qui se peuvent chanter devant et après le repas. Nouvellement composées (la plus part) par maistre Thomas Crecquillon et maistre Ja. Clemens non papa & aultres bons musiciens. Nouvellement imprimé. [Antwerp: T. Susato, Oct. 1549.] [14]

The texts are the well-known *O Souverain Pasteur and Père éternel* by Marot. The words are again found in harmonizations by Clemens non Papa in the

> Septiesme livre des chansons à quatre parties, de nouveau reveu, corrigé et de plusieurs autres nouvelles chansons (lesquelles jamais n'ont esté imprimées) augmenté. . . . [Louvain: P. Phalèse, 1570.]

In the words of Professor Bernet Kempers, the settings of *O Souverain Pasteur* and *Père éternel* "are fine examples of the art of Clemens." [15] They were reprinted in collections of 1597 and 1636.

Harmonizations of *O Souverain Pasteur* (called *Consécration de la table*) and *Père éternel*, were made by Andries (André) Pevernage and issued by the famous printer of Antwerp, Christophe Plantin, in 1589, in *Chansons d'André Pevernage Maistre de la chapelle de l'Église Cathédrale d'Anvers. Livre Premier, contenant Chansons spirituelles à cincq parties.* [Antwerp, 1589.]

Marot also wrote a *Bénédiction devant manger* that made its initial appearance in the *Miroir de treschrestienne Princesse Marguerite de France* in 1513. The words, *Nostre bon Père tout puissant qui gouverne ta créature*, were used for a grace by Jacques Buus in his *Canzoni francesi a cinque voci* (Venice, 1550). Thematically the tune suggests Psalm 134 (Old Hundred), while the polyphonic treatment is that of an elaborate Catholic motet. The opening of this splendid piece is included here: [16]

Bénédiction devant manger

Clément Marot   Jacques Buus

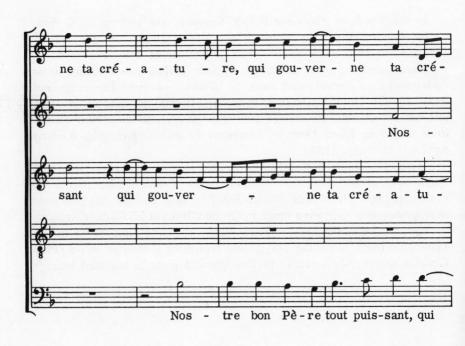

Other French texts used at the time, their authorship unknown to me, were *Dieu, Père, Créateur, gouverne de ta main Ton peuple; A Toy seul à jamais, à Toy gloire et honneur; Bénis, Seigneur, les biens que Tu nous donnes; Bon Dieu, bénis nous;* and *Rendons grâces à Dieu, vous toutes nations.*[17] The first two are found in Louis des Masures's *Vingtsix Cantiques chantés au Seigneur* (Lyons, 1564); the third is composed as a *Cantique à 3* in Jean Servin's *Second Livre de Chansons nouvelles* (Lyons, 1578), while the other two appear in Claude Le Jeune's *Pseaumes en vers mesurez* (Paris, Ballard, 1606).[17]

A canon for four voices by Orlando di Lasso,[18] which may have been intended as a grace, is based on the simple phrase, *Célébrons sans cesse de Dieu ses bontés*. This piece, first published in 1576, was reprinted without acknowledgement to Lasso in Thomas Ravenscroft's *Pammelia* in 1609 (2nd edition, 1618). In the same English collection there is a six-part Latin round to the words, *Benedic, Domine, nobis his donis tuis quae de tua largitate sumus sumpturi*. I have not been able to identify the composer of this grace.

Thomas Crecquillon produced two pieces for the imperial table of Charles V that were published in Tylman Susato's *Liber Quartus sacrarum cantionum quatuor vocum vulgo moteta vocant, ex optimis quibusque huius aetatis musicis selectarum* (Antwerp, 1547). The first is a two-part motet for four voices entitled *Benedicite*, and the second a *Jubilate Deo* for the *Deo gratias* following the repast. Both are among the more elaborate compositions of the period that are connected with table blessings, and the composer makes use of *Eleison* shouts and, in the first piece, in a passage later than the one shown in our example, introduces a section of the *Vater unser*.[19] (For the example, see below.)

As a matter of fact, it was not uncommon at more formal occasions to have the *Pater noster* and the *Domine Deus, Pater coelestis* sung after the *Oculi omnium in te sperant*. Nicolas Gombert has two motet settings of *Oculi omnium*, one *a 5* and the other *a 6*, both of which appeared in 1539. The five-part composition is worked out with great care, and occasionally there are passages of three against two in the voice lines. There is a *Secunda pars*, which begins *Qui edunt me adhuc esurient* (Ecclesiasticus 24: 29-30) and thus suggests that it was also appropriate for communion. Since the piece is a good example of the motet style during the second quarter of the 16th century and illustrates the type of music heard before princely repasts, a few measures are quoted on pages 251 and 252.[20]

Ex. 5

Benedicite

Thomas Crecquillon
(Transcribed by Edward Lowinsky)

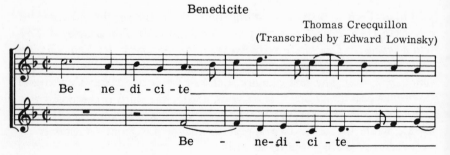

249

Oculi omnium

Nicolas Gombert
(Transcribed by Eleanor Lawry)

A composition by Orlando di Lasso on the same text, also *a 5*, was included in 1573 in the first volume of the *Patrocinium musices*, the magnificent choir-book publication of Adam Berg sponsored by Duke William of Bavaria.[21] Since the collection was designed by the composer to show the range of his technique and of his means of expression, this *Tischgebet* reaches a remarkably high level. To lend greater emphasis to the ceremony, the composer added a second part, *Justus Dominus in omnibus vivis suis* (Psalm 145:17-18), written with both fervor and technical mastery. The collection also contains a brilliant four-part *Pater noster*, in which running passages flow in the upper and lower voices, presumably to provide an additional solemn reminder of the Lord's bounty. If both pieces were performed in full before the feast, a truly remarkable musical *hors d'oeuvre* was heard at the princely board.

William Byrd in his *Gradualia*, Book I, Part II, No. 2, London, 1605, in providing music for the Roman rite for Corpus Christi, included a setting of *Oculi omnium* and of the succeeding *Alleluia*.[22] He concluded the piece according to custom with St. John 6:55-56. The "final" quality of the tonic ending of the first *Alleluia* suggests that the section beginning *Caro mea vere est cibus* may have been omitted by Christians wishing to sing *Oculi omnium* as a grace. Certainly it is much more appropriate as a table blessing than the canon *Non nobis Domine—*

attributed to Byrd in some late sources, perhaps without foundation—frequently sung as a grace, despite the fact that the words have no relationship to food.

It is not easy to find and recognize early graces; texts and music were not always marked *Benedictio mensae* or *Gratiarum actio*. For instance, the five settings of *Agimus tibi gratias* by Orlando di Lasso were unmistakably intended to be sung after meals, though the average student is unaware of this. Some of the notes in Haberl's portion of the *Sämmtliche Werke* do indicate such a use, but the comments are fragmentary.[23] In order to make the present study more useful, a list of pertinent texts is included in the Appendix.

There were a number of new Latin versions of the Psalms during the Reformation, one of the most popular in the later 16th century being by the Scottish schoolman, George Buchanan; his appropriate table verses, after Psalm 145, begin *Te volucrum pecundumque,* and a simple setting of this text was made in 1585 by the German Statius Olthof.[24]

It is amusing to read the instructions to children regarding grace. British Museum Harleian MS. 3362, fols. 6 and 10, has specific admonishments:

> Non lotis escam manibus non sumperris unquam.
> Nemo cibum capiat, donec benedicio fiat . . .
> Assumptoque cibo reddatur gratia Christo
> Privetur Mensa, qui apreverit haec documenta.[25]

British Museum, Cotton MS Titus A xx, fol. 173, admonishes:

> Extersis manibus, dentes non mappula tergat,
> Interea grates solvantur cuncta Regenti.[26]

The interest in young people is also demonstrated by six graces in Melanchthon's *Benedictio mensae in usum suorum discipulorum.*[27]

Besides the grace quoted in connection with the *Apostolical Constitutions* (see note 1 *supra*), Erasmus cites another in the *Convivium religiosum*, this grace also being taken from St. Chrysostom:

> Gloria tibi, Domine, sancte; gloria tibi, Rex; quoniam dedisti nobis escas. Imple nos gaudio et laetitia in Spiritu Sancto, ut inveniamur in conspectu tuo acceptabiles; nec pudefiamus, quando reddes unicuique secundum opera sua. Amen.[28]

And in the *Convivium profanum*, the boy pronounces a third:

> Quicquid appositum est, et quicquid apponetur, felix ac sacrum esse iubeat, qui sua benignitate pascit universa. Amen.[29]

The reliance on tradition in the Renaissance cannot be overstressed. For instance, Prudentius's *ante cibum* and *post cibum* hymns, *O Crucifer bene lucis sator* and *Pastis visceribus ciboque*, which we found set to plainsong melodies in the 13th century (cf. pp. 237 f.) were harmonized by Lucas Hordisch (who provides two settings of *O Crucifer*) in a collection issued at Leipzig in the early 16th century: *Melodiae Prudentianae et in Virgilium magna ex parte nuper natae et per Nicolaum Fabrum typographum expressae* (Leipzig, 1533).

O Crucifer was set again the next year by one of the leading musical figures of the day, Ludwig Senfl, who paid tribute to the classics in his

Varia carminum genera, quibus tum Horatius, tum alii egregii Poëtae, Graeci et Latini, veteres et recentiores, sacri et prophani usi sunt, suavissimis harmoniis composita, authore Ludovico Senflio Helvetio, illustrissimi Boiorum principiis Giuilelmi etc. musico primario. [Frankfurt-on-Main: Christian Egenolff, 1534]

Senfl's version was reprinted in a retrospective collection brought out under the editorship of Peter Nigidius nearly two decades later:

Geminae undeviginti Odarum Horatii melodiae, quatuor vocibus probe adornatae, cum selectissimis carminum, partim sacrorum, partim prophanorum, concentibus: additis circa finem aliis item cantionibus, matutinis, meridianis, et serotinis: paedagogiis recte institutis, ac scholis, quibuslibet pro exercenda iuventute literaria accomodatissimis. [Frankfurt-on-Main: Christian Egenolff, 1551-1552]

The Latin style of Prudentius was imitated by the Passau humanist Philipp Gundelius, who served several years as professor *für Dichtkunst* in Vienna, and both Senfl and his distinguished older colleague, Paul Hofhaimer (whose face is so familiar to us through the drawing of Dürer), made settings of Gundelius's *Hymnus post cibum, Rerum creator maxime*. Actually there are two completely different versions by the famous Swiss master, the first of which appeared in the *Varia carminum* (reprinted in the *Geminae undeviginti*) while the second is included, along with Hofhaimer's contribution, in

Harmoniae poeticae Pauli Hofheimeri, et Ludovici Senflii, musicorum praestantissimorum una cum selectis ad hanc rem locis, e poetis accommodatioribus, seorsim tum decantandis, tum praelegendis. [Nuremberg: Johann Petreius, 1539]

Another contemporary Latin grace printed in the *Varia carminum* and the *Geminae undeviginti* was the work of Joachim Camerarius who taught at the St. Lorenz School in Nuremberg. His *Hymnus post cibum*, *Frequens ad esto parve grex*, is still admired for its poetical qualities. Since it was included in the *Varia carminum*, one would normally suppose that the music was by Senfl. Arnold Geering and Wilhelm Altwegg, however, the editors of the Swiss composer's complete works, believe that Camerarius made the musical setting for his own text— thus providing another example of Renaissance versatility.[30]

The pedagogical insistence on the ceremony of saying grace carried over into the New World, and the vice-provincial of the Dominicans on the island of Hispaniola, Fray Pedro de Córdoba, provided two Latin table blessings in his *Doctrina Christiana para Instrucción y Información de los Indios*. Pedro de Córdoba died in 1521, and the work was only published in Mexico in 1544, with slight modifications by Bishop Juan Zumárraga and Fray Domingo de Betanzos. It is not unnatural to speculate on the emotions of the aborigines when they intoned these prayers:

> *La Benedición de la Mesa:*
> Nos et ea quae sumpturi sumus: benedicat Deus trinus et unus Pater et Filius; et Spiritus Sanctus. Amen. Pater noster.

> *Las Gracias después de comer:*
> Laus Deo: gloria sanctis: pax vivis: requiem defunctis per infinita saeculorum saecula. Amen. Pater noster. Ave Maria.[31]

There were many more table blessings sung in Latin during the Renaissance; one finds for example, in Louis des Masure's *Vingtsix Cantiques chantés au Seigneur* (Lyons, 1564), *Plus un Hymne latin, & des semblables prières pour la table faictes en vers latins*. I have not yet identified the author of the text, *Larga qui terrae genitor feracis* (*Mensae benedictio*) and *Optimis grates agimus parenti* (*a Mensa gratiarum actio*) from this Protestant collection.

Among the most fascinating Latin graces are several preserved on the blades of knives of the early 16th century, probably French or German, though they have sometimes been considered Italian. The *Benedictio Mensae* text reads: *Quae sumpturi sumus benedicat trinus et unum. Amen* and the *Gratiarum Actio: Pro tuis beneficiis Deus gratias agimus tibi*.[32] Samples are found in the Cluny Museum, the Victoria and Albert Museum, the Sheffield City Museum, the Musée de Dijon, and the Pennsylvania Museum. The handles are of ivory, decorated with strips of ebony, green stained ivory, and brass with silver knobs at the end. Apparently the knives were more for decorative than utilitarian purposes (unless saying grace is a kind of insurance); at any rate, if the blades were wiped with a napkin at the end of a hearty meal, the *Gratiarum Actio* would have been completely legible. The *Pro tuis bene-*

ficiis Deus gratias agimus tibi printed here reproduces the music on the
knives at the Cluny Museum.[33]

Ex. 7   **Gratiarum Actio**

Mention should naturally be made of the Hebrew practice of singing
Psalm 137 ("By the waters of Babylon"), the well-known *Al naharot
Babel*, as a grace on week days. There is a free setting of this text by the
17th-century Italian Jewish composer, Salomone Rossi, in his *Ha-*

Shirim Asher Li Shelomoh . . . (Venice, 1622). The rabbis of the period objected to the introduction of Rossi's music in the synagogues, and this piece was undoubtedly meant for use in the home.[34]

Sung table prayers or *Tischgebete* flourished in Germany, and a glance at Schöberlein, Wackernagel, or Zahn will reveal dozens of settings of numerous texts. Among the most popular, again deriving partly from the psalms, were *Lobet den Herrn, denn er ist sehr freundlich; Nun lasst uns Gott dem Herrn; Danket dem Herrn;* and *Aller Augen warten auf Dich, Herre.* Such fashioners of religious verse as Cyriacus Schneegass, Martinus Behm, Adam Hamel, Nicolaus Boye, Ludwig Helmbold, and Nicolaus Herman wrote stanzas that were frequently set.[35] Martin Luther's *Betbüchlein* (1522) and his *Kleiner Katechismus* (1529)—which also appeared the same year in two Latin editions, one entitled *Enchiridion piarum precationum* and the other *Parvus Cathechismus pro pueris in schola*—included graces. *Dem grossen Gott sey Dank für diese seine Gaben* to the tune *O Gott, du frommer Gott* is particularly well-known.[36] In the last hymn book published under the reformer's supervision, the *Geystliche Lieder. Mit einer newen vorrhede D. Mart. Luth.*, issued in two parts by Valentin Babst (Leipzig, 1545), No. XXXVIII by Johann Horn, is entitled *Das Benedicite vor dem Tische*, and begins:

> Almechtiger gütiger Gott
> du ewiger Herr Zebaoth
> Aller augen warten auff dich
> Und du speisest sie gnediglich.

No. XXXIX is the even better known hymn, also written by Johann Horn:

> Dancket dem Herren denn er ist sehr freundlich
> Denn seine Güt und Warheit bleibt ewiglich.

There was a distinct German influence in England and Scotland at this time, and one of the three Wedderburn brothers of Dundee had studied with Luther at Wittenberg. Already by 1540 the Scotsmen had translated a number of German hymns, some by the great reformer himself, which were published in Edinburgh as *The Gude and Godlie Ballatis.* This collection went through many editions, which were so popular that they were literally worn to pieces. Most of them had a section entitled *Certane Gracis to be sung befoir meit or efter.* The edition of 1567 contained five metrical table blessings and a rhymed version of the Lord's Prayer, *Christ learnit us, on God how we suld call,* with which they were to be combined. Three texts clearly show German influence. *We thank our God baith kynde and liberall* stems from *"Das gratias,"* *Wir dancken Gott dem Herren*, a text written by the Saxon *Sänger-meister* and friend of Luther, Johann Walther; *All Creature on the Lord dependis*, to be sung "befoir supper," derives from the Low German *De Ogen aller Creatur* of Johannes Freder; while *We thank Thé God of Thy Gudnes*, "ane grace to be sung," is a translation of Nicolaus Boye's *O Gott wir dancken deiner Güt*. The opening "Grace befoir Meit," *All meit & drink was creat be the Lord* is a touching thirteen-line prayer, while *To our gude God, of warldis Lord and King*, to be sung "efter supper," is rather a paean to the King of Heaven than a prayer of thanks for food partaken. Some of these graces deserve to be revived.[37]

Praetorius printed over twenty-five graces, Melchior Vulpius more than fifteen. There are settings by Mattheus Le Maistre, Sixtus Dietrich, Joachim a Burck, Seth Calvisius, Johann Staden, Adam Gumpelzheimer, Prince Moritz von Hessen, Samuel Scheidt, Johann Hermann Schein, and many more. *Tischgebete* were so popular that Bartholomäus Gesius (Barthol Göss or Gese) issued in 1605 a collection of over 300 pages called *Christiliches Haus- und Tisch-Musica* in four parts. Like Goudimel and Le Jeune, Heinrich Schütz made various settings: (1) a note-against-note harmonization (published in 1661) of verse 6 of Psalm 145, as translated by Cornelius Becker; (2) a setting *a 6* of Ludwig Helm-bold's *Nun lasst uns Gott dem Herren;* (3) a series consisting of three prayers before the meal: *Oculi omnium in te sperant, Pater noster, qui es in coelis,* and *Domine deus, Pater coelestis,* and two prayers to follow the meal: *Confitemini domino, Pater noster* (as above) and *Gratias agi-mus tibi,* the five pieces being Nos. 36-40 in the *Cantiones Sacrae* (1625); (4) a similar group in the *Zwölf geistliche Gesänge* (1657), beginning with *Aller Augen warten auf Dich, Herre,* followed by the *Vater unser* and *Herr Gott, himmlischer Vater, segne uns und diese deine Gaben.* The *Gratias nach dem Essen* leads off with *Danket dem Herren, denn er ist sehr freundlich;* then comes the *Vater unser* (paralleling the *Pater noster* in the Latin series), the whole ending with a setting of the text, *Wir danken Dir, Herr Gott himmlischer Vater.*[38]

As might be expected, Johann Sebastian Bach harmonized some of the traditional tunes associated with such texts as *Danket dem Herrn; Den Vater, dort oben; Nun lasst uns Gott, dem Herren; Nun preiset alle Gottes Barmherzigkeit;* and *Singen wir aus Herzensgrund,* all of which are to be found in the standard editions of his chorales. It is sur-prising how few people outside of Germany realize that these magnificent settings may serve as *Tischgebete* in the home as well as for more gen-eral congregational singing in church. Graces sung in German were brought to the New World by the "Pennsylvania Dutch" in colonial times, and collections containing *Tischlieder* were published on this side of the Atlantic by the Lutherans, the Moravians, the Schwenk-felders, and the members of the Reformed Church. It should not be forgotten that Count Zinzendorf, who was active in the Moravian settlements in America from 1741 to 1743, wrote two prayers to be sung at table: *Lobt und erhöht des grossen Gottes Güte* and *Gib, Heiland, dass ich Dich geniess.*[39]

In England, the primers for children during the 16th century made a great point of table blessings, and Psalm 145 was available in settings by William Pearson, Thomas Causton, William Damon, John Cosyn, Richard Allison, Edmund Hooper, and others. In *The School of Vertue* (London, 1557), Francis Segar introduced a short section: *How to order thy selfe syttinge at the table* and *How to behave thiselfe in serv-ynge the table.* From the latter come the rhymed instructions:

> When thy parentes downe—To the table shall syt
> In place be ready—For the purpose most fyt:
> With sober countinaunce—Lokynge them in the face,
> Thy handes holdynge up—Thus begyn grace.

The hortatory grace must have been written by the teacher:

> Geve thanks to God—With one accorde
> For that shall be—Set on this borde
> And be not carefull—What to eate,
> To eche thynge lyvynge—The Lord sendes meate;
> For foode he wyll not—See you peryshe
> But wyll you fede—Foster and cheryshe
> Take well in worthe—What he hath sent.
> At this tyme be—Therewith content.
>   Praysynge God.[40]

In 1571, there appeared in London a collection entitled:

> Songes for three, fower, and five voyces composed and made by Thomas Whythorne, Gent. the which songes be of sundry sortes, that is to say, some long, some short, some hard, some easie to be songe, and some betweene both. Also some solemne, and some pleasant or mery: so that according to the skill of the singers (not being musi-tians) and disposition and delite of all the hearers, they may here finde songes for their contention and liking.

Whythorne, whose autobiography—the earliest known in English—has only recently been published,[41] furnished his collection with two pertinent pieces, a "Grace before Meate," *Almighty God, Thy loving care* and a "Grace after Meate," *O Our Father we yelde to Thee, for all Thy giftes most thankful prayse.* Fortunately the author-composer gives particulars in his autobiography regarding their inception. After speaking of the "pestiferous time" he had undergone in 1563, the musician informs us that he left London

> to remain in the country with purpose to disburden me of the late cares that I had in the city; and also to recover if I could some part of my health, the which was so much impaired . . . And after I was a little while settled in a gentleman's there, whereas, although not for profit, yet for good and friendly entertainment, diet and lodging, I never came in the like before, I could not be idle from reading and writing somewhat, beside the pains I took in teaching of their only daughter. And among all my other writings I wrote two Graces, the one to be said before dinner and the other to be said after dinner, because that I was partly spoken unto the same. [The verses of both table blessings which were printed with music in 1571 are then given.]

Although in the autobiography Whythorne writes that the graces were "to be said," the conclusion that they were sung is inescapable, particularly as the daughter of the house was being taught music by the visitor.[42]

There is a text suitable for grace in the *Bay Psalm Book*, the first book published in what is today the United States. As many readers will remember, this metrical version of the Psalter, the work of a committee of ministers, was issued in 1640 and was "revised and refined" between 1647 and 1651 by President Richard Dunster of Harvard and one of the tutors, Richard Lyon. The *Admonition to the Reader* explained: "The verses of these psalms . . . may be sung to . . . tunes, as they are collected out of our chief musicians by Tho. Ravenscroft." For this reason Psalm 145, as versified in New England, appears opposite in the musical setting that Edmund Hooper provided for that Psalm in the *Whole Book of Psalmes: with the Hymnes Evangelicall and Songs Spirituall Composed into 4 parts by Sundry Authors, with such severall Tunes, as have beene, and are usually sung in England, Scotland, Wales, Germany, Italy, France, and the Nether-lands: never as yet before in one volume published . . . Newly corrected and enlarged by Tho: Ravenscroft Bachelar of Musicke* (London, 1621; second edition, 1633).[43] The harmonization of the "Playnsong," which is in the tenor, has a quiet dignity, eminently suited to the words. Hooper was organist of Westminster Abbey from 1606 until his death in 1621.

A number of graces were written by George Wither, one of the minor poets of 17th-century England. In a publication entitled *Haleluiah or Britain's Second Remembrancer*, which appeared in 1641, the versatile man of letters, soldier, and politician, made two contributions de-

Ex. 8   My God, O King, I'll Thee extol

Words from Psalm 145   Edmund Hooper
Verses 1-2, 15-16.

scribed as 1) *A Hymn before Meat. God is praised for furnishing our Table And that when we are full, we may be mindfull of the Poore* and 2) *God Almightie having fed our Bodies; is here besought to feed our Soules also; and desired that whether we Feed or Fast, he may be glorified thereby.* Both are to be sung to the *Magnificat* tune that is associated with English psalmody, and Ravenscroft's Psalter again comes to mind since its second edition is the closest in time to *Haleluiah.* The setting shown below was made by John Farmer, distinguished for his harmonizations of the twelve canticles and hymns prefixed to the Psalms proper in East's *Whole Booke of Psalmes,* issued in 1592, 1594, and 1604. In 1621, the arrangement was either slightly modified by the author or "corrected" by Ravenscroft, and this second version is the one presented in Ex. 9. Dr. Burney in the 18th century admired Farmer's settings: "The counterpoint is constantly simple, of note against note, but in such correct and excellent harmony as manifests the art to have been very successfully cultivated in England at that time.[44] To Verse 1, included in Ex. 9, we add Verses 2 and 3, printed below.

Verse 2

> And, whilst the Flesh her nourishment,
> From Thy good Creature takes;
> Let not, into our Souls, be sent,
> What there, a leanesse makes.
> But, whether want, or thrive we shall,
> Or Fast, or take our Food;
> Unto Thy praise, convert it all:
> And all things to our God.

Verse 3

> With Health and Plentie, blesse this place;
> From Error keep us free:
> And let Thy Gospel, and Thy Grace
> Our Portion always be.
> Preserve Thy Church; protect our King;
> And all his Kingdomes blesse:
> That, we may at our Table sing,
> And eat our Bread in Peace.

The number of texts devoted to grace expanded greatly during the 18th and 19th centuries. For instance, a special tract of twenty-six *Graces before Meat* was published by Charles Wesley in 1746, each being assigned a tune from John Lampe's *Hymns for the Great Festivals,*

Ex. 9　　　　　A Hymn after Meat to the Magnificat tune

George Wither　　　　　　　　　　　　　　　　　John Farmer

We praise O God! we hon-our Thee, By whom␣

␣␣we now are fed! And, we ac-know-ledge that from Thee,

We have our dai-ly bread. As with ex-ter-nal Food, O

Lord! Thou feed'st our bod-ies now, Ev'n so Thy

Blest In-car-nate word Up-on␣␣our Souls be-stow.

which appeared in print the same year. These are distinct from the seven graces included in John and Charles Wesley's *Hymns and Sacred Poems* (London, 1739; Philadelphia, 1740).[45] John Cennick's "Hymn before Meat," *Be present at our Table, Lord,* and "Hymn after Meat," *We bless Thee, Lord, for this our Food,* which first appeared in his *Sacred Hymns for the Children of God, in the Days of their Pilgrimage* (London, 1741) have become the best-known metrical graces in the English-speaking world. The former was embossed on John Wesley's huge Wedgewood teapot, which could hold a gallon of tea. One might name the authors of many more table blessings, for instance, William Hammond, the American Indian Samson Occom, Robert Burns, the Moravian Bishop John Gambold, William Cowper, James Montgomery, James Martineau, and so forth. It is not our purpose, however, to carry the story down to the present.

In this study little has been said about the musical qualities of the works. Many of the names of the composers themselves, however, where examples have not been given, are so well-known to musicians and students of cultural history that it scarcely seems necessary to stress that the pieces under discussion form a splendid repertory of vocal music. It would be hard to exaggerate the effect that graces had on those who took part in them. Like the psalms of David and other spiritual songs, table blessings offered both a musical and a religious experience for everyone who sang them. As was written in *The Gude and Godlie Ballatis* (edition of 1621), when the people "heir the true word sung, or singe it themselves into their vulgar toung with sweet melody: then sall they love their God, with hart and minde." [46]

The enthusiasm for spiritual songs, particularly in the countries affected by the Reformation, brought music into the home, and people urged one another to sing from the moment they arose to the time that they went to bed. George Wither's *Haleluiah* contains verses for *When we first awake, When Day-light appears, A Hymn whilst we are washing, When we put on our Apparel, When we put off our Apparel, When we cannot sleep, A Hymn for a House warming*—yes, even a hymn *For them who intend to settle in Virginia, New England, or the like Places* . . .—all in all, over a hundred and thirty poems, including the graces cited above, some to be sung to psalm tunes, others to folk songs.[47]

Charles Lamb has a curious essay on *Grace before Meat* and like George Wither, whom he greatly admired, felt that there were many other occasions to express thanks and gratitude for the "good things of existence." As he confessed:

I own that I am disposed to say grace upon twenty other occasions in the course of the day besides my dinner. I want a form for setting out upon a pleasant walk, for a moonlight ramble, for a friendly meeting or a solved problem. Why have we none for books, those spiritual repasts—a grace before Milton—a grace before Shakespeare? [48]

The point is well taken, and I can only observe that most people are neither so reflective nor so grateful for their manifold blessings as the gentle English essayist. Yet music that grows naturally out of our daily life should be one of the goals for which we are striving. Let us remember the practice of singing the blessings of the Lord at table. We can raise our voices as often as three times a day and give ourselves the joy of praising the Maker of all things in graces by the world's finest poets and composers.[49]

Notes

1. Editions of the works of Clement of Alexandria exist in Greek, Latin, English, and German. A scholarly, modern publication under the editorship of Otto Stählin is in process. An older collected edition of the *Opera* in 4 vols. was made by Wilhelm Dindorf (Oxford: Clarendon Press, 1869). Those desirous of comparing the Greek and Latin texts of this passage from the *Paedagogica* may consult *Clementis Alexandrini Opera graece et latine, quae extant . . . à Friderico Sylburgio collectae* (Paris, 1641). This edition does not divide the text by paragraphs; the quotation is on p. 165, lines 31-36.

The *Apostolical Constitutions* have been frequently published, translated, and quoted. The oldest texts are in Greek, Syriac, and Latin, the first being the original. Our English translation is taken from Irah Chase, *The Work claiming to be The Constitutions of the Holy Apostles, including the canons; Whiston's version, revised from the Greek . . .* (New York: D. Appleton & Co., 1848), p. 196. The Latin version, given below, deserves comparison with that of St. Chryosostom's prayer, printed on p. 237 above:

> Benedictus es Domine, qui nutris me a pueritia mea qui das escam omni carni: imple gaudio et laetitia corda nostra, ut semper omnem sufficientiam habentes, abundemus in omne opus bonum, in Christo Jesu Domino nostro; per quem tibi gloria, honor, et imperium, in saecula. Amen.

The only basic difference affecting translation is that St. Chrysostom's last phrase following "Christ Jesus, our Lord" should be rendered: "to whom with the Holy Ghost one and indivisible be all honor and glory. Amen." The greatest of the Greek Fathers tells us that he heard the prayer sung after meals by the Eastern monks living in the desert. This is the same grace that Erasmus quotes in the *Colloquia familiaria (Familiar Colloquies)* (Basle, 1522). Eusebius in the *Convivium religiosum* (The Religious Banquet) tells his friends:

Christ Himself gave us this example, that we should sit down to
the table with a Hymn; and I take it from this, that we frequently read
in the Evangelists that He blessed or gave thanks to His Father before
He broke bread, and that He concluded with giving of thanks. And,
if you please, I will say to you a grace that St. Chrysostum commends
to the skies in one of his homilies, which he himself interpreted.
(Translation of the *Familiar Colloquies* by N. Bailey, London, 1725,
p. 105.)

Eusebius then proceeds to recite it. For St. Chrysostom's grace, see *Homilia*
on St. John, Nos. LV-LVI, 5, in J. P. Migne, *Patrologiae cursus completus*
(Paris, 1857-1880), 161 vols., *Series graeca*, Vol. LVIII (1680), *Monachorum
laus et vitae genus*, p. 545, where the Greek and Latin texts are printed on
opposite pages.

2. The literature on table blessings leads to Migne, *Patrologiae cursus . . .
Ser. latina*, Vol. III of the *Indices generales*, col. 952f (*De orationis tempore et
loco*); Hugues Ménard, Notes to LII of the *Concordia regularum* of St. Bene-
dict of Aniane (*Patr. lat.*, Vol. CIII, col. 1153-1154); and Eduard Freiherr von
der Goltz, *Tischgebete und Abendmahlsgebete in der altchristlichen und
griechischen Kirche* (*Texte und Untersuchungen*, Ser. 2, Vol. XIV, Leipzig:
J. C. Hinrichs, 1905). See also W. E. Scudamore, "Grace at Meals," in William
Smith and Samuel Cheetham, *A Dictionary of Christian Antiquities* (Boston:
Little, Brown & Co., 1875), Vol. I, pp. 745-746; W. T. Brooke, "Metrical
Graces," in Julian's *A Dictionary of Hymnology*, revised edition (London:
John Murray, 1913), pp. 446-448; L. Gougaud, "Notes sur les prières chré-
tiennes de la table," in *Rassegna Gregoriana*, VIII (1909), Nos. 11-12, pp. 524-
527. The best general history of the texts is Henry L. Dixon, *Saying Grace*
(Oxford & London: Longmans, 1903).

The three short prayers, the second and third from the *Bobbio Missal*, may
be translated:

Bless, O Lord, Thy gifts, which we are about to receive from Thy
bounty.
May Thy gifts be blessed to us, O Lord, which have been bestowed
of Thy bounty, who livest and reignest.
We give thanks to Thee, almighty, eternal God, who hast vouch-
safed to satisfy us with Thy gifts by the hand of these Thy servants.
Render to them, O Lord, great things in return for small, everlasting
rewards in return for temporal, who livest and reignest.

Muratori prints the texts of the early graces in *Liturgia romana vetus*
(Venice, 1748, 2 vols.), Vol. I (devoted to the "Sacramentarium Gelasianum"):
Orationes ante cibum, col. 745-746; *Orationes post cibum*, col. 746; in Vol. II
(devoted to the "Sacramentarium Gregorianum"): *Orationes ante cibum*, col.
229; the *Orationes super mensam*, col. 229-230; and the *Orationes post cibum*,
col. 230. The *Bobbio Missal* is also found in Muratori, Vol. II, where the
Benedictio ad mensam appears in col. 959, and the *Benedictio post mensam
levatam*, as quoted above, in col. 230.

3. G. Vale, "Nota intorno alle Preghiere Cristiane della Mensa," in *Rassegna Gregoriana*, IX (1910), Nos. 1-2, pp. 60-61. The texts of the hymns of
Prudentius are found in Migne, *Patr. lat.*, Vol. XLI, col. 796-813. A rather
Victorian translation of *Hymnus III*, in which the five-line stanzas are short-
ened to four lines, reads:

To Thee, O Father, when the day shall break
At noon and when the fading sunlight dies,
When the bell sounds and we our food partake
Let tuneful hymns from gladsome hearts arise.

And since our breath is warm; and through our veins
The secret heart's blood quivers; and our tongue
From hollow cell may give forth echoing strains
To God on high let Praises loud be sung. (Dixon, *op. cit.*, p. 26.)

Prudentius also wrote verses to be sung after fasting, *Hymnus VIII, Post jejunium*, beginning *Sufficit, quidquid facias vocato*.

4. St. Martin, Archbishop of Braga, *Opera omnia*, edited by Claude W. Barlow (New Haven: Yale University Press, 1950), Vol. XII of *Papers and Monographs Published for the American Academy in Rome*, containing No. LXV of the *Canones ex Orientalium Patrum Synodis*, known as the Canons of St. Martin. Translation according to Dixon, *op. cit.*, p. 37: "Neither clergy nor religious laymen should begin to feast till the third sacred hour of the day be past, nor should the clergy ever eat bread until a hymn has been sung, and after meat they should return thanks to God the author of the feast."

5. Alcuin's blessing, intended for the Refectory of the Monastery of Noailles, is also given in a rhymed translation by Dixon, *op. cit.*, p. 47:

Bless Thou, O Christ, the social feast
Here on our table spread,
And every gracious gift of Thine
Upon Thy servants shed.
By Thee alone let these be blest,
Each gift Thou dost bestow
And all are good, for they are Thine,
And Thou art good, we know.
And you, O guests, I also ask
To sing to Christ your praise,
And hymns of peace and saving grace
Unto his honour raise.

6. Transl.: Moreover, whoever comes not to table before the verse is said (that all may say the verse and pray together, and approach the table at one time), whoever has failed to do so through his own negligence and fault, shall be reproved the first and second time; if afterwards he does not improve his ways, he shall be debarred from taking his place at the common table, and separated from the company of his fellows, shall take his meal alone, being deprived of his portion of wine, until such time as he shall have made satisfaction and given proofs of amendment. The same penalty shall be attached to the man who fails to be present when the verse after meals is recited. (Dixon, *op. cit.*, p. 36.)

7. L. Gougaud, *op. cit.*, p. 527.

8. The words from Psalm 145 may be literally translated:

Bless ye the Lord, the eyes of all put their trust in Thee, O Lord, and Thou givest them their food in due season. Thou openest Thy hand and satisfiest every creature with Thy blessing.

This note continues on p. 268.

The second prayer signifies:

Bless us, O Lord, and these Thy gifts, which we are about to receive from Thy bounty.

The third:

But Thou, O Lord, have pity upon us. Praise be to God. All Thy works acknowledge Thee, O Lord, and Thy Saints bless Thee.

The *Agimus tibi gratias:*

We give thanks to Thee, almighty God for Thy all-embracing liberality, who livest and reignest for ever and ever.

9. Paris, Tournai, Rome: Desclée & Soc., 1926. "Die Melodie zum Tischgebet in unserem *Proprium Missarum et officii* habe ich zwei Handschriften (codices) in Rom entnommen. Sie stammen beide etwa aus dem 14. Jahrhundert. Die eine ist in der Biblioteca Vaticana, die andere in der Biblioteca Angelica, der ehemaligen Bibliothek unseres Generalshauses St. Agostino in Rom . . . Unsere Melodie stellt eine völlig unserem Orden eigene dar und hat mit der benediktinischen nichts zu tun." Communication from the editor, Father Adalbero Kunzelmann, Münnerstadt, April 20, 1955.

Latin graces today begin with the word *Benedicite* stated twice, which may seem redundant. This may be an outgrowth of a mutual greeting, asking for a blessing. It was common in the refectories of the monasteries for the younger priests to ask a benediction of the Superior. St. Benedict even suggested that a monk who met a stranger inside the abbey should request his blessing. The custom must be very old, and the Psalms indicate indirectly that it antedates Christian practice. "Neither do they which go by say, The blessing of the Lord be upon you: we bless you in the name of the Lord." Ps. 129, 8.

10. Dixon, *op. cit.*, pp. 161-210, prints the texts of over eighty Latin graces from Oxford and Cambridge and more than a dozen from such public schools as Eton, Westminster, and Charter House. The best known university graces were composed in the second half of the 17th century. Dr. Benjamin Rogers' *Te Deum Patrem colimus*, which was printed in the Appendix to Hawkins' *History*, dates from 1653 and is sung daily in Magdalen College Hall as grace after dinner. John Reading's celebrated *Wykehamist's Grace* was written in 1675, the year he was appointed organist of Winchester Cathedral. It is printed in Philip Hayes's *Harmonia Wiccamica* (London: 1780). Both pieces are available in *Graces, before and after Meat*. Novello's Glee-Hive Vol. II (1851), No. 34, which is still in print.

11. Concerning the various sources, see Otto A. Baumann, *Das deutsche Lied und seine Bearbeitungen in den frühen Orgeltabulaturen* (Kassel: Bärenreiter-Verlag, 1934), I. Paumann's setting is printed in F. W. Arnold, *Das Lochheimer Liederbuch nebst der Ars Organisandi* (Leipzig: Breitkopf & Härtel, 1926), p. 211; The Buxheimer settings are given in Bertha Wallner's edition, *Das Erbe deutscher Musik* (Kassel: Bärenreiter-Verlag, 1958), Vols. XXXVII-XXXIX, pp. 41, 84, 86, 88, 281. The complete text is in Philipp Wackernagel, *Das deutsche Kirchenlied*, 5 vols. (Leipzig: B. G. Teubner, 1867-1877), Vol. II, Nos. 600 and 601.

12. In the *Denkmäler der Tonkunst in Oesterreich*, Jahrg. IX¹, Bd. 18

(Vienna: Artaria & Co., 1902) (text, p. 33, Nos. 51 and 52; music p. 152, No. 29a, and pp. 152-153, No. 29b). For the second *Gratias* text, see *Lochamer Liederbuch*, No. 224.

13. Only the bassus part of the Bourgeois print of 1554 has survived; it is at the British Museum. The best recent study of Calvinist psalmody is Pierre Pidoux, *Le Psautier Huguenot du XVIe siècle, Mélodies et Documents*, 2 vols. (Basle: Bärenreiter-Verlag, 1962). Regarding Bourgeois, see Vol. II, pp. 73-74, 171-172. Two indispensable guides are Robert Eitner *et al.*, *Bibliographie der Musik-sammelwerke des 16. und 17. Jahrhunderts* (Berlin: Liepmannssohn, 1877) hereinafter referred to as Eitner, *Bg*, and *Répertoire International des Sources Musicales, XVIe-XVIIe siècles*, I. *Liste Chronologique* (Munich-Duisburg: G. Henle Verlag, 1960), hereinafter referred to as RISM. When the second volume of RISM appears, with an alphabetical list of the text incipits of the contents of 16th- and 17th-century collections containing the works of more than one composer, a number of graces that are now unknown should come to light.

14. Regarding the Susato compositions in *L'Unziesme livre*, see Eitner, *Bg* 1549k, and RISM 1549 [21], fols. 2 and 16; regarding the Clemens non Papa settings from the *Septiesme livre*, see Eitner *Bg* 1570d and RISM 1570 [8], fol. 36.

15. Letter of Professor Bernet Kempers dated July 30, 1963. The two chansons will soon appear in Vol. XI of the *Opera omnia* of Clemens. Concerning later editions of the *Septiesme livre*, see Eitner *Bg* 1597h (=RISM 1597 [9]) and *Bg* 1636.

16. The *Bérédiction devant manger* is the last piece in the collection, No. XXI. See 'The '*Chanson Spirituelle*,' Jacques Buus, and Parody Technique" by Howard Brown in *Journal of the American Musicological Society*, XV (1962), No. 2, pp. 145-173. There is also a setting by Jean Crespel, *Le Bénédicité*, No. XXIIII in the *Quatriesme livre des chansons à quatre parties nouvellement composez et mises en musicque* . . . (Louvain: Phalèse, 1552). The tune is unrelated to that of Buus. I am indebted to Professor Brown for sending me scores of the Buus and Crespel settings of the *Bénédiction devant manger* as well as photographs of the original editions.

17. Among settings by other composers, attention should be called to four-part ones by Antoine de Mornable, Pierre Colin, Jean Le Gendre, and Pierre Certon, published at Paris in 1546, 1550, 1552 (2nd ed. 1556), and 1555 respectively, as well as collections by Philibert Jambe de Fer and Richard Crassot, both of which appeared at Lyons (1559 and 1564), and two Geneva imprints, the first by Guillaume de la Moeulle (1554), the second by Hugues Sureau (1565). There is a freely elaborated two-part treatment of the familiar Marot texts by Antoine de Hauville at the end of the Crassot collection, and there are several three-part settings by Barthélemy Le Bel in *Le Second Livre des Pseaulmes et Sentences, tirées du Psalmiste Royal que des autres Saincts Prophètes: Mis en Musique en forme de Motetz, par divers excellens Musiciens* (Paris, 1555). Both the Le Jeune prayers are printed in Henry Expert, *Maîtres Musiciens de la Renaissance française*, Vol. XXI (Paris: Leduc, 1905) pp. 24-25, 26-27.

18. Lasso, *Sämmtliche Werke* (Leipzig: Breitkopf & Härtel), Vol. XVI pp. 162-163. The Lasso canon and anonymous round may be consulted in Peter Warlock's modern edition, *Pammelia and other Rounds and Catches* (London: Oxford University Press, 1928), Nos. 48 and 89.

19. Professor Edward Lowinsky has very kindly called my attention to Crecquillon's *Benedicite*, besides sending me a score copied by his wife. See

Lowinsky, *Das Antwerpener Motettenbuch Orlando di Lasso's* (The Hague: Nijhoff, 1937); also published in *Tijdschrift der Vereeniging voor Nederlandsche Muziekgeschiedenis*, XV (1937), pp. 1-43 and 94-105. Latin versions of the *Lord's Prayer* differed slightly, and there were hundreds of settings. One put to music by M. C. Bodenschatz (published in 1613) begins *O Pater coelestis, o qui regna coelorum*, modern ed. in Ludwig Schöberlein, *Schatz des liturgischen Chor- und Gemeindegesangs nebst den Altarweisen in der deutschen evangelischen Kirche*, 3 vols. (Göttingen: Vandenhoeck & Ruprecht, 1865-1872), *Anhang* (*Tischgesänge*), pp. 710-711.

20. Eitner *Bg* lists the five-part Gombert version in several editions, the oldest being in the *Primus liber cum sex vocibus . . . Mottetti del frutto a sei voci* (Venice: Gardano, 1539), p. 23, the latest being in the *Novum et insigne opus musicum, sex, quinque, et quatuor vocum, cuius in Germania hactenus nihil simile usquam est editum* (Nuremberg: Berg and Neuber, 1558). The score from which our quotation is taken was kindly made for me from the 1558 source by Dr. Eleanor Lawry. This setting appears also in Eitner *Bg*, 1549d (=RISM 1549 [2]), where the *Qui edunt* is presented as a separate composition, and in *Bg* 1554h (=RISM 1554 [2]). Since Gombert's five-part *Pater noster* is also included in the 1554 edition (Louvain: Phalèse), this piece, in which the traditional plainsong permeates the polyphony, may have been combined with *Oculi omnium* for more festive table blessings. The six-voice treatment of the text without the second part from Ecclesiasticus) was printed in the *Cantiones quinque vocum selectissime, a primariis (Germania inferioris, Galliae, et Italiae) musices magistris editae . . . Mutetarum liber primus* [Strasburg: P. Schöffer, 1539] and *Musica Excelentissimi Nicolai Gombertii vulgo Motecta quinque vocum nuncupata in qua facile comperies quantum in hac arte, inventione aliis omnibus praevaleat* (Venice: Scotto, 1539). See Joseph Schmidt-Görg, *Nicolas Gombert Kapellmeister Kaiser Karls V: Leben und Werk* (Bonn: Röhrscheid, 1938) pp. 350-366.

21. The Lasso *Oculi omnium* is reprinted in the *Sämmtliche Werke*, Vol. VII, pp. 122-124.

22. Byrd's piece is in Vol. V, pp. 8-17 of the collected edition prepared by Edmund H. Fellowes (London: Stainer & Bell, 1938).

23. For the first of the Lasso *Agimus tibi gratias* pieces *a 3*, which appeared initially as No. 46 of the *Magnum opus musicum* (Munich, 1604), see the *Sämmtliche Werke*, Vol. I, pp. 59-60; for the second, No. 74 of the *Magnum opus musicum*, see *ibid.*, pp. 131-132. The five-part settings, which date from 1576 and 1568 respectively, are printed *ibid.*, Vol. V, pp. 98-100 and 100-102. A practical edition of the latter was brought out by the Schola Cantorum, Paris, 1954. The *Agimus tibi gratias a 6* was reprinted in *Sämmtliche Werke*, Vol. XIII, pp. 103-104. Haberl notes of the last: "Aus dem kirchlichen Tischgebet nach dem Mittagessen . . . feierlich, kräftig, originelle Modulation." It initially appeared as No. 21 of the *Patrocinium musices* in 1573 and is the counterpiece to *Oculi omnium*, No. 10. Some readers may remember the *Agimus tibi gratias* cf Cipriano de Rore found in August Reissmann's *Allgemeine Geschichte der Musik* (Munich: Friedrich Bruckmann's Verlag, 1863), *Notenbeilage*, Vol. I, pp. 24-27, described as "ebenso vortrefflich declamiert, als er ein treues Bild der harmonischen Darstellung der Kirchentonart gibt." There is no mention of its being a table blessing. Also to the same text is a setting in Grammatico Metallo's *Il Primo Libro de Motetti* (Venice, 1602). In general, however, graces are rare in Italian publications.

24. Regarding Olthof, see *Psalmorum Davidis paraphrasis poetica Georgii*

Buchanan Scoti argumentis ac melodiis explicata atque illustrata, reprinted in *Vierteljahrsschrift für Musikwissenschaft*, V (1888), pp. 290-321, specifically p. 313. It is also found in Maurice Frost, *English & Scottish Psalm and Hymn Tunes c. 1543-1677* (London-New York: Oxford University Press, 1953), this setting being No. 452. The first complete edition of Buchanan's psalms was published by Henri and Robert Estienne at Paris in 1564 or 1565 and is remembered for its graceful dedication to Mary Queen of Scots:

> Nympha, Caledoniae quae nunc feliciter orae
> Missa per innumeros sceptra tueris avos;
>
> Accipe (sed facilis) cultu donata Latino
> Carmina, faticidi nobile regis opus.

Jean Servin had been inspired by the Latin paraphrases of the Caledonian humanist a few years earlier and his *Psalmi Davidis a G. Buchanano Versibus expressi nunc primum modulis, IIII., V., VI., VII., et VIII. vocum, a I. Servino decantati* (Lyons, Charles Pesnot, 1579) were dedicated to King James VI, the son of Queen Mary of Scots. Only the initial forty-one paraphrases were published but there is reason to believe that Servin composed music for all of King David's Songs of Praise, including Psalm 145. It may still exist in manuscript.

25. "You must not ever take up your viands with unwashed hands. Let no one take any food until the Blessing shall be given. And when the food has been taken, let thanks to Christ be given And let him be forbidden the table, who shall spurn the lesson." Dixon, *op. cit.* p. 64.

26. "Having wiped your hands, do not use the napkin for cleaning your teeth, Meanwhile let thanks be given to the Ruler of all things." Dixon, *op. cit.* p. 65.

27. Republished in *Philipp Melanchthon Opera quae supersunt omnia*, ed. by Karl Gottlieb Bretschneider, 28 vols. (Halle-on-the-Saale: C. A. Schwetschke und Sohn, 1836-1860). Vol. X contains *Carmina Lib. I* and *IV, His epulis donisque Tuis benedictio, Christe; Quae nunc sumemus membris alimenta caducis; O Deus, appositis apponendisque, precamur; Corpora qui solito satiasti nostra cibatu; Quod sumus utilibus dapibus potuque refecti;* and *Gratia magna Tibi, Pater et Rex inclyte rerum.* All six are found in the 1564 edition of the *Preces privatae*, but their composition must be from an earlier period, as Melanchthon died in 1560. Two other graces that deserve mention are a *Precatio ad mensam*, beginning *Quod sumus et tegimur, dulces quod carpimus escas*, and a *Gratiarum actio post cibum sumptum discipulis suis praescripta*, which commences *Postquam epulis exempta fames, mensaeque remotae.* No musical settings of these texts are known to me, but I believe they may have been sung as well as spoken. According to Zahn, *Die Melodien der deutschen evangelischen Kirchenlieder*, 6 vols. (Gütersloh: C. Bertelsmann, 1889-1893), No. 966 text b, *Dicimus grates tibi* by Melanchthon (?) was sung to Tritonius's *Iam satis terrae nivis* (1507). I have been unable to find this text attributed to the preceptor of the Lutheran Reformation in the Halle edition.

28. "Glory to Thee, O Lord, O Holy One; glory to Thee, O King; as Thou hast given us meat in our bodies, so replenish us with joy and gladness in Thy Holy Spirit that we may be found acceptable in Thy sight, and may not be made ashamed when Thou shalt render to every one according to his works. Amen." (Slightly modified from N. Bailey's translation, London, 1725.

Erasmus's *Homilia LVI* (Migne, *op. cit.*, Vol. 58, p. 545, gives both Greek and Latin Texts.)

29. "May what is or what shall be set upon this table be commended to the happy blessing of Him who feeds all things with his bounty. Amen."

30. Senfl's setting of *O Crucifer* is No. 30 in the *Varia carminum* and No. 52 in the *Geminae*, RISM, 1551[17]. Modern reprint in Ludwig Senfl, *Sämtliche Werke* (Wolfenbüttel and Zürich: Möseler Verlag, 1961), Vol. VI, No. 30, pp. 86-87. His versions of *Rerum creator maxime* are (1) No. 29 (text b) of the *Varia carminum* (*Geminae undeviginti*, No. 51); modern reprint in *Sämtliche Werke*, Vol. VI, No. 29, p. 86, and (2) fol. D 7 recte in *Harmoniae poeticae*, *ibid.*, Vol. VI, No. 38, p. 91. Paul Hofhaimer's setting is also in the *Harmoniae poeticae*, reprinted in Hans Joachim Moser, *Paul Hofhaimer* (Stuttgart and Berlin: J. G. Cotta'scher Buchhandlung Nachf., 1929), *Noten-Anhang*, p. 127, No. 33. *Frequens ad esto parve grex* by Camerarius in *Varia carminum*, No. 31 (*Geminae undeviginti*, No. 53) is not available in a modern score. The text is reprinted in Senfl, *Sämtliche Werke*, Vol. VI, note 30, p. 116, "mit heute üblicher Rechtschreibung und Zeichensetzung." For the musical attribution, "Von Camerarius stammt also wohl nicht nur der Text, sondern auch die Musik, so das das Stück nicht in unserer Senfl-ausgabe gehörte," see *ibid.*

31. *Benediction at the table:* "May God the three in one, the Father and the Son and the Holy Ghost, bless us and those things which we are about to receive. Amen. [The Pater Noster was then sung.]" *Grace after the meal:* "Praise be to God. Glory to His Saints; peace on earth. May the dead rest [in peace] for ever and ever. Amen. [The Pater Noster and Ave Maria followed.]" See modern facsimile reprint by the University of Santo Domingo, Ciudad Trujillo, 1945, with a preface by E. Rodriguez Demorizi.

32. "What we are about to receive may the Trinity and Unity bless. Amen. For Thy benefits, O Lord, we give Thee thanks."

33. Consult T. Lea Southgate and Arthur Watson, "Knives with Music Inscribed" in *Musical News*, April 30, 1910, pp. 444-448; see also *The Antiquary*, February, 1895, pp. 21-22. Adrien de La Fage scored one of the sets for Antoine Elwart's *Histoire de la Société des Concerts du conservatoire* (Paris: S. Castel, 1860). Being a man of his time, he added a *Réduction pour l'Orgue-Harm: ou le Piano*. There is a short commentary on *couteaux de table* on p. 47, together with an engraving of one of the knives on the opposite page. No one to my knowledge has thus far satisfactorily established the provenance of the knives.

34. See *Cantiques de Salomon Rossi*, ed. by S. Naumbourg (Paris: S. Naumbourg, 1877), *Partie I*, p. 27, and the same in a photographic reissue *Out of Print Classics. Series of Synagogue Music No. 16* (New York: Sacred Music Press, 1954) p. 27.

35. Concerning Schöberlein, Wackernagel, and Zahn, see notes 19, 11, and 27, *supra*. Wackernagel, *op. cit.*, Vols. I and II lack adequate indexes; in Vol. III, see *Vor und nach Tische:* Nos. 229, 245, 377-379, 443-445, 642, 731, 829, 985, 1060, 1100, 1101, 1290, 1291, 1382, 1383; Vol. IV, *Vor und nach Tische:* Nos. 182, 269, 272, 283-287, 293, 366, 447, 664-666, 685, 687, 688, 728, 741, 743, 785, 804, 932, 1118-1120, 1214, 1215, 1291, 1304, 1474, 1528, 1529, 1585; Vol. V, *Tischgebete:* Nos. 157, 204, 205, 311, 312, and Roman Catholic table blessings: 1262, 1263, 1409, 1421, 1422, 1452.

36. There are various melodies given in Zahn for *O Gott, du frommer Gott* (Nos. 5144-5151), some of which were later set by J. S. Bach. These do not, however, include the one that Luther apparently had in mind. Luther's

enthusiasm for *Tischgebete* is also shown by the number of prose table blessings that he included in his publications. See Vol. 30, Part I, of the Weimar edition, pp. 262-263, 322-337, 394-396. There is a facsimile print of the Bapst *Geystliche Lieder* (Kassel: Bärenreiter, 1929). Many modern German collections include early *Tischgebete*. See Fritz Jöde, *Frau Musica* (Berlin: Deutsche Buch-gemeinschaft, 1929) pp. 43-48; *Lose Blätter der Musikantengilde* (Wolfenbüttel: Kallmeyer) Nos. 56, 169 6-7, 186 7-11, 255 13-14; and *Handbuch der deutschen evangelischen Kirchenmusik*, ed. by Carl Gerhardt, 3 vols. (Göttingen: Vandenhoeck & Ruprecht, 1941-42).

37. Horn's *Almechtiger gütiger Gott* (Zahn, *op. cit.*, No. 362) was slightly modified by Bapst (Zahn, 362 b). This is No. 443 in Wackernagel, *op. cit.*, Vol. III. *Dancket dem Herren* is Zahn No. 12 and Wackernagel, Vol. III, No. 445. For the text of *Certane Gracis*, see pp. 18-21 and the notes on pp. 244-245 of A. F. Mitchell's edition of *A compendious Book of Godly and Spiritual Songs commonly known as "The Gude and Godlie Ballatis" Reprinted from the edition of 1567* in *The Scottish Text Society Publications*, Vol. XXXIX (Edinburgh: W. Blackwood and Sons, 1897). The table-blessing lines, paraphrased from Psalm 145, are quaintly spelled:

> All mennis eine, O Lord, do thé abyde
> Thow feidis thame in all tyme and tyde:
> Thow oppinnis furth thy hand full graciuslie,
> And satisfyis all flesche aboundantlie.

One may also consult *A Compendious Book of Psalms and Spiritual Songs, commonly known as "The gude and godlie Ballates"* . . . *Reprinted from the edition of 1578*, ed. by David Laing (Edinburgh: George Robb, 1868) as well as the more recent *The gude and godlie ballates, edited by Iain Ross* (Edinburgh: published for the Saltire society by Oliver and Boyd, Ltd., 1939). The rubric for *Wir danken Gott dem Herren*, as given in Wackernagel, *op. cit.*, Vol. III, No. 229, reads: *Das Gratias. Eine Christliche Dancksagung, Johannis Waltheri des Eltern letztes Gedicht. Nach der Melodey: Lobet Gott ir frommen Christen, etc. Oder nach der Melodey, Von der Gottfürchtigen Dorothea und Susanna zu singen.* Its rhythmic scheme is 7.6.7.6. D; that of the Scottish adaptation is 10.10.10. 10. 10. 10. *Ein Benedicite (De Ogen aller Creatur), ibid.*, Vol. III, No. 245, follows an 8.8.8.7.8.8.7 pattern, the Edinburgh version a 9.10.10.10.10.10.10 meter. *O Gott wir denken deiner Güt, ibid.*, Vol. III, Nos. 1060-1061, a *Lobgesang nach dem Essen*, sung to the tune *Nu frewet euch*, Zahn No. 8143, was first published in 1553. Its 8.7.8.7.8.8.7 meter was changed by the Wedderburns to 8.8.8.8.8.8.8. If the German tunes were used in Scotland, they were undoubtedly modified. More light is thrown on this subject by A. F. Mitchell, *The Wedderburns and their Work, or, The Sacred Poetry of the Scottish Reformation in its Historical Relation to that of Germany; a Lecture* . . . (Edinburgh: W. Blackwood and Sons, 1867).

38. For (1), see Schütz, *Sämmtliche Werke* (Leipzig: Breitkopf & Härtel, 1885-1927), Vol. XVI, pp. 126-127 and 185, and *Neue Ausgabe sämmtlicher Werke* (Kassel: Bärenreiter, 1955), Vol. VI, p. 149. For (2), see *Sämmtliche Werke*, Vol. XVI, pp. 188-189. For (3), *ibid.*, Vol. IV, pp. 135-144, and *Neue Ausgabe*, Vol. IX, (1960), pp. 116-127; this group of settings appeared separately as Bärenreiter Ausgabe 1963. For (4) see *Sämmtliche Werke*, Vol. XII, pp. 171-178.

39. The first of Zinzendorf's *Tischgebete* was written about 1720; the sec-

ond dates from 1741 and may have been composed in America. See *Geistliche Gedichte des Grafen von Zinzendorf gesammelt und gesichtet von Albert Knapp* (Stuttgart: J. G. Cotta, 1845), pp. 14 and 153. Three collections will serve to illustrate the transplantation of the Old World practice. 1) The *Gesangbuch worinnen sowohl die Psalmen Davids nach D. Ambrosii Lobwassers Uebersetzung hin und wieder verbessert, als auch 730 auserlesener alter und neuer Geistreichen Lieder begriffen sind . . . welche sowohl bey dem öffentlichen Gottesdienste in den Reformirten Kirchen der Hessisch-Hanauisch-Pfältzisch-Pensilvanischen und mehreren andern angräntzenden Landen, Als auch zur Privat-Andacht und Erbauung nützlich können gebraucht werden . . . (Germantown, bey Christoph Saur 1763), Zweyte Auflage,* contains four *Tischlieder vor dem Essen* and five *Nach dem Essen* (besides, of course, Psalm 145). 2) A Schwenkfelder manuscript, gathered and copied by Rosina Dresher Hoffman "zusammen getragen 1727 und aufs neue abgeschrieben 1753" reads: *Tägliches Gesang-Büchlein. Das ist: Morgen- Tisch- und Abend-Lieder. Samt einer Einrichtung und Ordnung was man Vor- und Nachmittags; sowol auch dess Abends, nach den Tisch-Liedern nach Belieben singende betrachten kan: sowol auch Sonntags-Lieder welche man bey einem häusslichen Gottes-dienst zu dem Anbett; wie auch Vor- und nach der Predigt, zu singen pfleget.* The title page is reproduced in *Publications of the Pennsylvania Society of the Colonial Dames—IV. Church Music and Musical Life in Pennsylvania in the Eighteenth Century* (Philadelphia: printed for the Society, 1927), Vol. II, p. 106; there is a description on p. 108. The original Ms is in the Schwenkfelder Historical Library, Pennsburg, Penn. 3) A more formal Schwenkfelder collection, the *Neu- eingerichtetes Gesang-Buch . . . (Germantown, bedruckt bey Christoph Saur, auf Kosten vereinigter Freunden,* 1762), lists seven hymns to be sung *Vor dem Essen,* four *Nach dem Tisch-Gebät,* and ten *Nach dem Essen.*

Pennsylvania also saw the publication of English table blessings inspired by German practice, for instance, the seven previously unpublished graces in John and Charles Wesley's collection of *Hymns and Sacred Poems* (Philadelphia, 1740; reprinted from the 1739 London edition). The brothers had been impressed by the *Tischlieder* of the Moravian emigrants during their sojourn in Georgia from 1735 to 1737.

40. Francis Segar (Seagar), *The School of Vertue,* reprinted in F. J. Furnival, *The Babees Book . . . , The Early English Text Society Original Series,* No. 32 (London: N. Trübner & Co., 1868).

41. *The Autobiography of Thomas Whythorne,* ed. by James T. Osborn (Oxford: Clarendon Press, 1961), modern spelling edition (London: Oxford University Press, 1962). For the quotation, see section XV, pp. 130-131, of the latter.

42. Both the Whythorne graces were transcribed and edited by Peter Warlock and appeared in 1927 as Nos. 358 and 359 in the Oxford University Press series, *Choral Songs from the Old Masters.*

43. The Cantus and Tenor or Playnsong of Psalm 145 face the Medius and Bassus on pp. 252-253 of both editions. The entire collection, consisting of settings of the words of Sternhold and Hopkins, appeared in a slightly confusing score over a hundred years ago: *A Reprint of all the tunes in Ravenscroft's Book of psalms, With introductory remarks,* ed. by the Rev. W. H. Havergal (London: J. A. Novello, 1845). For Psalm 145, see p. 55. A modern scholarly edition is long overdue. The melody is printed in Frost, *English &*

Scottish Psalm and Hymn Tunes, No. 169. The words of Ex. 8 are taken from the revised version.

44. There were several editions of *Haleluiah* in the 19th century: *Halle-lelujah . . . or Britain's Second Remembrancer . . . Composed in a three-fold volume, by George Wither, With an introduction by Edward Farr* (London: J. R. Smith, 1857) and one preserving the original spelling, *Haleluiah or Britans Second Remembrancer* (Manchester: Spenser Society, 1879), 2 vols. (being Nos. 26 and 27 of the *Publications of the Spenser Society*). The table blessings are Hymns 34 and 35 of Part I. The tune is given in Frost, *op. cit.*, No. 4. Wither's more elaborate graces, Nos. 32 and 33, might be further described. The rubric for No. 32 is "Hymn before or at a Feast. Feasts are useful to cheer our minds by a plentiful enjoying of the creatures in a neighborly society, when times and good occasions allow the same. And this Hymn offers to remembrance some cautions to sanctify, and keep harms from such refresh-ings." The first line is "What plenties, O thrice gracious Lord." The poem was to be sung to the tune for Psalm 4. This was the tune, *Low Dutch*, in Ravens-croft, called *English* in the Scottish Psalters; it was recast twice by Playford under the name *Canterbury*. The rubric for No. 33 reads: "A Hymn after a Feast. We are here remembered to be thankful for our refreshments; to acknowldge God's bounty in giving His creatures as well for delight as neces-sity; and to use His good blessings with temperance." The musical instruction is "Sing this as the former Hymn." In his introductory remarks *To the Reader*, Wither speaks of the simple rhythmic scheme of his verses: ". . . this I have done also, that they may be sung to the common tunes of the Psalms, and such others as are well known [he suggests for a number of hymns the popular songs *In Sad and Ashy Weeds, The Hermit Poor*, and *I loved thee once*]; to which I have directed my reader not to confine him to such tunes, but that he may have those until he be provided of such as may be more proper; which, perchance, may by some devout musician be hereafter prepared." Some years before, in 1623, Orlando Gibbons had supplied fourteen excellent tunes with a bass for Wither's *Hymnes and Songs of the Church*. Mention should be made again of the 17th-century Latin graces written by the English composers Ben-jamin Rogers and John Reading. See note 10, *supra*.

45. See note 39 *supra*.

46. See article by T. C. L. Pritchard on "Psalter, Metrical: Scottish" in *Grove's Dictionary of Music and Musicians*, 5th ed., ed. by Eric Blom (New York: St. Martin's Press, 1959), Vol. VI, p. 972.

47. Wither, *op. cit.* The seven hymns listed are Nos. 2, 3, 6, 4, 19, 20, and 43 in Part I and No. 61 of Part III, respectively.

48. Charles Lamb, No. XIX of the *Essays of Elia* (1823). Actually Wither wrote hymns for most of Lamb's categories: *When we walk to the Church, When we walk from Church, When we are walking in a Garden, When we are walking in the fields, When we depart from Home, When we return Home, When we ride for pleasure, In a clear starry night, In a dark night, When kindred meet together, When kindred depart from each other, When our hopes are obtained. Op. cit.*, Hymns 36, 37, 30, 31, 11, 12, 22, 15, 16, 38, 39, and 106 in Part I.

49. Since the writer is preparing a volume on table blessings set to music, suggestions will be welcome from anyone who reads this contribution in honor of the memory of a great teacher, scholar, and friend.

Appendix

A partial list of text incipits associated with table blessings

Latin

Ad panem medicum currite
Agimus tibi gratias omnipotens Deus

Benedicam Dominum in omni tempore
Benedicantur nobis Domine dona tua, quae de tua largitate sumus
    sumpturi
Benedic, Domine, dona tua quae de tua largitate
Benedic, Domine, et haec tua dona quae de tua largitate
Benedic, Domine, nobis his donis tuis
Benedic, Domine, nos et haec tua dona
Benedic nobis Domine Deus atque illis donis tuis
Benedicite Dominus. Omnia te expectant domine et des illis escam in
    tempore
Benedicite, oculi omnium in te sperant
Benedictus Deus in bonis suis
Benedictus Deus qui me pascis a juventute mea
Benedictus es Domine, qui nutris me a pueritia mea
Benedictus sit Deus in donis suis

Christe Deus nostrae benedic convivia mensae
Confiteantur tibi, Domine, omnia opera tua
Confitemini Domine, quoniam bonus, quoniam in eternam (saeculum)
    misericordia eius, Qui dat escam
Corpora qui solito satiasti nostra cibatu

Dicimus grates tibi
Domine Deus Pater coelestis, benedic nos et haec dona

Frequens ad esto parve grex dei proles

Gloria tibi, Domine sancte; gloria tibi, Rex, quoniam dedisti nobis escas
Gratia magna tibi, Pater, et Rex inclyte rerum
Gratias agimus tibi, Domine Deus Pater
Gratias tibi agimus, omnipotens, aeterne Deus

His epulis donisque tuis benedictio, Christe
Hic patriarcha pius sedeat sumusque sacerdos

Laus Deo; gloria sancti; pax vivis

Nos et ea quae sumpturi sumus, benedicat Deus trinus et unus

O Crucifer bone, lucis sator
Oculi omnium in te sperant
O Deus, appositis apponendisque, precamur
Omnes gentes laudent Dominum
O Pater coelestis, o qui regna coelorum tenes

Pastis visceribus, ciboque sumpto
Postquam epulis, exempta fames, mensaeque remotae
Pro tuis beneficiis Deus gratias agimus tibi

Quae nunc sumemus membris alimenta caducis
Quae sumpturi sumus benedicat trinus et unum
Quicquid appositum est, et quicquid apponetur
Quod sumus et tegimur, dulces quod carpimus escas

Rerum creator maxime

Sufficit, quidquid facias vocato

Te canunt omnes Nicolae
Te Deum Patrem colimus, Te laudibus prosequimur
Te volucrum pecundumque
Tu autem, Domine, miserere nobis; Deo Gratias

French

A Toi seul à jamais, à Toi gloire et honneur
Bénis Seigneur, les biens que Tu nous donnes
Bon Dieu, bénis nous
Célébrons sans cesse, de Dieu ses bontés
Dieu, Père, Créateur, gouverne de Ta main Ton peuple
Notre bon Père tout puissant qui governe Ta créature
O Souverain Pasteur et Maître
Père éternel qui nous ordonnes
Rendons grâces à Dieu, vous toutes nations
Ton règne, o Dieu, est un règne à toujours

German

Ach Gott, dass (der) Du uns hast so mild
Allmächtig Gott, Herr Jesu Christ
Allmächtiger, gütiger Gott, Du ewiger Herr Zebaoth
Aller Augen auf dich, O Herre, warten
Aller Augen, O Herre Gott
Aller Augen warten auf Dich
Auf Dich allein, O Herre Gott
Auf Dich die Augen sehen von allen Seiten
Auf Dich warten mit ganzem Fleiss
Auf, lasset uns dem Herrn fröhlich singen
Auf, lobt den Herren und dankt für seine Gaben

Benedictus. Gesegnet sei die Frucht, Trank, Essen, Wein und Brot
Bescher uns, Herre, das täglich Brot

Dank Du hast uns wohl gespeiset
Dank sag wir Dir um alles, das wir in Speiss und Trank genossen haben
Danket dem Herren, der allem Fleisch Speise gibt
Danket dem Herren, der uns all thut nähren
Danket dem Herren, denn er ist sehr freundlich
Danket dem Herren, er thut uns ernähren
Danket dem Herren fleissig
Danket dem Herren heut und allzeit
Danket Gott dem Herrn
Das Gratias das singen wir, Herr Gott Vater
Dem grossen Gott sei Dank für diese seine Gaben
Dem Herrn danket allezeit
Dem Herrn danket aus Herzensgrund
Den Vater dort oben wollen wir nun loben
Der Mensch lebt nicht allein im Brodt
Dich bitten wir deine Kinder
Die Augen aller Kreatur
Dir Gott Vater sagen wir Dank
Dir sei durch Jesum Christum Dank
Du Schöpfer Himmels auf der Erden

Ehrt, lobt und dankt mit grossem (ganzem) Fleiss

Fröhlich lasst uns erheben
Für dein Empfangen, Speiss und Trank

Gesegn uns, Herr, die Gaben dein
Gesegnet sei die Frucht, Trank, Essen, Wein und Brot
Gib Heiland, dass ich Dich geniess
Gib uns heut, unser täglich Brot
Gott, Vater, der Du deinen Sohn
Gott, Vater, der Du uns ernährst
Gott, Vater, Sohn, heiliger Geist, O unser einiger Gott
Gott, wir danken deiner Güt
Gott wollt uns vorneigen
Gratias: Wohlauf als das zu Himmel sei
Grosser Gott wir arme Sünder
Grossmächtiger ewiger Gott

Herr Gott, dein Gut man billig preist
Herr Gott, himmlischer Vater
Herr Gott, nun sei gepreiset
Herr Gott, Vater in Himmelreich
Herr Gott, wir wagen Dir Lob und Dank
Herr Jesu Christ, dich zu uns neig

Komm, Herr Jesu, sei unser Gast
Kommt herzu, lasst uns jetzund Herz, Gemüthe, Seel und Mund

Lasset uns den Herren preisen
Lobet den Herren, denn er ist sehr freundlich
Lobet den Herren und dankt ihm seine Gaben
Lobet den Herren und preiset ihn
Lobet Gott, unsern Herren
Lobt und erhöht des grossen Gottes Güte
Lob, Ehre und Dankbarkeit

Nun freut euch lieben Christen
Nun lasst uns alle Gott
Nun lasst uns Gott, dem Herren danksagen
Nun lobet all Gott den Herrn Zebaoth
Nun preiset all Gottes Barmherzigkeit

O Gott, wir danken deiner Güt
O Herr, tu auf Dein milde Hand
O Herr, wir sagen Dir Lob und Dank
O treuer Gott, wir danken Dir
O Vater aller Frommen

Segne Vater diese Speise
Segne Vater, unser Essen
Speis' uns Vater
Singen wir (all) aus Herzensgrund

Vater, aller Frommen, geheiligt werd' dein Nam'
Vater im höchsten Thron

Weil wir gegessen haben
Weil wir nu gessen haben
Wir danken Dir, Herr Gott, (himmlischer) Vater
Wir danken Gott für seine Gaben
Wohlauf als das zu Himmel sei
Wohlauf ihr lieben Gäste

Zwei Ding, O Herr, bitte ich von Dir
Zu Gott wollen wir uns kehren

English

All eyes wait on Thee, and their meat
All creature on the Lord dependis
All mennis eine, O Lord, do thé abyde
All meit and drink was creat by the Lord
All ye here now that present be
Almighty God, Eternal King
Almighty God, Thy loving care
Almighty God, Whose wondrous hand
As to the sick all pleasant things

Be present at our Table, Lord
Bless the Lord in all lands
Bless these Thy gifts most gracious God
Bless we our Lord which of his grace
Blessed be the Father celestial
Blest be the God whose tender care

Christ learnit us, on God how we suld call

Dust, earthy ashes is our strength

Expecting Thee each creature's eye attendeth

Father of mercies by Whose love abounding
For spreading, Lord, our Table, thus

Geve (Give) thanks to God with one accorde
God bless our meat, God guide our ways
God gives not only corn for need
God, that His brede brake
Good Lord for Thy grace meekly we call

He that is king of glory, and Lord over all
Here a little Child I stand

Jesus' mercies never fail

Let us give thanks to God our Lord
Like as Thou hast almighty God
Lord we again lift up our eyes

Man's life preserved is by food
My God, O King, I'll Thee extol

Now that our bodies refreshed be
Now we have both meat and drink

O blessed God and most high king
O lamb of God, Christ which takest away
O Lord, bless us and this our store
O Lord our God to Thee we pray
O Lord, that art my God and King
O Lord, the merciful and good
O Lord, to Whom all praise is due
O our Father we yield to Thee
O Thou, in whom we live and move
O Thou who kindly dost provide
Of Dives and Lazarus

Parent of God, whose plenteous grace
Pray we to God, the almighty Lord

Receive your meat without grudging

Sweet is the memory of Thy grace

Thank and praise the Lord in everlastingness
Thanks to that Lord that all hath sent
The eyes of all do wait on Thee
The eyes of all things, Lord, attend
The Lord does them support that fall
The Lord helps those that fall
Thee I'll extol, my God and King
Thee let us taste in all our food
Thee will I laud my God and King, and bless Thy name for aye
To eat and drink doth small avail
To our gude God, of warldis Lord and King

We bless Thee, Lord, for this our food
We give Thee thanks, O Father Almighty
We praise, O God! we honour Thee
We praise Thy name, for Thou, O Lord
We thank our God both kind and liberall
We thank Thee God of Thy Gudness
What God gives and what we take
What plenties, O thrice gracious Lord
What praise to Thee, my Saviour
When is it fitter to begin
With longing eyes Thy creatures wait *

* A number of these graces have not been found with music, but being metrical they naturally lent themselves to singing. A few initial lines of middle stanzas have been included. It is hoped that this alphabetical listing will reveal more table blessings set to music.

ES IST GENUG, SO NIMM

HERR MEINEN GEIST:

300 YEARS IN THE HISTORY

OF A PROTESTANT

FUNERAL SONG

Karl Geiringer (Santa Barbara, California)

$\mathcal{T}$he treasure chest of Lutheran chorales contains many hymns notable for their ancient origin, forceful text, or melodic beauty. But only a few provide the material for as interesting a chronicle as does the funeral song *Es ist genug*, written three hundred years ago. In the following study an attempt will be made to outline the history of this remarkable tune.[1]

The First Book of the Kings in the Old Testament reports the futile attempts of the prophet Elijah to suppress the Israelites' worship of idols. Persecuted by his enemies, he gives up the fight in despair and prays to the Lord in words reminiscent of the utterances of the agonized Job and of Jonah: "It is enough; now, O Lord, take away

283

my life." [2] This outcry inspired the young German poet, Franz Joachim
Burmeister (1633?-1672) of Lüneburg, to write a funeral song in five
stanzas "Über die Sehnsuchtsworte des Elias" (On Elijah's Words of
Longing). Burmeister, a friend of the North-German theologian Johann
Rist (1607-1667), who played an important part in the growth of the
Protestant church song, here contributed a poem imbued with genuine
feeling. The two most significant stanzas of the forceful song, the first
and the last, read as follows:

Es ist genug, so nimm Herr, meinen Geist zu Zions Geistern hin.
Lös' auf das Band, das allgemählich reisst, befreie diesen Sinn,
der sich nach seinem Gotte sehnet,
der täglich klagt, der nächtlich thränet:
Es ist genug,
es ist genug.

Es ist genug, Herr. Wenn es dir gefällt, so spanne mich doch aus.
Mein Jesus kommt, nun gute Nacht o Welt! Ich fahr' ins Himmels-Haus.
Ich fahre sicher hin mit Frieden,
mein feuchter Jammer bleibt hienieden.
Es ist genug,
es ist genug.[3]

Johann Rudolf Ahle (1625-1673), organist in Mühlhausen, Thuringia,
set this moving text to music, and the song appeared in 1662 in a collection, *Drittes Zehn Newer Geistlicher Arien.*[4] The composition is for
six voices (2 cantus, 1 altus, 2 tenors, 1 bass) and consists of three
musical phrases, each of which is presented twice. The initial phrase,
intended for the first and second lines of the text, is the most extensive
one in the composition and starts in sedate half notes, changing soon,
however, to quarter-note motion. Ahle divides his six voices into two
groups to achieve half-choirs of different range, and he has the phrase
uttered first by the upper voices and then, in a kind of antiphonal effect,
one octave lower by the two tenors and the bass.

Ex. 1

Band,   das all-ge-mäh-lich reisst, be-frei - e die-sen Sinn.

The more concise second phrase, written for the third and fourth lines of the hymn, moves almost entirely in quarter notes, thus giving increased urgency to the passionate supplication. This phrase, like the first one, is presented by the upper and then by the lower voices. The last and shortest phrase, which merely sets the text's three initial words as a kind of refrain, is again in a somewhat calmer mood, although syncopations and dotted quarter notes in the middle voices still reveal some of the former unrest. All the voices join in singing this refrain, applying to the text-repetition a dynamic echo effect, prescribed in the old print. The most impressive feature of the song appears at the beginning, with its peculiar leaning towards the Lydian mode. In the melody three whole tones follow each other, and simultaneously in the harmony the supertonic chord with raised third succeeds the tonic chord. Ardent longing for death could hardly have been expressed more forcefully and stirringly.

The song was soon widely adopted in Protestant congregational singing. In 1682, Gottfried Vopelius, cantor of St. Nicholai, Leipzig, included it in his book of hymns, which was regarded as a sequel to the *Cantionale* by Schein, and in the following two decades the hymn may be traced in more than thirty different publications.[5] It is noteworthy, however, that the music was subjected to not inconsiderable changes, which may be illustrated by two characteristic examples. The *Geist- und Lehr-reiches Kirchen- und Hausz-Buch*, published in 1694 at Dresden,[6] shows the typical process of simplification applied to the tune in later editions. Ahle's subtle use of six voices is replaced by a setting for a melody and figured bass only. The alternation between an upper and a lower choir is no longer to be found, and the *Kirchen- und Hausz-Buch* is satisfied to provide simple repeat-signs at the end of the first and of the second phrase. In addition, the initial melody has lost much of its power and character. Ahle's expressive first phrase is changed in the Dresden hymnbook to:

Ex. 2

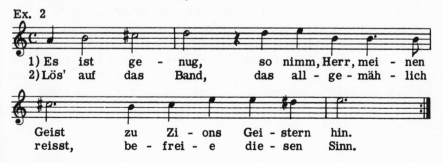

1) Es ist   ge - nug,   so nimm, Herr, mei - nen
2) Lös' auf   das   Band,   das all - ge - mäh - lich

Geist   zu   Zi - ons   Gei - stern   hin.
reisst,   be - frei - e   die - sen   Sinn.

The significant tritone of the original has disappeared,[7] since the editor apparently feared that the congregation would resent the use of the "diabolus in musica." A somewhat different method of avoiding the offensive interval is used in another group of arrangements, as may be illustrated by the *Neues Geist-reiches Gesang-Buch . . . herausgegeben von Johann Anastasio Freylinghausen . . .* , Halle, 1714.[8] This version is also set for melody and figured bass only and uses the familiar repetitions:

Ex. 3

For the arranger's peculiar manner of eluding the tritone,[9] Ahle might himself have supplied the model. The composer thought it advisable to emphasize the startling whole-tone progression only once and to veil it in the repetition of the initial phrase. Although the first tenor utters the same four notes as the first cantus sang a few measures before, the effect is neutralized by the second tenor, whose part crosses that of the first tenor (see Ex. 1, meas. 4).

It would lead too far afield to trace all the numerous adaptations of Ahle's song. Some differ so greatly from the original that one finds it difficult to decide whether they are free arrangements or completely new compositions,[10] and, with a single exception, their artistic value remains far below that of the model.

The imposing new version of the hymn by J. S. Bach belongs to a category of its own. As is well-known, the cantor of the St. Thomas Church wrote two cantatas on the chorale *O Ewigkeit, du Donnerwort* (Nos. 20 and 60). The shorter of the two, composed, according to new research, in 1723,[11] starts with a dialogue between Fear (alto) and Hope (tenor), which are subsequently joined by the voice of Christ.[12] As a surprising conclusion, a four-part chorale on Ahle's song is presented, using as a text the last and most impressive stanza of the hymn. Bach's chorale arrangement compensates for 18th-century rhythmic atrophy by the unusual harmonic richness of its setting. The repetition of the phrases leads here to systematically fresh harmonizations; each of the melodic lines is presented twice, the chordal support of the second statement always being a new one. Thus Bach succeeds, within the formal framework of his time, in achieving by different means the antiphonal effect envisioned by Ahle. Moreover, he is by no means willing to mitigate the harshness of the tritone at the beginning. He

seems to revel in the emotional outburst as he underlines the whole-
tone progressions in the soprano by a related device in the bass
and, in addition, exposes the tritone once more when repeating the
phrase with changed harmonization.

Ex. 4

Es   ist ge - nug.   Herr, wenn_____ es Dir__ ge -
fällt,   so   span-ne mich doch__ aus. Mein   Je - sus kommt,

Bach aims in this chorale at the strongest interpretation of the text, a
tendency revealed in the octave skip in the alto, the violently down-
ward-rushing middle parts at the cadence, and the chromatically descending bass line illustrating the words "mein grosser Jammer bleibt
darnieden."

Ex. 5

mein gros-ser   Jam - mer bleibt dar - nie   -   den.

With the help of bold melodic leaps, harsh dissonances, an abundant
use of altered chords, passing tones, anticipations, and retardations, he
paints a Michelangelesque picture of the horrors of earthly existence
and expresses an overwhelming longing for liberation from worldly
bondage.

This version was included in the collection of J. S. Bach's four-part chorale arrangements edited by J. P. Kirnberger and C. P. E. Bach,[13] and it appeared also in numerous subsequent editions of these chorales. In ordinary hymn books, however, it is hardly ever found, as Bach's harmonization is too daring for congregational singing. In the concert hall, however, the significance of Bach's chorale arrangement and its connection with Ahle's song were pointed out by an amateur musicologist of the 19th century. Johannes Brahms, appointed conductor of the Gesellschaft der Musikfreunde in Vienna in the fall of 1872, tried to make his concert programs more interesting by including older compositions. Music by Eccard, Isaac, Stradella, and Gallus was performed under his baton, and the concert of December 7, 1873, offered Ahle's *Es ist genug* and Bach's arrangement of it in immediate succession.[14] Brahms's manuscript scores made for this concert have survived in the archives of the society and were published by the present author in May 1933 in celebration of the centenary of Brahms's birth.[15] Brahms had no difficulty in obtaining the source material for his performance. As a fervent admirer of Bach, whose works he thoroughly studied and frequently performed, he certainly knew Vol. XII[2] of the Bach Gesellschaft edition,[16] where the final chorale, *Es ist genug*, of Cantata No. 60 appears as the last item. Most likely he saw Ahle's composition in Winterfeld's *Der evangelische Kirchengesang*, or possibly one of his musicologist friends, such as Pohl or Nottebohm, may have directed his attention to the old song. In any event, it may be considered a remarkable achievement for a creative artist thus to have carried out a project in applied musicology.

Brahms did not change any notes in the original scores, but, as a true son of the 19th century, he did liberally supply dynamic signs for his performance. In the Bach arrangement, he even provided different expression marks for each phrase-repetition, while leaving out most of the *fermate*.

Ex. 6

In the 20th century, Ahle's enduring hymn has found remarkable employment as part of a monumental work in which Baroque, romantic, and contemporary features are brought into a highly significant fusion.

In the 1930's, the Viennese composer Alban Berg was commissioned by the American violinist Louis Krasner to write a violin concerto.[17] Berg, who was at heart a dramatic composer, seemed at first unable to make real progress with his work, until a tragic event in his circle of friends inspired him to conceive his Concerto as a kind of tone poem with a programmatic meaning. In April 1935, the eighteen-year-old Manon Gropius,[18] a dear friend of both Berg and his wife, died of infantile paralysis, and the composer decided to erect a monument to her in the Concerto. Now the work progressed rapidly, but shortly after its completion the composer himself died in December, 1935.[19]

Berg dedicates the Concerto [20] "to the memory of an angel." In the first movement, he describes the innocent and gay life of the young girl and, in the concluding second movement, her death and her transformation into a spiritual being. Each movement contains a pre-existent melody that conveys a clear symbolic meaning. In the second half of the first movement, a Carinthian folk dance expresses Manon's joy in life; near the end of the second movement, Bach's hymn indicates that she is exchanging her terrestrial for a celestial abode. The hymn is allotted an important part not only in the conclusion of the Concerto; even at the beginning, the twelve-tone row that seems to form the germ cell of the whole work, presents in its last four notes the whole-tone progression [21] so characteristic of Ahle's melody.

Ex. 7

After the monumental death scene, the hymn is intoned in its entirety, and a footnote in the score refers to Bach's Cantata No. 60 and indicates that all the fragments of the chorale quoted by the soloist or the orchestra are marked with the letters "CH." In addition, the score refers in meas. 152 to Bach's harmonization, and the fifth stanza of Burmeister's poem is placed underneath the notes played by the instruments. At the outset, the first phrase of the hymn is intoned by the solo violin in the key of B♭ major, transposed a half tone up from the original key of A, the accompanying countermelodies being provided by Berg. Then the woodwinds repeat this phrase, uttering it in Bach's harmonization. Likewise the second and ultimately the third phrase are first presented by the solo violin with Berg's counterpoints and subsequently by the woodwinds in Bach's version. Since the older composer had offered every phrase in two versions, while the later composer used only one, Berg had a choice between two alternatives for each of his quotations. Obviously the 20th-century artist chose in each case the more daring and harsher-sounding chords. (The first phrase is based on Bach's meas. 1-4 and 10-11, the second on meas. 15-17, the third on meas. 18-19.)

It is noteworthy that Berg not only took over parts of Bach's harmonization, but at the same time adopted Ahle's antiphonal setting, to the extent that he presented the tune in the form of a dialogue between the accompanied solo violin and a chorus of woodwinds. It cannot be ascertained whether Berg knew Ahle's original version; but this is quite possible, since the present writer had presented the old hymn two years earlier in the widely circulated *Zeitschrift für Musik*. However this may be, Berg, either through musicological knowledge or through artistic instinct, produced a kind of fusion of Ahle's and Bach's ideas in assigning each phrase first to one and then to another group of performers, while at the same time changing its harmonic setting. The hymn is regarded by Berg as a theme to which, like an artist of the Baroque period, he adds two variations. In the course of these variations, the expression is increasingly enhanced until a climax is reached in the middle of the second one. Bach's harmonies are no longer used, but in both variations the complete melody is intoned by instruments in the tenor or baritone range (cello, trombone, horn, etc.). In the first variation the tune is offered in its original form, in the second in strict inversion. The antiphonal presentation of the phrases is still maintained and, in order to stress the contrast between the different melodic sections, Berg usually spaces the entrances at the interval of a fifth. A canonic imitation of the chorale's initial phrase in the first variation might be intended to express the soul's obedience in following divine leadership. Clearer is the symbolic meaning of the inversion of the theme in the second variation. Longing for death reverts to a longing for life. At this point, with greatest delicacy, the solo violin and the orchestra conjure up a vision of the Carinthian folk dance played in the first movement of the Concerto. But, while the solo violin accompanied by the other violins dreamily intones the dance tune in harmonic notes, the trombone utters delicately, but with unmistakable decision, the whole tone sequence of the chorale.

Ex. 8

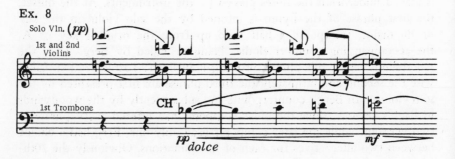

The attraction toward life in this world is overcome, and the soul turns away from it toward life in the heavenly abode. For the last time, in aching sweetness, the chorale melody is intoned in Berg's own harmonization. Thus a secular composer of the 20th century gave new meaning to the old church tune. His unorthodox version rounds off the chain of events begun during the Baroque period by a modest Thuringian organist.

Notes

1. The author feels greatly indebted to Dr. Karl-Heinz Köhler, Director of the Music Division of the Deutsche Staatsbibliothek, Berlin, and to Dr. Hedwig Mitringer, Archivdirektor of the Gesellschaft der Musikfreunde in Vienna, who kindly helped him obtain photographic reproductions from hymn-books and manuscripts in their charge.
2. I. Kings 19:4. These words were also set to music by Mendelssohn in his *Elijah* (No. 26).
3. In the English translation of Henry S. Drinker (*The 389 Chorales of Johann Sebastian Bach*, Merion, Pa.: Association of American Choruses, 1944, p. 60) these stanzas read:

It is enough; so take my soul to Thee, with Thine elect to be;
Loose Thou my bonds, and set my spirit free; O God deliver me;
I yearn for Thee, awake or sleeping,
By day in tears, by night in weeping.
It is enough,
it is enough.

It is enough; Lord, when it pleases Thee, do Thou unshackle me.
My Jesus comes; I bid the world farewell, and go in peace to dwell.
In Heaven's house I soon will find me,
My cares and troubles all behind me.
It is enough,
it is enough.

4. Printed at Mühlhausen. The piece is reprinted in Carl von Winterfeld, *Der evangelische Kirchengesang*, Leipzig: Breitkopf & Härtel 1843-47, Vol. II, Appendix, 134; and in *Denkmäler deutscher Tonkunst* V, edited by Johannes Wolf (Leipzig: Breitkopf & Härtel, 1901; reprint Wiesbaden, 1957), p. 47.
5. Cf. Joh. Zahn, *Die Melodien des deutschen evangelischen Kirchenliedes* (Gütersloh: C. Bertelsmann, 1891), Vol. IV, pp. 315-318, and C. von Winterfeld, *op. cit.*, Vol. II, pp. 308, 320-321, 549.
6. P. 76. Copy in the Deutsche Staatsbibliothek, Berlin. In this hymn, the bass is not completely figured, so that the choice of harmonies is partly left to the organist.
7. The same was true of the Vopelius edition, published twelve years earlier.

8. Pp. 728, 729. Copy in the Deutsche Staatsbibliothek, Berlin. The words are not underlaid in the music, but are printed below it. As here given, the text represents an altered and decidedly weakened version of Burmeister's poem.

9. Similar adaptations of the hymn may be found in C. H. Dretzel's *Evangelisches Choral-Buch* (Nuremberg, 1731), p. 667, and in the collection, *Melodeien zu der Wernigerodischen Neuen Sammlung Geistlicher Lieder* of 1767, p. 66. Copies of both works are in the Deutsche Staatsbibliothek, Berlin.

10. Zahn, *op. cit.*, offers a fair sampling of various versions up to the beginning of the 19th century. Characteristic of the sweetly Mendelssohnian idiom favored by choir directors in the second half of the century is the setting by Friedrich Riegel in Ludwig Schoeberlein, *Schatz des liturgischen Chor- und Gemeindegesangs* (Göttingen: Vandenhoeck & Ruprecht, 1871), Vol. II, p. 875.

11. Alfred Dürr, "Zur Chronologie der Leipziger Vokalwerke J. S. Bachs," *Bach-Jahrbuch*, 1957, p. 63.

12. The interpretation of this part, in the old Collected Edition, as the voice of the Holy Ghost seems rather far-fetched. In all likelihood this utterance of a bass voice represents the words of Christ. (Compare also Arnold Schering, *Über Kantaten Johann Sebastian Bachs*, Leipzig: Köhler & Amelang, 1942, p. 145.)

13. *Joh. Seb. Bachs vierstimmige Choralgesänge*, Leipzig, 1784-87.

14. Cf. R. von Perger and R. Hirschfeld, *Geschichte der k. k. Gesellschaft der Musikfreunde* (Vienna: A Holzhausen, 1912), p. 305.

15. *Zeitschrift für Musik*, C (1933), No. 5, p. 465.

16. Edited by Wilhelm Rust in 1863.

17. Cf. H. F. Redlich, *Alban Berg* (London: J. Calder, 1957), chap. VIII, p. 203 ff.

18. She was a daughter of the architect W. A. Gropius and of Gustav Mahler's widow, Alma.

19. A parallel to the events connected with the creation of Mozart's *Requiem* and Brahms's *Vier ernste Gesänge* could easily be established.

20. Published by Universal Edition, Vienna, in miniature score in 1936 and in piano score in 1938.

21. In a letter to Arnold Schönberg, however, Berg claimed that this connection was quite accidental. Cf. the facsimile reproduction of the letter (dated August 28, 1935) in *Melos* for February 1955.

MOZART'S SIX QUARTETS

DEDICATED TO HAYDN

Louise E. Cuyler (Ann Arbor, Michigan)

$\mathcal{T}$he chapters and volumes written these many years about Mozart's music might well have exhausted the subject, so that, so far as literary comment is concerned, it were better laid to rest. There remain, however, many tantalizing questions, many unexplored avenues. Haydn is popularly regarded as "father" of the string quartet, in part, perhaps, because in sheer volume of output he far surpassed his contemporaries. There is no denying his tremendous influence, nor that the string quartet fully supplanted the *continuo*-based ensemble during the middle years of his life. But to regard Mozart's quartets, especially the later ones, as in the shadow of works by his elder contemporary (as is done continually), to see intensely personal compositions like the six quartets dedicated to Haydn as a kind of afterglow, a facile *Schnörkel* to Haydn's "Russian" quartets—these attitudes seem unwarranted.

Certain quite early circumstances are responsible for this state of things: Mozart's affectionate regard for the older master, his humble, touching letter committing his "children" to Haydn's fatherly care, Haydn's own prophetic remarks when first he heard three of the quartets, all have contributed to a certain blindness about many qualities in the Mozart works. Mozart was one of the most individual of composers, as well as the most absorptive; what he took from Haydn and

293

numerous others emerges in his own works transformed, and often cloaked in deceiving ingenuousness.

For numerous reasons, the six quartets of Haydn's Op. 33 made a profound impression upon Mozart, whose situation at the time he began his own series of six (late 1782) was especially disturbed and insecure. Mozart had written no quartets in about ten years, and, since church music in particular was enmeshed in his dispute with Archbishop Colloredo, he was probably happy to escape into this most detached of mediums. Certainly there is initial obeisance, in the quartets dedicated to Haydn, both to tradition and, immediately, to the Haydn works whose existence provided models. Once this has been accomplished, however, Mozart produces some of the most daring passages to be found in any of his music. Many movements of these quartets are highly personal, amazingly plastic, and infused with chromaticism the more remarkable because it is intrinsic rather than functional or decorative, in the manner of the day. Mozart's six quartets (K.387 in G, K.421 in D minor, K.428 in E♭, K.458 in B♭, K.464 in A, K.465 in C) will be considered in this article as autonomous works, with only passing reference to any quartets that preceded them. They are regarded here as more prescient of the future than indebted to the past.

Strings were never a favorite medium for Mozart. Perhaps, as a modern psychiatrist might suggest, he held an instinctive resentment against his father's profession. Leopold was a hard taskmaster, distressingly ready to exploit his gifted children; and scant sympathy between father and son survived after the early years. More important in Mozart's attitude, however, was his obvious preference for mediums embodying a dichotomy, or the *concertato* principle: notably opera and the pianoforte concerto. The string quartet, most homogeneous of mediums, is conspicuously lacking in the element of "jousting" that Mozart found so necessary. He had to supply it, to shape and forge it from other components besides timbre. Herein may lie an explanation for much that is remarkable in the quartets dedicated to Haydn: bold juxtaposition of chromatic and diatonic elements, abrupt rhythmic transformations, and the choice of vivid tonal levels for portions not involved in traditional thematic relationships.

As has been implied, the period 1780-1785 was one of the least stable of Mozart's entire life, full of disappointments, insecurity, and emotional involvement. The long-standing feud between Archbishop Colloredo of Salzburg and his youthful court organist at last erupted into an open break; the affair with Constanze Weber finally resulted in marriage— Mozart did not thrive in domesticity; and, of happier import, Mozart experienced his first intimate acquaintance with the works of J. S. Bach. All of these events combined to make a comparatively fresh new medium especially opportune. Church music had, for the time being, unhappy associations; opera and concerto were long familiar, deeply subjective types; but the string quartet, just emerging into early maturity, was vital and full of unexplored potential, and it provided an ideal opportunity for Mozart to put to use what he had learned from Bach. Thus the twenty-seven-year-old composer must have experienced both stimulation and welcome escape from his habitual mediums when, during late 1782 and 1783, he wrote the earlier of the six Quartets. (K.387, K.421, K.428).

A sense of freedom is apparent immediately in the gay, jaunty *Allegro vivace assai* that opens the G major quartet, K.387. Its two principal subjects, standing in conventional tonic-dominant key relationship, are fresh, uncomplicated, and infused with enough decorative chromaticism to smooth the angular diatonic shape of the lines. The Development section commences in archaic fashion with allusion to the opening subject at the dominant level, a procedure encountered continually at about the middle of so many bipartite sonata movements of the earlier 18th century. The remainder of the movement, likewise, is conventional.

The *Menuetto (Allegretto)* in G major shows two traits that are to be characteristic of Mozart's best mature style: contrasting length of motive or phrase units and sharp juxtaposition of diatonic and chromatic elements. The opening statement illustrates both of these. An angular, two-measure motive is complemented immediately by a supple, chromatic unit of six measures plus two measures of cadence material. The chromatic motive, basically two measures in length, is enlarged in masterfully simple fashion: stated in the first violin alone, it is immediately repeated in sequence, a second lower in the same instrument, then a tenth lower by the cello in mirror fashion, while the three upper instruments provide counterpoint. A quasi-reprise of the opening statement is full of contrapuntal device, as it extends to a total length of eighteen measures. The remainder of the *Menuetto* is built up in similar manner, and achieves a rather large (ninety-three measure) tripartite design. The G minor Trio has more symmetrical units and leads directly to the *da capo*.

The C major *Andante cantabile* is a lyric piece of great beauty that is cast in the type of small sonata-allegro design greatly favored by both Haydn and Mozart for slow movements. This *Andante* illustrates graphically one of Mozart's basic plans for the Exposition section: Area I states the principal subject and enlarges it to considerable length; Area II is a large intermediary section separating the two principal subjects, often containing highly individual material, sometimes commencing in the "new" key, sometimes achieving it *en route;* Area III presents the second principal subject, often tersely, and then moves on to material designed to close the Exposition section. The deviation of this from the conventional sonata-allegro is, obviously, the reserving of the second subject for use near the end of the Exposition section, in much the same manner that a so-called "closing theme" is introduced in later and larger sonata designs. In this movement, Area II (meas. 15-30) has a vivid digression to G minor, arrived at suavely by a chromatic semitone (meas. 22-23) in the first violin. By contrast, the G major second principal subject (meas. 31) sounds fresh and vigorous.

The finale (Molto Allegro) is cited frequently as a movement combining both contrapuntal and classical-homophonic textures. The overlying sonata-allegro design manifests still another Exposition plan used repeatedly by Mozart. This is basically a two-area plan, in contrast to the three-area one described above. Area I is a very large unit, cast in a fully autonomous tripartite design; Area II, appearing near the close of the Exposition, presents the second principal theme tersely, plus a flourish of some sort for the cadence. The characteristic of this Exposition plan is the conspicuous imbalance in length between the two principal sections. In this finale, Area I (meas. 1-91) is a well-developed, tripartite design, each of whose three principal sections commences with a point of imitation followed through in all four voices. By contrast, Area II is brief (thirty-two measures to the Exposition cadence), and has a catchy, naive theme in the dominant key. The Development section in a design of this sort always presents problems, since so large a portion of the principal sections is devoted to enlargement of ideas. The solution in this movement is particularly apt: immediate introduction of a new chromatic motive, use of a remote key level (B♭ minor) for initiating a brief development of the opening subject, minimal total length, and elimination of the entire first portion of the conventional Recapitulation section. The Recapitulation commences dramatically in meas. 175 after a long general pause, resuming primary material at a point corresponding to meas. 23 in the original, and transposed to the subdominant key.

The second quartet, K.421 in D minor, is the only one of them set in the minor mode. Mozart's only other string quartet in a minor key, also D, is the last of his earlier quartets, K.173. In every aspect and every movement this is the most conventional of the six quartets. In the opening Allegro moderato, the phrase units are squarely symmetrical, the areas devoted to the two principal subjects are contiguous and of almost equal length. Such symmetry is rare in Mozart's mature style. The most striking moment of the entire movement comes when the Development section commences, abruptly, with a colorful allusion to the principal subject at the vivid level of E♭.

The second movement, Andante in F major, is a tripartite design of ingenuous charm, whose middle section in A♭ is approached through a C-minor bridge. The *Menuetto* reverts to D minor and has a D-major Trio, characterized by the "Scotch snap" rhythm of the first violin. The finale, a set of five variations upon a D minor theme in 6/8, furnishes at least two noteworthy episodes. Variation II appears to be a result of Mozart's study of earlier models than those of Father Bach, for its rhythmic intricacies suggest the 16th century: in actual effect, the first violin has 3/8 time, the second violin 12/8, the viola and cello the prevailing 6/8. Variation III features the viola, a rare incident in 18th-century chamber music. Speaking as a lifelong quartet enthusiast, I still recall with pleasure the thrill this portion gave, many years ago, to a neophyte violist who was weary of filler parts and after beats.

The third quartet, K.428 in E♭, is an extraordinarily exciting work in several respects. The *Allegro ma non troppo* commences boldly with a four-measure phrase, stated by all four instruments in octave and unison, and employing nine of the twelve semitones in its brief span. The complementary phrase, following immediately, is seven measures long, has no chromatics at all, and is written in conventional quartet texture. These two phrases, placed in sharp juxtaposition, have a most exhilarating effect. Next, the initial four-measure phrase returns, with significant mutations: only the first violin states the original nine-tone theme, while the other three instruments supply counterpoint that embraces the three tones missing in the original phrase (*F♯, D♭ D♮*), for a complete twelve-tone segment. A long bridge passage establishes, eventually, a strong B♭ cadence (meas. 40), in conventional preparation for the second subject. This subject, which follows immediately, is anything but conventional, however, since it commences in G minor and passes through both F major and C minor en route to a B♭ cadence. The effect is fresh and arresting. The remainder of the movement follows along conventional lines.

The second movement, *Andante con moto* in A♭, is an enigmatic, elusive one that anticipates the texture of some of Beethoven's later quartets, especially the second movement of Op. 127. Interweaving parts, overlapping phrases, constant use of syncopation, all combine to obscure the partite "seams" of the design. Movements of this sort are more subtly prescient of the future than others filled with more obvious device.

The remaining movements of K.428 are conventional in most respects and serve to emphasize the untypical qualities of the first two.

The fourth quartet, K.458 in B♭, is popularly known as "The Hunt." The sonata-allegro design of its first movement shows striking departure from conventional form. A section based upon a single rhythmic figure commences in F major at meas. 42, extends to twenty-nine measures, mostly through imitative procedures, and stands entirely in lieu of the traditional second principal theme of the Exposition section. This contrapuntally developed portion is interrupted abruptly at meas. 71 by a passage in longer note values, commencing *Fp* and employing all twelve semitones in its four-measure extent. A brief codetta brings the Exposition to a full close in F major. At once after the double bar, the second principal theme, withheld from the Exposition section, commences. It is in the key of F major and is presented in the simple format of a repeated period, so often encountered in statements of themes in classical style. Once this is finished with a full cadence in meas. 106, the Development section pursues a traditional course. The one exceptional feature of the remainder of this movement is the use of a large Coda in conclusion. This is introduced by abrupt chromaticism at meas. 232 and develops to the unusual length of forty-eight measures.

The *Menuetto* is entirely traditional, as is the E♭ *Adagio*, a movement that contains exceptionally beautiful figuration, mostly in the first violin, but occasionally, by imitation, in the cello.

The finale, *Allegro assai*, is in a sonata design, with rondo allusions through return of the initial theme to conclude both Exposition and Recapitulation sections.

The opening *Allegro* of the A major quartet, K.464, is the most unconventional and intricately planned of all the first-movement sonata-allegro designs. It has three distinct themes and three firmly established key levels in both Exposition and Recapitulation sections; and it alludes to initial material toward the close of both these principal sections, as does the B♭ quartet. Throughout the movement there is intrinsic, logical motivic expansion, a process of enlargement regrettably uncommon in late 18th-century classical style and likely to produce excursions into remote tonal areas. In K.464, this process may be noted first between meas. 17 and 24, where three dovetailed imitative entries, combined with accidentals, serve first to obscure tonality, then to lead to C major. The brief but sturdy second subject in C commences immediately and dissolves into a bridge to the third subject in the traditional dominant key of E. The constant reference to opening material in the closing portion of the Exposition has been cited already. In the Recapitulation, measures 178 to 197 are interesting because a transposition of the area described above leads to statement of the second subject in F major. The remainder of the movement follows a predictable course.

The A major *Menuetto* and the D major *Andante* are written in Mozart's typical quartet style—which is certainly no disparagement!

By contrast, the finale, *Allegro non troppo* in A, is a wonderfully concocted movement, essentially sonata-allegro in design, but so totally derived from four simple factors that larger aspects of the design tend to be obscured. Three of these factors are stated within the first three measures: the opening four-note chromatic motive; the rhythmic motive

♩ ♪♪♪|♪♪ and a second rhythmic motive ♪. ♫♪. The fourth factor is pedal point, which is introduced frequently, ingeniously, and with happy effect. Virtually the entire movement, including the second principal area, takes form through adroit combinations and permutations of these basic factors. Any Development section could easily seem redundant in a movement of this sort. This one is saved by two arresting moments: one at meas. 85, where the pedal point G commences abruptly, after an F♯ major triad and general pause; one at meas. 114, where a brief, choral-like interlude in D intervenes, after a C♯ major triad. Each of these is, in fact, a "deceptive" resolution of a dominant triad—but context, especially the dramatic pause, makes them sound like something far more complex.

As Einstein has so aptly remarked, the opening *Adagio* of the sixth quartet, K.465 in C, has set many a pen in motion. Considered by itself, this *Adagio* is surely the epitome of free chromaticism in Mozart's day. Considered in context with the ensuing *Allegro*, it is the ultimate in juxtaposition of chromatic and diatonic elements—the logical end of briefer and less spectacular use of the same type of contrast, as applied, for example, in the *Menuetto* of K.387 and the first movement of K.428. This Adagio depends upon four structural factors: a descending eighth-note figure in the cello that comprises a four-measure unit and is twice repeated in sequence to arrive at E♭ in meas. 12; constantly maintained eighth-note motion that precludes any firm cadence points; lines whose contours are shaped by a sense of direction instead of vertical considerations, so that any of the twelve semitones are logical potentials; total movement from initial repose in the cello's opening C to high expectancy in the G major triad of meas. 16. The remainder of the *Adagio* comprises a six-measure intensification of the dominant implication of meas. 16, concluding on the full dominant-seventh chord with *appoggiatura* and *fermata* at meas. 22.

That the *Allegro* which follows, as well as the three other movements of the quartet, are genial and uncomplicated could be predicted through an understanding of Mozart's liking for sharp juxtapositions and relationships based upon a dichotomy of elements.

The discussion contained in the past several pages has cited, from the quartets dedicated to Haydn, some of the more extraordinary passages in which Mozart has applied studied craftsmanship. That these passages were the result as much of experiment and revision as of intuition may be ascertained through examination of the manuscripts of these quartets. Apparently they cost Mozart as much travail as any of his mature works. Regardless of the processes involved in their creation, they have long been the treasure and joy of chamber-music enthusiasts—and are likely to remain so.

C. P. E. BACH AND

ARNOLD SCHOENBERG:

A COMPARISON

Dika Newlin (Madison, New Jersey)

*A*rnold Schoenberg would have been surprised, to say the least, by the topic of this discussion. His attitude toward Bach's sons was always a very negative one, for he felt that they had, in a sense, betrayed the great traditions of their father. Humorously he once said in class, "He should have spanked them oftener!" Yet there is reason to believe that this negative assessment rested on a rather limited knowledge of the works of these composers. In particular, had Schoenberg delved more deeply into the clavier works of C. P. E. Bach, he might have reacted very differently. For certain of these works—far indeed from the superficialities of the *style galant*—in their improvisational fervor foreshadow the Expressionism of the young Schoenberg.

Well-known are the contemporary descriptions of C. P. E. Bach at the clavier. Reichardt said, "Bach would become lost for hours in new ideas and a sea of fresh modulations. . . . His soul seemed absent from the earth. His eyes swam as though in some delicious dream. The lower lip drooped over his chin, his face and form bowed apparently lifeless over the keyboard." [1] And Burney wrote, ". . . he grew so animated and *possessed*, that he not only played, but looked like one inspired. His eyes were fixed, his under lip fell, and drops of effervescence distilled from his countenance." [2] Such emotions are reflected in keyboard music like the *Prussian Sonatas* or like the *Probestücke* appended to the *Versuch über die wahre Art das Klavier zu spielen*. At certain moments in these works, we seem to see improvisation captured on the printed page. We cite here a few such examples.

From the second movement of the Prussian Sonata No. 1, the following passage of recitative is noteworthy. We are to imagine it rendered with the utmost freedom.

Ex. 1

A little later in the same movement, this similar passage occurs:

Ex. 2

But these improvisational passages are surpassed by certain episodes of the *Probestücke*. Thus we hear the following free passage in the second movement of the fourth sonata from this group:

Ex. 3

The culmination of this type of writing is found in the last movement
of the sixth sonata. It was this famous piece to which H. W. von Gersten-
berg (1737-1823) set his translation of "To be or not to be"; he also
wrote his own version of Socrates' meditation before drinking the hem-
lock, which he conceived to be recited to the accompaniment of this
composition. A representative section gives us an idea of the almost
chaotic character of this music—well-nigh impossible to capture in
notation:

Ex. 4

Such music could easily find its justification in esthetics and philosophies of C. P. E. Bach's day. The doctrine of Nature as expounded by

Rousseau could lead to the following of impulses and vagaries of the moment in art. In music, the Rousseauian esthetic had no place for double fugues and "other difficult fooleries that the ear cannot endure nor the reason justify"; these, according to the feeling that Rousseau expressed in his *Lettre sur la musique française*, are mere relics of barbarism and bad taste. The C. P. E. Bach works that we have cited above eschew such complexities in favor of an untrammeled expression of emotion.

Does not a passage like this, from Rousseau's *Rêveries du promeneur solitaire*, parallel the kaleidoscopic shifts of mood that we find, let us say, in Ex. 4?

> Everything on earth is a continual ebb. Nothing can keep a fixed and constant form; and our affections, attached to external things, necessarily change with them. Always before or behind us, they recall the past, which is no more, or anticipate the future, which perhaps will never be; in all there is nothing solid to which the heart can cleave. Neither have we here below scarcely any other than passing pleasure; as to continual happiness, I doubt if it is known. There is hardly a single instant of our liveliest enjoyments of which the heart can truly say, *I wish this instant would last for ever.* And how then can we call a fugitive state happy which leaves uneasiness and void in the heart, which leaves regret for something preceding, and hope for something after it? [3]

In truth C. P. E. Bach, in his improvisatory passages, was master of these "fugitive states" so tellingly described by Rousseau.

For similar outpourings in the music of Schoenberg we have to look to that period of his music when he had transcended tonality but had not yet discovered the discipline of the "method of composition with twelve tones related only to one another." In discussing this music we shall deliberately avoid the term "atonal," which has no place in descriptions of Schoenberg's works. Schoenberg himself rejected this term violently. He interpreted it literally as meaning "without tone," and extended this meaning to include the concept "without relation between tones." But such a concept is impossible, for no two tones can be played together or consecutively without a relationship arising between them. Thus, "atonality" does not exist. Instead, Schoenberg preferred the term "pantonality," which he conceived as representing the inclusion of *all* possible tone-combinations rather than the exclusion of any. This concept of *inclusion* rather than *exclusion* was an important part of Schoenberg's thinking during his dodecaphonic period also—something that certain of his disciples tend to forget.

With Schoenberg's transcending of tonality, new expressive possibilities were opened up to him. The emancipation of the dissonance placed at his disposal an entire new spectrum of harmonies. Motifs

became short, highly varied—though with repetition where it was necessary to insure unity. (The concept that the *Six Little Piano Pieces*,
Op. 19, are without repetition is erroneous. I—in common with Schoenberg—also consider the designation "athematic" which has sometimes
been applied to works like *Erwartung* a misnomer.) Compositions
became very short; in the case of longer pieces, unity was insured by a
text (*Erwartung, Die glückliche Hand*) or series of texts (*Pierrot lunaire*). Very large or very small intervals were preferred. Excessive
rhythmic regularity or "squareness" was avoided. (Compare the complete rhythmic freedom of the C. P. E. Bach passages quoted above.)

How does all this serve expressive purposes? A good example of a
piece from this period in which Schoenberg desired to express a particular emotion is the last of the above-mentioned *Six Little Piano Pieces*
(1911).[4] Here, Schoenberg was under the spell of a particular event—
the funeral of Mahler. On this occasion, the bells were tolled in the little
parish church of Grinzing. The day had been an overcast one, but at
the moment when the coffin was lowered into the grave a ray of sun-
shine struck through. All this is reflected in the evocative harmonies
of Op. 19, No. 6. We might note a few points: 1) the six-toned chords,
which suggest the ringing of the bells; 2) the use of very high and
very low registers of the piano; 3) the "floating" rhythm, seemingly
unbound by metrical considerations; 4) the extremely delicately nuanced
dynamics (later to be adopted by Webern); 5) the extreme brevity of
the piece. All of these things contribute to an overall expressiveness of
great intensity through subtlety.

Here it is appropriate to quote Ferruccio Busoni. His sketch "Schön-
berg-Matinée" (written in Berlin in 1911 and reprinted in the collection
of essays *Von der Einheit der Musik*) gives in vivid fashion his highly
subjective impressions of this music:

> Might sentimentality be undergoing a rebirth? After listening to
> (and playing through and studying) Arnold Schoenberg's piano pieces
> and songs, it almost seemed that way. Suppressed tears, windy sighs,
> gusts blowing through trees of sorrow;—here and there a short burst
> of defiance or the reflection of a rapidly disappearing late-winter sun.
> In between, a few merry pranks [*Eulenspiegeleien*]. Lonely voices flow
> along in recitative-like fashion, in unexpected intervals—we scarcely
> sense their coherence any more. Bold harmony, which, in its con-
> tinuity, yet resolves itself—brevity of the movements—most frequent
> pauses to take a breath and listen—naiveté almost to the point of bar-
> barism. And again, so much spontaneity, insight and integrity.

Could we not almost imagine that we are reading a description of
an improvisation by C. P. E. Bach?

When we look for even more heightened expressiveness in the works of this period we have not far to seek. Perhaps the most intense emotional experience is to be found in *Erwartung*. This work was written between August 27, 1909, and September 12, 1909, at bewildering, almost trance-like speed. The text by Marie Pappenheim was admirably suited to evoke emotional expression of the highest intensity.[5] In kaleidoscopic transformations of motif and orchestral color, each psychological nuance of the libretto is depicted with uncanny accuracy. Almost any passage from the work would illustrate this; here I choose the beginning, where the woman—the work's sole character—commences her haunted wandering through the woods in search of her lover. Again as in a C. P. E. Bach improvisation—though in far different harmonic-melodic diction—every "fugitive state" of emotion is captured in sound. The printed page gives but a weak idea of this.

Ex. 5

Later, Schoenberg was to bring such emotional impulses under the discipline of the twelve-tone method. Some have felt that, in these later works, the expressive intensity dwindles in favor of an overriding interest in constructive factors. With this judgment, I would disagree. In certain of the earlier twelve-tone works—e.g., the Wind Quintet— Schoenberg seemed less concerned with expressiveness *per se* than with the constructive possibilities afforded by the new method. However, as he became more familiar with these, he no longer needed to be concerned with them at the expense of expressiveness. Thus we see, in his later twelve-tone works—as diverse as the Piano Concerto, *A Survivor from Warsaw*, or the String Trio—that marvelous balance between "heart" and "brain" which is so characteristic of the finest of his work always. Here Expressionistic and Classic elements appear in a new and powerful blend.

In many ways C. P. E. Bach turned away from the traditions of his father. Schoenberg, on the contrary, revered J. S. Bach while minimizing the contributions of his son. Yet both C. P. E. Bach and Schoenberg made giant steps forward into new musical and expressive domains. C. P. E. Bach is today seen as the great forerunner of Beethoven—perhaps somewhat to the detriment of our appreciation of his music in its own right. Some, today, would like to see Schoenberg as a forerunner of Berg and Webern, not to mention the "electronic" composers. Such a conception must one day be rectified in favor of a more just appreciation of his unique contribution. Thus, as we see the proper place of each of these original innovators in music history, their inner relationship is also seen.

Notes

1. J. F. Reichardt, "Autobiographie" (*Allgemeine Muşikalische Zeitung*, January 12, 1814.)

2. Charles Burney, *The Present State of Music in Germany*, 2nd ed. (London: T. Becket, 1775), Vol. II, pp. 235 f.

3. Jean Jacques Rousseau, *Rêveries du promeneur solitaire*. Translation quoted from *The Living Thoughts of Rousseau*, presented by Romain Rolland (London: Cassell Co., Ltd., 1939), p. 50.

4. The reader may consult the complete composition in the edition of Associated Music Publishers.

5. The subject and format of this "monodrama" were *not* suggested by Schoenberg, as has often erroneously been stated.

PIERROT LUNAIRE

George Perle (New York)

*A*lbert Giraud, Belgian disciple of the Parnassian movement that flourished in France in the second half of the 19th century, was only twenty-four years old when his *Pierrot lunaire* was published in 1884. The Italian Commedia dell'Arte had brought Pierrot to Paris more than three hundred years earlier, along with Harlequin, Columbine, Pantaloon, and the other stock characters of pantomine and puppet show. Pierrot, white-faced doltish peasant boy in a baggy white suit with enormous buttons, known in Italy as Piero, Pedrolino, Pagliaccio, was given a new romantic soul early in the 19th century by Jean-Gaspard Deburau, "actor without passion, without words, and almost without a face, who," in the words of his biographer, Janin, "says everything, expresses everything, mocks everything." It is Deburau's Pierrot that is at the core of the innumerable Pierrot creations of poets, playwrights, painters, and musicians that appeared in the latter half of the 19th century and the first decades of the 20th. Baudelaire, writing in 1855, nine years after Deburau's death, describes Pierrot as "the personage of pallor and silent mystery, supple and mute as a snake, tall and rigid as a gallows, that mechanical man operated by strange springs, to whom the much-to-be regretted Deburau had accustomed us."

Giraud's Pierrot is a *fin de siècle* product, a decadent version of the romanticized clown. Characteristic motifs of French decadent literature are found: the painted dandy, hallucinatory landscapes, religious—and sacrilegious—ecstasies. In keeping with the deliberate artificiality of language and form of the original, Schoenberg used number symbolism in his selection and arrangement of the poems. His *Pierrot lunaire* comprises settings of only twenty-one of Giraud's fifty poems, in agreement with the opus number of the work, and these are grouped into three parts of seven poems each. Schoenberg's use of magic numbers has, of course, no intrinsic musical significance. Since each of the poems consists of thirteen lines, an unlucky number, perhaps he thought it well to organize the whole according to two lucky numbers, three and seven. Whatever his motives, in the use of number symbolism in musical composition the composer had many distinguished predecessors. Schoenberg calls attention to his artifice in the full title of the work: *Dreimal sieben Gedichte aus Albert Girauds Pierrot lunaire*.

The sequence of the pieces does not derive from Giraud, nor does it represent the order in which they were composed. Though the individual numbers are not grouped according to any strict principle, there are family resemblances among the images evoked within each of the three parts. Part One shows us the moondrunk poet, the anxious lover, the dandy daubing his face with moonlight; Part Two concentrates on images of crime, guilt, and punishment; Part Three, as though in reply to the author's *Gebet an Pierrot* in the second number of Part Two (*O gieb mir wieder, . . . Pierrot—mein Lachen*), describes Pierrot's homesickness and re-enacts the grotesqueries of the old Italian pantomime, concluding with an evocation of the *alter Duft aus Märchenzeit*. The overall impression produced by the work is that of an inverted romanticism. If any single work can be regarded as an epitome of the romantic ideology, it is Wagner's *Tristan und Isolde*, a work which is central to that world of musical and emotional experience in which Schoenberg had his beginnings as a composer and in reaction to which, in one way or another, the various tendencies of what we call "contemporary music" first appeared. The realization expressed by the two lovers in the love duet of the second act of *Tristan*, "I myself am the world," is implicit in *Pierrot lunaire*, but it is no longer the inner world of the tragic hero that is represented but that of a puppet, whose inner world is as illusory as his whole existence. The inner world is symbolized by night in *Tristan*, and so it is in *Pierrot lunaire*. But the inner life that is illumined by the cold light of the moon in *Pierrot lunaire* consists only of hallucinations and trivial obsessions—Pierrot's desperate attempt to pluck a blossom of moonlight for his sweetheart, his furious effort to rub away a spot of white moonlight from his black jacket, his fear that the crescent moon is about to decapitate him, etc.

Each of the poems is a rondeau of thirteen lines, with lines one and two repeated as lines seven and eight, and line one repeated again as line thirteen. The strict refrain pattern assures a certain formal clarity and overall unity in itself. (Schoenberg's setting employs the Hartleben translation into German, which, fortunately, ignores the rhyme scheme of the original.) To offset the rigid uniformity of the twenty-one poems, each setting is related to the refrain pattern of the text in an individual manner. Even the pauses separating the pieces are differentiated: there are measured pauses of various durations, unmeasured pauses of various durations, conclusive pauses, anticipatory pauses, interludes, transitions. The style of vocal declamation used throughout is *Sprechstimme*, a type of recitative invented by Schoenberg, in which the vocal part is *spoken* to exact time values, with the vowels momentarily touching the indicated pitch and at once rising or falling away from it. The vocal treatment creates a certain uniformity of sound throughout, and this is compensated for by providing each piece with its characteristic timbre. In fact, the structural coherence and direction of the work as a whole is mainly dependent on an overall instrumental conception that is entirely original.

From the five players and eight instruments (piano; flute and piccolo; clarinet and bass clarinet; violin and viola; cello) highly varied instrumental ensembles are drawn, each uniquely characterizing a single number, or even a section of a single number. A solo instrument accompanies the voice in two of the movements—the flute in the final number of Part One and the piano in the first half of the final number of Part Two. The use of the piano alone in the one-measure transition between Nos. 10 and 11 and in the two-measure transition between Nos. 17 and 18 calls attention to its paramount role in the work as a whole. There are four instrumental duets: violin and piano for the first tempo of No. 2, clarinet and piano for No. 9, viola and cello for all but the last two bars of No. 12, and cello and piano for No. 19. The following trios are found: No. 1, first section—flute, violin, piano; No. 3—piccolo, clarinet, piano; No. 4—flute, clarinet, violin; No. 5, first section—flute, clarinet, piano; No. 5, second section—flute, bass clarinet, piano; No. 6, Bars 1-20 and Bar 22—flute, bass clarinet, cello; No. 6, conclusion—violin (*arco* only), cello, piano; No. 8—bass clarinet, cello, piano; No. 12, conclusion —piccolo, viola, cello; No. 15—clarinet, violin, piano; No. 16, beginning —violin (*pizzicato* only), cello, piano. Instrumental quartets are employed as follows: No. 1, second section—flute, violin, cello, piano; No. 2, conclusion—flute, clarinet, violin, piano; No. 10—flute, clarinet, violin, cello; No. 13—bass clarinet, viola, cello, piano; instrumental interlude between Nos. 13 and 14—flute, bass clarinet, viola, cello; instrumental interlude between Nos. 15 and 16—piccolo, clarinet, cello, piano; No. 17 —piccolo, clarinet, viola, piano (except for five bars in which piccolo is exchanged for flute). All five players are simultaneously employed for the first time in No. 11, which is for an ensemble of piccolo, bass clarinet, viola, cello, and piano. Another quintet—piccolo, clarinet, violin, cello, piano—is required for *both* Nos. 16 and 18, while No. 20, the second half of No. 14, and the conclusion of No. 19 all call for a quintet of flute, clarinet, violin, cello, and piano. Far from being an exception to Schoenberg's general scheme of uniquely characterizing each number in its instrumental treatment, a comparison of these appearances of the same combination of instruments in several numbers proves that Schoenberg perseveres in his plan with remarkable thoroughness, each appearance of the same ensemble being differentiated from the others in some way. In No. 20 the violin and cello are muted throughout; at the conclusion of No. 19 (bars 46-51) there is no *Sprechtstimme* and the violin plays *pizzicato;* in No. 18 the clarinet in B♭, replacing the clarinet in A, makes its only appearance in the whole composition, a change that can have no perceptible audible effect, nor, so far as I can tell, any practical value, and which can be explained only as a conceit of the composer, comparable to his selection of an opus number that corresponds to the number of movements in the work (or vice versa), but even more esoteric. An inspection of the distribution of the various ensembles throughout the work as a whole shows that the texture tends to get fuller and the instrumental variety richer as the work progresses. Part One concludes with the movement that is texturally lightest, No. 7, for flute and *Sprechstimme* only. Otherwise it comprises mainly trios. In only one movement (No. 6) of Part One are all five players required, but nowhere in the movement are they employed simultaneously. Four of the numbers of Part Two require the services of all five instrumentalists, though in only two of the numbers do they form quintets. In Part Three every movement except No. 17 employs all five instrumentalists. In Nos. 16, 18, 19, 20, and 21 they form quintets, the final number, 21, requiring not only all five players but also all eight instruments.

It is consistent with Schoenberg's emphasis on means of differentiating the individual numbers of *Pierrot lunaire* that each of the pieces, so far as its tone-material is concerned, is autonomous, with a single exception—the long instrumental coda that follows No. 13, which incorporates extensive portions of No. 7. In No. 13, *Enthauptung*, Pierrot imagines that the crescent moon is about to decapitate him. No. 7, *Der kranke Mond*, describes a deathly pale moon, fatally ill of an unappeasable yearning for love. One can only speculate about the extra-musical significance of this single return to the music of an earlier number, but certainly the musical reference, at this point, to a moon that is frustrated unto death by repressed longings for love is a suggestive one. Other, less problematical, instances of textual illustration pervade the score. At the conclusion of *Galgenlied* a flourish of the piccolo represents Pierrot's anticipated end on the gallows. The *alter Duft* in the final number is musically evoked by parallel thirds and an E major triad. In No. 19 the text describes Pierrot's performance on the viola. Such a plain reference to a musical instrument or device in the words of a song can be embarrassing to a composer: the use of the viola to accompany a verbal description of Pierrot playing the viola is too literal, and therefore inartistic, and yet one cannot ignore, in a musical setting, the musical references in the text. Schoenberg solves this problem with a magnificent solo in the cello. At one point the words tell us that Pierrot "sadly plucks a pizzicato." This mournful pizzicato is performed by the cellist, but not at the point where it is mentioned in the text. The significance of the canons in *Parodie* and *Der Mondfleck* is more esoteric. In the former the imitative writing symbolizes the moonbeams mimicking an aging lovesick duenna waiting for Pierrot in an arbor. In *Der Mondfleck* Pierrot discovers a white spot of moonlight on his coat. A retrograde canon commences at the precise instant when Pierrot discovers the spot and concludes when he finally, in the early dawn, supposedly rubs it off.

To a certain extent even the basic compositional techniques exploited in the different pieces are of an individual nature. This should come as no surprise to anyone who has studied the three pieces of Op. 11, Schoenberg's earliest atonal work, or the *Fünf Orchesterstücke*, completed in the same year, 1909. Some of the numbers of *Pierrot lunaire* tend toward the so-called athematic style, whose best-known example is *Erwartung*. Whatever unifying details one can discover here have only immediate associations within a constantly fluctuating context. An example is the middle section of No. 13, with its 16th-note figures in the bass clarinet, viola, cello, and piano. Traditionally, in a contrapuntal passage of this nature, all of these figures would have been based on characteristic motivic elements, and in all probability they would have been more or less similar in contour, or even identical. Here, on the contrary, the shape of the different figures seems completely fortuitous. The principle that governs the choice of notes here appears to be the *avoidance* of any stable referential pattern, however temporary. At the opposite extreme is the employment throughout No. 8 of a single generative cell of three notes—a procedure that anticipates certain aspects of the twelve-tone system, which Schoenberg was to evolve eleven years later. Two pieces, Nos. 1 and 2, are mainly based on ostinati. In other pieces, on the contrary, whatever repetition appears is non-literal, as in No. 5, with its approximate rather than exact sequences (flute, bars 9-11). Except in the two canonic numbers, imitative writing that is consistent in one respect will be inconsistent in another. Thus in No. 5, bars 16-19, the clarinet imitates the flute at the lower octave, but shifts its temporal distance from one sixteenth to two sixteenths back to one sixteenth. The use of a strict polyphonic structure in *Der Mondfleck* is a new departure in Schoenberg's atonal music. The piano presents a three-part fugue. (The imitative writing in the fugue is somewhat obscured by the crossing of voices and occasional supplementary notes.) Clarinet and piccolo form strict canons in diminution with the first two voices (in order of entry) of the fugue. A third canon, independent of the others, is formed by violin and cello. Midway through the piece the clarinet and piccolo, having proceeded at twice the speed of their canonic associates in the piano, run out of notes and thereupon reverse their direction, so that they form, for the remainder of the movement, retrograde canons in diminution with the two fugal voices. The independent canon in violin and cello is also reversed at this point. Thus, in only five instruments, a three-part fugue, a double canon in diminution, and a triple retrograde canon are simultaneously unfolded.

Composed in 1912, *Pierrot lunaire* is almost exactly contemporaneous with a number of other masterpieces of 20th-century music which were also regarded as revolutionary at the time. The preceding year had seen the first performances of Ravel's *Daphnis et Chloe,* Mahler's *Das Lied von der Erde,* Strauss's *Rosenkavalier,* Sibelius' *Fourth Symphony.* In the following year came Stravinsky's *Le Sacre du printemps.* Among all of these *avant-garde* works that appear in the years immediately preceding the first World War, only *Pierrot lunaire* remains problematical, the only one whose implications are still being investigated today in the work of advanced composers everywhere in the world. "I already feel the opposition that I shall have to overcome," Schoenberg had written in 1909, in a program note for the première of his earliest atonal works, *Drei Klavierstücke,* Op. 11, and *Das Buch der hängenden Garten.* Nevertheless, the three years between these works and the composition of *Pierrot lunaire* must have been happy ones for Schoenberg, for they represent a period of creative vitality that has very few parallels. In these few years he wrote, in addition to the works just mentioned and several shorter pieces, the *Fünf Orchesterstücke,* the monodrama *Erwartung,* and the greater part of the short music drama, *Die glückliche Hand. Gurre-Lieder,* interrupted in 1901, was finally completed. With the publication of his famous textbook on traditional harmony in 1911 and the appearance of the first important works of his two most distinguished disciples, Berg and Webern, his importance as a teacher was established. His creative exuberance led him into painting and literature as well. *Die glückliche Hand* is based on his own text. As a painter he was identified with the Expressionist school of Marc, Kokoschka, and Kandinsky. *Pierrot lunaire* is the culmination of these amazing years soon to be followed by many years of silence that came to an end only with his discovery of new organizing principles for atonality—the twelve-tone system—in 1923.

THE IMAGE

OF ITALIAN MUSIC

AND ART PRESENTED

IN GERMAN LITERATURE

Walther Vetter (Berlin)

1

*H*ow possible is it to differentiate the characteristic quality of Italian musical style, which has been called Mediterranean or Southern, from the musical language as understood by the Germans? This question goes beyond the determination of the personal style of this or that composer. And knowledge of a composer's relation to the style of a particular period may well tell us nothing about the common ground that binds him to musicians of any other periods, even if they created in the same geographical area. Nor does it necessarily disclose anything about dissimilarities. If this is true, it certainly will not reveal what differentiates a composer of a certain period from a composer active at any other time under another constellation. The common ground that binds together composers of the same geographical area is perhaps best revealed where the personal styles of two or more composers contrast sharply. Dissimilarities, on the other hand, may be especially well observed where there is musical borrowing or adaptation, illustrated, for example, when Bach accepts a Vivaldi violin concerto or when Richard Strauss in *Rosenkavalier* places a page of Italian music in the hands of the tenor.

It is not enough, however, to determine similarities and differences, models and indebtedness, even though this surely belongs to the technique and the toil of music history. What is required, rather, is penetration into the specific characters of the arts as they thrive in different climates. Only then will the necessary light be shed upon the relationship between an original and its reworking by a foreigner, a relationship of which Grillparzer [1] in principle approved when he declared that the artist in whom originality is the primary characteristic belongs, because of this, to the second rank. On the other hand, the artist who follows foreign models will save himself from complete loss of identity if he can preserve some contact with his native soil. J. A. Hasse, for example, did not wrestle with the Italian ideal; he did not come to terms with it; he simply accepted it and made it his own. This is not to say, however, that he renounced the German way of perceiving form. He rather overemphasized a trait that stands out in the history of every German art, namely, the inclination toward the foreign—the spiritual and mental capacity to identify oneself with the artistic experiences of the "other side" and the readiness to incorporate it. It is understandable that the German Hasse became the *caro sassone* of the Italians. He composed in a manner more Italian than that of the Italians themselves. In Hasse's arias there is almost nothing that the Italians did not practice: constant syncopation, pauses entering on strong beats, brilliant coloratura, sensuous singable melody, light treatment of text, rich vocal flourishes, and instrumental ornaments. With the Italians, however, the apportionment is different, the disposition simpler, the dosage more conservative, and the whole plan less conscious. Hasse's originality lies in his overcultivation of *Formgefühl*, in his outdoing the Southern *Formgefühl*.[2]

In connection with Heinrich Wölfflin's thesis of the special and separate *Formgefühl* of the nations,[3] one should first differentiate between the musical idioms of the individual nations, which approach musical creation from divergent mental and spiritual premises.[4] In seeking to understand the prerequisites that are standard for Southern art, we can also arrive at an understanding of those of German music. One should not be satisfied, in making this attempt, with a formal-technical analysis, even if it can do good service. Musicology, proceeding alone, cannot afford us the range of vision for the entire task. It will have to co-operate with art history and literary history, and naturally have a good look at their subjects of research in order to achieve a proper perspective.

Naturally no music historian wishes to pose as a specialist in literary history, and just as little in the history of the visual arts. The musical, artistic, and literary problems, however, are so intertwined that proper musicological activity is conceivable only in partnership with allied studies.

II

J. N. Forkel, the first important German music historian, wrote in the year 1788: [5]

> No branch of the culture of our minds can go on by itself. The relationship between all the powers of the human spirit is too intimate for an isolated culture to be possible. No one power can be aroused without the others. From this interconnection of the powers of thought and feeling one can account for the mutual ties that bind all types of knowledge and art. No one of them may reach its highest fulfillment without the others.

About 130 years after Forkel, Guido Adler, in his *Methode der Musikgeschichte*,[6] brought to the fore, in the light of newer times, some ideas which in principle signify the same thing as did Forkel's. He stressed the idea that scientific research must investigate the connection with artistic activities as well. Musicology must take into consideration the whole of mental and spiritual life insofar as it can be pursued in music. It must involve everything within and outside of music that can serve to clarify its development. Forty-five years have passed since this declaration was made. During this time musicology has tended more and more to take general history into account and to investigate the interaction between musicians and their social milieu.[7]

Adler referred to art history and called upon the trail-blazing personality of Wölfflin. When Adler stressed the possibility of investigating the experiences and results of stylistic analysis in art history, he acted along lines similar to those of Curt Sachs and Robert Haas. He did not, however, as did Sachs, transfer specific rules of formal analysis from art history to music history. It was a clever tactical stroke that Adler did not emphasize the question of which methodological devices musicology could borrow from art history. Rather, he chose the opposite procedure and asked what the science of general history, which had already respectfully accepted the results of art history, was prepared to accept from musicological research.[8] Furthermore, he demanded categorically that musicology be ranked equally with art history and justified this demand by pointing to analogies and interactions between the two disciplines. Again Adler refers to Wölfflin, who, though an art historian, still remains the most important guide to those engaged in the scholarly investigation of the manner in which two great areas and nations perceive their own and each other's musical styles. It should be added that Wölfflin himself placed musicology in the foreground as that intellectual discipline which should join art history in questions of such methodological importance as perception of form and stylistic feeling.[9]

III

Neither knowledge nor scholarliness can secure for the ordinary Northerner a complete understanding of the music of the South; they cannot teach him to hear with the ears of an Italian. The poet's intuition is capable of more, and the poet can convey to us what he has intuitively grasped. It does not matter whether he chooses the form of a poem, story, novel, report, essay, drama, or any other favorite form. Ippolito Nievo has his lad see the ocean for the first time: [10]

> Still farther beyond—how could I have dreamed it?—there stretched an endless blue space, as if a piece of blue had fallen from the sky and lay flat on the earth; a clear blue shot through with silver streaks that far, far off flowed into the paler blue of the air.

Here the poet of the South describes the sea of the South. He does not reflect upon it, deliberate or ponder the matter; he does not philosophize, and does not wish to instruct. Quite simply (so it seems, but in fact not so simply) he describes his sensory impression.

Grillparzer ventured the journey from the North to the South, as did Goethe before him, and wrote much that may interest the musician. He, too, wrote about the sea.[11] He meets the sea with a certain mistrust; he is afraid of being disenchanted and actually is disenchanted. The reality seems to him less forceful or powerful than the image of the sea that he has made in his own fantasy. Still, he finds the sea "indescribably beautiful." And it is then that the poet Grillparzer begins to ponder and reflect. The impression of the sea not only involves his senses, it stirs his imagination:

> How it lay there, a gracious picture midway between a green rolling field and the quiet blue sky, so soft to the sight that our speech has no word to denote it, so gentle and mild, that unstirring, untamed element, which is like a tranquil beloved, who is doubly beautiful if

first she storms and rages and then caresses her lover in soothing embrace.

The difference between Nievo and Grillparzer, between South and North, is so clear that it requires no comment. It is the very same difference as exists between Palestrina and Josquin, Giovanni Gabrieli and Michael Praetorius, Vivaldi and Bach, Verdi and Wagner.

Grillparzer has also celebrated the sea in poetry, in the lines *Zwischen Gaeta und Capua*, which he penned on April 27, 1819, in Capua.

Trotz'ger Poseidon!	Headstrong Poseidon,
Wärest du dies,	Is it you down below
Der drunten scherzt und	Frolicking there,
Murmelt so süss?	Gently murmuring so?
Und dies, halb Wiese, halb	And this I behold,
Äther zu schaun,	Half meadow, half ether,
Es wär' des Meeres	Is this the sea
Furchtbares Graun?	In its frightful terror?

The poem declares the self-same thing as does the journal entry. The sea does not speak directly to his senses. He remembers former illusions and is disillusioned. This and the antithesis of thoughts, the mythological allusion to the earth-shaker Poseidon, the astonishment of the writer hailing from the Alpine foothills when he finds that he does not shudder at his first glimpse of the sea, the depth and richness of his ideas—all these stand in such clear contrast to Nievo that, again, further comment would be superfluous.

As an *Italienfahrer*, Goethe, too, experienced the sea of the South. In Venice, on October 8, 1786, he wrote: [12]

I heard a loud noise: it was the sea, and I soon saw it as it washed up against the shore and receded again in the ebb-tide of noon. And it finally happened that I saw the sea with my eyes, and on the lovely threshing floor that it leaves behind in receding, I followed after it.

How clear, how simple, how beautiful. He *hears*. He *sees*. On the threshing floor left behind by the sea, he *feels* in the damp sand the effect of the sea. He harnesses his senses to receive an impression, and as he walks he feels the sea floor yield beneath his feet. He had already often seen the sea—from within. Today, he declares that he is seeing it with his eyes. He abstains from all reasoning; in his declaration itself, however, there is a soft restraint which reveals the fact, though it is half suppressed, that the great man comes from the North, even though the words themselves could be those of an Italian. Goethe belongs to

those Germans who have a predisposition for what is alien. While most
German artists, however, prove such a predisposition by a more or less
creative imitation or, like Hasse, by outdoing Southern *Formgefühl,*
Goethe is satisfied to receive the acoustical and optical phenomena of
Italy, to hear and see them like an Italian, and to report directly from
such sensory perceptions. Hence the clarity, the simplicity, the beauty.

IV

That which characterizes the spiritual and atmospheric climate of
Italy and which is for the Northerner both enticing and repelling has
not been felt as vividly or formulated as precisely by any German
writer of the present time as by Thomas Mann. By his excess, he experienced the justification of Wölfflin's warning against rushing to Italy
and, as it were, partaking of a meal immediately in the field of art; this
would surely upset one's stomach. Obviously, the author of *Budden-
brooks* did not resist the longing expressed in Mignon's "Kennst du das
Land?" The young man went quite early to Palestrina; in this little
country town, he spent "a long, burning hot Italian summer" [13] with
his brother, Heinrich, the author of the novel *Die kleine Stadt.* In the
winter, the brothers left for Rome. Thomas, as he confesses, was not
living there for the sake of the South, *which he basically disliked.* He
expressed himself on the subject of Italy in a typically German fashion:
"The historical-esthetic impressions . . . I received with respect, though
not quite with the feeling that they were mine or could benefit me
directly." He enjoyed what he called the ostentatious humility of the
Mass-reading cardinal and state-secretary Rampolla. He deplored for
esthetic reasons the fact that this man who, according to his taste, had
such a decorative personality was hindered diplomatically from becoming
the pope.

Ten years later, Heinrich's *Die kleine Stadt* appeared. A half century
after that, Thomas wrote *Doktor Faustus* and had the German composer
Adrian Leverkühn seek out a town in the Sabine Hills in order there
to introduce him to the devil incarnate. (The importance of the whole
novel for the investigation of German musical *Formgefühl* is too far-
reaching to be considered here.) The little town, *die keine Stadt* of Heinrich's title, the mountain hamlet, are all the same place. They are
Palestrina, where Pierluigi was born; the Praeneste of antiquity; and
Prince Colonna's Penestrino, mentioned by Dante in canto XXVII of
the *Inferno.* All this is sufficiently steeped in history and pregnant with
meaning to move Heinrich to honor the tiny Italian town with the dedication of *Die kleine Stadt,* a novel of classic compactness and composi-

tional mastery, which the publisher viewed as a reflection of the social movements of the time.[14] Undoubtedly, the town also inspired Thomas to rise to the pivotal point of his career, the high point and turning point of his late work—*Doktor Faustus*. For him the word *Palestrina* symbolized at the same time the significant experience of becoming acquainted with a 20th-century opera—Pfitzner's *Palestrina*—to which he dedicated the most penetrating words that have ever been uttered or written about it.[15]

The whole world is the scene of action of the literary works of Thomas Mann. Germany, however, stands in the center of that scene of action, and, whenever things revolve around Germany, they also revolve around German music. Nevertheless, he did not completely yield to that urge toward the South which gave so much stimulus, drive, and dimension to the course of German music history. Although he is aware that for German art, and also for himself, there is no getting along without Italy, yet his North-German artistic intelligence counsels reserve. Munich is for him not only biographically but also spiritually a halfway house. He is aware that acquaintance with Italy is a requirement that every German artist must fulfill, and this vexes him. He is not able to come to terms with the South or make an "arrangment" with it, as did Mozart or even Goethe. Thomas Mann is more ponderous and, in this sense, more German; he is mistrustful of pure feeling, and would rather listen to reason; he tends toward mockery and employs irony. He uses too many automatically functioning defense mechanisms against the sensory impressions that overwhelm the Northerner who journeys to Italy in order that the spirit of some higher learning may influence him. He recognizes the slight possibility of his assimilating Italian artistic feeling into his own creative style, and his intellect keeps him from allowing his own creative efforts to approach the Italian. This he does not do even in his Renaissance piece, *Fiorenza*. He is on guard expressly against the supposition that in *Fiorenza* he is the glorifier of the Italian Renaissance.[16] "Here," he explains, "I am from the first word to the last a critic of the Renaissance," and he appeals to the fact that he has portrayed the "representatives of pagan beauty as an amusing band of swaggerers, jesters, fauns, and children." Admitted that someone familiar with the work may raise certain objections—that is not the point. The idea is rather that an analysis of Renaissance art undertaken by a Northerner may very well disclose comic, faunlike, and childish features, in an objectionable sense, features which, moreover, the Italian has also noticed, but to which he has no objection. Nevertheless, Thomas Mann, in criticizing the Italian Renaissance, shows a deeper understanding of it than do many people of the North who admire it wholeheartedly.

The author of *Fiorenza* is a keen observer; as such, he separates and differentiates the phenomenon of the South from every comparable manifestation in the North. His portraiture of the "divine Fiore" is wholly in keeping with stylistic trends of the South; in its own way, it is a complete description of a certain Italian feminine type of the time. Who does not think of Leonardo da Vinci's *Gioconda* or of Botticelli's *Caterina Sforza* [17] when he sees the Fiore of Thomas Mann step forth, "her arms bent at right angles, hands clasped at her waist, standing erect and slender"? She is "of precious and wonderfully artistic beauty. Her appearance is strictly linear, serenely symmetrical." Wölfflin speaks of the noble *calm* of the Italians, to whom the *asymmetry of the North* seems arbitrary and formless. In Thomas Mann's rendering, Fiore's hair flows just as does that of *Gioconda* and *Caterina Sforza*, symmetrically "to both sides of the cheeks in blond, even locks." Wöfflin stressed the clarity of the Renaissance; Thomas Mann speaks of the "clearly outlined lips" of Fiore, which are closed in an "ambiguous smile," obviously the smile of Mona Lisa. We shall easily recognize comparable features in Italian music.

Fiorenza is a poetic drama of ultimate artistic refinement, but it is not typical of Thomas Mann; this highly polished work of art lacks the representation of the personal. Not so the two totally German, and therefore un-Italian, tales, *Death in Venice* and *Mario and the Magician*. Here the phenomenon of Italy as the North-German writer experiences and judges it is particularly clear. The character, Gustav Aschenbach, "author of the lucid and vigorous prose epic on the life of Frederick the Great," the artist and "weaver of the richly patterned tapestry entitled *Maia*—a novel that gathers up the threads of many human destinies in the warp of a single idea"—[18] is the reflection of the author of the sketch of *Frederick the Great and the Grand Coalition* and many other richly populated novels, such as *The Magic Mountain* and *Confessions of Felix Krull*. In Italy, in Venice, death overtakes Aschenbach. Shortly before his departure for Venice, at the tram station in the Ungererstrasse in Munich, he is transfixed by the fiendish apparition of a man in a straw hat baring his teeth. The Northerner who sees the devil does not meet any redeeming angel in the South, but only a handsome lad who destroys his soul and profanes his identity.

In Italy, the writer learns disturbing things about *form as divine thought;* [19] he discovers also, while learning, "that the sun turns our attention from intellectual to sensuous things." Thus a basic concept of the South and of Southern art is formulated. Down there, reason and remembrance, the attributes of the North, become confused and bewitched. If any Northern artist, be he a writer or composer, finds himself unexpectedly confronted by Southern beauty, the same thing may happen to him that happened to the author Aschenbach.

The tale of *Mario and the Magician* is no *roman à clef;* the writer reports on himself and his family. He does not join the ranks of those sweating fugitives from the North, the Italy-enthusiasts; he renounces revelry in recollection and declares right at the outset that the memory of the Torre di Venere has an unpleasant atmosphere. No other story of Thomas Mann's begins in this illusion-shattering manner, whether its setting be Germany, France, Portugal, Denmark, Flanders, Artois, the Norman islands, Switzerland, Greece, Egypt, India, America, or the Holy Land; this Italian short story constitutes an exception, an exemplary special case. Thomas Mann complains, he suffers under the solar reign of terror:

Certainly, it is the South, it is classic weather, the climate of the flowering of human culture, the sun of Homer, and so forth. But after a short while—I can't help myself—I am easily persuaded that it is dull. The glaring *emptiness of the sky* day after day soon begins to trouble me, the dazzle of *colors* and the tremendous *simplicity* and unbrokenness of the light certainly arouse festive feelings . . . ; yet, without one's taking account of it at first, all this leaves the deeper, more complex needs of the Northern soul devastatingly unsatisfied.[20]

As distinctly as Wölfflin, Thomas Mann sets the brightness of the sky, the simplicity, the unbroken light of the South, against that depth and non-simplicity of the North, which need not always be complicated, but which has gained the reputation of inducing vagueness and creating unrest. His ambivalent feelings toward Wagner's "enchanting work," which accompanied the author throughout his life,[21] his vast understanding for the *"urnordische Heroik"* [22] of the man from Bayreuth, allow him at times to enter into a festive mood, but cause him to see in the clear Italian sky nothing but blankness. The faces of Mona Lisa and the features of Caterina Sforza must have seemed equally empty to him; also many aria texts by Metastasio and their musical settings.[23]

Thomas Mann contrasts the style of *The Magic Mountain*, emitting English humor, with the austerity of *Death in Venice*.[24] Not only are the atmosphere and content of this short story austere, but also the opinions passed in it together with certain self-critical utterances. There is hardly another literary work that so sharply reflects Italian sentiments within a German framework. The events of *The Magic Mountain* take place not only actually but also figuratively on neutral soil. The writer from the North transplants us not to Italy, but to Switzerland, there to bring in the representative of the South, Ludovico Settembrini, the man of letters with the refined, lively, critical air, the humanist with the pedagogical streak—at once Satan, a wind-bag, and an organ grinder (none of these three, of course, in a literal sense). And this magnificent example of all that is Southern, Mann puts into those ever-the-same coarse-fibred jacket and checkered trousers. This man of letters champions a most valiant ethos but, as an Italian, he places the emphasis upon grace and charm of form, on elegant fencing with dialectic, all of which stand in lasting contradiction to the profundity, the moralizing philosophy, and the dignity of artistic catharsis that lie so close to the heart of the author. In his characterization of Settembrini, which is lively yet solid, almost humorous, Mann himself remains a son of North Germany, whose stylistic characteristics are dear to him even in their weaknesses. These he overcomes in recognizing them.

V

Two such different minds as Goethe and Grillparzer both attest to the discord arising within themselves in their experiences with Italian art. Nevertheless, they react quite individually. The morose, embittered Grillparzer is censorious in the extreme; at times its seems as if nothing in Italy can please him. This is not so, however; for, as a rule, he ends up by being satisfied. He finds the external aspects of the ceremonies of Holy Week in Rome without significance and without spirit.[25] They do not appeal to his reason. One must be acquainted with Grillparzer's blunter and more spiteful attacks, such as the one against Weber's *Euryanthe*,[26] in order not to be shocked by his comparison of cardinals and prelates with street boys, and by much else. He denies that the dome of St. Peter's has any churchly character, nonetheless acknowledging its splendor and majesty. He warms up not so much to the Sistine Chapel itself as to its music: [27]

> Without the accompaniment of instruments, it is performed by men's voices which are thoroughly admirable, and of which the discant and alto were sung by *castrati*. The singing of the latter, in its strange and penetrating quality, strengthens the total effect greatly.

Thus the discord aroused in the *writer* by the *architect* is resolved by the *music*. Here it is not the rigor of Northern style perception that is manifest, but rather its capacity for sympathetic understanding.

The Sistine Chapel and St. Peter's generate divided feelings in Goethe as well, but he avoids hasty criticism. He finds the chapel bright and serene, the paintings well illuminated; he can only see and gaze in astonishment. The size and splendor of St. Peter's, which receives the most beautiful light from the bright sky, delight him. Of himself and Tischbein, he says: "We enjoyed ourselves . . . without letting ourselves be put out by overly fastidious or clever taste, and we suppressed every sharper judgment. We delighted in the delightful." [28] Wölfflin, in his own words, said much the same thing.

Goethe saw Italian beauty and saw through it. As far as the dependability of taste and the natural limitation of the intellect are concerned, his mind was made up. We do not need to investigate here in what respect he, too, was and continued to be a man of the North; if he did not remain one, Wölfflin's theory would fall like a house of cards.

Goethe sharpens his judgments on Italian art through a study of the writings of Andrea Palladio [29] and an examination of Palladio's structures. He finds something divine in Palladio's plans and compares them, significantly enough, to the form of the great writer, who out of truth and untruth creates a third entity that enchants us through its fabricated existence.[30] Under the influence of Palladio's art and his admiration for Roman antiquities,[31] Goethe declares himself free of his erstwhile fervently admired Gothic, whose "ornaments," "tobacco-pipe columns," and "flower scallops" he now reviles. It was he who, in 1772, looking at the Strasburg cathedral, wrote:

> This is German architecture, our architecture, of which the Italian cannot boast . . . : approach it, and perceive the deepest feeling of truth and beauty of proportions, produced from the strong, rugged, German soul . . .[32]

This turnabout in Goethe's heart is one of those results of his Italian journey that concern the music historian directly, because they are also mirrored in his relationship to music. I have in mind his *Singspiele*.

Erwin und Elmire and *Claudine von Villa Bella*, both of them originally dramas with merely incidental music, became in Italy *Singspiele*, because in the Italian sun their author set up new requirements for himself. It is not so much a question of whether the "Italian" or the "German" version is superior, as it is a matter of what is German in the one and Italian in the other. In Italy, Goethe consciously disavows the *comédies mêlées d'ariettes* and also the French operetta. At this time, he feels completely like a native Italian and, more as an Italian than as a German, seeks to refine the dialogue. He does not join in the senseless inveighing against Italian opera texts; it is clear to him that they are light, gay, unpretentious—and suit the needs of the composer. And he does not hesitate to choose as a model Giovanni Bertati's libretto for Cimarosa's *Il Matrimonio Segreto*. He also notices what Thomas Mann formulated much later,[33] namely, that in the South even the little man attempts to turn a phrase, for language, insofar as he uses it consciously, becomes for him an ingredient in the pleasure of living. Thomas Mann speaks in this connection of light-heartedness and pleasantness; and it is these that Goethe wished to acquire for his *Singspiel* style.

For over a decade, before the trip to Italy, the Claudine work was a "prose essay, interwoven with songs." One can, in general, compare the change of the old version into the new to the development of the prose piece *Iphigenie* of 1781 into its iambic form. Goethe reports: [34]

> During my sojourn in that musical country, I thought carefully about the true Italian opera form and its advantages, and I practiced it well; therefore, I undertook with pleasure to recast metrically *Claudine von Villa Bella* and also *Erwin und Elmire* and to present them to the composer for light-hearted treatment.

The comedy-mixed-with-songs, in the French taste, became—with the sympathetic understanding of the Italian style—a piece into which the lyricism was organically interwoven. In Italy, the musical element was extended and broadened, first, through the inclusion of rhythm and sound in the text and, second, through increased possibilities for musical composition afforded by the text. The whole is conceived à la Metastasio.

In his remarks to Rameau's nephew, Goethe wrote fully about music. With high-minded eagerness for learning and knowledge, he immersed himself, in Italy, in the problems of Southern *Formgefühl*. In his opinion, the Italian looks upon music as an independent art, cultivates it in himself, and enjoys it through *refined sense perception*, while the Germans, French, and Scandinavians perceive music in relation to *reason*, *feeling*, and *passion* (these are Goethe's words). Goethe knows the talent of the Germans, which is also his talent. From the clarity and precision of his knowledge, he derives the strength to overcome such limitations and restrictions as this talent reveals. In Italy, his experiences give him the ability to wed his spiritual being to the Italian character without, in so doing, jeopardizing in the slightest what is natural to him and in him.

Goethe holds that one can only "deal successfully with the history of the newer music" if one "takes careful notice" of the two arts, that of the South and that of the North. On the music of the South, he says:

> The Italian will devote himself to the loveliest harmony, the most pleasing melody; he will enjoy the sonority and movement as such; he will consider the singer's voice and stress in the happiest manner what the latter can perform in the way of sustained or running notes and so . . . charm the ear of his compatriots. He cannot, however, escape the reproach [of certain critics] that he treats his text—for, after all, he must have a text for singing—too lightly.

But Goethe does not share in this reproach himself. He is far too seriously concerned with understanding Italy and the Italians to censure them for what seems good and beautiful to them. All this, notwithstanding the fact that he himself composed "texts," *Singspiel* texts, and used to have serious oral and written consultations with his then favorite composer, Philipp Christoph Kayser. He accepted the fact that the Italian composers would at times bypass the text if, in the process, something beautiful resulted. And he remained intent upon maintaining an agreeable give-and-take with the composer who set his own verses.

Goethe, however, does speak critically of the disadvantage suffered by his dramatic texts when song is added. It is true that, in many instances, the *Singspiel* version of a work entails a certain devaluing of the drama. In the first version of *Erwin und Elmire*, for example, the social and political questions that excited the minds of the time were dealt with in an emphatic manner, and this was in no way disadvantageous to the play. True to life is the talkative Olympia who has sunk to slovenliness, the typical mother-in-law who "does not understand." Also realistic are the sidelights dealing with the general and musical educational methods of the day. The combination, in a musical stage work, of such subject matter with the true lyric poetry of songs would hardly have pleased the Italian. And this Goethe takes into account, not because he is ready to make concessions, but because he spent a good amount of time under the rays of the Southern sun. In 1787, he wrote that he had cast aside the extremely dull dialogue of *Erwin und Elmire*, because it was a patchwork.

Goethe differentiates between a usable libretto and a spoken drama of high quality, but his attitude with respect to the adaptation of either is unchanged. He knows that what is beneficial to the spoken drama may be harmful to the sung piece. In a fundamental respect he is in agreement with Grillparzer, who wrote: [35] "A basic principle is: No opera should be considered from the standpoint of poetry, but rather from the point of view of music." There is less agreement between the two writers, however, when the younger one formulates the Nordic view in this extreme fashion: "Poetry wishes to corporealize the spiritual, music wishes to spiritualize the sensuous." Goethe is on far too good terms with the sensuous not to grant it, in all its variety, a place in his writings; he favors it too much not to be suspicious of a one-sided spirituality. That music must at all costs spiritualize the sensuous would, in any case, seem absurd to him. Because Goethe, in this instance, is identified to a large degree with Italy, the South was for him an inspiring and stimulating experience and he, himself, became a mediator between the *Formgefühl* of the South and that of the North.

(Translated by Mildred Pearl Parker.)

Notes

1. Grillparzer, *Sämtliche Werke*, ed. by Moritz Necker (Leipzig: M. Hasse, 1903), Vol. XV, p. 142.

2. See further the section on Hasse in my article about Gluck and his Italian contemporaries in Walther Vetter, *Mythos-Melos-Musica* (Leipzig: Deutscher Verlag für Musik, 1961), Vol. II, pp. 222-228.

3. It would be a misunderstanding of Wölfflin, however, to limit the application of *Formgefühl* nationally in all cases.

4. For an understanding of musical *Formgefühl* of the various nations, a knowledge of the following articles of mine may be useful: "Deutschland und das Formgefühl Italiens," in *Deutsches Jahrbuch der Musikwissenschaft*, IV (1959), pp. 7 ff; "Zur Stilproblematik der italienischen Oper des 17. und 18. Jahrhunderts," in *Festschrift für Erich Schenk* . . . (Vienna: Hermann Böhlaus Nachfolge, 1962); "Der deutsche Charakter der italienischen Opern Georg Christoph Wagenseils," in *Festschrift Karl Gustav Fellerer zum sechzigsten Geburtstag am 7. Juli 1962* . . . ed. by Heinrich Hüschen (Regensburg: Gustav Bosse, 1962); "Italienische Opernkomponisten um Georg Christoph Wagenseil," in *Festschrift Friedrich Blume zum 70. Geburtstag*, ed. by Anna Amalie Abert und Wilhelm von Pfannkuch (Kassel: Bärenreiter, 1963).

5. In paragraphs 49 and 50 of his introduction to his *Allgemeine Geschichte der Musik*.

6. Leipzig: Breitkopf & Härtel, 1919, pp. 12 ff.

7. Ernst Hermann Meyer, *Musik im Zeitgeschehen* (Berlin: Henschel und Sohn, 1952).

8. With regard to research into the music of antiquity, I have in my article "Warum erforschen wir antike Musik?," *Mythos-Melos-Musica*, Vol. II, pp. 355-356, examined the possibility that musicology may sometimes be of help to classical philology.

9. Heinrich Wölfflin, "Das Problem des Stils in der Bildenden Kunst," *Sitzungsberichte der Preussischen Akademie der Wissenschaften, Jahrgang* for 1912, *Halb-Band* 1, p. 578. Cf. also *Deutsches Jahrbuch der Musikwissenschaft*, IV, p. 9.

10. *Le Confessioni di un Ottuagenario (1867)* in *Opere*, ed. by Sergio Romagnoli (Milan: Riccardo Ricciardi, 1952), p. 100. One should have access to the original verson, which actually cannot be fully translated but only paralleled: "Ma più in là ancora l'occhio mio non poteva indovinar cosa fosse quello spazio infinito d'azzurro, che mi pareva un pezzo di cielo caduto e schiacciatosi in terra: un azzurro trasparente, e svariato da striscie d'argento che si congiungeva lontano lontano coll'azzurro meno colorito dell'aria."

11. *Tagebuch auf der Reise nach Italien (1819)*, *Sämtliche Werke*, Vol. XVI, pp. 126-127.

12. Goethe, *Italienische Reise, Sämtliche Werke*, ed. by Ludwig Geiger (Berlin, 1883), Vol. XXV, p. 66.

13. Thomas Mann, *Lebensabriss, Gesammelte Werke* (Berlin: Aufbau-Verlag, 1955), Vol. XII, p. 388.

14. Heinrich Mann, *Ausgewählte Werke in Einzelausgaben* (Berlin: published under the auspices of the Deutsche Akademie der Künste, 1951), Vol. III, p. 414.

15. Thomas Mann, *Betrachtungen eines Unpolitischen*, in *Gesammelte Werke* (Berlin: S. Fischer, 1922), pp. 410 ff.

16. *Gesammelte Werke*, Vol. XII, p. 348.

17. Cf. Hanns-Conon von der Gabelentz, *Frühitalienische Malerei* . . . , Bildende Kunst (Dresden: Verband Bildender Künstler Deutschlands, 1961), p. 808; in addition, see the picture on the back of the jacket.

18. The lines quoted in the present paper are from the translation by H. T. Lowe-Porter and appear in Thomas Mann, *Stories of Three Decades* (New York: Knopf, 1948), p. 382.

19. *Gesammelte Werke*, Vol. IX, p. 502. According to Erika Mann, the author is supposed to have given Aschenbach the external features of Gustav Mahler (Thomas Mann, *Briefe*, Vol. I, Frankfurt-on-Main: S. Fischer, 1961, p. x).

20. *Ibid.*, Vol. IX, p. 717.

21. *Ibid.*, Vol. X, p. 410.

22. *Ibid.*, Vol. X, p. 396.

23. When Richard Hamann, in his *Geschichte der Kunst* (Berlin: T. Knaur Nachfolge, 1933), pp. 498 ff, describes the portrait of Mona Lisa and speaks of the *lazy* crossing of the hands, the *calm* presence, and the *state* of inward poise, he employs terms that have Wölfflin's imprint.

24. *Gesammelte Werke*, Vol. XII, p. 437.

25. Grillparzer, *Sämtliche Werke*, Vol. XVI, p. 145.

26. *Ibid.*, Vol. XV, p. 203.

27. *Ibid.*, Vol. XVI, p. 146.

28. Goethe, *Sämtliche Werke*, Vol. XXV, p. 106.

29. *I Quattro Libri dell'Architettura*, 1570-81.

30. *Sämtliche Werke*, Vol. XXV, p. 37.

31. Palladio also wrote *Antichità di Roma*, 1554.

32. *Sämtliche Werke*, Vol. XXXVII, pp. 9-10.

33. In the story *Mario and the Magician*, *Gesammelte Werke*, Vol. IX, p. 732.

34. In the *Annalen*, *Sämtliche Werke*, Vol. XXIX, p. 9.

35. Grillparzer, *Sämtliche Werke*, Vol. XV, p. 193.

FRAGMENTS FROM DIARIES WRITTEN

DURING A LECTURE TOUR

IN THE NEW WORLD (October 4, 1955—March 3, 1956)

AND A TRIP TO AUSTRALIA (May 15—August 28, 1959)

Jaap Kunst (Amsterdam) †

U. S. A.

Chicago, Friday, 18th Nov. 1955

In the evening I went by bus to the home of Emiko Suzuki, a Japanese music student from Hawaii. I arrive there exactly on time, in other words, too early. But that gives me the opportunity to follow the preparations for dinner in all their subtleties. I am delighted to observe how my hostess makes seafood of all sorts, mushrooms, pickled "mouse ears," large fresh shrimps and small dried ones, little meat cubes, peas in the pod, cucumber, bean sauce, and root tubers of a kind unknown to me, among other things, into exquisite dishes. A Russian friend, Elena Korsakoff, and I lend her a helping hand. A little later, a most distinguished Japanese couple arrives, Mr. and Mrs. Kagani, who are social workers; then, after having removed our shoes, we take our places on cushions around a low table. In front of each of us is a bowl of rice and a cup of delicious Chinese tea, and we all help ourselves to the various dishes to our hearts' content. The three Japanese eat with chop sticks, the two "Caucasians" use their forks. The conversation is lively and amusingly varied, carried on mainly in English, which is familiar to all of us, but sometimes in Russian and Japanese as well. We are in excellent spirits; Suzuki San is a perfect hostess. She (like her house companions Miss Korsakoff and the Austrian Miss Sauer, who is to turn up later in the evening) practices piano and singing here in Chicago, which does not mean, however, that she has forsworn the music of her native country. We hear in the course of the evening some excellent recordings of this Japanese music, while nibbling crisp noodles of salted seaweed.

After the meal, Suzuki—one of the three living experts in the field of ancient Hawaiian court dances (which have nothing to do with the vulgar and nowadays completely commercialized *hula-hula*)—gives us a demonstration of the dances that used to be performed before the king and the king's consort on solemn occasions. The accompaniment consists of the dancer's own voice and of drumming, imitated, for lack of a real drum, by Miss Sauer on a rectangular object sewn inside a piece of cotton print, which turns out to be a book printed on so-called unsized paper. The book in question is, as Miss Suzuki somewhat maliciously observes, Willi Apel's (excellent) *Harvard Dictionary of Music*, for which she has thus found a useful purpose of her own. It never comes out of its cover and it produces melodious and unobtrusive sounds.

We see agile movements of feet, hips, and arms, movements flowing into one another with singular grace. The choreographic figures of the king's dance are clearly distinct from those performed before the queen.

Next comes a sitting dance, accompanied not only by the dancer's voice, but also by a clapping instrument of split bamboo—identical with the Buginese *apó* or *bulu laé-laé*—manipulated with consummate skill. With this instrument, Suzuki taps in rapid and ever unexpected succession, now on the palm of the left hand, now on her right shoulder, or on the floor.

In another dance, she accompanies herself with *ili-ili*, little black oval-shaped flat stones with rounded edges; she holds a pair of these in each hand between her fingers, tapping them against one another in the manner of castanets.

And finally, there is a dance to the accompaniment of the *uli-uli*, a rattling calabash containing small pebbles (or grains of rice?) and decorated on the outside with a shock of red and yellow feathers. She also demonstrates the rattling technique of this instrument, which is more complicated than one might expect: for its high-pitched crisp sound should by no means be allowed to falter, but should be continuously audible, rushing gently and yet rhythmically as a result of proper movements of the wrist.

The songs Suzuki performs afterward are quite melodious, give the

impression of being more or less diatonic, and have a limited range. The
first song, for instance, moves through four notes only, within a range
of slightly less than a tritone; similarly, the second song moves within
a range of something less than a fifth. Always there is a clearly dis-
tinguishable *mesē*, used as a reciting tone.

Chicago, Saturday, 19th Nov.

At half past nine, Yury [Dr. Arbatsky] and I, together with his
Greek friend Tom Paganis and a lady friend of his, drive to the Pan
Hellenic Restaurant, which is situated in an exclusively Greek quarter
with signs everywhere written in the Greek alphabet. The owner has
a reserved table for us close to the orchestra which consists of a cim-
balom; a long-necked strumming-instrument with eight pegs (though
only strung with 3+2+2 strings), which is called a mandoline or *buzuka*
and which resembles the Indian *tambura;* a clarinet; a jingling tambourine;
and a *darbuka* (an Arabic one-headed vase-drum). The tambourine and
the *darbuka* are played by ladies.

The music performed is partly Greek, partly Turkish, and belongs
unmistakably to the kind of "café-music," which Yury loathes and which,
according to him, has very little to do with the original folk music.
To the ears of a West European musician, however, the music sounds
Oriental enough to be interesting on account of its typical and often
rather intricate rhythms. I note at one time, for instance, periods of
3+4+3; at another time the melody moves on a basic pattern of 3+3+2,
3+2+3, 2+3+3, so that a three-bar period can be distinguished in which
the component rhythmic elements shift and in which the eight eighth-
notes in each bar are combined in a manner strange to Occidental ears.

In the Greek music, simple West European harmonies are used; the
Turkish music is strictly monophonic. Both kinds of music make use of
the well-known "Oriental" scale with augmented seconds and a downward resolving leading note.

The two ladies, with good though rather shrill voices, alternately
sing before the microphone; in the Turkish songs, the long-sustained, as
it were trill-like, notes strike me as remarkable.

Occasionally, the ladies perform a dance, with or without the assistance of gentlemen—or sometimes with the assistance of additional ladies
as well—from the audience. As in one big family, everybody knows
everybody else here. When there is a group dancing—usually three
people (two men and one woman between them)—they form part of a
circle, two at a time holding on to the corners of a handkerchief. The
dancers never touch each other physically. It is an extremely decent
entertainment and musically very good. It is touching to see how even
old men, who, judging by their appearance, are petty bookkeepers or

employees of some drugstore, seek companionship here on weekend nights and have their fling at exercise, music, and singing. At the close of each number the guests never fail to drop their dollar bills on the floor before the orchestra.

One of the lady musician-dancers, good-looking and well-dressed, joins our table for a while. She tells me that in the daytime she works as an assistant in a chemical laboratory and that she joined this music- and dance-group to earn a little extra money. She can sing in four languages: Greek, Turkish, Armenian, and Serbian, and is, though she does not say so herself, an excellent *darbuka* player and a graceful dancer. Though she enjoys doing this kind of work, she is thinking of resigning her job here, since she actually finds it too tiring in addition to her professional work.

Earlier that evening we heartily enjoyed a quite savory Greek dinner; we began with a thick rice-soup with veal-liver cubes; then there was a dish with that stimulating combination of salted fish, colvi turnips, young white curdle-like cheese, olives, tomatoes, and olive oil; after that, another dish with cut-up liver and sweetbreads. And, of course, that somewhat rough, but spicy Greek wine.

It is getting late. Fortunately, however, Mr. Paganis had said that this was to be *my* evening and that it was up to me to give the signal of retreat. At half-past twelve I feel that without being rude I can safely suggest that we leave. I have such busy days ahead of me!

Los Angeles, Tuesday, 29th Nov.

In the afternoon, Mantle [Dr. Hood] drives me over to the Music Department. There we meet, among others, Mrs. Anna Bender-Brink of Johannesburg. Mrs. Brink is a pianist and works for the Broadcasting Company in Johannesburg. In view of the fact that she usually accompanies the artists that come to South Africa, she must be a very good pianist. I discover that she knows all my African musical friends: Professor Kirby, Dr. du Plessis, Willem van Warmelo, Professor Bon, and Hugh Tracey. . . .

That evening there is a rehearsal of the gamelan society that has been formed within the Music Department, in the so-called "pendopo" (which, of course, is not a real *pendopo*, but a small auditorium). Though the instrument collection does not yet contain all the instruments normally included in a gamelan orchestra, it is already sufficiently large to allow reasonable performances of both *pélog* and *sléndro* compositions.

Among the musicians—a devoted team—I notice Professor Petran (organist and acoustician of the University of California at Los Angeles); our friend, the musicologist Harry Edwall; a colored lady, the gracious

Mrs. Gertrude Robinson, who plays remarkably well; the architect Mr. Stevens; Miss Ann Robinson, a violoncellist, who is in charge of the *rebab;* Shirley Hood; and Elizabeth May, a graduate music student.

First we hear the society's "signature tune," the *gending Udan mas* (from which the society derives its name), played in two versions, to wit, first in *pélog*, then in *sléndro*. It is amazing how much this group, under Mantle's spirited leadership, has managed to achieve in so short a time— in less than a year, in fact. The teamwork is really good; even the *stringendi (sesekan)* and final *ritardandi (suwook)* are played with remarkable precision and certitude, difficult as they are. When, in time to come, *bonangs* are available to the society, playing together will no doubt be easier and consequently there will be a gain in consistency and homogeneity.

After *Udan mas* the delightful *Srimaléla* is played, in *pélog barang;* the curious *Tlosor,* in *sléndro manyura,* which so cunningly conceals its *patet* for a long time; the *pélog* piece *Chandra sari;* the *sléndro* piece *Gonjong sèrèt,* characterized by graceful *ngentjot*-figures (anapaests); and finally—played with fanatical sincerity—the famous *Gangsaran,* which begins and ends in a fascinating and overwhelming one-tone period.

The society's repertoire is still limited, but it is gradually being extended. As was the case with respect to Bernard Ijzerdraat's experimental ensemble "Babar layar," so in this group the musicians change places after each number in order to master all the various instruments.

Los Angeles, Thursday, 1st Dec.

About noon we set off to the Music Department, where I have been invited to attend a meeting of the faculty board. Practically all the members are present.

After we have gone through the brief agenda, a discussion develops based on the pros and cons of a combined scientific institution and conservatory, such as exists in several universities in this country. In European countries, at least in France, the Netherlands, and Germany, this combination is unknown. One of its drawbacks—in the U. S. A. sometimes a painful actuality—is that one of the two departments, usually the conservatory, gets the upper hand and claims the lion's share of the funds and space available; the drawback of *not* combining is that musicological students run the risk of losing touch with living music, and that the students of the conservatory become too specialized and acquire too little general knowledge (as, alas, often occurs at the Netherlands conservatories).

Furthermore, the value of studying and practicing non-Western music at a Western musical institution, for example, Javanese music (among others) at U.C.L.A., also comes up for discussion. We agree that a more penetrating study of foreign music can broaden the horizon of a musician and bring home to him the fact that his own art is but one of many modes of expression; in addition, composers may find elements among the foreign musical patterns that they may use effectively in their own creations, not by slavish imitation, of course, but by "translating" them, so to speak, into their own idioms. Mention is made, in this connection, of Debussy, whose music would certainly have been of a different character, had he not come into contact with Javanese music at the Paris World Fair in 1889.

After the meeting I hurry home to change, and then we go to Schoenberg Hall, where I am to deliver a lecture at four on "Some Sociological Aspects of Music."

The auditorium is not quite full, but still there are about 200 people. The microphone is out of order. Fortunately, the acoustical qualities of the hall are excellent, so that my voice carries easily as far as the last rows. . . .

Los Angeles, Sunday, 4th Dec.

In the afternoon I had a visit from Boris Kremenliev, who is writing an article about musical folklore and wishes to discuss one or two things concerning it with Mantle and me. It turns out that Boris's treatise concerns the "Functional Aspects of Folk Song," and as a result "du choc des opinions" we come to the conclusion that every folk song can be called functional, taking the term in its widest sense—to the extent that it gratifies the minds of both singers and listeners, or perhaps has an invigorating effect, or sustains the solemnity of an occasion—but that the term, as commonly used, is very hard to define and consequently had better not be used at all: a song, of which the text deals with, let us say, forging, is not necessarily functional to the blacksmith's trade. The functional quality of a song can be bound up with the melody as well as with the contents of the text. A marching song, so far as its melody is concerned, is, no doubt, functional with regard to the soldiers who sing it, but the text usually is far from being functional. Is a religious song functional? When sung at a religious meeting it probably is; when sung in the street it usually is not. A ballad . . . is not functional, unless the text improves the listener as a person or is intended to do so; also, a lullaby is functional when sung at the cradle, since it helps make the baby fall asleep. However, it is impossible to draw a strict line between songs that are, and those that are not functional (in the common, narrow sense of the word), for this depends not only on the text and the

melody, but also on the circumstances under which the song is sung . . .
Only of dance songs can it be said that they are usually functional—that
is, when they are sung to actual dancing.

Los Angeles, Saturday, 17th December
I am engaged in reading Editha and Richard Sterba's *Beethoven and
his Nephew*, a fascinating psychoanalytical work. It has always bothered
and surprised me somewhat that Beethoven's enigmatic personality has
never been studied from a psychoanalytical point of view, since everything in his behavior indicates that in this respect a more promising
subject could hardly be found. Without exception, the existing biographies fail to give an adequate explanation for the often quite strange
utterances and reactions of the great composer. Had I not lacked the
required knowledge and training, I would long ago have applied myself
to the task of writing a psychoanalytical biography of Beethoven. This
book by the Sterbas provides the necessary supplement to and correc-
tion of the biographies by Schindler, Thayer, and Becker. The Sterbas
detract nothing from the greatness and "Einmaligkeit" of Beethoven's
works. On the contrary, they show the greatest admiration for them;
but whoever prefers a romantic "Idealbildnis" of the great master and
cannot do without hero worship had better not read the book. At the
same time, this work gives a belated, much needed re-evaluation of Beethoven's much maligned nephew Karl.

Los Angeles, Wednesday, 28th Dec.
A few days ago Mantle made contact with an acoustician who lives
somewhere beyond the Santa Monica mountains in Los Angeles and who
Mantle hopes will be able and willing to help him with the construction
of some *gendèr*s that are to be built for his *gamelan* orchestra. From
*gendèr*s the conversation on the telephone leads to *gamelan*s in general,
and from them to Java is but a step. It turns out that this acoustician has
himself been to Java. Mantle then asks him whether by any chance he
has met me. It happens that he has. He hopes that Mantle is able to give
him my address, as he would like to ask me a few things. He is delighted
when he learns that I am staying with Mantle and invites us to visit him
in his studio. His name is Claire Omar Musser.
I knew Mr. Musser as a marimba virtuoso, the leader of the "one
hundred piece marimba band" at the Chicago World's Fair in 1933, and
as the agent of the vibraphone firm, Deagan & Co., in the same city.
Through him, Mangku Negara VII at one time had acquired a vibraphone for his best *gamelan*, the Kangjeng Kyahi Kanyut Mèsem, and I

had forwarded the vibration numbers of this vibraphone to Chicago. That was in 1928.

It seems that Mr. Musser has now started a business of his own, but devotes himself mainly to research. He must have prospered. His marvelous home, situated on a hilltop, overlooks a good part of the Los Angeles plain as far as the San Bernardino Mountains; a panorama of unparalleled beauty lies below us. But yet more impressive, one might almost say, is the music room that Musser has had built for himself. Every part of it has been calculated with a view toward the acoustical effect. The floor, as well as the ceiling, has all the properties of a first-class stringed instrument; that is to say, for instance, that the floor is hollow and, though when struck it has the fundamental C itself, it will respond like a good soundboard to any other fundamental pitch as well. It is, so to speak, a singing floor, and the acoustical results are perfect; never did I hear the grand piano sound with such sonority; on the other hand, the tones never encroached upon one another because of a resonance that lasted too long.

In addition, there are a couple of vibraphones of a large model in the room and a xylophone, supplied, like the vibraphones, with sound-tubes. The xylophone is of a quality I did not know could be attained in a percussion instrument of this type. We never tire of listening to its rich, warm, and yet wood-like cascades of sound. Moreover, Musser, with the two pairs of sticks—of which he ever varies the angle—and his dazzling technique, knows well how to demonstrate every possible effect of which the instrument is capable. His chords and modulations are a joy to the ear; I would never have thought the things he does possible on a xylophone.

But another, still more important surprise is yet in store for us. I tell Musser, who is interested in all kinds of keyboard instruments—especially those from Southeast Asia—about that curious lithophone which was found by Mr. Condominas in Annam a few years ago at the excavation of a prehistoric tomb and which is now one of the most treasured objects at the Music Department of the Musée de l'Homme in Paris.[1] And, to my immense surprise, Musser's reaction to this piece of information is to tell me that he himself is in possession of such a lithophone—consisting of six slabs—also from Annam. A friend of his, an engineer attached to the Smithsonian Institution in Washington, had found it, when, in overseas service during World War II, he had a bull-dozer remove the soil for road-making. Later on he forwarded it to his friend Musser. Musser shows one of the slabs to us; it is approximately 24 inches long, 3 inches wide, and one inch thick and is made of a slate-colored unweathered kind of stone. We press Musser most strongly to

measure without delay the pitch of this set of slabs with his Stroboconn
and to send the results, together with all the details concerning their discovery, that is, as much as is known to him, to the head of the Music
Department of the Musée de l'Homme, Mr. André Schaeffner.

Musser, who is an amateur astronomer, has in the course of time collected a great number of meteorites, some of them weighing many
pounds and some of them rich in ore, especially nickel. Some huge specimens are piled up in one corner of his studio. He is planning to build
a vibraphone, using meteorite metals exclusively. If that is not going
to bring forth heavenly music, then nothing ever will.

Los Angeles, Friday, 30th Dec.
A day of leave-taking. But not a day entirely without the presence
of the Muses: at the Youngs' I listen to Bartók's sixth (and last) string
quartet, a work which, in my opinion and to my ears, can be ranked
with the best of Mozart's and Beethoven's quartets. Especially most
touching is the last movement; it could have been a picture of the
Crucifixion expressed in music: it is as if we hear the last cries of
despair and then drops of blood, falling slowly—all this raised to a level
of incomparable grandeur.

In the afternoon I go through Mantle's treatise, *Paṭet and the Pane-
rusan in Javanese Music*, the logical sequel to his thesis, *The Nuclear
Theme as a Determinant of Paṭet in Javanese Music*. It is a clear analysis of the instrumental parts that carry the musical ornamentation in
Central Javanese orchestral music, and is based mainly on a score of the
genḍing Pangkur, written down and stenciled by the Kerawitan conservatory of Surakarta. Mantle has surpassed himself in the way he has
set forth this far from simple matter. I suggest that he permit the
Anthropological Department of our Institute [the Royal Tropical Institute in Amsterdam] to publish this treatise and he gladly falls in with
the idea. I will write to Prof. Bergman about it immediately; we must
not fail to have the name of our Institute attached to this essay, which
bears witness to great originality.

Los Angeles, Saturday, 31st Dec.
In the morning a visit from Claire Omar Musser. He has carefully
measured the six slabs of his Anammese lithophone with the Stroboconn,
and I lose no time in calculating, with the aid of von Hornbostel's cent-
table, the intervals formed by this tone series. The results

1473.6		1241.09		1173		1008.7		959.2		841		(736.8)
I	297	II	97½	III	261½	IV	87½	V	227½	VI	231	I

do not allow us to draw immediate conclusions about the nature of the scale, but it seems to me that we should look rather for a connection with the (heptatonic) *pélog*-group than with the pentatonic group, the more so as there was yet a seventh slab belonging to this series; the slab, however, was crushed by the bull-dozer that brought the series to light and therefore was not sent to Musser. The position of this seventh tone could very well have been in one of the larger intervals and so have helped to form a heptatonic scale.

COSTA RICA

San José, Wednesday, 4th Jan., 1956

At half past five my Dutch folk-song performance begins. This is to introduce the solemn inauguration of the newly founded Hall of Folk Music in the Museo Nacional. Although it is customary in San José to arrive 15 to 30 minutes late at public meetings, the auditorium this time is filled to the last seat at the officially appointed hour, and scores of visitors have to be content with standing-room. There are no late comers at all! The entire Dutch colony is present, that is to say, the Chargé d'Affaires Mr. de Waal, with Mrs. de Waal; the first secretary of the legation, Mr. Daniels, with Mrs. Daniels; the deputy consul, Mr. Bijleveld, with Mrs. Bijleveld; and many others, whose names I cannot remember. The President of Costa Rica, who has sent word that to his regret he is unable to be present on account of the serious illness of his daughter, and the Costa Rican government are represented by Mr. Usla-dislao Gamez, the Minister of Education. Furthermore, there are many members of the Corps Diplomatique present. Then there are also all the people I met last year or in the course of these last few days and—for the first time at such a function in the history of Costa Rica—a small group of full-blooded Indians. I do not think that I have ever had a more international and racially varied audience before me.

When "Don Carlos" (Mr. Balser) with a pleasant and effective voice has read my speech, which was the day before translated with great care into Spanish by Mrs. Stone and Mr. de Waal, I sing and play my songs and dance pieces, each preceded by a word of explanation by Balser, so that the people know what I am singing about. Señor Murillo's accompaniment leaves nothing to be desired. The songs "sell like hot cakes"; the performance is, if I may say so, a great success. That afterward in some of the newspaper reports I am taken for a Dane and the songs for Indonesian music, does not alter the case in the least. The audience, especially, of course, the Dutch among them, eagerly joins in some of the choruses. Together with Mrs. Daniels I demonstrate some dances of the island of Terschelling.

Strange how these simple tunes, time and again, wherever I have sung and played them (in Holland, Sweden, Denmark, the U.S.A.,

Indonesia, Brazil, Surinam, Curacao, Aruba, and now here), have invariably given moments of unclouded happiness to so many people. At the
time when I collected them, in 1913, and harmonized them for publication during the years from 1914 to 1919, I could not possibly have
anticipated this, nor that they would become a permanent part of my
whole life.

At the close of the performance I—on behalf of both myself and
the Royal Tropical Institute of the Netherlands—present Mrs. Stone with
a copy of my *Music in Java* as a first acquisition for the new department's future library of folk music, and the whole party then repairs
to the recently completed hall. The light blue ribbon strung across
the entrance is cut through by Mrs. Gamez, the wife of the Minister
of Education, amid a volley of flashlights from the press photographers.
The whole performance passes off without a hitch; it all fits beautifully.
Not a single jarring note—apart, perhaps, from some in my singing—
has occurred this afternoon. Everybody is grateful and delighted to have
had this experience. Doris Stone and Charles Balser are particularly
pleased, and I am happy that I have not been a disappointment to them.

San José, Thursday, 5th Jan. 1956
At seven we drive to the country house of the Stones. There we
meet many other guests; all in all, there are sixteen of us.

How can I find the proper words to describe this evening? After
a pleasant dinner—I had been seated next to Doris Stone—we pass
the time merrily with music and dance. The Stones have engaged two
well-known Costa Rican guitarists, who form a wonderfully harmonious team; two Spanish girls, Pilar and Martha, and Doris herself, perform some dances with castanets; the repertoire is partly native Costa
Rican, partly pure Spanish, sometimes Panamanian. At one point,
Caribbean music is played, and we, in a mood of intensified rhythmical
sensitivity, accent the time on various native drums; the girl Pilar sings
wonderful Costa Rican folk songs with a curiously deep alto voice, now
and then assisted by Mrs. Balser, while the two guitarists really show
their worth: for the duration of one, too short, evening I live in a
typically South-Latin world.

Doris shows me a few earthenware ocarinas; sometimes two are
identical and make a pair. They have all been found in prehistoric
Indian graves; many of them are in the shape of animals, and the largest,
with two rows of three finger-holes, is of a type that up to now has
been quite unknown to the scholarly world. Another ocarina has the
shape of a small, one-headed vase drum. Some of these instruments have
a surprisingly beautiful tone.

The hours fly, and we feel like carefree children. Of course, it gets

very late and, when I finally lie in bed, I can still hear, in blissfully free
and relaxed sleep, this melodious and at the same time so stimulating
guitar music.

MALAYA   Singapore, Thursday, 4th June, 1959
My wife and I take our leave of the company to visit the Raffles
museum and its library by ourselves. To us, who have known the excellent museum and well-stocked library of the Bataviaas Genootschap at
Jakarta, this visit is somewhat disappointing.

The library contains about 150,000 volumes, which for the greater
part are fiction. Science, or "non-fiction," as the library—in a manner
so characteristic of the local point of view—prefers to call it, is posi-
tively insufficiently represented—indeed, the collection is so defective
that no one who has to depend exclusively on what is available here
could possibly produce a well-grounded scientific treatise.

As for the museum: we see, arranged in a rather old-fashioned way,
some valuable collections of Malayan and Dyak ethnographical material,
some excellent bronzes from Brunei, some china, and some conveniently
arranged palaeolithic and neolithic collections, partly gifts from our
compatriots, van Stein Callenfels and von Koenigswald.

I am particularly interested in the musical instruments and mainly
for the following reason:

The Śailéndra dynasty, whose rule saw the tremendous growth of
civilization in Central Java in the 8th century A.D.—think, for example,
of the caṇḍi [temple] at Sari and of those at Sèwu, Mendut, Kalasan,
and Barabuḍur, as well as of many others—, was, unless all evidence
pointing in that direction fails, also responsible for the introduction of
the *gamelan sléndro* (=*gamelan Śailéndra?*) and the *wayang purwa* into
Java. It is supposed that this dynasty originally came from Malaya, so
one would expect to find traces there of a once flourishing world of
music with *sléndro*-orchestras, and consequently remainders of that
world among the collections of the Raffles Museum. On the contrary,
however, we come across only a couple of showcases containing a few
bamboo instruments from the peninsula, partly of Malayan, partly of
Negrito or Semai origin; furthermore, there are a couple of drums, a
coconut-leaf oboe, a three-stringed *rebab* (from Kelantan) and finally
one single so-called *kromong* of five sound-pots of a none too good
quality hailing from Negri Sembilan.

The scale of the last instrument, the sound-kettle series, turns out to
be approximately as follows (I have no measuring instrument handy):

B-D-E-F-G-A

It is clear that this scale bears no relation whatsoever to the *sléndro*-
or to the *pélog*-gender (the latter well-known among some proto-

Indonesian tribes of the Indo-Chinese highlands, particularly one or two of the Moï-tribes).

I note down the names of various bamboo instruments: the Negrito name for the mouth organ is *yanggoing;* the Semai name for the nose flute (with three finger-holes) is *pensôl;* the transverse flute is called *peningyong* by the Negritos, *pinyong* by the highland Semai, *lei-o bangsi* by the lowland Semai, and *samoje* by the Jakun tribe from Pahang; the Semai name for the flute with a central hole is *tu'ôl;* the Jakun name for the many-stringed bamboo idiochord is *sirdam.*

We see a wind-driven musical scarecrow in the shape of a two-winged propeller, fitted at the end of the wings with notched bamboo flutes of unequal length (and consequently of unequal pitch); these are differentiated into a masculine flute (the lower one in tone) and a feminine flute, and they make a sound as soon as the propeller is put into motion. We also see a pair of single-headed mosque drums (*beḍug*), one from Kelantan, the other from Trengganu; the way in which the skin is stretched on the drums is identical with that of the Toba-Batak *tataganing-* (*gondang-*) drum groups. These, too, have a rattan hoop that keeps the drum-skin tightly stretched and is tied down to the drum-bottom by means of rattan cords. The drum-bottom itself is not connected to the drum-body. Between the drum-bottom and the drum-body, a great number of conical plugs are inserted; these, when driven in further, stretch the skin more tightly over the drum-body, so as to give it the desired pitch or at least the desired clear sonority.

AUSTRALIA   Sydney, Friday, 19th June, 1959.

At the appointed hour of eleven we arrive at Mr. Trevor Jones's bureau. In addition to Mr. Jones, we meet there Dr. Steele, the music historian at Sydney University. Trevor Jones, who is the counterpart of our South African friend, Professor Percival Kirby, in his incredible knack for getting sounds out of the most divergent kinds of instruments, acquaints us with the sound of the Australian *didjeridu.* He is capable of producing not only an extremely low sound on the unwieldy instrument, but also, by over-blowing, the tenth. In other words: a) the lowest tone produced on the *didjeridu,* however low it may sound, is the upper octave of the real fundamental tone, and not that fundamental itself; b) the twelfth (partial No. 3) and the octave of the octave (partial No. 4) are skipped, although the instrument is not "closed" (German: *gedackt*) at the distal end and therefore should have been able, theoretically, to produce all partials, including the octaves. A plausible explanation of the skipping of the two partials has not yet been found. Actually, it is possible to bring forth partial No. 4, but then the player has to sing that tone at the same time that he is blowing.

All things taken together, to play on this seemingly simple instrument in the correct way requires a quite complicated technique. This proves once more that the culture of the aborigines—appearing so primitive to us Westerners—is in its own way far from primitive. Think also, for instance, of the incredibly complicated system of clan and family relationship among Australian tribes, which they still have managed to maintain, in spite of the disastrous impact of Western "civilization."

Sydney, Thursday, 25th June

To Sydney in the afternoon to meet Mrs. Alice Moyle at the Department of Anthropology, as arranged. This meeting is most pleasant. Mrs. Moyle turns out to be a middle-aged woman (she has a daughter who works at the University library) of great erudition and intelligence and is evidently very well informed in her special field. She shows me the manuscript of a book she is writing about Australian music; this promises to become a welcome addition to the still rather scant literature on the music of this continent because of its numerous music examples, the notation of which immediately bespeaks the expert. She then plays for us some tapes that she recorded herself in various regions of Australia. She points out to us the variations in style, character, and melodic structure, clearly perceptible even to someone who knows little or nothing about this kind of music. First, we hear music from East Arnhemland, marked by a clear organic unity between the voice part and the *didjeridu* accompaniment, the two going hand in hand from beginning to end without interruption. Then comes music from West Arnhemland, in which the voice is much less closely connected with the *didjeridu* part and in which the vocal melody is frequently interspersed with instrumental interludes. Next, from the region of Alice Springs, we hear Central Australian songs that have a range of an octave (occasionally of some more tones) and no instrumental accompaniment. These songs are, much more obviously than the music of Arnhemland, of the type to which von Hornbostel has given the name of *Treppenmelos* and Sachs of "tumbling strains." And finally there are songs, also unaccompanied (except for hand-clapping, if I remember well), from more southwesterly regions of Central Australia; these are characterized by melodies of a very limited range (as a rule no more than a third or a fourth), these melodies being at once repeated one octave lower.

Sydney, Monday, 6th July

An interesting afternoon with Mrs. Moyle at Sydney University, for she played some recordings for us—the only ones extant—of songs once sung by the Tasmanians, long since extinct (read: exterminated by the white settlers). These recordings, made on wax cylinders, in the years 1899 and 1903, respectively, contain songs sung by Fanny Cochrane Smith, a half-caste born on Flinders Island not far from Tasmania, whose mother was a full-blooded Tasmanian. By lucky chance, a few of these cylinders have been preserved—and, believe it or not, are still in playable condition—in the museum at Hobart, the capital of Tasmania; there, a couple of years ago, copies were made on tape, and from these gramophone records were made by the Australian Broadcasting Committee.

In their predominant use of "tumbling strains" and in their delivery, most of the recorded songs bear a strong resemblance to the music of the Papua tribes of the Van Rees Mountains in West New Guinea and the coastal districts north of those mountains; only one recording—purely pentatonic—bears a different character. On the other hand, I could discover no direct affinity with Australian aboriginal music and, what is more, neither could Mrs. Moyle, who is so much more at home in this field.

I have been told that a publication about these recordings by Mrs. Moyle can be expected before long.

Melbourne, Wednesday, 22nd July

In the morning, first to the National Museum. Spencer's recordings, played for us there through the good graces of the museum's director, Dr. Brazenor, are all from the Northern Territory (Catharine River, East Arnhemland, Desert Island, Bathurst Island). Apart from some one-tone recitatives, rhythmic shouts, and "yells," all the songs heard can be classed under the heading "tumbling strains." The usual range is one octave but occasionally it is no more than a fifth. Most of the songs are accompanied by rhythmic beats with sticks, one or two by the *didjeridu*, and some by hand-clapping. Now and then I hear some interesting cross rhythms, which, as a rule, are the result of a ternary vocal melody with a binary accompaniment of beats (3/4 against 6/8). One of the songs is in 5/8 time.

As these recordings will be available on L.P. records before long, with commentary by Mrs. Moyle, I will not discuss them any further for the moment.

Note

1. See a discussion of this lithophone in Curt Sachs, *The Wellsprings of Music* (The Hague: Martinus Nijhoff, 1961), pp. 106 ff.—*Editorial Note*

DANCE IN MODERN

AMERICAN CULTURE

Gertrude Prokosch Kurath (Ann Arbor, Michigan)

$\mathcal{T}$he question "whether ethnology includes all forms of the dance must be emphatically answered in the affirmative." Thus wrote Curt Sachs in a letter of July 7, 1958. His knowledge of folk dance and music of many peoples sharpened his appreciation of the Commonwealth of Art, the function of the fine arts in any culture. He would agree that art dance, commonly termed "Modern Dance," is not a folk art, but it shares some of the patterns and objectives of folk dances, draws on topics within our culture, and has a place in modern life.

THE PRACTITIONERS

Who Dances

A relatively small percentage of the American population actively participates in creative dancing, but the numbers have greatly increased since the early stages about 1920. Theoretically, many teachers would like to see everyone thus engaged. In the preface to her Seminar, *The Function of the Dance in Human Society*, Franziska Boas states that "Dance must be thought of as an expression of communal activity, and its constructive influence on the individual must be realized and promoted." She would open it to "all age groups and all types, the healthy and the physically handicapped, the mentally integrated and the neurotic, people in every sort of occupation and industry." (1944: 6.) * Others are in agreement, from Margaret H'Doubler, the pioneer, to young Barbara Mettler.

Although male participants are, of course, essential, they have remained relatively scarce. The idea is still strong that dancing is effeminate. The men must be reminded that in ethnic dances they are more important than the women (Sachs, 1937: 172). They must be convinced that dancing is a man's game (Martin, 1960) and akin to athletics. Ted Shawn has championed the cause of male dancing by forming a male group during the 1930's and by starting a hierarchy of professionals in his pupil, Charles Weidman, and *his* pupil, José Limón. The professional ranks enlist an increasing number of able men, the veterans, Alwin Nikolais and William Bales, the aspirants, Alvin Ailey and Roni Arnold. Amateur groups in colleges and elsewhere have members of both sexes.

Pre-teen children swarm to dancing schools. In addition to the large numbers who have joined folk dance or Indian dance groups and the smaller number who dance in school rooms, they or their parents have created an increasing demand. They register in summer courses of recreation departments beyond the capacity of the staff (Joel, 1960). This problem and the special problems of child teaching will be dealt with separately.

All classes are open to people of all occupations, but there frequently are special courses designed for groups such as garment workers or singers. Daniel Nagrin has helped cadets discover dance (Martin, 1960). Likewise, all races and nationalities take part. Children and adults of Chinese, Irish, and Jewish descent work together amicably. Several Negro dancers have achieved prominence.

Why They Dance

The motivation for dancing varies greatly between laymen and professionals, as well as between individuals. Barring ladies who need exercise and children dragged by mothers, the usual reason is joy in dancing. Variants might be termed recreative, social, and artistic.

Since Margaret H'Doubler perceived before 1920 that dance could fulfill "the relation between body and soul as expressed in regulated rhythm" (1925: 3), many teachers have perceived the need for making

* Citations refer to items listed in the bibliography at the end of this article.

it "available to the average person as pure movement experience" (Mettler, 1956:1). The first stage is physiological relaxation, which brings mental stability. The effects are thus recreative and therapeutic. Some individuals find most joy in acquiring high technical facility, others find fulfillment in an exuberance often approaching ecstasy. This mystic state appears to Sachs as a basic goal of dance. "The dance, inherited from savage ancestors as an ordered expression in motion of the exhilaration of the soul, develops and broadens into the search for God" (1937: 4).

The individual as well as the group experience has been called "self-expression" and "creativity." Brodie considers this basic, "arising from the psychological make-up of the human being. In this respect the artist is different from other human beings not in motivation, but only in facility and sensitivity. The layman too needs a certain amount of creative experience." (1948: 4.) It is up to the group director to guide the ideas.

There is much difference of opinion about the fate of these creations. Bird Larson, who trained both amateurs and professionals between 1917 and 1927, believed in "using energies for introspection rather than outward show" (Moulton, 1959). That is, the active creativity is an end in itself. Others believe in spectators. Mettler thinks that the enjoyment "can be shared actively by watchers as well as dancers." (Communication.)

How They Dance

The balance of feeling and form has been a prime problem of modern art dance. H'Doubler observed that the individual's growth evolves from dancing for joy to mastery of technique to the art of communication (1940: 103). The same evolution characterizes the art as a whole. When Sachs wrote his *World History of the Dance*, he was justifiably concerned over "too much egotism and too little ability." (1937: 447.) In the earlier decades there prevailed "the school of thought which supports the theory that the externalization of emotion is the only essential consideration" (Hayes, 1955: 2). This attitude still exists, alongside an increasing emphasis on form. Since about 1930 there have been many theories and experiments. The search for a sound basis has investigated the human body, the surrounding space, and principles of structure.

The physiological theories consistently sought to free dancers from a restricting vocabulary and at the same time provide a scientific and healthful set of exercises. The first teachers were physiologists and based their systems on laws of anatomy and weight. The precursor was an American, Genevieve Stebbins, who took her methods to Germany around the turn of the century. Her pupils, Bess Mensendieck and Hade Kallmeyer, again influenced the European dancers, Dora Menzler and Hans Wiener (Menzler, 1924: 16-17). H'Doubler and Larson independently evolved similar ideas in Madison, Wisconsin, and in New York. The basic principles were radiation from the spinal center and dynamic alternation of tension and relaxation.

Before 1920 the Hungarian artist, Rudolf Laban de Varaljas, first realized and analyzed space. In fact, he based his system of dance notation on theories derived from his analysis. Before 1930 his pupils and their pupils brought them to America. "Space consciousness can be passive and responsive or active and creative. The former is the reaction in mood and movement to surroundings. . . . But the creative artist, whether dancer or architect, fills the empty space with forms. The dancer . . . moves in certain directions, cuts lines in the air with his body, weaves a pattern in the air; and with these lines and forms evokes the desired emotional response in the spectator." (Prokosch, 1931:4.) This principle has been fully exploited in the class work of Mary Wigman (Bach, 1933: 25, 40, 53), Hanya Holm, Hans Wiener (Jan Veen), Barbara Mettler (1956: 44-9), and Elizabeth Hayes (1955: 31-45).

The structural legacy of music has been spatial as well as temporal. Rhythmic aspects lie in the time dimension. Gifted dancers have always kept time with the musical accompaniment and sensed the quality of the rhythms. But a musician, Jaques-Dalcroze, devised a system of analysis in kinetic terms, as early as 1910. He moved his school from Geneva to Dresden-Hellerau. His pupils applied his theories more intensively to dance, both abroad and in America. Else Findlay of New York carried rhythmic experiments into excellent dance compositions, before 1930. She and others have experimented with reciprocity of dancer and musician, using percussion instruments other than the piano, realizing with Sachs that "motor impulses pass from the moving limbs to the accompanying music, only to revert from voices, clappers, and drums as a stronger stimulus to the legs and torsos of those who dance." (1953: 38.) Bold use of rhythm and tempo with unorthodox instruments was initiated by Wigman and her pupils in America, Hanya Holm, Franzisca Boas, Barbara Mettler.

The Topics

What They Dance

Not only the techniques but the topics have in little more than four decades undergone a tremendous change. In 1915 creative dance was budding, but very modestly. So far as the general public was concerned, Robert Lowie was justified in an unfavorable comparison with American Indian dancing.

> To put it briefly, our dancing appears in the same context with restaurants, hotels, débutantes, attempts at a social rapprochement of the sexes. In Indian society, dancing is largely connected with war and agriculture and the chase, magical performances and religious observances, in short, with the serious affairs of life. (1915: 95.)

With much thought and daring, American dancers have enlarged the scope to include almost every conceivable topic. Walter Terry makes an incomplete statement in saying that

> Thematically, modern dance may deal with sex impulses, man's need for God, race hatred and evils, lynching, marriage problems, democracy, biography and it may deal with its problems in terms of tragedy, satire or abstraction. (1949: 311.)

Christian Religion

In 1917, Ted Shawn danced an entire service in the Interdenominational Church of San Francisco, including Opening Prayer, Doxology, Gloria, Anthem, Twenty-third Psalm, a sermon, a hymn, and Benediction. In 1920, Dr. William Norman Guthrie commissioned Bird Larson to train a group for Easter dances in St. Mark's-in-the-Bowerie, New York. Ecclesiastical turmoil and excommunication did not deter him. After Larson's death, the pastor's daughter, Phoebe Guthrie, produced *The Book of Job* after William Blake, excerpts from Khalil Gibran's *The Prophet*, and other dignified and beautiful group dances for the church, without, however, audience participation.

Since then Ruth St. Denis and others have performed in services. In 1932, Erika Thimey directed a Nativity scene and taught dances at the Meadville Theological School in Illinois. These pupils spread the idea and she transferred her activities to Boston.

The Burlington Council of churches sponsored lectures and dancing by Julia Lepeschkin, and the South Congregational Church of Hartford invited the Eastern Sacred Dance Guild for conferences. This Guild is directed by professionals, such as Louise Mattlage and Myra Kinch, and includes members of various faiths, such as the Jewish Aviv dancers. They have continued performances. Mattlage was asked to explain their credo to the Yale Divinity School: "dance and religion are translations of faith into activity" and "share in the importance of living." (1958: 119.)

There have been other groups, and also productions based on Biblical themes in other places than churches. Some New England summer camps engage youthful students in reverent enactments, *Sign of Jonas* and *O Ye Daughters of Jerusalem*. Most active are the Fairfield County Modern Dance Workshop and the Indian Hill Workshop in Stockbridge, Massachusetts (Affelder, 1959). In 1959 students of Marylhurst College, Portland, Oregon, choreographed *O Antiphons* to Gregorian chants.

Americana—American Indian Themes

Dancers as well as anthropologists have appreciated the ritual content of much Amerindian dancing and have drawn on their lore for occasional choreography. Soon after 1920, as part of his suite of American Sketches, Ted Shawn performed an *Invocation to the Thunderbird*, music by Sousa. He also directed his professional group in two dance dramas, an Aztec *Xochitl* to music by Homer Grunn and a Hopi *The Feather of the Dawn* to music by Charles Wakefield Cadman. These he based on research and observation.

Several other productions have remained fairly close to the source, as in 1936 my *Marriage of the Moon*, an Indian legend, with students of Pembroke College and the Providence Symphony Orchestra, and in 1952 Esther Brown's *It's Spring in the Desert* with students of Santa Barbara College. Other productions have been impressionistic and have used modern technique with an Indian idea. In 1947, William Bales and Martha Hill directed students of Bennington College in *When the Two Came to Their Father*, based on a Navajo legend; in 1960 Pearl Lang's New York group danced *Sky Chant*, inspired by the Navajo Mountain Chant. Elizabeth Waters has drawn upon Pueblo material for performances by her dance club at the University of Albuquerque.

American Negro Dance and Song

Ted Shawn was also the first to introduce American Negro topics. He choreographed *Juba* by Nathaniel Dett ten years before Tamiris began composing her series of Negro spirituals. Between 1928 and 1932, she devised solos and trios to *Joshua Fit the Battle of Jericho, Nobody Knows the Trouble I've Seen, Go Down Moses, Little David,* and others. Her approach was free and creative, as was the approach of other choreographers. In 1928, the New World Dancers, pupils of Bird Larson, produced *Go Down, Death,* with reading by James Weldon Johnson and with Esther Junger as soloist. In 1937, a Negro group, the Southland Quartet, danced and sang *I'se Been Hammerin' on Dis Mountain* under my direction (see plate 1), and the Creative Dance Guild of Rhode Island later on expanded the patterns with a larger group. In 1942 the Negro dancer, Pearl Primus, freely interpreted a poem by Lewis Allen, *Strange Fruit.*

There have also been dance dramas inspired by the jerks and exuberance of Negro revivals, which worried ministers in 1804 and delight dancers in 1960. The most recent composition, in 1960, is the work of a young Negro dancer, Alvin Ailey. His *Revelations* includes ring shouts and holy blues.

American History

Ted Shawn's suite of pioneer dances, to Eastwood Lane's music, was a novelty in 1924. Members of the Denishawn company exploited early Americana, as simple dance or as epic, but not until years after establishing their independence. Martha Graham composed her solo, *Frontier,* in 1935, a group work, *American Document,* in 1938, and a stupendous dance drama to music by Aaron Copland, *Appalachian Spring,* in 1944. Her pupils took up the idea, Jane Dudley with her *Ballad of Molly Pitcher* in 1939 and the whimsical *Harmonica Break-down* in 1940; Sophie Maslow with *Folksay* and *Dustbowl Ballads,* 1943. Doris Humphrey choreographed *Shakers* in 1931 and *Song of the West* to music by Roy Harris in 1941, and she advised José Limón regarding his *Western Suite* of 1942. Ballet companies modified their technique to express the Wild West, Eugene Loring successfully produced *Billy the Kid* (Copland), in Chicago, 1938, and New York, 1941. Agnes de Mille introduced a hand-clapping square dance in the zestful *Rodeo* (Copland) of 1942 in New York. Her *Fall River Legend* (Gould, 1948) shows a grim side of New England.

Directors of amateur groups have found such topics appropriate.

PLATE 1

Drawing by Gertrude Kurath for her choreography for *I'se Been Hammerin' on Dis Mountain* (Negro song).

In 1940, I produced the *Legend of Sleepy Hollow* to music by Walter Legawiec at a program of the Rhode Island Creative Dance Guild; in 1941, I coached children in *Li'l Abner* (Guion). College productions were: 1941, *Comin' Round the Mountain*, University of Rochester, Elsie Bockstruck, director, *Square Dance*, New Paltz Normal School, Louise Mattlage; in 1942, *Swing Like Thunder*, University of Southern California, Lois Ellfeldt. At Interlochen Music Camp, Michigan, in 1951, Hildegarde directed *Song of the Plains*, with music by Virgil Thomson, in a dance depicting a pioneer family crossing the Plains. In 1940, Frances Wright produced *Ballad for Americans* (Earl Robinson). Lincoln and the American people were symbolized by a speaking soloist and dancing groups. Folk dances were stylized. The cast included youngsters of varied ages and abilities. At Indiana University, Jane Fox directed a suite of *Folk Ballads* in 1956 and *Spoon River Anthology*, music by Cola Heiden, in 1957.

In 1956, the Philadelphia Orchestra commissioned a program, *America in Music and Dance*, choreographed by Nadia Chilkovsky and professionals as well as amateurs of the Philadelphia Dance Academy. Scenes depicted early New England, vaudeville, Negro influence, a southern tale, and a contemporary satire, to music by G. Rochberg. The first was "based on witchcraft in American colonial days, material gathered from sermons of Jonathan Edwards, rebuttals of Roger Williams to public records of Judge Sewall of Salem, Mass." (Communication.)

Contemporary Scenes

The realistic trend did not start until after 1930, but it has gained momentum. Radir gives the reason for the emphasis on modern scenes: "Dancers have looked upon America and have discovered its traditions. They have made a new dance out of what they have seen. This dance emerges not only with a content new to dance, but with a new range and arc and quality of movement. . . . For the expression of ideas that are close to the everyday lives of common people, dance has found a straightforward, direct vocabulary of movement that is close to the earth." (1944: 14.)

New York professionals usually couch their comments in satire, as happens in Dudley's *In the Life of the Worker, Time Is Money*, 1934, and *Middle Class Portraits* (Parnass), 1935, and Holm's *Metropolitan Daily*, 1939.

My dance drama, *Hurricane*, based on the New England hurricane of 1938 and produced in 1940, contained tragic and comic episodes— the hurricane itself, refugees, searchers, looters, sightseers. The special

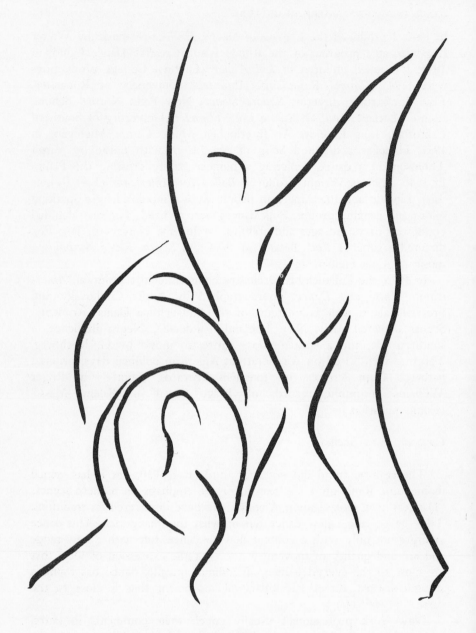

PLATE 2

Drawing by Gertrude Kurath for her choreography for "Basket Ball
Game" in her *Holiday Suite*.

music by Arthur Hitchcock was performed by the WPA Providence orchestra. The next year I directed teenagers in a *Holiday Suite* with work and play (see plate 2). Also in 1941, Genevieve Lucas directed *Work Song* and *The City* with students of Battin High School, N. J. The second world war inspired Ruth Radir's *Times Change*, Alice Hayden's *March of Americans for National Defense* with Winthrop College dancers in 1941, and Betty Lynd Thompson's Oregon State College *Suite of American Dances*, 1942, including dancers from the Selective Service. Fun is poked at the immediate environment in Else Bockstruck's *Campus Suite*, 1941, University of Rochester, and Alice Gates' Swarthmore College *Candy Flavor, City Savor, Big City Blues*, 1942. Jane Fox directed many similar topics at Indiana University: in 1942, *Campus Trials* (from registration turmoil to athletic section); in 1952, *House on Fire;* 1956, *Busy Day* (Britten); 1957, *City Beat*, with policeman, traffic, and shoppers.

For a while this fad waned. But within a year two teachers of children treated realistic themes of very different kinds. In 1958, Julie Lepeschkin of Burlington produced *Festivals—Beach Dance, Night Sky, Basketball Game*. In 1959, Blanche Evan of New York directed choreography by children of all ages, in *Symbols of Now*. This is "a composite of dance episodes derived from an awareness of emotional conflict typical of now . . . the line of action winds through and around the children of today." (Communication.) The eighteen episodes include titles such as *Delinquent, Restlessness, Many Alones, Stifled Aggression, Low Self-Esteem;* that is, the dances deal with pyschological problems.

Jazz

Some of the domestic scenes used jazz rhythms in the later years. Jazz themes were slow in taking hold in the world of art dancers, despite their popularity on the stage. Jazz was considered "trivial pastime by couples or vaudeville entertainment" (Shawn, 1926: 89). Shawn made a distinction between Negro themes like Juba and the social dance types. He expresses his opinions in no uncertain terms: "There has been a great deal of talk about jazz being the American dance—that our contribution to the history of dance is jazz, and I greatly resent that because I think it is the line of least resistance, that it is the negative side of American life expressing itself, not the positive" (*ibid.:* 47-8). His opinion was shared by others, such as Dean F. Louise Nardin who found H'Doubler's teaching a revelation "in the dark hour when the natural delight in rhythmic action had small chance of gratification. Fashion had reduced ordinary social dancing to a graceless lurching and tottering or lunging about" (in H'Doubler, 1925: xii). The "present degenerate condition of dancing" had been a worry for several decades (Scott, 1899: 198). But opinions gradually mellowed.

Sachs was no great admirer of jazz dancing, but he understood its social import, a revolt against restrictions at the turn of the century, motion to the point of distortion. His complaint lay in the dehydration of vigorous primitive style: "what we see here is not just a transformation but an inevitable disintegration . . . Thus has our standardized civilization extracted from these foreign dances everything in them that is primitive, forceful, and ecstatic." (1937: 445-6.)

By 1960, jazz dance had been lifted from a demoralizing influence to an anti-delinquency factor; it had invaded respectable circles, including anthropology. Marshall Stearns went to the other extreme in believing that "our choreographers are not using enough of the rich resources of jazz dance." (1959: 31.)

Jazz dance arrived on the concert stage by the back way, that is, through the music of Gershwin. In 1927, Tamiris choreographed the *Rhapsody in Blue* and, in 1931, Geneva Watson followed suit with the dance club of Ohio State University. In 1930, men and women students at the Yale School of Drama worked on Gershwin's *Concerto in F* under my direction. Then I danced to his *Three Preludes*, which have also been used by other dancers. I choreographed tunes of the day, Duke Ellington's *Creole Love Call* and the popular *Twentieth Century Blues* at the Rhode Island School of Design. One of my group members, Francesca Battastini, interpreted *Flatfoot Floogie* in 1935, and my entire group did *Boogie-Woogie* (Williams) in 1943. Colleges have used jazz topics, but professional reworkings have been more numerous. To mention a few: Dudley's *Jazz Lyric*, 1938; Esther Junger's *Torch Song* (Gershwin) and *Mr. Bach Goes to Town* (Templeton), 1939; Primus's *Hard Time Blues*, 1942; Ailey's *Fast Blues*, 1946; Nagrin's *Jazz Suite* and *Strange Hero*, 1959; and Roni Arnold's *Humor*, 1959 (see plate 3).

The treatment varies greatly, from fairly literal use of the style to extreme modification, from simple effervescence to expression of a character or story, as in Jerome Robbins' *West Side Story* (Bernstein), 1957. Mura Dehn approaches jazz as a serious study in her Academy of Swing in New York. Extremes of interpretation range from vulgarity to mysticism, from male-female duet to group counterpoint.

Nature

A few choreographers have considered nature as a part of human life. Humphrey's greatest interest is in people, but she recommends other dance topics: "Nature presents a never-ending panorama of wind and

PLATE 3

Humor, to music by William Grant Still, choreographed and danced by Roni Arnold of Philadelphia Dance Academy. (*Photograph by Ruben E. Hall.*)

cloud, shapes of growing things, animal life, plain and mountain and water." (1959a: 44.) She was probably the first choreographer to train professionals in dances derived from nature in her *Water Study* of 1928 and her *Life of the Bee* with accompaniment of humming on combs. Esther Junger's *Animal Ritual* of 1935 was a strange, eerie dance. Other productions were my *Four Elements* of 1927, as well as *Earth Mother* and *Earth Ritual* in 1931 and *Of the Earth*, directed by Bessie Schönberg at Sarah Lawrence College in 1948. There has been a tendency to associate nature with children's dancing, from my *Four Seasons* of 1922 to Julie Lepeschkin's *Quails and Hawks* of 1958 and her mimed animal poems (1948: 328).

The treatment of nature varies from realism to symbolism. Small children may be encouraged to hop as bunnies, but adult choreographers stylize the movements, as did Esther Junger, or imply a drama of forces and conflicts reaching into human relationship, as did Humphrey.

Science and Mechanisms

Another approach merges nature with scientific concepts. Thus Ruth Page danced the *Expanding Universe* in 1945 and Merce Cunningham molded the elements into *Galaxy*, 1957. With the aid of strange lights, Jeanne Parsons created the effect of the aurora borealis and of cosmic motion. Her *Intégrales* (Varèse) was actually danced by Karin Paulson at the 1960 dance concert, University of Michigan. Science fiction also has a place, in Murray Louis' *Incredible Garden*, 1957.

The rhythm of machinery has fascinated several choreographers. In 1928, Eugene von Grona electrified New York audiences with his *Machine*. Two years later, Virginia Roediger directed a group machine dance for a production at the Yale School of Drama, *Man and the Masses*. In 1933, students of the Rhode Island School of Design portrayed the motion of a mechanical loom, in Charleston rhythm. More frequently, mechanical qualities have been incorporated in various contexts, especially abstractions.

Abstractions

Earlier experiments with abstract topics had emotional connotations, for example, my musicless *Dynamo* and *Crescendo* with Riva Hoffman's Philadelphia group in 1926; Humphrey's *Color Harmony* (1928) and *Drama of Motion* (1930); *Unison* (1941) by Veen and Thimey. At the University of Wisconsin in 1957, Louise Kloepper used ropes to intensify her group's *Patterns of Forces*. Abstract dances with an exuberant quality have often been used to open programs.

With his group at the Neighborhood Playhouse, New York, Alwin Nikolais has tried to free things of their associations in his *Masks, Props, Mobiles* (1955), *Prisms* (1956), *Kaleidoscope* (1956), *Allegory* (1958), *Totem* (1959). He makes use of a battery of sets and props to dehumanize his dancers, for the eight parts of *Kaleidoscope*—disc, pole, box, skirts, bird, hoop, straps, cape. For the electronic accompaniment, he tapes every conceivable ear-splitting sound, such as riveting and the noise of "El" trains. What do audiences and critics think? Louis Horst suggested in a review in the *Dance Observer:* "A little less ga-ga and da-da. A little more choreo-gra-gra." Doris Herring regrets in the *Dance Magazine* that "We are forced to forget that they are people. And, in so doing, we are forced to forget that art in its fullest definition implies emotional involvement."

All degrees from mime to abstraction have their justification. They represent different attitudes, even different cultural values, as Sachs perceived. He connected the "image dance" and "the imageless dance" with psychological and personality types—extrovert, introvert; and he related them to cultural horizons (1937: 77-79). He made this dichotomy the theme of his *Commonwealth of Art* (1946), from pre-historic animal mime and round to modern program and abstract music. In our complex culture all points of view are represented.

RELATION TO THE OTHER ARTS

"Modern dance, like modern music or modern painting, writing, architecture, is an expression of contemporary life by contemporary artists" writes Chilkovsky (1954: 104). The dance parallels trends in the other arts.

Music

Followers of Isadora Duncan by preference interpreted art music, especially by nineteenth-century composers, and most preferably by Chopin and Schubert. After 1920, some progressives added Scriabine. Romantic music has remained in occasional use, but has generally given way to Renaissance and medieval music or to ultra-modern compositions. These were better suited to the new, angular technique. A musician, Louis Horst, studied "Pre-classic" forms, that is pre-Bach court and theater dances, their steps, rhythms, and musical structures. He was almost as expert on the ethnic aspects as was Sachs, but in practice he used the patterns as formal guides for choreographers.

It became a matter of course for accompanists to compose for exercises and choreographies, as did Mark Wessel for H'Doubler, Maurine Dewslap for Hayes, and Cola Heiden for Fox. New York professionals have repeatedly commissioned the leading American composers to provide music for every conceivable instrumental combination, often but not always on American themes. The musicians include not only the "Americanists," Copland, Harris, Gould, but also "Traditionalists," Nordoff, "Eclectics," Thomson, "Experimentalists," Cage, and "Twelve-tone Composers," Riegger (Chase, 1955, Ch. 24-28). The composers have worked closely with the dancers, to provide suitable rhythm, tone color, and structure (Gottlieb, 1959).

In addition to more orthodox accompaniments there have been experiments with innumerable devices, including self-accompaniment and even complete silence. The simplest self-created sounds are stamping, clapping, cries, and singing by the dancers. These devices of primitive tribes (Sachs, 1937: 177) have been in vogue since 1925 (Mettler, 1956: 33-43; Haack, 1960). Percussion instruments—drums, gongs, rattles, etc. —were introduced largely by Wigman's pupils, Boas Holm, and Mettler, but also by Dalcroze teachers. They have opened up possibilities of interaction between dancing and accompanying groups as well as sound qualities. (Boas, 1938; Tula, 1948.)

Before 1930, dancers insisted on live music at least for public programs. With the improvement of recording techniques, they began to resort to "canned" music and were quick to change over to tape recordings, which do not scratch or break irreparably. Electronics have opened up possibilities beyond the recording of instrumental or vocal accompaniments. Choreographers have devised taped scores from sounds they hear.

Symptomatic of the increasing interest in American native scenes has been the employment of folk music—Amerindian, Negro, Hillbilly—, sometimes straight, sometimes modified or used as thematic material, sometimes live, sometimes sung by dancers, sometimes recorded.

In all this variety and change there has been one constant—the music of Bach. My earliest memories are dances to Bach Suites and Chorale Preludes, and the most recent programs continue to honor him. In 1935, entire programs were dedicated to the music of Bach and Handel. Doris Humphrey's last composition was to a Brandenburg Concerto. In 1943, the critic, John Martin, objected to her all-Bach programs, but Norman Cazden promptly rose in defense of the use of his music, perfectly constructed for dancers (1943: 31-2), and referred to what he claimed was the "close kinship of Bach's ideals and those of the modern dance."

Speech and Poetry

The word has accompanied dance throughout its modern development. Sometimes a text is spoken by the dancer, as in Graham's *Deaths and Entrances*. More freqently prose or poetry is entrusted to a reader. Guthrie, Shawn, and the religious dancers draw on biblical excerpts. Other dancers use all kinds of poetry, with a special liking for Federico García Lorca. But American poets are the favorites, starting with my *Caliban in the Coal Mines* by Louis Untermeyer (1927). Walt Whitman, Carl Sandburg, James Weldon Johnson, and Vachel Lindsay are as popular now as they were in 1930. There are many pitfalls in accompaniment by poetry, because not all poetry has suitable imagery and rhythm.

Theater Arts

In theatrical productions, movement joins the word. Plays for dancers, such as the series by William B. Yeats, have offered dancers opportunities for collaboration with actors. Larger productions have increasingly required choreography of all stage action and of special dances—plays, operas, Broadway shows. Many modern dancers have been thus employed. Juana de Laban has experimented with techniques at the Waco Civic Theater. Rachel Yocum and Gertrude Shurr have collaborated with the drama department at Utah State University Summer School, as have dancers in other colleges.

Other theatrical aspects affect the stage dancer. Costume, properties, décor, lighting, and scenery (if any) must be carefully planned to enhance the mood and movement. About 1930, dancers shed all nonessentials, simplified costumes and background along with their movement; but lately they have been designing more elaborate externals. Graham uses her many properties for expressive and symbolic purposes. Nikolais uses them for visual design. Often the choreographers engage professional designers and thus come into contact with the newest trends in painting.

Fine Arts

The fine arts may enhance stage productions. The combination of movement and color thus often resembles a modern painting. The effect of Graham's dances has been compared to Picasso and that of Hawkins' dances to Dubuffet. This is coincidental. But sometimes dancers attempt to reproduce the quality of a work of art, from medieval tapestry or sculpture to cartoons by William Steig or James Thurber. Modern architecture has also inspired patterns. Because of the close connection between the fine arts and the modern dancer's concepts of space and line, some schools and independent teachers, such as Katrine Hooper, include art history and appreciation or drawing in their curriculum. Students both paint and dance their ideas.

THE DANCE AND THE CULTURE

The place of dance in modern American culture presents problems, because both the art and the culture are complex and inconsistent. Isolationists feel no concern over the problems, but many dancers, especially teachers, believe that the "social relationship of an individual to his fellow beings, or of one group to another is a matter of utmost importance in every culture. This interrelationship of human beings provides the living source material for all dramatic expression." (Hayes, 1955: 106.)

The major aspects of the dance have passed in review. Now these may be matched with the anthropologist's picture of the culture. Leonard Mason concludes that

> Each individual must regulate his being within a system that separates social, economic, and religious activities, distinguishes between rural and urban and among lower, middle, and upper class, and combines the frontier spirit of Texas with the staid conservatism of New England. He is constantly urged to take the initiative, to assume responsibility, and to consider his own interests above those of his fellows. . . . Americans are quick to profess ideals of social democracy, freedom of expression for individual personality, and equality of opportunity unhampered by distinctions of sex, age, race, or religion." (1955: 1268.)

Democracy

The democratic ideal includes two aspects, the freedom of the individual and his attitude toward the society. A few dance directors ignore the group member's individuality, but the majority agree with Radir:

> The freedom of the individual to work out his way of life, according to his own beliefs, makes possible these varied technical developments. The individuality of the technique of modern dance is an outgrowth, also, of the experimentation that is permitted, and fostered, in a democracy. (1944: 15.)

Religion

It is conspicuous how individuals of various faiths or of no faith create together dramas from the Bible, the Shaker sect, Buddhism, or various primitive cults. The participants do not profess faith in all of the beliefs that are expressed, but they try to understand and reflect them, somewhat in the spirit of the ethnologists. In many cases the dancers have developed a mystic, non-sectarian attitude. "How to find substitutes for traditional religion, which will promote the feeling of solidarity and peace of mind which religion formerly produced, remains an unsolved ethnological problem." (Bidney, 1953: 687.) But this is not true for the dancer.

Current Events

The increasing concern with Americana reached its apex in the compositions on surrounding life and current events. Often they grew out of immediate experience, but just as often they referred to people and happenings miles or years away. The treatments do not indicate political convictions, though after 1930 several New York dancers danced their worry over the worker's plight and other issues. Here again the choreographer reflects rather than influences the issues.

Science and Nature

"Physical nature is something which must be controlled and harnessed to man's advantage. Americans have faith that this can be done through the application of scientific knowledge." (Mason, 1955: 1268.) Dancers show this attitude in two ways, artistic and technical. Though they sometimes approach natural phenomena ritualistically, more often they interpret them through the eyes of the zoologist or astronomer. The very methods have scientific foundations in physics and physiology.

Machines serve several functions. They furnish topics for dances. They are exploited for accompaniment or choreographic experiments. Films and television are used not only for recording, but for novel creations of patterns. Pauline Koner has been a pioneer in choreography for television.

Economy

So far the issues refer to the dancers' behavior and function as a mirror of society. Now the discussion shifts to problems that demand

solution. Professionals may perform dances for the earth and its cultiva-
tion, but few derive a livelihood in that way. The urban artist in
particular is caught in a monetary economy and must make his living
by charging for classes or performances. Positions at schools and
colleges help to solve this problem, but the independent dancer is
confronted with a public attitude that the artist should be glad to teach
and perform free, and with theater owners who charge high prices.
(Selden, 1935: 181-82.) He is sometimes deterred from fulfilling ideals
of design in space or of production because of inadequate facilities,
and he must enter into unhappy competition with colleagues.

Therapy

Objectives of recreation and therapy affect the laymen but are in
the hands of trained teachers. The recreative and thereby therapeutic
effect of most dancing has already been mentioned. Dr. Shailer Upton
Lawton agrees with dancers about the beneficial effects along "neuro-
logical, psychological and physiological lines" (1949: 134). Both dancers
and physicians would agree with Blanche Evan that much "modern
dance has been taught in a personal stylistic manner that has been
detrimental to health." (Communication.) Specialists have done research
and made experiments.

One approach is the analysis of healing techniques in tribal rituals.
The ecstatic circle dance is therapeutic. "In the healing of the sick,
the relation of the circle dance to the world of the ecstatic, visionary
mental state becomes most impressive." (Sachs, 1937: 63.) Certain
tempi and pulsating rhythms aid recovery (Kurath, 1952). Franziska
Boas has applied vibration and other tribal techniques to normal and
psychopathic pupils.

Representative of another approach are experiments at the University of Wisconsin in "psychomovement" involving adjustment by
emotional release and, again, dance composition on psychiatric themes.
The University of Illinois has similarly trained specialists, such as
Margery Turner. One of the leaders is Blanche Evan in New York.
She has devised methods, which she hands on to prospective teachers.
She differentiates methods for the normally healthy student, normally
disturbed, neurotic, psychotic, and disabled. While she believes that
the exercises must have a scientific basis, she also wishes the partici-
pant "to revere her art and to cherish it as her mainspring of inspiration"
(1959).

There are teachers who have specialized in certain problems, such
as children's speech defects (Stephenson, 1959). There are women who
have worked with acute cases, at Bellevue Hospital, Manhattan Hospital,

Eastern Pennsylvania Psychiatric Institute, and St. Elizabeth's Hospital, Washington, D. C. There are others who have made use of certain Laban notation symbols, called Effort symbols, in analyzing abnormal motion and its remedy. The teachers have observed with gratification the transformations of introverts and hypochondriacs, but they require more cooperation with psychiatrists (Rosen, 1957).

Education

Dance teachers encounter different problems in classes of lay and professional students. They find the problems intensified in the training of children. The leaders in education have held a consistent ideal of giving boys and girls a philosophy of life. "It is the development of human nature, of personalities, that is the important consideration." (H'Doubler, 1925: 8.) "The teacher of dance is concerned not merely with the presentation of subject material. He is also concerned with the students as individuals who have varying personalities and who are at different stages in their artistic development." (Hayes, 1955: 5.) The teachers resent the use of "some of the major techniques for professional training in modern dance and ballet, and the application of the principles of these techniques to children." (Stodelle, 1960: 70.)

These experts and others have devised special approaches. Mettler uses an adaptation of her methods of relaxation, improvisation, and invention through guidance (Eastman, 1954). Other successful child specialists are Evelyn Davis, Washington; Bruce King, Adelphi Children's Theater; Steffi Nossen, Larchmont; Julie Lepeschkin, Burlington; Virginia Tanner, Salt Lake City; Martha Nishatani, Seattle.

Frances Wright has taught for many years in Wichita, Interlochen, and Ann Arbor.

> Dance in the last ten years has produced more technically well-trained dancers than ever before. But if one student in five hundred reaches the height of dance in the professional world this is good and gratifying to the teacher . . . If the child is forced into a rigid technical practice in the first dance experience he may well become discouraged and even repelled before he has had a chance to know the satisfaction of the work which makes good dancers. . . . To introduce children to other art forms through the medium of dance in education is far more important than attempting to produce master technicians in the first years. The majority will go into other fields, and if teachers can give a knowledge that consequently affords intelligent appreciation, then dance for the many children is of immense value. (Communication.)

Dora Dubsky, a graduate of the Dalcroze School at Hellerau-Laxenburg, emphasizes the musical approach in her classes at the New York

Y.M.H.A. "There are many who believe that the emphasis on sound, and the knowledge of music which such training brings, are a necessary part of any young child's education" (Leddick, 1959: 40). To piano and other orthodox accompaniments she adds experiments in self-accompaniment by percussion. Her system resembles that of the musician, Bruce Haack (1960).

At Quaker Ridge School, Scarsdale, New York, Rita Chazin uses jazz music.

> Whether in the pre-teen or teenage classes, the children use the jazz material in a wholly unsophisticated, even primitive way. It is subordinated to the structure of the creative dance class—being used as a device which has proved successful in evoking a complete kinesthetic response to music. By integrating elements from the child's own background and environment, the total dance program has a richer, more meaningful appeal. (Levart, 1959: 49.)

Recreational dance programs in parks, civic centers, etc., thrive. But the mushrooming attendance means huge classes and sometimes incompetent teachers who harm the children physically and artistically (Joel, 1960). The National Recreation Association is working on the problems of educating our future dancers and citizens.

Is the Dance Expendable?

Dancers have been holding their debates and making their experiments in a culture that separates the arts and practical matters. They wistfully regard the ideal societies in which dance is an expression of all cultural activities (Sachs, 1937: 4-5). Idealists have .made futile attempts to reintroduce dancing in churches. More successfully, progressive schools integrate the arts in their curriculum. But virtuoso fusions of ballet and modern techniques appal educationalists.

Since its lowly status at the turn of the century, dance has risen in prestige and has increased its circle of participants. New methods can benefit health and mental adjustments. New themes reflect American life, folklore, events, and problems. Scientific preoccupations transcend continental boundaries. Productions utilize mechanical inventions.

As a special phase of the culture, dance can bring pleasure and benefit. As an art, it inevitably develops manifold and changing forms, derived from Europe and from our own land's distinctively non-European peoples.

Bibliography

Affelder, Paul. 1959, "The Bible as a Theme for a Summer Project," *Dance Magazine*, XXXIII, 4: 57-59.

Bach, Rudolf. 1933, *Das Mary Wigman Werk*, Reissner, Dresden.

Bidney David. 1953, "The Concept Value in Modern Anthropolgy," in *Anthropology Today* (ed. A. L. Kroeber *et al.*), 682-99, University of Chicago Press, Chicago.

Boas, Franziska. 1938, "Notes on Percussion Accompaniment for the Dance." *Dance Observer*, VI, 5: 71-72.

――――. 1944, *The Function of Dance in Human Society*, Author, New York.

Bode, Rudolf. 1922, *Ausdrucksgymnastik*, Beck, Munich.

Brodie, Joan. 1948, "Modern Dance and the Layman," *Dance Observer*, XVI, 1: 4-5.

Cazden, Norman. 1943, "On Dancing to Bach." *Dance Observer*, X, 3: 31-32.

Chase, Gilbert. 1955, *America's Music*, McGraw-Hill, New York.

Chilkovsky, Nadia. 1954, "The Modern Dance," in S. Spaeth, *Music and Dance in Pennsylvania, New Jersey, and Delaware*, New York Bureau of Musical Research, New York, 104-05.

Chujoy, Anatole. 1949, *Dance Encyclopedia*, Barnes, New York.

Eastman, Marcia. 1954, *Creative Dance for Children*, Mettler Studios, Meredith, N. H.

Evan, Blanche. 1959, "Therapeutic Aspects of Creative Dance," *Dance Observer*, XXVI, 9: 135-36.

Gottlieb, Jack. "1959, "Let There Be Music," *Dance Magazine*, XXXIII, 4: 52-53, 78-80.

Haack, Bruce C. 1960, "A New Approach," *Dance Magazine*, XXXIV, 7: 47-49.

Hayes, Elizabeth. 1955, *Dance Composition and Production*, Barnes, New York.

H'Doubler, Margaret. 1925, *The Dance and Its Place in Education*, Harcourt Brace, New York.

――――. 1940, *Dance: A Creative Art Experience*, Appleton, New York.

Horst, Louis. 1940, *Pre-Classic Dance Forms*, Dance Observer, New York.

Humphrey, Doris. 1959a, "Choreographers are Special People," *Dance Magazine*, XXXIII, 6: 42-44, 81.

――――. 1959b, "The Art of Making Dances: The Stage Space," *ibid.*, 43-45, 91.

————. 1959c, *The Art of Making Dances,* Rinehart, New York.

Joel, Lydia. 1960, "Protest; the Problem of Recreational Dance," *Dance Magazine,* XXXIV, 5: 16.

King, Eleanor. 1945, "Indian Dance in the Northwest," *Dance Observer,* XII, 9: 111-14.

Kurath, Gertrude P. 1952, "Therapeutic Dance Rhythms," *Dance Observer,* XIX, 10: 117-18.

Lawton, Shailer Upton. 1949, "Dances as Therapy," *in* Chujoy 1949, 134-36.

Leddick, David. 1959, "With Emphasis on Sound," *Dance Magazine,* XXXIII, 10: 40-46.

Levart, Herman H. 1959, "Jazz, Dance and the Child," *Dance Magazine,* XXXIII, 7: 46-49.

Lepeschkin, Julie Wilson. 1948, "Dance Education for the Growing Child," *Journal of Health and Physical Education,* XIX, 5: 326-28, 381-83.

Lowie, Robert H. 1915, "American Indian Dances," *American Museum Journal,* XV, 95-102.

Martin, William J. 1960, "Cadets Discover Dance," *Dance Magazine,* XXXIV, 6: 52-53, 65.

Mason, Leonard. 1955, "The Characterization of American Culture in Studies of Acculturation," *American Anthropologist,* LVII, 1264-76.

Mattlage, Louis. 1958, "Faith Dancing," *Dance Observer,* XXV, 8: 117-19.

Mayo, Margot. 1943, *The American Square Dance,* Sentinel Books, New York.

Menzler, Dora. 1924, *Die Schönheit deines Körpers,* Dieck, Stuttgart.

Mettler, Barbara. n.d. *Nine Articles on Dance,* Mettler Studios, Boston.

————. 1956, and June Warner, *Basic Dance on a College Level, ibid.*

Moulton, Robert H. 1959, "Bird Larson, the Legend," *Dance Observer,* XXVI, 4: 53-54.

Murray, Ruth L. 1953, *Dance in Elementary Education,* Harper, New York.

Prokosch, Gertrude. 1931, "Space Consciousness and Movement," *Design,* XXXIII, 64-70 (Columbus, O.).

————. 1934, "Dissonance and Harmony in Dance Design," *Design,* XXXVI, 8-9.

Radir, Ruth. 1944, *Modern Dance for the Youth of America,* Barnes, New York.

Rosen, Elizabeth. 1957, *Dance in Psychotherapy,* Columbia University, New York.

Sachs, Curt. 1937, *World History of the Dance* (English translation by

Bessie Schönberg, New York, Norton) of *Eine Weltgeschichte des Tanzes*, 1933, Reimer, Berlin.

———. 1946, *The Commonwealth of Art*, Norton, New York.

———. 1948, *Our Musical Heritage*, Prentice Hall, New York.

———. 1953, *Rhythm and Tempo*, Norton, New York.

Scott, Edward. 1899, *Dancing in All Ages*, Swan, London.

Selden, Elizabeth. 1935, *The Dancer's Quest*, University of California Press, Berkeley and Los Angeles.

Shawn, Ted. 1920, *Ruth St. Denis, Pioneer and Prophet*, Howell, San Francisco.

———. 1926, *The American Ballet*, Holt, New York.

———. 1940, *Dance We Must*, Author.

Shurr, Gertrude and Rachel D. Yocum. 1949, *Modern Dance Techniques and Teaching*, Barnes, New York.

Stearns, Marshall. 1959, "Is Modern Jazz Dance Hopelessly Square?" *Dance Magazine*, XXXIII, 6: 30-35.

Stodelle, Ernestine. 1960, "Reflections on the 1959 Conference of Creative Teaching of Dance to Children," *Dance Observer*, XXVII, 5: 70-72.

Terry, Walter. 1949, "Modern Dance," *in* Chujoy 1949, 309-11.

———. 1956, *The Dance in America*, Harper, New York.

Tula. 1948, "Dancer-Accompanist-in-One," *Dance Observer*, XV, 5: 53-54.

Winther, Fritz. 1914, *Körperbildung als Kunst und Pflicht*, Delphin-verlag, Munich.

GESTALT HEARING

OF INTERVALS

Mieczyslaw Kolinski (New York)

*O*ne of the cornerstones of Gestalt psychology is the thesis that a whole is not necessarily equal to the sum of its parts, since physically identical parts will be perceived differently, depending upon their function within an organic whole or "Gestalt." For example, the multivalent function of intervals and chords is a characteristic aspect of melodic and harmonic structure. Equally well-known is the flexible intonation of tone steps, due to their specific function; a good example is the sharpening of the leading tone. The resulting step will generally be perceived as a regular semitone in spite of its compression. Normally the melody-Gestalt will not considerably affect the evaluation of the size of intervals. However, the test described in the present paper shows that under certain "laboratory" conditions the melody-Gestalt may extensively influence the evaluation of the size of both tone steps and simultaneous intervals.

The test under discussion was carried out about 1930 within the framework of a seminar on sound psychology, held by Erich M. von Hornbostel at the University of Berlin. At that time, I had the opportunity to experiment with two metallophones, which were used to demonstrate the division of the octave into five and into seven strictly equal parts. The tunings of the two instruments were supposed to represent the "ideal" Javanese *sléndro* scale and the Siamese scale. The limiting octave tones (*c'-c"*) were tuned identically in both instances. In the present paper, the tones of the two metallophones are shown in Western notation representing the equal-tempered scale and are adjusted by means of the cent system (one octave = 1200 cents). The figures placed *above* the staves designate the number of cents to be added to or subtracted from the individual (equal-tempered) notes in order to obtain the right pitches, that is, the pitches of the metallophones. The figures that are placed *below* the staves show the number of cents that lie within intervallic distances. The size of each interval of the five-tone scale is 1200:5 = 240 cents; that of each interval of the seven-tone scale is 1200:7 = 171.43 cents. In the following two charts, the upper row represents the cent adjustments, as explained above; the lower one represents the intervals between the lowest note (*c'*) and the note shown above each number:

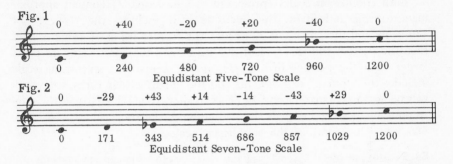

Fig. 1

| 0 | +40 | −20 | +20 | −40 | 0 |

| 0 | 240 | 480 | 720 | 960 | 1200 |

Equidistant Five-Tone Scale

Fig. 2

| 0 | −29 | +43 | +14 | −14 | −43 | +29 | 0 |

| 0 | 171 | 343 | 514 | 686 | 857 | 1029 | 1200 |

Equidistant Seven-Tone Scale

The superimposition of these two scales yields an artificial "scale" which includes an additional number of interval sizes, such as the microtonal interval of 34 cents (514 — 480), the semitone of 103 cents (960 — 857), or the neutral interval (i.e., in this instance, neither a major third nor a perfect fourth) of 446 cents (686 — 240). The material used for the present experiment consisted of eight short musical phrases based upon this compound scale. They are designed to determine how the melody-Gestalt may influence the evaluation of the size of intervals. Participating in the test were eleven advanced students of Professor von Hornbostel, as well as Hornbostel himself, who was eager to join the students. The test consisted in writing down the musical phrases played by me on the two metallophones. The participants were informed that the opening note of each phrase was a *C*, but no other pitch was named; they were asked to use diacritical signs (+ and −) to indicate deviations from the pitches they wrote down; if the deviations seemed slight, the diacritical signs were to be enclosed in parentheses. The phrases were played at medium speed. Each phrase was repeatedly presented as a whole and, whenever it seemed advisable, in musically meaningful sections. The playing of isolated tone steps or simultaneous intervals, taken out of their musical context, was consistently avoided. In the present paper, only Hornbostel's notation will be reproduced and analyzed because of his outstanding skill and great experience in transcribing non-Western material. But it might be added that his notation did not differ basically from the ones furnished by the students. In the following examples, the upper staves represent the phrases (Ph.), as played by me on the two metallophones, while the lower staves show their transcriptions (Tr.) by Hornbostel. In these examples, as heretofore, the figures preceded by + or — signs represent cent adjustments needed to obtain the pitches on the metallophones. For the convenience of the reader, the present author gives in cents, below the bottom staff—in Exx. 1-4—the actual sizes of intervals that were sounded between successive notes.

Both equidistant scales (presented in figs. 1 and 2) contain approximate fourths and fifths: the five-tone scale includes the "fourth" of 480 cents and the "fifth" of 720 cents, the former being 18 cents smaller than the perfect fourth (3:4) of 498 cents, and the latter being 18 cents larger than the perfect fifth (2:3) of 702 cents; the seven-tone scale includes the "fourth" of 514 cents and the "fifth" of 686 cents, the intervals being 16 cents larger and 16 cents smaller, respectively, than the corresponding perfect intervals. Ex. 1 combines the four values (480, 514, 686, and 720 cents) of the equidistant scales:

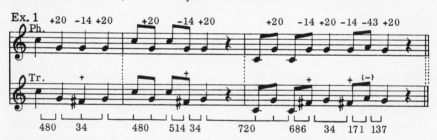

As the transcription shows, the intervals of 480 and 720 cents are perceived as regular fourths and fifths; however, the interval of 514 cents is interpreted as a narrow diminished fifth and the interval of 686 cents as a large augmented fourth, although these two intervals differ by only 16 cents, respectively, from the perfect fourth 3:4 and from the perfect fifth 2:3. As a matter of fact, the intervals notated as C-F♯ *plus* actually deviate slightly less from the perfect fourth and the perfect fifth than do those notated as C-G (which deviate by 18 cents from the corresponding perfect intervals). This interpretation is all the more remarkable since the tritone differs from the perfect fourth and perfect fifth not only in its size but also in its specific character: the tritone is a basic dissonance, the fourth and fifth are basic consonances. It is obviously the musical context that leads to this paradoxical evaluation. The microtonal interval of 34 cents is not small enough to be perceived as a mere intonational shading. In measure 1, note 3 functions as an auxiliary note and appears, therefore, to form a narrow semitone with the two surrounding notes. Since the first interval of 480 cents is interpreted as a regular fourth, note 3 appears to form a narrow diminished fifth with note 1. As a consequence, the actual intervals of 514 (= 480 + 34) cents and of 686 (= 720 − 34) cents, played in measures 2 and 3, are bound to be perceived, respectively, as a narrow diminished fifth and a large augmented fourth. Perceiving the two intervals in this way results, in turn, in an evaluation of the final step as a slightly narrow whole tone, although its size of 137 cents is far closer to a semitone than to a whole tone.

The main feature of Ex. 2 is the notating, at the end of the phrase, of the neutral third of 343 cents as a regular major third and that of the neutral sixth of 857 cents as a regular minor sixth:

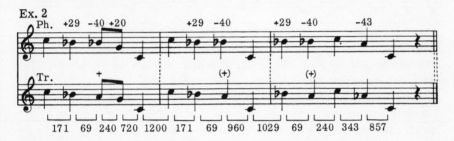

Ex. 2

This interpretation results from the structure of the preceding portion of the phrase. In measure 1, the octave c'' - c' is perceived in a normal division, that is, as consisting of an upper tetrachord and a lower fifth; however, the tetrachord c'' - g' consists of 480 cents, and the fifth g' - c', of 720 cents, the former thus deviating by 18 cents from the perfect fourth of 498 cents, and the latter deviating by 18 cents from the perfect fifth of 702 cents. Note 3 of measure 1, notated as a' *plus*, divides the fourth c'' - g' of 480 cents into two equal parts (of 240 cents each); however, the subdivision of the upper half into a narrow "whole tone" of 171 cents and a narrow "semitone" of 69 cents results in the interpretation of the upper half of the tetrachord as a narrow minor third (c'' - a' *plus*) and of the lower half as a large whole tone (a' *plus* - g'); in turn, the interval between notes 3 and 5 of measure 1 (960 cents) is perceived as a large major sixth (a' *plus* - c'). By the elimination of g' in measure 2 the interval of 960 cents appears as only a *slightly* enlarged major sixth, although its actual size is closer to that of a minor seventh than to that of a major sixth. The upper note of the interval reappears in measure 3 and is, therefore, again notated as a slightly high *a'*. Since note 4 of measure 3 lies a comfortable whole tone of 103 cents below note 2 of that measure, it is perceived as an *a♭'*. This note divides the octave *c'' - c'* into a major third and a minor sixth, although actually the two intervals are neither major nor minor, but neutral.

As in the phrase of Ex. 2, the first two tone steps of Ex. 3 consist of a narrow "whole tone" of 171 cents and a narrow "semitone" of 69 cents; but this time the steps move in the direction opposite from that taken by the melody at the opening of Ex. 2.

Ex. 3

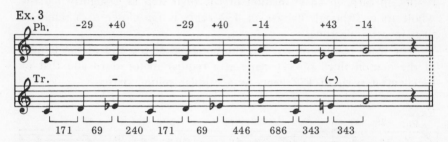

The subsequent step of 240 cents, which leads back to *c'*, is equal to the combination of the opening "whole tone" and the "semitone" and is, therefore, perceived as a narrow minor third, although in size it is less close to a minor third than to a whole tone. Note 1 of measure 2, *g'*, appears as a normal fifth above the "root" *c'*, although the interval *c' - g'* is 16 cents narrower than the fifth 2:3. Since the closing note of measure 1 is interpreted as a low *e♭'*, the subsequent neutral interval of 446 cents assumes the function of a large major third. The last two steps of the example represent an equidistant subdivision of the "fifth" *c' - g'* of 686 cents into two neutral thirds of 343 cents each. The subdividing note appears as a slightly low *e♮'* because it lies a semitone of 103 cents above each note that is notated in measure 1 as low *e♭'*. As a result, the neutral broken triad of measure 2 is interpreted as a major chord with a slightly narrow major third. Incidentally, the interval of 686 cents, notated in the beginning of measure 2 as a regular fifth, is exactly the same interval which, in measure 3 of Ex. 1, was perceived as a large augmented fourth.

In the construction of phrase 4 (which constitutes Ex. 4), the interval of 1029 cents is interpreted as a narrow major seventh, in spite of the closeness of its size to that of a minor seventh (996 cents) and in spite of the contrast in character between the major and minor sevenths.

Ex. 4

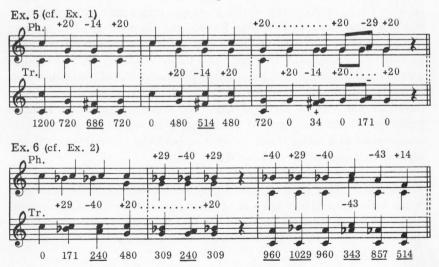

The neutral sixth of 857 cents in measure 1, which ends on the level of the opening *c'*, is perceived as only a slightly narrow major sixth because of the interpretation of the three preceding steps as a perfect fourth, a regular whole tone, and a slightly narrow whole tone. The closing leap of measure 2 corresponds structurally to that of measure 1, but since it is larger by a semitone of 103 cents, it appears as a regular minor seventh, in spite of its narrow size of 960 cents. As a result, the interval of 1029 cents at the end of measure 3, which is 69 cents larger than the corresponding step of the preceding measure, is interpreted as a narrow major seventh and not as a minor seventh (996 cents), to which it is actually closer. In Ex. 2 the same interval of 1029 cents (between measures 2 and 3) was, in fact, notated as a regular minor seventh.

The remaining examples are variants of the preceding four phrases; they served to test the effects of melody-Gestalt on the evaluation of simultaneous intervals with respect to size and type. No major differences between the interpretation of tone steps and that of simultaneous intervals could be observed; however, the influence of melody-Gestalt seems to be stronger with regard to the evaluation of simultaneous intervals than to that of melodic steps. Exx. 5-8 will illustrate this point.

Ex. 5 (cf. Ex. 1)

Ex. 6 (cf. Ex. 2)

Ex. 7 (cf. Ex. 3)

Ex. 8 (cf. Ex. 4)

These are organized like the earlier examples, except that the figures under the lower staves now indicate the number of cents between simultaneously rather than successively sounded notes. It will be observed that the interval of 240 cents is interpreted both as a major second (*g'-a'* in Ex. 6) and as a minor third (*a'-c''* in Ex. 6); the interval of 343 cents both as a minor third (*e'-g'* in Ex. 7) and as a major third (*ab'-c''* in Ex. 6, and *c'-e'* in Ex. 7); the interval of 514 both as a perfect fourth (*c'-f'* in Exx. 6 and 8, and *d'-g'* in Ex. 7) and as a diminished fifth (*f♯'-c''* in Ex. 5); the interval of 686 cents both as an augmented fourth (*c'-f♯'* in Ex. 5) and as a perfect fifth (*c'-g'* in Ex. 8); the interval of 857 cents both as a minor sixth (*c'-ab'* in Ex. 6) and as a major sixth (*c'-a'* in Ex. 8); the interval of 960 cents as a major sixth (*c'-a'* in Ex. 6) and as a minor seventh (*c'-bb'* in Ex. 8); and the interval of 1029 cents as a minor seventh (*c'-bb'* in Ex. 6) and as a major seventh (*c'-b'* in Ex. 8). Thus we see not only that intervals of equal size may be evaluated in a completely different way, depending on the melody-Gestalt, but that intervals differing in their size by more than 100 cents may be perceived as intervals of identical size. The second observation is illustrated by the interpretation of both the 240-cent interval and the 343-cent interval as a minor third, and that of both the 857-cent interval and the 960-cent interval as a major sixth.

After the test was completed, Hornbostel agreed to take a supplementary test. This time all tone steps and simultaneous intervals, used in the main test, were taken out of their musical context (Gestalt) and presented for notation in isolated fashion. The evaluations now matched the actual sizes with all the closeness that one would expect from such a prominent transcriber.